Urban Development
Its Implications for Social Welfare

Urban Development
Its Implications for Social Welfare

PROCEEDINGS OF THE XIIITH INTERNATIONAL
CONFERENCE OF SOCIAL WORK
WASHINGTON, D.C., UNITED STATES
SEPTEMBER 4-10, 1966

Published 1967
for the INTERNATIONAL COUNCIL ON SOCIAL WELFARE
by COLUMBIA UNIVERSITY PRESS
NEW YORK AND LONDON

Foreword

IN SELECTING the theme for the XIIIth International Conference
of Social Work, many considerations have played a role. The interest reflected by the theme is world-wide, even if the problem
itself does not appear everywhere in the same light. The theme is
common territory to many disciplines, reflecting the fact that
progress in welfare can result only from the constructive cooperation of many forces and many specialties. It has special significance
for the host country of the XIIIth Conference, the United States
of America, whose citizens have made an outstanding contribution
to the success of the Conference, intellectually as well as in terms
of organization. But above all, the city is a subject of growing
importance. It is because of this orientation toward the future,
toward the time when, foreseeably, most of the people on this
earth will be living under conditions which we today still distinguish by the adjective "urban," that the theme of the city was
chosen from a host of possibilities.

Not only the city, however, was at the center of our attention
this time. We were not discussing the city simply as a fact, as a
natural phenomenon, so to say; we were not restricting ourselves
to the sociological, economic, administrative, or other analysis of
the process of urbanization in the world. We are interested in the
implications of that process for social welfare. And, to that extent,
we are committed. We are committed to the human value of welfare, to a positive state of individual and social well-being and
dignity shared equally by all people in all countries on this planet
which is our common home.

This goal, this value commitment, implies a clear knowledge
that in the world as it is today there is considerable inequality,
within countries and among countries. These inequalities may be
the consequence of causes which we consider natural, such as
different stages of development, different economic capabilities
and cultural conditions, or they may be the result of interest-
inspired human action, of the domination of the powerless by the

powerful. In any case, they are incompatible, in the final analysis, with welfare as a world-wide concept. As general technological capabilities of the human race increase, there is no natural reason why the benefits of this technology should not be available to every man and woman and to every child in the world. There are social reasons, however, for the present state of affairs. It is our commitment to understand these reasons and to change them.

With regard to the problem of the city, our commitment means that we should seek ways and means to promote welfare through conscious social intervention in the process of urbanization, through urban development. It means also that we should find methods appropriate for all the various stages and situations of general economic and social progress in various parts of the world. Our concern is with the life we and our children are going to lead in the cities of the future.

But, in order to live in cities we first must live—and in order to live we must live in peace. It is therefore, finally, our greatest and foremost common responsibility to strengthen the forces of reason and of peace by emphasizing our common human tasks which are important for all of us and which we can accomplish only by acting together. It is the hope of all of us that the XIIIth International Conference of Social Work has contributed however little to this great and essential cause.

EUGEN PUSIĆ
President

Contents

Foreword   *Eugen Pusić*   v

PLENARY SESSIONS

Welcoming Address   *Ellen Winston*   3
Highlights of the Report of the Pre-Conference
    Working Party   *Helena Junqueira*   10
The Social Impact of Urbanization   *Robert C. Weaver*   18
The Social Impact of Urbanization as a Universal
    Process   *Asoka Mehta*   25
Insuring an Enriched Urban Environment   *L. Hugh Wilson*   35
Remarks   *Hubert Humphrey*   48
Developing a Sense of Community in Today's Urban
    Areas   *Whitney M. Young, Jr.*   54
Strengthening Human Relationships   *Jane M. Hoey*   67
Problems of Future Urban Development   *Lucien Mehl*   78

GENERAL MEETINGS

Mental Health Aspects of Urban Life   *T. Adeoye Lambo*   100
    Discussion: Implications for Services   *Louis Miller, M.D.*   112
What Are the Social Priorities for the Modern City and
    How Do We Achieve Them?   *Elizabeth Wickenden*   117
Towns within a Town: a Proposal for Greater
    Athens   *P. Vassiliadis*   130
Urban Development in Atlanta, Georgia   *Duane W. Beck*   138
Social Implications of Advanced Urban Planning and
    Development   *Michel de Chalendar*   147
The Social Welfare Program of Norway   *Lilian Bye*   152
The Impact of Urbanization on Rural Areas
    Part I. *J.-B. Lanctot*   163
    Part II. *H. P. Van Roosmalen*   179

Social Services as Social Utilities   *Alfred J. Kahn*   189
New Trends in Client Participation in Urban Development
   I. A View from the United States   *Bernard M. Shiffman*   208
   II. A View from Southern Italy   *Albino Sacco*   217
   III. A View from a Developing Country   *Ali Akbar*   227
Social Planning and Urban Development   *Wilbur J. Cohen*   237
The Paradoxes of Urbanization and Regional
   Development   *Gerald Hodge*   246
Reports on Research
   I. Working Mothers and Family Life   *K. N. George*   257
   II. Research in Germany   *Arno Kosmale*   264
   III. Four Social Welfare Programs in Israel
       Jona M. Rosenfeld   267
Demographic Factors in Urban Development   *Milos Macura*   273
Urban Development: Implications for Training Social
   Work Personnel   *Ellen Winston*   283
   I. In Europe and Africa   *Jean Iliovici*   296
   II. In Latin America   *Virginia A. Paraiso*   300
   III. In India   *N. F. Kaikobad*   306
Highlights of the International Congress of Schools
   of Social Work   *Robert A. B. Leaper*   311
Techniques and Methods of Coordinating Public and
   Voluntary Services at the Neighborhood Level
   I. In Japan   *Yuichi Nakamura*   319
   II. In the United States   *Abner D. Silverman*   322
   III. In the United Kingdom   *Elizabeth R. Littlejohn* 332
The United Nations Program of Regional Development
   Julia J. Henderson   338
The Special Needs of Young Children in Shantytowns
   I. In Brazil   *Maria Luiza Moniz de Aragao*   348
   II. In Hong Kong   *Patricia Nye*   358
   III. In Nigeria   *G. N. Agbim*   364

COMMISSIONS

   I. The Impact of Urbanization   371
   II. Social Policy and Strategy for Urban
      Development   376
   III. Patterns of Intervention—Structures and Process for
      Urban Development   382

IV. Maximizing the Participation of Citizens in
    Urban Development 386
V. Interrelatedness of Urban and Rural Development 393
VI. Social Aspects of Urban Renewal and Redevelopment 398

STUDY GROUPS

1. Shelter 403
2. Employment and Unemployment 406
3. Health 409
4. Income Maintenance 412
5. The Role of the School 416
6. Leisure 419
7. Family Life 422
8. Government Structures 425
9. Groups Needing Special Attention: Children 429
10. Groups Needing Special Attention: the Aging 432
11. Groups Needing Special Attention: the Physically
    Handicapped 436
12. Groups Needing Special Attention: Juvenile Delinquents 440
13. Groups Needing Special Attention: Newcomers to
    Urban Centers 443
14. Use of Multipurpose Workers at the Local Level 446
15. The Role of Social Work with Other Disciplines in
    Providing Service in Urban Areas 450

SPECIAL MEETINGS

1. Pre-Conference Seminar on Social Welfare in the
   United States 454
2. Representatives of Social Welfare Ministries Concerned
   with International Social Welfare 455
3. Municipal Social Welfare Officers 457

APPENDICES

Countries and International Organizations Represented 461
Organizing Committee 463
Program Committee 464
Executive Committee 465

Urban Development
Its Implications for Social Welfare

Welcoming Address

ELLEN WINSTON

COMMISSIONER OF WELFARE, U.S. DEPARTMENT OF
HEALTH, EDUCATION, AND WELFARE

WE HAVE all been looking forward to the arrival of this, the opening day of the XIIIth International Conference of Social Work. For the United States members of the Conference there is the special pleasure of welcoming our colleagues from abroad. We are keenly aware of the honor paid to us and to our country in your selection of the United States as the site for a conference devoted to such a crucial issue as urban development. Many of us, having attended the Conference meetings in other countries, are equally aware of the high standards of hospitality and service which have been set by those countries. We cherish many memories of our experiences as guests in your lands, and it is our fondest hope that you will find your visit here an equally rich and rewarding experience.

Our planning groups have tried to foresee your needs and interests, and if there is anything more we can do to make your visit all that you had hoped it might be, please voice your wishes to your host committee. Every effort will be made to fulfill them.

Most of all, we hope that we will be able to convey to you the essence of life in the United States. Although we will be discussing problems, because that is the purpose of social work meetings, we would not want you to leave with the impression that our country is a nation of problems. Overtowering its problems are its beauties, natural and man-made, its achievements, its aspirations. Only by seeing our problems in their true perspective can you understand both our confidence in successfully coping with them and our impatience to get on with the job more rapidly.

I bring you greetings from the Secretary of the Department of Health, Education, and Welfare, Dr. John W. Gardner. He had hoped to be with us this evening and asked me to tell you how deeply he regretted his inability to do so.

I regret his absence particularly because he had planned to tell you of the many programs of the Department, beyond those of the Welfare Administration, which I direct, that deal with urban development. Indeed, I think it no exaggeration to say that every one of the hundreds of programs administered by the seven operating agencies which comprise the Department of Health, Education, and Welfare (HEW) contributes directly or indirectly, and most of them quite directly, to the solution of urban problems.

The Public Health Service gives strong support to state and local health department programs which deal with the prevention and control of both chronic and communicable diseases. It is also deeply involved, as are its state and local counterparts, in the control of air pollution, accident hazards, and other facets of our urban environment.

The Office of Education plays an increasingly important role in the improvement of the nation's schools, with special emphasis on the educational needs of children in the slum areas of our cities.

The Social Security Administration, which handles the social insurance for old age, survivors, and disability, and, as of this year, the new hospital and voluntary medical insurance for persons over sixty-five, popularly known as "Medicare," provides the basic protection against income losses which, in a money-based urban economy, would be disastrous to family life.

The other agencies of HEW, aside from the Welfare Administration, are the Food and Drug Administration, the Vocational Rehabilitation Administration, and the Administration on Aging. These agencies also meet needs that are particularly important to urban dwellers because, unlike the inhabitants of rural, pioneer America, people today must depend upon organized, systematic measures for meeting their needs, such as the protection of their food and drug supplies or the more personalized help required to equip a disabled person to become self-supporting or to offer a meaningful future to our almost twenty million elder citizens. And because all these agencies are welded into a single department, they work closely together toward the goal of coordinated programs of aids and services in all our cities as well as in our small towns and rural communities.

There are four principal ways in which the programs of these HEW agencies are carried out. Basic are the grants in aid which channel federal funds into every state and local jurisdiction. More than $6 billion a year in federal funds is administered by the HEW agencies in grants to states, a bulwark of support for a broad range of public services in every community.

A second important measure is research. Some of this is carried out directly by HEW agencies, but they also support a vast number of research and demonstration projects conducted by voluntary as well as public agencies and institutions throughout the nation. Altogether, nearly $2 billion in HEW funds is allocated for intra- and extramural research and demonstrations each year.

A third important measure is the training of personnel. This too is supported by grants to voluntary and public organizations as well as by institutes and conferences sponsored by the federal agencies themselves. Construction of facilities for training is financed in part through some of these HEW programs.

Finally, a very basic part of the HEW program is consultation and technical assistance. We frequently refer to our programs as "partnerships." They are very active, working partnerships to which local, state, and federal personnel have all contributed. The most direct and constant contact is maintained through HEW staff in nine regional offices, but many members of the Washington staff are also in the field much of the time.

I realize that nothing can be more boring to a visitor than a description of a government bureaucracy, and I have given this brief outline only because I believe that our United States representatives as well as our foreign colleagues will find it a useful framework for many of the discussions that will be held during the week.

Perhaps the most important thing to keep in mind is that whereas a large share of the financing of welfare and related services comes through federal funds administered by HEW, basic responsibility for administration rests with the states, which in turn delegate some of this responsibility to the local communities.

This explains why there is no typical or uniform way in which activities are carried out, why you will hear of so many variations and differences as you talk to our social workers about their programs. Federal requirements are minimal and are designed mainly to assure that money which comes from all parts of the country as tax funds brings equal benefits to people in equal circumstances. For example, neither a public nor a voluntary agency can receive any federal aid if it denies services to anyone on the basis of race, color, or national origin. Similarly, in our public assistance programs, a service cannot be available only to rural people or only to city people; it must be available to anyone in the state who meets the eligibility requirements set by the state.

Increasingly, however, a major portion of all the programs in which the HEW agencies participate are becoming city programs for the very simple reason that a major portion of the population have become city people. Our task as federal officials, a task which we share with state and local officials, is to help give direction to our cities as they grow and develop, to make certain that human factors are taken into consideration at every step of the planning and execution of change. One might say that HEW is the federal agency primarily interested in the human side of urban development just as the Department of Housing and Urban Development is the federal agency primarily interested in the physical side of urban development. Yet, the physical and the humanitarian aspects are interrelated and cannot be separated, and there is the closest possible cooperation and collaboration between the two departments.

One of the most serious problems of American cities today is the isolation and even alienation of a seriously deprived minority of their populations, people who for various reasons, ranging from age and infirmity to lack of education and skills, can find no meaningful role in our essentially work-oriented society. It is the problems of these people that most concern the Welfare Administration—the discouraged fathers who, unable to find work, leave their wives and children dependent upon public assistance; the teenagers whose youthful energies find outlets in delinquent behavior; the lonely old people who eke out their days in shabby rooming houses; those who have been denied opportunities because of their race or color despite our intensive efforts and our progress in this area; the misfits, the lost, the bewildered. The very efficiency of our modern economy tends to bar relatively small and yet important segments of our population from the main stream of our society. If the upward trend in their numbers is to be reversed, we must bring about changes in both the tangible and the intangible qualities of urban life so that these people will find within their environment as well as within themselves the resources to make their lives worth living.

How to bring about such change is a problem being studied with increasing urgency, not only by official bodies but by thoughtful citizens throughout the land.

It is most opportune that the ICSW is meeting here just at the time when a Senate subcommittee under the chairmanship of a former HEW Secretary, Senator Abraham Ribicoff, is holding public hearings on big-city problems. Although the committee is concerned with a wide spectrum of problems, I think you will find in the reports of the hearings that the situation of the deprived and alienated is the crucial problem.

Another pertinent study is the one made by a citizens' Advisory Council on Public Welfare, and I call your attention to the report which the Council released just two months ago. It contains some extremely practical suggestions of what can be done, and done now, for the fifth of the nation who live below our defined poverty level in a generally flourishing society.

On a more technical level, officials of federal, state, and city public welfare agencies have been scrutinizing the operation of public welfare programs in key cities during the past year. Teams assigned to a project which we called "Operation Big City" surveyed programs in six major cities about a year ago, bringing to light certain problems common to these and probably to all large cities. Subsequently, the administrators of public welfare programs in large cities, together with their state administrators, met with us in Washington for two days on the same basic problems.

All these studies, both lay and technical, point up similar problems, the seriousness of which is underscored by the fact that these same problems are frequently the ones which have sparked explosive, or potentially explosive, protest movements among the deprived.

The most dramatic unmet need is for emergency services. Emergencies seldom fall into the neat little categories of need provided for in laws and regulations, nor do they always occur during normal working hours—it is, of course, their very unusualness that makes them emergencies. Yet, if a city offers no succor at time of direst need, it becomes a cold and heartless place indeed.

The ambulance in the night carrying a mother to the hospital, leaving small children alone in their tenement home; the babies in the hospital wards, abandoned by their desperate mothers; the family whose monthly check has been lost or stolen and who can get neither money nor credit for another long month—these are just a few of the emergencies that occur in big cities to people who have no nearby friends or relatives, and no knowledge of where they can turn for the help they so urgently need.

The need for a system for offering prompt and effective emergency help is one of several reasons for the growing interest in the proposal, made by the Advisory Council on Public Welfare and other agencies, to locate service centers in every low-income neighborhood. These would be friendly places, housing a broad range of programs, which would quickly be known to everyone in the area as the place to go when one is in trouble. They would be places where, regardless of the kind of trouble, someone would stand by, either providing the necessary service or seeing that it was received from some other source. One would never find its door locked or its telephone unanswered.

A distribution of these centers in every large city would probably do more than any other single action to put heart into the modern city.

You will hear more about these centers and other measures being developed in this country as the week progresses. You will hear about many promising and innovative projects being undertaken through the antipoverty programs initiated by the Economic Opportunity Act of 1964, through the public welfare services supported by the Social Security Amendments of 1962 and 1965, and through other recent social legislation. We hope that, as our guests from abroad, you will discover among these projects some that can be adapted to the problems of the big cities of your home countries and we hope especially that we of the United States will learn from you about developments that can be adapted and incorporated into our plans and programs for the future.

It is this exchange, across geographic and cultural boundaries, this shared concern for like problems of people wherever they live, that gives an extra measure of excitement and stimulation to a great international conference. No national meeting, however important and interesting, ever has quite this special quality.

Out of it all, it is my hope and, I am sure, your hope as well, that we and all the people of the many countries we represent will gain much—in knowledge of how to enrich the human side of urban life and in determination to keep the needs of people, and especially of deprived people, a top priority in urban development. If we can act now, the cities of tomorrow, throughout the world, may come close to realization of the dream of the writer of a great American anthem in whose vision "alabaster cities gleam, undimmed by human tears."

Highlights of the Report of the Pre-Conference Working Party

HELENA JUNQUEIRA

CHIEF, DIVISION OF SOCIAL WORK OF SÃO PAULO, BRAZIL

THE SUBJECT of urban development and its implications for social welfare is becoming more and more relevant to public administration and to the thinking of modern social scientists because of the challenge it represents both for the developed countries and for those going through the developmental stage.

Mankind as a whole has undergone virtually the entire process of urbanization since the late eighteenth century. In our present century the rate has become exceedingly high. In 1900 only 5.5 percent of the world's population lived in towns numbering more than 100,000 inhabitants, but the percentage reached 13 in 1950. Over the past 150 years the rural population has increased at a constant annual rate of 0.5 percent, while in the same period the urban population has shown an annual increase of 2 percent to 2.5 percent.

This phenomenon must be considered not only from a demographic standpoint but also in relationship to the industrialization process—a very important factor in social change as well as one of its immediate consequences.

The process of urbanization is in some countries almost spontaneous, chaotic, while in others it is deliberately stimulated by national policies and programs. In all countries, however, urbanization brings problems that need planned action at national, regional, and municipal levels. The conscious confrontation of these problems is commonly known as "urban development," and this implies that the philosophy and techniques of physical, economic, and social planning are to be applied to the process of urbanization.

The ICSW at its 1958 meeting in Japan adopted the practice of calling together a Pre-Conference Working Party to prepare a document that would serve as a resource for commissions and study groups. The 1966 working party met in the lovely historic town of Charlottesville, Virginia, from August 21 to 28, at the National Red Cross Training Center. Delegates from twenty-one countries and representatives of five international agencies were included.

Since it was not our intention to duplicate the work of the study groups and commissions; the reports prepared in advance by the national committee were the basis of our discussions.

After a general discussion, the group was divided into four committees which elaborated the first version of the final document. The introductory chapter was written by the workshop's *rapporteur*. Later on the material was reformulated by the group, and the final document was approved for presentation to all members of the conference.

The Introduction explains how the subject was focused; common aspects and differences found in studying situations in different countries are described, and the more significant problems are stated. The first chapter is devoted to an analysis of concepts and processes; the second, to social policy; the third, to social welfare implications; and the fourth, to the implementation of urban development programs, followed by closing remarks.

After analyzing the main characteristics of urban development, the Introduction details some aspects of urbanization and related problems. It points out that from the reports one gains the impression that rapid urbanization is likely to outdistance economic, physical, and social development. Problems of both the inadequacy of development efforts and of their imbalance were reported. Inadequacy, it was found, took at least two different forms. One was that of insufficient or inadequate attempts at planning for such development, with consequent neglect of methods which might prevent random, chaotic, and uneven growth. The other was not so much a lack of planning as a lack of resources to keep up with needs, such as the physical infrastructure, as new communities developed or old ones grew rapidly. Imbalance, on the other hand, was reported most frequently in terms of an overemphasis on economic and physical planning and an underemphasis on social planning.

The reports brought out a widely expressed conviction that

more attention should be given to social development, and that such development should be undertaken positively and aggressively instead of being in large part a secondary response to the undesirable consequences of economic development and urbanization.

A composite problem mentioned by almost all countries was housing, growth of slums, poverty, and inadequate social opportunities. Others were the lack of coordination among various agencies engaged in urban development and the question of how to obtain citizen participation in urban development. Every national report commented on the fundamental importance of citizen participation, but they seldom pointed to methods or systems actually in use.

The first chapter analyzes the three aspects of urban development.

The economic aspect has to do with provision of industrial opportunities—broadly conceived—through which individuals can earn sufficient income, through which public services and facilities can be financed, and through which goods and services can be made available for consumption. Economic development activities include policy decisions, often at the national level, concerning the allocation of industries to different cities and to different regions, as well as policies regarding their intracity or intraregional dispersion or concentration.

The physical aspect of urban development, which perhaps is the one most widely known because of its visibility, includes tangibles like street patterns, drainage, sewerage, transit facilities. Yet the participants of the workshop, as well as the national reports, indicated that there is a widespread lack of adequate physical planning.

The social aspect of urban development concentrates on the provision of those facilities and services which produce a healthier and richer life and opportunities for individual expression. It is important that they be made available to the total population and no longer remain inaccessible to all but a privileged few.

The great promise of urban development will more likely be achieved as it begins to take place not in an atmosphere of crisis planning, as a mere reaction to formidable urban problems, but as a means of coordinating efforts in a positive direction so that opportunities are available for individuals and groups to realize their full potential.

It is recognized that physical planning must be governed by social needs and that the physical aspects of urban communities should, therefore, be organized in such a way as to facilitate the different functions that the town performs.

From the analysis of urban development policy presented in Chapter 2 certain points should be mentioned. A review of the national reports indicates that there are three important types of hindrance to urban development: conflicts of interest; lack of co-ordination; and difficulties regarding land use.

In the process of economic growth, economic development, or industrial location, men are often still regarded as physical objects and not as spiritual entities. But human beings constitute the very essence of the community, and social planning should therefore never be considered of secondary importance when plans are being prepared or executed.

Developing countries, however, are often faced with a vicious circle; for resources are not optimally exploited and less developed organizational structures make planning both necessary and difficult. In these countries, the elementary physical infrastructure—water supply, electricity, transportation, and communication—is not yet sufficiently developed to bring people to higher economic, social, and cultural levels.

Many of the national reports stated that in a modern, industrialized society it is necessary to take into account the quality of life, measured not only in goods and services but also in environmental factors. In considering the quality of life, one should pay particular attention to the social and cultural needs of a given society. In a society where different ethnic groups live together, there should be opportunities for them to maintain their distinctive cultural values and at the same time to integrate with new patterns of culture and with the community as a whole.

Inasmuch as urban development planning should be a permanent process, calling for continuous collaboration, whether permissive or mandatory, it would seem essential that some cultural coordinating secretariat, council, committee, or other authority be created within the structure of government, particularly at high levels, to undertake or delegate research, to consult with the interested parties, including the ultimate consumer, to draft preliminary plans, to propose appropriate standards, to provide for the administration of such standards, and in every proper way to encourage the growth and implementation of policies and programs.

Some of the most interesting considerations from Chapter 3 were the following. Social welfare objectives need to be formulated in accordance with underlying basic value assumptions. These basic values may be different in different parts of the world, and sometimes they even differ within one nation. Though it is necessary to make a distinction between basic values and cultural social and political attitudes, it is not intended to ignore or minimize the fact that there is a relation between values and attitudes. We are also conscious that in a changing society and under changing conditions new values will emerge, and that this fact might cause conflicts between values.

In large urban centers in developing countries social welfare generally deals with mass problems. The needs that arise are mainly basic human needs related to health, labor, housing, and education. The emphasis should be placed on developmental types of social welfare programs. In particular, attention has to be given to certain kinds of educational programs, such as prevocational training and a required minimum of general education so that the people will be able to adapt themselves to new ways of living.

Provision would have to be made to offer opportunities for work, to care for the children, and to establish suitable housing conditions. One of the great tasks of social welfare in such a situation is to stimulate and even to create "community feeling," "community spirit," and help to form a "community" out of a mass of people.

In the more developed countries, there will be problems of minorities and of disadvantaged groups. Here the task will be to integrate individuals and small groups into the existing community life.

Chapter 4 studies the implementation of urban development programs.

There is no infallible prescription for the successful implementation of planned change, but the experience of numerous countries suggests that the observance of certain basic sequences and procedures improves substantially the chances of success. A first requirment is knowledge of the social structures, value system, and felt needs of the population in question; for it is only on the basis of such knowledge that realistic plans and programs can be formulated. Provision should be made at the earliest opportunity to represent the views of the people affected and to furnish full and reliable information on the proposed changes.

Reference is made in the report to the necessity for teamwork among the various professions engaged in urban development. A common complaint is that administrators and policy-makers show insufficient appreciation of the social aspects of economic and physical development. This is no doubt due in part to the difference in values and priorities of the various professions. It may also have something to do with the failure of the social welfare system to systematize and articulate its knowledge of the impact of urbanization on human welfare. In spite of the difficulties, there is urgent need and scope for the cost-benefit type of analysis in the social aspects of urban development.

One valuable element for implementation is citizen participation. Although it is clear that citizen participation may take a variety of forms, and serve a number of purposes, most reports understand it as being much the same as individual cooperation, usually expressed through group representatives, in the identification and resolution of common problems. Citizen participation may be viewed as a means of achieving popular support for policies and programs that have already been decided upon by some higher authority, or it may be seen as a way of enabling individuals and groups to share in the shaping of decisions that affect their lives.

A special problem noted in a number of developing countries, and in developed countries as well, is the lack of participation of young people in civic affairs. Considerable scope is needed both in the educational systems of most countries and in the voluntary services to provide students and other young people with a better understanding of the problems of urban development and an opportunity to take part in their resolution. The concept of genuine citizen participation in social development is relatively new and holds vast potential for creative innovation and change.

The importance of the problem of urbanization induced one developed country to state that "the metropolitan problem is perhaps the greatest single problem facing man in the second half of the twentieth century." Although the matter could not be stated in the same terms for the developing countries, since their greatest single problem is mainly economic and social development, these countries nevertheless face the most serious consequences of rapid and uncontrolled urban growth, hampered by lack of adequate resources to fulfill the basic needs of the population.

One can neither deny nor regret that the problems of urbanization are enormous. It is noteworthy in how many cases the reverse of a loss in human well-being represents a potential gain, given an appropriate response on the part of society. Thus, the disorganization resulting from a loosening of traditional family and group ties can be a prelude to the emergence of greater personal autonomy and the growth of more mutually respectful personal relationships, given, among other things, a physical environment which permits these qualities to appear. Similarly, although the very vitality which impels the migration of people to the cities is a source of much squalor and disorder, it has the potential for enormous productive effort and achievement if investment is made in these human beings on their arrival.

The concept of city planning as meaning only physical planning should be enlarged to encompass urban development which, besides comprehending economic and social aspects of city planning, will be considered as a part of a country's over-all planning, thus including norms for land use and appeals for better distribution of population as well as planning for economic and social development. It will only be possible within this framework to establish the basis for effective urban development.

A new and very significant concept is that of "social infrastructure," which implies the provision of such basic services as sufficient housing, adapted to the needs and sociocultural levels of the population; sociocultural facilities, such as educational, religious, social, and recreational institutions; high job potential for people of various socioeconomic groups; the possibility of using the land, whether by local government or private enterprise, for the benefit of the whole population. This concept of social infrastructure should overcome the traditional infrastructure concept that means only physical equipment and should become a basic condition for urban development.

To equate the difficult problems resulting from an accelerated process of urbanization with the possibility of a creative use of the dynamics of this changing process brings up the need to review the whole philosophy, the policies, and the working techniques. It is evident that urban development is primarily a government responsibility carried through political decisions and implementation of programs. But it is the responsibility of the professions concerned to speak up for integrated planning for urban development; to help deepen the connotations of social welfare; to review the functions and methods of social work in order to arrive at a better definition of the role that each profession has to play; and to bring more emphasis to interdisciplinary cooperation. On the other hand, there is also a need for systematic use of research and social studies, including those of an operational nature, together with the elaboration of new methods and techniques that will prove to be more adequate to the challenges of urban life to meet human needs and aspirations.

The Social Impact of Urbanization

ROBERT C. WEAVER

SECRETARY, U·S. DEPARTMENT OF HOUSING
AND URBAN DEVELOPMENT

THE PHENOMENON of urbanization is truly a universal phenomenon, and the International Conference of Social Work can help to highlight for the American people the international character of what has come to be known in this country as the "crisis in our cities."

Americans could not and would not live as they do were it not for the level of industrial and urban development achieved in this nation. But Americans will not be able to continue to live as they do—let alone improve their living standards—unless and until they come to grips with the social consequences of urbanization.

This is the challenge which confronts our nation today. And, I expect, it is a challenge which confronts our world as well.

What are these consequences?

They are the consequences of being uprooted from the closed, static pattern of the rural agricultural community or the small town.

They are the consequences of being thrust into the uncertain turbulence of the city, where every man is a stranger and yet all are dependent upon each other.

They are the consequences of a culture, thousands of years in the making, disintegrating in a generation under the impact of new ideas, new concepts, and new values.

They are the consequences of learning to survive in an environment created entirely by men, yet beyond the ability of men to understand or control.

They are the consequences of losing the sense of community, of identification, of continuity.

They are the consequences of trying to find creative satisfaction in a life that often is the constant repetition of a specialized function, the signifiance of which can rarely be understood or explained.

The Johnson Administration has done more than any other in the history of this nation—and perhaps of any in the world—to help those who live in cities meet the problems of urbanization. Yet all that has been done up to now is but a small fraction of what must be done in the years immediately ahead.

This country, in common with nearly every other country, is confronted with the irresistible force of population growth. That growth will give this country, within the next generation, a population larger than that of present-day India.

Somehow all of us must find the capital resources to build housing, the community facilities, and the production facilities necessary to support this population growth. If we do, and if at the same time we can sustain the present momentum of technological progress, we can look forward to a period of prosperity beyond anything the world yet has known. If we fail to find these resources, or fail to maintain the momentum we now have in improving the efficiency with which we use those resources, that population growth can overwhelm us.

On the one hand, this growth—and the urbanization we know will accompany it—is our greatest hope for the future. The more people there are, the greater the demand for the goods and services which can be produced by an urban society, the more work there will be for those who produce those goods or render those services, and the greater the incentive to improve the efficiency of that production, the greater will be the potential for bettering the standard of living of all of us.

But population growth and urbanization can also destroy the world as we now know it. If productive capacity does not keep pace with population increase, if innovation fails to keep pace with demand, then less and less must be divided among more and more. And the standard of living of all of us will start to spiral downward. This may seem to be a grim alternative, but it is an alternative which must be recognized if it is to be avoided.

Although urbanization is a universal phenomenon, there are significant differences in the characteristics of its social impact. In the United States, for example, most of its adverse impact has been concentrated in the centers of cities; in many other countries, the adverse impact has been felt primarily in the suburbs.

One reason for the difference is that this country has, in recent years, adopted government housing programs which facilitated the rapid expansion of single-family housing on the outskirts of cities. Through mortgage insurance provided by the Federal Housing Administration, and mortgage guarantees provided by the Veterans Administration, such housing was brought within the financial reach of families with moderate incomes. As a result, many families left the cities and moved to this new housing in the suburbs, and many of those who intended to move to the cities found, instead, homes in the suburbs.

Much of the housing in the central cities was thus left to families with lower incomes—both those who stayed behind and those who were moving into the cities. To increase the number of housing units, apartments were frequently subdivided—resulting in overcrowding—and maintenance was deferred in order to increase the financial yield to the landlords. As a consequence, housing which was basically sound and desirably located—housing that in any other country would have been considered preferred housing for many years to come—was systematically exploited and destroyed.

In many countries, as the tide of urbanization swept in toward the city, it was halted on the outskirts. There was no room in the cities. So squatters seized land wherever they could and built homes with whatever they could find. Great agglomerations of shacks and shanties, with no sewers, no water supply, no transportation, grew up around the cities.

In those countries, the pressing problems of urbanization have been to provide decent housing and community facilities and political stability to break through the ring of poverty that is strangling the central city. In this country, by contrast, the problem has been to decongest the crowded housing of the central city, to demolish and replace what has deteriorated beyond repair, to rehabilitate what is still structurally sound, and to break through the ring of suburban isolation that surrounds the central city.

Another significant difference in the social impact of urbanization in this country lies in the characteristics of the poverty which it has brought to light. In a rural society poverty can be hidden. When the poor move to the cities they cannot and will not be hidden. We can try to sweep them into slums. We can try to escape to the isolation of gentler neighborhoods. But in a city all men are interdependent and interact. Some of the rich live off the poor. Some of the poor prey on the rich. And all of us are offended by and reproached by poverty in the midst of plenty.

There was a time in this country—and most of us have some memory of it—when we tried to blame poverty on indolence. In a rich, expansive country where land was readily available, the implements of production easy to come by, and nature kind, we liked to think that any man who was able and willing to work could provide a good living for his family. But there came a time, as cities grew with the spread of industrialization, when we were forced to recognize that industry and ambition alone were not enough to enable a person to rise out of poverty. Then the magic word became "opportunity"—the opportunity to get an education, the opportunity to get a job, and the opportunity to find a decent place to live within the means provided by that job. All our efforts to conquer poverty were directed toward providing these opportunities.

Now we are finding that opportunities alone will not wipe out poverty; for not everyone can take advantage of those opportunities or is motivated to do so.

Now we are being forced to come to grips with what we call the "hard core of poverty"—the poverty of disability and despair.

No longer can poverty be dismissed as a moral problem.

No longer can we regard it merely as an economic problem.

Now—in this country—we have to regard it as a social problem.

If poverty is to be overcome we must find ways to overcome the mental, physical, and emotional disabilities which make it impossible for some people to take advantage of the opportunities that are open to them. We must greatly expand and equalize opportunities for the neglected and the discriminated against.

And we must find ways to restore the faith and hope that give a man the desire to reach out for those opportunities.

This is the great opportunity and the challenge which faces

social workers. It is the reason that in this country, more perhaps than in any other country, we concentrate upon the problems which are the chief concern of social workers.

A third significant characteristic of urbanization in this country is a result of the racial composition of the United States. Urban problems here are inseparable from racial problems. And that is a fact of life with which we will have to live for a long time to come.

The Negro is the most urban dweller in this urban land. Although the Negro proportion of the population is not significantly larger than it was at the time of the American Revolution, nearly two hundred years ago, today a larger proportion of Negroes than of whites live in urban areas. But colored Americans do not have access to the whole metropolitan area. They are concentrated in the central cities and further, generally restricted to certain sections of the core districts. This enforced residential segregation extracts many social and psychological tolls. Its economic consequences are the inevitable results of restricting a group to a segment of a market. Negroes get less for their housing dollars than do whites.

Nearly twenty years ago I wrote a book documenting the growth of these compacted, concentrated Negro residential areas. I called that book *The Negro Ghetto*. Significantly, at the time that I wrote it, I was living in Chicago's Hull House, one of the shrines of American social workers.

Since then nonwhite ghettos have grown larger and more congested, their residents more alienated and more desperate. And day after day across this country what should be minor incidents trigger wild and senseless destruction and violence.

The toll taken by this violence is appalling.

No one can review all this without realizing that we are in the midst of a revolutionary situation. That revolutionary situation cannot be met with platitudes and palliatives. We are not going to solve the problems of Negro ghettos by putting shower heads on hydrants or erecting portable swimming pools. Temporary and emergency measures may help to restore a semblance of calm for the time being, but they leave the underlying grievances unsolved.

If we are going to bring real peace to our cities—and without that peace we have no hope of being prepared for the population explosion that lies ahead—we must move to meet the basic causes of this unrest.

The responsibility for meeting the challenge of urbanization involves government at all levels, private industry, and nonprofit, religious, and community organizations. Every American has a personal responsibility as well.

Yet the federal government must provide leadership and offer financial and technical assistance. This we are now doing:

1. In the Demonstration Cities bill lies a vital and bold new instrument to rebuild slum sections in American cities and to bring a new and better life to the people.

2. In the Rent Supplement Program lies the fulfillment of the dream of a clean and decent home for those who now live in squalor.

3. In the Urban Mass Transit Authorization bill lies the opportunity to continue to serve the growing needs of the cities for adequate transportation to jobs and recreation.

4. In Title IV of the Civil Rights bill lies the opportunity to banish discrimination from the sale and rental of housing, thus breaking a strong chain that binds the ghetto.

5. In the Teachers Corps lies the promise of providing skilled teachers to instill a quest for learning in those children who need it most.

6. In the Office of Economic Opportunity's Authorization bill lies almost $2 billion to prosecute the war against poverty by providing job opportunities, training, and a head start for the very young.

7. In the Child Nutrition Act lies the promise of breakfasts and hot lunches for poor children and the chance to reduce the school dropout rate and preserve a young child's desire to learn.

8. In the Allied Health Professions bill lies the means to help overcome a severe shortage of trained medical personnel so that proper treatment can be brought to people in our cities.

9. In the Hospital Modernization bill lies the promise of better hospital care for those citizens who need it most in our cities.

10. In the Group Practice Construction bill lies the chance to build group medical facilities to serve our cities.

11. In the minimum wage amendments to the Fair Labor Standards Act lies the chance for more American workers to earn a decent wage.

12. In the Unemployment Insurance bill lies the needed strengthening of the benefits for those of our workers who are temporarily out of a job.

13. In the Truth in Lending bill lies the promise of a clear disclosure of the cost of credit so that all customers, but particularly those who are poor, can be protected and informed.

14. In the Truth in Packaging bill lies the means to allow the hard-earned dollars of the poor to go further by protecting them against deception and making it easier to shop for values.

This, in brief, is a fourteen-point program for action. It represents our recognition of our urban status and it is designed to assist in building in our cities and towns an environment for man equal to the dignity of his highest aspirations.

This is the direction in which our country is moving to meet the urban challenge.

The Social Impact of Urbanization
as a Universal Process

ASOKA MEHTA

MINISTER OF PLANNING AND SOCIAL WELFARE

INDIA

I MYSELF am a product of the universal process of urbanization, a process which has not only unleashed the great movements for national freedom in many countries of Asia and Africa, including India, but which also increasingly characterizes their economic and social development. I live in the city of Bombay which, together with Calcutta and Lahore, sets the tone for our freedom struggle. I have seen with my own eyes how a great industrial city changes the contours of the life of the millions who are drawn into it, how it gives them hope and nourishment, but also how it often fills them with despair and despondency.

There is no doubt in my mind that the developing areas of the world today are experiencing the impact of urbanization much more acutely than the relatively more developed areas, if for no other reason than that they have to deal with much larger numbers, manage with much smaller resources, and have much less time before an urban explosion can very well set at nought their efforts to bring about an economic and social transformation. My own country, where one seventh of humanity lives, is no exception.

I regard urbanization as the process of human resettlement which follows the mass transfer of a people from primary to secondary and tertiary activities, a process which has undoubtedly characterized social life since the Industrial Revolution in the West. Modern industrialization means the introduction of the machine into the people's ways of working, in search of greater efficiency and better management. This has brought new patterns of industrial time use and led to a new rhythm of life pulsating outward from places of employment.

Not only have the ways of working become more diverse, leading to an endless variety of jobs in factories, trade and commerce, transportation, communication, and other services, but agricultural activity has also become more varied and complex with the application of science and technology and the various tools and implements and new skills that have come in their wake. All this has resulted in a new kind of human settlement, based on an ever growing industrial activity, producing much greater value than it consumes. The old dichotomy between town and country has broken down, and the two now represent merely transient stages of a fast-changing continuum.

This process started with the Industrial Revolution, which made possible the use of inanimate power and machine tools and the transformation of matter through chemical processes, bringing into existence in England what Mumford calls "coke towns." These raw-material-based urban configurations drew into themselves a great many industries because of the economies which they offered. An enlarging reservoir of skilled and semiskilled workers; the opportunity of sharing various economic and social overheads; the advantage of buying from, and selling to, one another; and common facilities of banking and marketing were some of the sources of these economies. These settlements multiplied with the passage of time and set up around themselves fields of forces which transformed the occupational structure of their economies. As a result of all this, the distance between town and country has shrunk, and with the ever widening scatter of consumer durables which is already evident in all advanced countries of the West, and is well on the way to becoming universal in Japan too, this distance is likely to be virtually obliterated in the future.

Urbanization today presents two distinct aspects. One concerns the process of industrialization which is sweeping the developing countries, mostly in Asia, Africa, and Latin America, where the majority of humanity is still struggling to establish an industrial society. The other aspect is that of a new trend in urbanization also evident in the developed areas of the world, but mainly confined to Western Europe and parts of America, where the transindustrial society based on light alloys, electronics, nuclear energy, and new biochemical processes is setting the norms for social and economic organization. Encompassing the two, however, is the global picture which can be summed up in a few words.

While the world population has doubled over the last 100 years, the urban population has increased five times. Around 1800 less than 2 percent of the population lived in towns and cities, of which there were hardly more than 50 that had a population of more than 100,000. Today, out of a population of 3,000,000,000, about 1,000,000,000 people live in cities. One third of them, or about 12 percent of the world population, live in shanty towns of more than 100,000 inhabitants on the fringes of our cities. Of the estimated world population of 6,000,000,000 by the end of this century, 60 percent are likely to live in urban areas.

In some of the European countries, like Great Britain, the Netherlands, Belgium, and Germany, where industrialization started more than a century ago, the rate of urbanization has slowed down since 1930. This really means that these countries have become, or are on the way to becoming, completely urbanized in the sense that 75 percent or 80 percent of their populations are concentrated in towns of more than 5,000 inhabitants. A secondary reason for this stabilization is that the birth rate in European countries has been steadily declining. The present European birth rate is 19 per thousand, as against 42 per thousand in Asia and 46 per thousand in Africa. In the U.S.S.R., however, where industrialization began later, the urban population has doubled in the last thirty years and is still increasing at a fast rate. By 1930 nearly half of the population of the United States lived within a radius of twenty to fifty miles of cities with a population of over 100,000; by 1950, they were in 168 urban areas with 50,000 or more people. More than half of the population of Australia lives in its seven capital cities.

Urbanization is proceeding at a much faster rate in the developing countries than in the developed areas. Japan presents a typical illustration. Its metropolitan population increased from 38 percent in 1950 to 68 percent in 1965. The three metropolitan regions of Keihin, Kinki, and Chukyo, which account for only 19 percent of the total area, absorb 48,000,000 people, or nearly half the total population.

Only 18 percent of the population of India lived in towns and cities in 1961. Between 1951 and 1961 the urban population increased by over 36 percent, nearly double the rate of increase of the rural population. About one third of India's estimated total population of 600,000,000 will live in towns and cities by 1981. This will mean a transfer from rural to urban settlement of 55,000,000 to 60,000,000 people. What is more striking is that about a quarter of India's total urban population 490,000,000 live in the seven metropolitan areas of Calcutta, Bombay, Delhi, Madras, Hyderabad, Bangalore, and Ahmedabad, and nearly one half live in towns and cities with a population of 100,000,000 or more.

The sharp increase in the tempo of urbanization in developing countries illustrated by Japan and India is reflected in the great rise over the last few decades in the population of certain major cities. The population of Bombay increased three times in the last twenty years, while that of New Delhi, Karachi, and Peking doubled. Inmigration accounted for two thirds of the total increase of Delhi's population. Of the population of Calcutta metropolitan district, which constitutes 7.5 percent of the total urban population of India, nearly one third live in slums with densities, in some instances, as high as 2,400 persons per acre. About 30 percent of its population share one room with two other families; 15 percent live in shops; and 17 percent have no home at all. Only 0.7 percent of the total area is given to parks and recreation places and only 5 percent to transportation uses, whereas in a modern city at least 5 percent to 10 percent of the area is normally given to recreation and 25 percent to 30 percent to transportation. In Africa, the population of Dar es Salaam doubled during the last ten years, that of Accra and Luanda trebled, and that of Conakry increased four times in the last five years. In Latin America the population of Santiago and Bogotá doubled between 1940 and 1960, that of São Paulo, Lima, and Mexico City increased threefold, and that of Caracas increased five times.

The impact on society of this ever growing cluster of humanity in urban areas has been great indeed. On the economic plane, urbanization has been associated with the full development of capitalism, including its reconstruction, socialism, banking, trade and insurance, unprecedented levels of construction, and employment of technical manpower. On the political plane, it has been accompanied by adult franchise, new forms of local government, and the rise and growth of political parties. On the cultural plane, it has set the trend toward universal literacy and mass enjoyment of leisure.

On the social plane, however, one of the important aspects of the impact of urbanization is the change of balance in the population structure. Because expectations rise much faster than opportunities, the rate of change in occupational structure set in motion by urbanization is often overtaken by the rate of geographical mobility from rural areas into towns and cities. The developing areas particularly face this problem. If migrations from rural to urban areas were matched by a planned training of people with low-productive agricultural skills so that they would have high-productive industrial skills, then the situation could be controlled. But the lack of planned industrial and regional development, useful skills, and urban facilities has made this a difficult problem for the developing areas. As a result, urban areas everywhere have been acquiring population quite often in excess of job opportunities and almost always in excess of existing civic facilities. The positive advantage of having a concentration of only a productive population in urban areas, people who produce more than they consume, is thus offset to a very large extent except in the developed areas.

An inescapable consequence of this is, therefore, the great mushrooming of slums and shanty towns which accompanies urbanization in the developing areas. Painful shortages of housing and civic amenities are bound to overlay the process of industrial development for many years to come. Historically, this is an old problem in the West, first met with in the wake of the Industrial Revolution. In the developed countries, it is being successfully dealt with through the creation of suburbs and neighborhoods, parks, modern housing, and zoning of industrial districts. It is true that it has not yet been possible even for some of the most advanced among them to remove pockets of poverty from their midst. But these pockets often owe their intractability to obstacles to interracial integration. Like the ghettos of old they continue to take scorn and neglect and, in turn, breed contempt and anger which can very well threaten the foundations of these societies. It is therefore heartening to see that a great battle, based on reason and patient effort, has been joined in the United States to overcome these grave threats to stability and progress. It is particularly reassuring to us in India; for we, in our own humble way, are struggling to bring back to our common stream of life nearly one fourth of our population whom 3,000 years of bondage have left traditionally underprivileged.

While it has been possible in the advanced countries by and large to separate living and working environments through the creation of new communities, neighborhoods, and rapid transit systems, many of these features are either absent or present only in a rudimentary form in the developing countries. It is true that where new industrial towns have been built a balance between living and working environments has been sought from the beginning. But in spite of every effort, as the new industrial towns of India show, the centripetal forces of population concentration in many cases prove too strong. This is mainly because in many of these countries regional planning has not yet gone beyond the location of selected industries.

Urban legislation in the developed countries over the last 100 years has covered a wide field, including sanitary regulations, health services, slum clearance, housing, job security, minimum wage provisions, free public schools, public parks and playgrounds, as well as public libraries and museums. In many developing countries such social legislation is only in its initial stages. It is not that these countries do not realize the importance of sanitation, pollution control, industrial health and safety, traffic control, vocational guidance and training, or recreational facilities. The real problem is their overwhelming lack of technical manpower and financial resources. Their general level of poverty also makes it difficult for voluntary efforts to be widespread and effective.

The psychological problems of urbanization are no less important than those of social organization. While in the advanced countries the gaps in urban living standards are being closed through a more or less uniform pattern of consumption of durables and services, the differences in living standards in urban areas of the developing countries are staggering. Limousines splash mud on pedestrians in rags and tatters while the new rich gorge themselves in fashionable restaurants within the sight of the starving or the semistarved. Fancy mansions raise their proud heads in exclusive park neighborhoods while ulcerous chains of jhuggis, callampas, and favelas sprawl within nodding distance. The coexistence of these widely divergent ways of living at close quarters blunts human sensibility to the point of accepting it as part of the natural order of things, making social changes even more difficult.

These glaring differences in living standards inevitably lead to differences in cultural standards. Torn from their original moorings the urban poor in the developing world either try to replicate their own cultural milieu by keeping to the same linguistic, religious, and racial grooves, thus defeating the objectives of a city life, or are totally lost to culture. On the other hand, the affluent afford the best in culture that money can buy.

These gaps in standards have been associated with another feature. While in the developed countries the urban dwellers have been liberated from a sense of localism and possess a common civic conscience, in the developing countries both the urban rich and the urban poor are apt to show a remarkable lack of community sense. Unequal living, segregated education, and a divergent culture have combined to prevent the growth of a common civic sense or a sense of participation in community activities.

Finally, all this is apt to result in a coarsening of the human fiber, not only of the deprived and the neglected but also of the rich and the successful. In the place of the diversified human relationships which urbanization has made possible in the developed countries, the relationships which govern rich and poor alike in developing countries are most likely to be money, food, and sex. The impersonality of social relations caused by the transiency of contact which urbanization implies has strengthened rather than weakened this tendency.

These are hard words to say, but anybody who is familiar with the dehumanizing processes at work in the metropolises of the developing world can hardly remain blind to these facts. And yet out of these sloughs of despond arises much that is beautiful and fascinating. These huge hives of humanity somehow make possible the flowering of a small number of men and women who are poor in wealth but rich in spirit and faith, an elite which is cosmopolitan and universal in its outlook and finds an echo of its faith in its counterparts in the developed countries of the world. Whether they adopt New York, London, or Paris, or Belgrade, Calcutta, or Caracas as their habitat, this new international elite is the true precursor of the world citizenry of tomorrow. Without parochialism, prejudice, or preconceptions, without bitterness or rancor, with the whole world as their home and all of humanity as their kith and kin to whose service they are dedicated, this small elite is probably the noblest fruit of urbanization.

In the last analysis, therefore, urbanization is much more than the process of growth of cities just as it is much more than the movement of people from the countryside into towns and cities. The rise of cities, conurbation, and the movement of people from country to town and from primary to secondary and tertiary activities are undoubtedly indices of this process. But they do not exhaust the process. Imbalances in the occupation structure, slums, confusion between living and working environments, as well as gaps in living standards, civic sense, and culture, may overshadow it in its initial stages. But given the time, the will, and the resources, the process goes much farther; for it is the process of transformation from the traditional way of life and work to the modern way of life and work. It represents a change in the value structure and culture of a society which increasingly claims the entire world as its domain. Whether the locus of his daily existence is changed or not, urbanization tends to transform a villager into a townsman and finally into a world citizen.

We have already seen how in the first phase of this transformation there is a movement from the countryside into urban pockets in the wake of industrialization and also how in its second phase the compulsions of a transindustrial society bring about a countermovement in the sense of the transformation of villages into urbanized neighborhoods and communities. In the greater part of the world—in Asia, Africa, and Latin America—the first phase is not yet over, while in the most advanced countries of the world—in Europe and North America—it is the second phase which is now beginning to unfold before our eyes. In the end, however, the first phase will gradually merge into the second, and the whole world will become urbanized. It is in this sense that urbanization is a universal phenomenon, a universal process which, though proceeding at different speeds in different parts of the world, nevertheless encompasses the whole world.

The social impact of the first phase of urbanization is going to prove much more staggering than that of the second. It will be too optimistic to expect the first phase to come to an end in most of the developing countries in Asia and Africa even by the end of this century. Many more towns and cities will come into existence, and their urban population will undoubtedly increase manifold, but it is not likely to be such as completely to change the contours of life in the country and set a pattern for the rest of the population. It is possible that the patterns of consumption in the countryside will be to a large extent influenced by those in the towns and cities, but its patterns of production are not likely to be completely superseded by those in the towns and cities. It is this dichotomy between the patterns of consumption and the patterns of production in the countryside and the consequent tension and painfulness of urbanization which holds much trouble in store for these countries.

Compared to this, the problem of further urbanization of trans-industrial societies in the advanced countries is much simpler. It is true that difficult social problems remain even there. Integrating racial minorities is one such problem; wiping out pockets of poverty which have escaped the process of industrialization and urbanization is another. In many of these countries the growing imbalance in the supply of technical manpower is still another problem. But all these problems are easily controlled because the resources available for controlling them are more than adequate.

Historically, cities have acted as focal points for many complex social activities which cannot be contained in the monotone of a pastoral or rural life. As shrines, citadols, political capitals and administrative headquarters, workshops, universities, and markets, sometimes many of those together, they have drawn to their vortices hundreds of thousands from the countryside and changed their way of life. From hunters, nomads, and peasants, people who have drifted into cities have turned into artisans and laborers, traders and bankers, teachers and writers, soldiers and politicians, and even brigands and professional assassins.

The ancient cities of Mesopotamia, Egypt, and the Indus Valley stood, on the one hand, for discipline and order and made their inhabitants control floods, repair storm damages, store water, and build monuments, riverways, and highways and create science, philosophy, and poetry. Many of them, on the other hand, brought in their wake ghettos, slavery, prostitution, and war and often an orientation toward death. Ur, Mohenjo Daro and Nineveh, Delhi, Peking and Cairo, Athens, Rome and London, have appeared as the great stereotypes of the process of urbanization. Many of the world's ancient cities have been destroyed by rude forces of nature or of history. Cities have died with the desiccation of fertile valleys; cruel conquerors have reduced them to rubble. The seeds of destruction of the world's new cities and urban settlements lie within, in their festering slums stalked by disease and death.

Insuring an Enriched Urban Environment

L. HUGH WILSON

CONSULTANT TO THE MINISTRY OF HOUSING AND
LOCAL GOVERNMENT, UNITED KINGDOM

THE URBAN environment represents a vast and all-too-little-understood subject, and yet it is of profound importance to us all; its improvement seems to me to be the major challenge of our time.

To take the example that I know best, if we in Britain are to deal with the problems of planning and building arising from the population explosion and the need to renew and modernize the obsolete urban environment of our towns and cities, we shall be involved in an investment approximating £200,000 million. Expressed in simple terms, we may well do more building between now and the end of the century than we have done in the whole of our previous history. The population increase alone may represent a new town of 100,000 people every ten weeks. At the same time, we have to grapple with ever increasing traffic congestion and we can expect a continued rise in the standard of living, major changes in leisure needs, and complex effects from changes in industry and commerce.

In Britain in recent years, urban renewal policies have hinged on the modernization of town centers, the emphasis being on comprehensive redevelopment to deal with traffic congestion, obsolescence, and lack of space for expansion. In housing, work has been concentrated on slum clearance and on building to deal with the population increase. Renewal of "twilight" areas surrounding the centers is expected to be started in the 1970s, together with urban road networks on new alignments routed through these outworn areas. In other words, towns were to be renewed outward from the center on the assumption that the structure would remain basically unchanged. Sprawl has been contained to some extent by green belts. In addition, there has been a vigorous policy of new town building to relieve overcrowding in the major cities. Although these basic urban planning pressures—population growth, traffic, and obsolescence—remain, a new urban planning policy is required in the light of current thought on the magnitude of these problems. I have no doubt that a similar story could be told in many countries.

Existing towns and cities are subject to obsolescence due partly to outworn buildings, roads, and services, lack of open space, conflicting land uses, and poor communal facilities, but just as much to changes in demand due to the rising standard of living. At one time we were able to plan towns with a reasonable degree of prediction in terms of the various elements of land use and the communications system. This is no longer the case; we are faced with much greater mobility, leading to diffuse patterns of travel to work and a greater range of shopping and leisure activities. Change is also reflected in the elements of towns; retailing methods and shopping habits are in a state of flux; there is more employment in service industries, often centrally located, and the spread of automation is leading to the rise of larger areas of land by fewer workers; open-space provision is conditioned by new leisure habits and opportunities; housing must be designed to take account of people's needs in the future. Above all, the increase in traffic in towns must lead to greater dependence on public transport and the possibility that new methods of movement will be found.

All these problems become graver and more extensive with the growing population. This leads to the often ill-considered expansion of suburban neighborhoods, in many cases regarded purely as a housing operation without provision of the essential communal facilities, and the redevelopment of town centers that encroach on the old residential areas surrounding the centers without regard to comprehensive planning. All this creates great and often insoluble problems of town structure and social and economic organization.

At the same time, the inadequacy of financial and administrative resources to meet the demands of rapid growth and change also leads to poor quality in the resulting work. Responsibilities are often divided among several local authorities since problems of land use and communications cover wide areas and there is often inadequate coordination among such authorities, between local and central governments, and even within central government.

It is important to keep in mind the need to maintain standards, even under short-term pressures. We must also adopt a comprehensive approach in which physical planning is coordinated with the other essential aspects. Urban planning must be firmly based on the social and economic sciences as well as concerned with the manipulation of buildings and spaces and movement systems and the arrangement and design of all the elements of town life. Planning is a continuous process, and the end product must respect the people's quest for better housing and education, better jobs and higher income, and a more complete social and cultural life; it must make possible the achievement of richness in the urban environment.

SOCIAL NEEDS

It is perhaps an impertinence on my part to refer here to the social needs of man in the urban environment. If I do so it is to offer a glimpse of the working of one planner's mind and to explain to some extent the basis of the solutions I shall suggest.

It is a commonplace to state that towns are for people and not monuments to planners. Nevertheless, I think we have to be particularly on our guard against "pattern-making" in town planning.

Many planners have felt that towns should be comprised of repeating elements consisting of groups of dwellings with the necessary community facilities. The self-contained neighborhood unit has also been a social planning concept much in evidence in postwar planning. Yet social studies in Britain have shown very little awareness of the arrangement of neighborhoods, and I would suggest that where they are examined, they have no meaning as social entities. In fact, social contacts are generally confined to the residents in small groups of houses or are enjoyed on a town scale by people with particular interests. (The upsurge in car ownership, however, has made people more mobile and thus able to satisfy their interests over a wider field.) Each activity has a particular catchment area served by primary school, church, club, political meeting place, and so forth.

It seems to me that the important thing is to site all the public and community buildings where they can be used to maximum advantage. The main town footpaths (I am assuming that pedestrains and vehicles are separated) can help to determine the location of a number of social facilities where they can contribute to the urban character of the town and introduce greater variety into the environment. This also brings up the question of the balance between the need for social integration and the need for privacy. Much can be achieved in the design of houses and layouts to insure privacy in open spaces and the main rooms of the dwellings whilst encouraging social contact in the public areas.

In following his various activities (home, work, leisure) man must be able to choose between a number of possible places, subject, of course, to reasonable traveling time and distance. He thus uses urban space to suit his own personal and social needs. With shorter working hours and greater mobility there will be a greater degree of choice. An important field of study would be the determination of possible patterns of family and collective activities and the way in which such patterns may develop under changing conditions. To take one example, the location and content of centers are important in urban structure, and a city region can be organized with specialist centers with a wide sphere of influence or with centers that contain a range of activities serving an area of lesser influence.

We have to decide whether the reduction in working hours will result in shorter working days or fewer working days. The answer to this question could be very important in planning; for facilities could be needed to a lesser extent for daily leisure and to a greater extent for weekend and annual holidays. Such requirements as weekend cottages, camping sites, and caravan centers come to mind, together with the resulting problems of weekend transport peaks.

PLANNING FRAMEWORK

The assessment of the planning process must be made at various levels—national, regional, subregional, and urban—if we are to make adequate policy decisions. In particular, I would stress the importance of a planning framework for the urban region to which can be related the various urban structure plans. Such a regional plan would set out the major planning policies, dealing with land use, green belt, overspill of population, distribution of industry, shopping facilities, and communications.

At the town level are the major planning problems of renewal and urban form and structure in new and expanded towns. Here the human environment is the end product, and this can only be created effectively on the basis of a well-conceived planning brief.

The problem of improving the quality of the urban environment must loom large in the future, and perhaps the major obstacle is that of traffic. Provision for moving traffic and the maintenance of good environment depend on two basic planning principles: (*a*) the routing of major traffic onto primary road networks designed specifically for traffic movement; (*b*) the establishment of areas in which traffic needs are subordinated to the quality of the environment.

The amount of traffic which can be accepted without detriment to the environment depends on the financial resources available. If the required scale of investment is not practicable, good environment can be maintained only by limiting the amount of traffic. A clear choice must be made.

The remainder of the field of environmental standards is largely uncharted. We need to know much more about people's requirements and about techniques for measuring them in planning terms. We must also think about such questions as the recognition of town character, the preservation of historic buildings, and the conservation of areas of special importance.

All these considerations must bring about profound changes in the structure of towns, in the relationship between land use and movement patterns, and in the need to plan for considerable land potential. Rapid change demands maximum adaptability and flexibility in urban development, and we need to work out methods which will provide these qualities in the design of new towns and in the renewal of existing towns.

Some of the work will depend on empirical methods of approach, and studies in depth of some of the problems can be undertaken in the process of preparing plans for new and expanded towns. But we also need a strong, coherent program of research aimed at filling the many gaps in our knowledge of the needs and behavior of people and the functional requirements of the various elements of land use and communications.

SOLUTIONS

The planning system.—To achieve worthwhile results we need a new kind of urban plan embodying a positive approach to urban design.

In England the Minister of Housing and Local Government appointed a committee, the Planning Advisory Group, to consider the future of the planning system. The solution put forward was to replace the present development plan by two new types of plan: one would be a broad statement of strategic aims, policies, and standards; the other, a detailed tactical plan to serve as a positive brief for developers. The strategic plan would consist mainly of a written document setting out the problems, the principles to be applied in their solution, and the policies to be adopted. It would cover such matters as land use, traffic generation, public transport and parking policies, population and employment patterns, social structure, and open-space standards. The map would be a simple document looking forward over a considerable period and indicating the grouping of environmental areas and the primary road network. Such a plan, providing the urban structure framework, would be augmented by a series of action plans to deal with the problems of areas to be developed or redeveloped over a much shorter period.

A procedure like this will result in a positive planning brief, but it will mean that local planning authorities will have to face up to the real problems of urban design. It has been suggested that it will require larger local authorities to be involved in planning at the subregional level so that there can be integration of land use and transportation policies covering travel to work, commercial and recreational patterns. Indeed, a commission is now considering the local authority set up in Britain. With reorganization of local government there should also be coordinated policies in central government on investment and building programs.

Manpower.—A bad planning system can prevent good urban design solutions, but a good system cannot prevent bad design. Quality in execution will depend on many factors; the most important, perhaps, is an adequate supply of skilled manpower. Quite simply, good design depends on good designers who are given the right opportunities. At the present time there is a serious shortage of manpower in the design professions in most countries. The more sophisticated the techniques the greater the need for high-caliber men to operate them. Planning is a team operation and must involve a range of skills depending on the scope of the work being carried out. If we are to raise the standards of design in urban development, the full use of all manpower resources is perhaps the most potent method.

Housing.—Housing is the major land user in a town and must be the pacesetter in urban development. Housing programs should be viewed not only from the standpoint of existing housing and new population pressures but also in terms of environmental and transport policies. If full advantage is to be taken of the increasing number of building programs, all major operations should be related to an over-all planning concept so that the impetus and scope of the program can be exploited to improve the whole urban environment.

I illustrate this point by reference to a recent housing redevelopment project near the center of Sheffield, England, where whole slum sections have been replaced by deck-access blocks of flats in a bold, imaginative way. The hilly sites have been exploited to produce a first-class housing environment, and the decks provide a basis for social integration that has been most successful. At the same time, the center of Sheffield has been transformed. Here is an example of comprehensive design on a massive scale which uses housing as an essential element of city regeneration.

CUMBERNAULD

Cumbernauld, in Scotland, one of four new towns proposed in the Clyde Valley Regional Plan, was started in 1956, nearly six years after the last of the first series of new towns in Britain. This fact was important to its over-all design since the planners were able to draw on experience gained in the earlier new towns.

The population proposed was 50,000, and later plans allowed for 70,000. Cumbernauld was destined to be a unique new town if only because of its unusual site on a hilltop of very limited area exposed to prevailing southwest winds. Although within fifteen miles of Glasgow it was to be self-contained, with its own industrial estates; this was a fundamental principle of the regional plan.

Cumbernauld occupies a central position in the lowland industrial belt of Scotland, and the designated space comprises some 4,150 acres. The form of the hilltop led to the general planning concept of the town as a compact urban site with surrounding recreation areas, the whole set against the background of open hilly country.

Cumbernauld was the first complete town to be planned on the basis of a high level of car ownership and usage, with the maximum separation of pedestrians and vehicles and with a separate footpath system to enable people to walk to the center, to the schools, or to the open space without having to come into contact with main traffic. The development of these principles of compactness and the freedom to walk in safety led to abandonment of the neighborhood unit pattern, and the central area was planned to contain all the principal shopping, commercial, and public buildings. Local facilities—primary schools, churches, meeting halls, shops—were placed on the main footpath system and related to the needs of the various groups of people.

The principle of the separation of vehicles and pedestrians was also applied to the design of the housing areas; the most common form layout is that in which the service roads and footpaths interlock. Traffic moves outward to join the distributor roads, while the pedestrians move inward along the local paths to the main town footpath, which provides a direct route to the town center or the open space, passing on the way schools, churches, and shops.

Apart from two main industrial districts, north and south of the hill, some factories are sited in the housing areas but with direct access from the distributor roads. These provide jobs for women who can walk to work from the nearby houses. Now that so many industrial processes are clean and quiet I see no reason why such a policy should not be adopted. I think we have gone too far in the rigorous zoning of industry.

The central area was designed after considerable study of shopping habits and retailing methods and with particular reference to provision for parked cars and to the maximum separation of pedestrians and vehicles. The final design is of a multideck structure with roads and parking underneath and pedestrian areas above. The center is located along the ridge of the hill; the main road runs under the center and gives access to car parks and unloading areas. After parking the car, driver and passengers are able to move to the pedestrian decks by escalator, lift, ramp, or staircase. Goods are taken directly from the loading docks into storage space under the shops. All the floor levels above the roads and car parks are for the exclusive use of pedestrians and have direct access from the town footpaths on either side of the center. The decks are laid out in squares and terraces; some are covered and enclosed to provide shopping halls and others are open. There is also provision for restaurants, hotel, cinema, dance hall, public houses, offices, town hall, library, and so forth, and above are terraces of flats.

Here at Cumbernauld it is possible for the first time to study on a town scale solutions to the problems of the motor age in which we live.

Planning for growth.—Cumbernauld was conceived as a finite town, an element in a regional plan, which is now being developed in city-region terms. But so many of our problems arise from population growth, and a program of finite new towns and town expansions must limit the population which can be accommodated in any area. The advantages of concentration—better public facilities; greater choice in leisure, shopping, and employment—cannot be obtained with a population which is dispersed throughout the countryside. This could result in a policy of large new towns and town expansion schemes in relatively small selected areas where they could form an interrelated pattern of growth.

In relation to a study we carried out in England in the Northampton, Bedford, Bletchley area, astride the motorway between London and Birmingham, we considered the advantages of alternative forms of urban growth to meet the needs of an eventual population of up to one million. In particular we investigated linear groupings of new developments which could be related to other major towns and offered the possibility of infinite and interrelated growth. We looked at possible patterns from the regional and urban aspects and also in terms of the constituent parts of the structure.

One of the most important aspects of linear planning is the organization of communications, and this in turn depends on the relative use of public and private transport. There will always be some people who wish to use public transport and this could become more efficient and economical in operation if it could be used extensively for journeys between home and work during the peak hours.

All forms of public transport move along a line and collect or set down passengers at stopping places which become the focal points for the surrounding areas. These can be divided into two concentric zones: that from which people would walk to the stopping place and that from which they would normally drive to it. The distance that people would walk was estimated at about one third of a mile, and the required time at five to seven minutes.

A public transport system, therefore, has definite implications for town structure in that development can be in the form of areas based in part upon walking distances, and containing residential, industrial, commercial, or recreational sections, connected to each other by the public transport line, roads, and footpaths. The system can be likened to a necklace, the string being the transport line and the beads the areas of development.

To allow for growth, the extent of which may well be unknown, it is important that the structure relate the traffic facilities to development in such a way that the capacity can maintain an acceptable level at all stages without overprovision. Since free movement of the motor car becomes more and more difficult with its increasing size, the system must accommodate the possibility of a change from private to public transport as the city grows and, indeed, from one form of public transport to another. The latter consideration suggests that the public transport should have a separate tract, thus allowing change from bus to rail or monorail and avoiding delay due to congestion on overcrowded roads.

The catchment areas form environmental areas from which extraneous traffic is excluded. Designs for these should be based on the separation of pedestrians and vehicles, with pedestrians moving inward to the public transport stop and community facilities and vehicles outward to the peripheral main road system.

Here I return to the dangers of pattern-making and of forcing people into molds. It is important that each village, town, and city should have its own character and identity. Wide variations in personal taste lead to demands for many forms of environment, of different types and sizes. Patterns such as I have described could accommodate a range of urban units related to site conditions—levels, trees, water, and so on. Indeed, the necklace can have several strands making a directional grid of development with linear and transverse movement patterns, as in our Northampton expansion plan.

Ease of movement within the regional city could have a considerable effect on the social organization. Thus a person could belong to several social groups and enjoy special activities in various centers, each covering a wide catchment area.

Such a planning concept can be most effectively applied to new settlements or to major expansions of existing towns, but our study of Northampton has suggested that it is possible to achieve some restructuring of existing towns. Certainly, our cities are not going to remain static. In Britain about one third of the population growth will be in new towns; the remainder is likely to be accommodated in existing cities. It is necessary to consider whether this growth should be distributed peripherally or in a linear or finger form, departing from the traditional concept of compact urban areas, separated where necessary by green belts. Growth of this order raises major questions, of course, on the future distribution of employment and on the need for any pattern to fit in with subregional policies. We need to consider, for instance, whether there should be a planned dispersal of central area developments and what would be the effect of this on present public transport facilities, particularly in relation to travel to work. If a finger concept could be applied to an existing town it might well be advantageous to redevelop inner areas of poor housing at lower densities, linked with an urban structure plan designed to bring green "lungs" into the city.

If I have appeared to dwell overmuch on the problems of movement in towns it is because I believe that until we have some improvement in conditions and can face with more confidence the vastly more serious situation which will inevitably arise in the coming years, it will be impossible for us to enjoy the richness in urban life which could be ours. I hold strongly to the view that a town should be a meeting place and that this essential function is not possible unless the pedestrian can regain his freedom. He should be protected from the danger, the noise and fumes, and the visual intrusion of the motor car; at the same time, he should be able to use it to serve his own ends. That is the problem we tried to solve at Cumbernauld.

If we can provide an adequate framework for a town in terms of environmental areas and road networks, we can concentrate on quality in design with some chance of success. Fine buildings can have the maximum impact; the spaces between them can provide safe, beautiful, and healthy surroundings for the people who use them.

I realize that I am expressing personal views; in the end, towns are for people, and it is their wishes that really count. From all our modern survey techniques and our computer processes we know so much about the conditions of yesterday. But we know so little about tomorrow, let alone the end of the century for which we are planning today.

So many questions come to mind:

Is it possible to deal with traffic in towns and create a good environment?

Would people rather have access than environment?

Do they care about environment at all?

What is the basis for a rich life?

Anybody who works on the urban environment must have a feeling of humility but also a deep sense of conviction in the rightness of what he is doing. He must have all the information that is available but then he must work by hypothesis and evaluation to produce the best possible results. But techniques and methods are only tools, and in the end he must rely on his judgment of values and qualities; this is where skill and experience are needed.

Let me remind you that this is where social workers must help. You could do so much to interpret human needs to us but so often you only tell us afterward where we have gone wrong; you have plenty of opportunities for that, I admit. I ask you, instead, to take your place on planning teams and to join in the creative process of evolving the plans and policies which will lead to richness in the urban environment. I can think of no better cause.

Remarks

HUBERT HUMPHREY

VICE PRESIDENT OF THE UNITED STATES

I AM INDEED privileged to bring the greetings of the government and people of the United States to the delegates from more than seventy countries attending the XIIIth International Conference on Social Work.

This is the first time since the Second World War that from all parts of the world persons concerned with social welfare have met in our country to discuss common interests and concerns. We have been honored by your presence, and I am confident that your deliberations have been challenging and productive.

Your sessions have focused upon a significant and important subject. Your findings will be studied and applied by persons in many lands who are striving to perfect the quality of urban life in the face of rising counterpressures—population growth, the rural-urban migration, food shortages, lack of development capital, insecure political institutions, and the dehumanizing forces of technology and industrialization.

Few nations are exempt from the threat of runaway urbanization. The growing complexity of life, the rising interdependence among people in this age of specialization, almost dictates that men shall live together in vast metropolitan areas in search of a more just, secure, and happy life.

Historically, the growth of cities and the rise of democratic societies were closely linked. The economic and social freedom, not to mention the political opportunities, encountered in the city were essential factors in evolving a new social order based on mass participation.

Today, with the value of widespread political and economic participation well-established, we face another and equally vital challenge: to insure the sanctity of human values and individual action in the midst of this process of mass urbanization.

Urban centers too often resemble a kind of living hell where individuals are systematically and ruthlessly deprived of any real opportunity to exercise meaningful choice in these vital areas of life. They should, instead, be places where all men can experience the humanizing impact of creative and worthwhile employment, refreshing leisure activities, stimulating education, satisfying home surroundings, and efficient public services.

In America we are in the midst of a great national effort to rescue our cities—and the people who inhabit them—from decay, deprivation, and discrimination. As President Johnson said recently:

... one word can best describe the task that we face ... and that word is "immense." In less than 40 years, the urban population of this country is going to double, and we will have to build in our cities as much as has already been built since the first settler arrived on these shores.

And we know that more than bricks, mortar, glass, and steel are involved. Again to quote our President: "It is the *people* who live in our cities and the *quality* of the lives they lead that should concern every public servant today."

We are all acutely aware of the violence and civil disorders which have taken place in some American cities over the past several years. We know that in most cases these outbreaks involved Negro Americans or other minority groups who live in the poorer, more deprived areas of our large cities.

We decry and deplore this violence and strife. We know that only under conditions of civil peace and domestic tranquillity can we hope to achieve the progress which will guarantee to all men full equality and opportunity in their daily lives.

But we also know that the lives of those who live in these areas bypassed by our national prosperity and affluence must be changed; hard, visible evidence must be forthcoming that a new day of opportunity and achievement is at hand: hard, visible evidence in terms of self-respecting job opportunities and the education and training necessary to hold those jobs; hard, visible evidence in terms of decent housing and recreational facilities which respect rather than destroy the unique character of neighborhoods; and hard, visible evidence in terms of a welfare system which preserves a sense of human dignity and provides the motivation and stimulation for generating self-support and self-respect.

Generations of poverty, discrimination, and despair have left scars which cannot heal in a day, a month, or a year. Unremitting effort, expanded resources, patience, and understanding on all sides are required, but the job can, and *will*, be done.

There is, however, this additional question which must be faced in America and elsewhere: In the process of meeting basic material needs, how is the vitality of the human spirit preserved in the impersonal urban environment—especially among people who have been on the bottom rung of our urbanized society's social and economic ladder?

Physical slums alone do not produce the problems concentrated in our urban ghettos. If it were possible to replace overnight the tenements in our cities with new housing, we would not overcome simultaneously the unemployment, juvenile delinquency, drug addiction, poor education, ill health, and family breakdown.

A recent study revealed that most of the rioters in Watts, California, last year *were* employed and lived in reasonably decent housing. Yet these people struck out blindly and senselessly against forces which seemingly denied them all opportunity to become real persons—in their own eyes and in the eyes of society. In the terrible rioting and violence which occurred, we actually discovered individuals attempting to achieve a sense of identity and selfhood.

Yes, it is one thing to provide food and shelter to those in need. It is quite another to perfect a substance and style of life which preserve those human attributes necessary to the maintenance of a civilized and rewarding life.

Almost two centuries ago our founders spoke about the right to "life, liberty and the pursuit of happiness." Today this promise has penetrated into the remotest corners of our urban ghettos, and people are sensing the full and complete meaning of these historic words.

This concept of freedom has never been restricted to the original thirteen colonies huddled on the eastern coast of this continent. Indeed, from our earliest history we have viewed the cause of freedom in America as the cause of all mankind. And today the affirmation, "We shall overcome!" or the cry, "Freedom now," is not just on the lips of our heroic civil rights workers, it is echoed by people everywhere. Therefore, whether we succeed or fail *here* in our efforts to achieve a humane *and* humanized urban society will have an impact far beyond the borders of this nation.

We admit frankly that many of the answers have not been found. But some vital ingredients to success are known.

First, we must attack simultaneously the problems generated by the physical environment and by the socioeconomic conditions if lasting progress in either realm is to be achieved.

A wide spectrum of social and welfare services combined effectively with physical improvements can upgrade both personality and environment, transforming the downward spiral of poverty and despair into a rising curve of self-sufficiency and faith in the future.

Second, persons who suffer from deprivation of both body and spirit must participate directly in prescribing and administering the cure.

There are great reservoirs of latent energy, talent, enthusiasm, and insight to be tapped if we but possess the skill, common sense, and faith to do so. We are, in fact, witnessing throughout America a magnificent rebirth of freedom in our urban and rural slums. People are being offered the chance—and the responsibility—to help mold their future and the future of their neighborhood and city.

Third, we must emphasize those government and nongovernment programs which demonstrate to people in the context of daily living that they really count, that society has a place for them.

Elements of the antipoverty program like neighborhood legal services, health centers, and VISTA have this capacity to tear down walls of ignorance and doubt which bar meaningful participation in society at large. The National Teacher Corps and educational advances stimulated by the Elementary and Secondary Education Act can help young minds otherwise destined to remain closed and stagnant to experience the marvelous excitement of learning and discovery. And for those who require financial aid and related social services, they should be provided as a matter of *right* and not as the result of complex, sometimes incomprehensible, administrative criteria and requirements.

Finally, in our efforts to develop area-wide responses to the physical problems of housing, transportation, and urban redevelopment, we must not ignore the smaller dimension wherein the individual can experience the rewards of a rich and varied life.

Government policy must be directed toward encouraging the creation—or preservation—of vibrant and living neighborhood communities. A city cannot simply be a place to live, to work, to exist. A city must be a *community* in the richest sense of the word, a combination of material and spiritual resources which gives every person a chance to express his unique talents and personality.

This involves an eye for humane and intimate details as well as a determination to conquer the major social and economic ills. This means a concern for the small park, play area, corner store, and neighborhood center. We are, in short, coming to see that the process of urbanization can be directed toward securing the betterment of man both materially and spiritually—if we possess the wit to direct and control these forces for the fulfillment of human objectives.

Through such proposals as the Demonstration Cities bill, the rent supplements program, the Omnibus Housing Act of 1965, the Elementary and Secondary Education Act, and the many facets of the war against poverty, this nation is seizing the initiative on a number of fronts to stop decay of people as well as of buildings. We are involving all levels of government and urging full participation by private foundations, universities, service groups, and individuals.

One fact must remain in our thinking: America today is blessed with the material and human resources to accomplish this goal.

We also know that some nations have initiated programs and approaches which are more imaginative and effective than those we have attempted in the United States. We welcome the opportunity to learn from your experiences, we solicit your counsel and advice.

In the same manner, we hope that you can learn from us as President Johnson's vision of the great society takes form and substance through legislation, executive decisions, and action programs at all levels of government and in the private sector.

What task is more vital than liberating millions of our fellow men from a life of misery, poverty, and defeat or enabling them to exercise qualities which are uniquely human—the ability to create, to judge, to accept rights and responsibilities, to use freedom, to acquire dignity and self-respect?

With this sense of common purpose and identity among the peoples of the earth, we cannot doubt the eventual victory of the human spirit or the achievement of human freedom even as we build cities worthy of man's highest aspirations.

Developing a Sense of Community
in Today's Urban Areas

WHITNEY M. YOUNG, JR.

EXECUTIVE DIRECTOR, NATIONAL URBAN LEAGUE

SOME YEARS AGO Dr. Howard Thurman, University Minister-at-Large and Professor of Spiritual Resources and Disciplines at the School of Theology, Boston University, made this statement:

It is a strange freedom to be adrift in the world of men without a sense of anchor anywhere. Always there is the need of mooring, the need of a firm grip on something that is rooted and will not give. The urge to be accountable to someone, to know that beyond the individual himself there is an answer that must be given and cannot be denied. The very spirit of man tends to panic from the desolation of going nameless up and down the streets of other minds where no salutation greets and no friendly recognition makes secure. It is a strange freedom to be adrift in the world of men.

Always a way must be found for bringing into one's solitary place the settled look from another's face, for getting the quiet sanction of another's grace to undergird the meaning of the self. To be ignored, to be passed over as of no account and of no meaning, is to be made into a faceless thing. It is better to be the complete victim of an anger unrestrained and a wrath which knows no bounds, to be torn asunder without mercy or battered to a pulp, than to be passed over as if one were not. For here at least one is dealt with, encountered, vanquished, or overwhelmed—but not ignored. It is a strange freedom to go nameless up and down the streets of other minds where no salutation greets and no sign is given to mark the place one calls one's own. For a name marks the claim a man stakes against the world; it is the private banner under which he moves which is his right whatever else betides. A name is a man's water mark above which the tides can never rise. It is the thing he holds that keeps him going whenever a light has failed or a marker has been destroyed. It is the rallying point around which a man gathers all that he means by himself. To be made anonymous and to give to it the acquiescence of the heart is to live without life, and for such a one, even death is no dying.

Thurman further defines community as the intent of creation. He says that community is the experience of realizing the fulfillment of one's self, the actualizing of potential; that community is a part of the racial memory of man; that in all the accounts of creation the basic notion is present that there was a time when there was harmony—harmony and an order of innocence. He draws a distinction between innocence, which has been lost, and goodness, which is an achievement. Mankind, according to Thurman, must win the right to move back into the garden. Today, the goal we seek, the achievement of goodness, lies, perhaps for the first time, within theoretical reach.

In the United States and the other technologically advanced nations of the world the problem in dealing with the urban complex is how to minimize deprivation, and perhaps how to approach the experience of a community in all its ramifications, with a maximum of resources to draw upon. In underdeveloped countries, the problem is the converse: how to arrive at human and humane solutions with a minimum of resources.

The pace of urbanization varies widely in different parts of the world; and while it poses similar problems, they appear in varying ratios. Today, 70 percent of the population of the United States lives in urban areas, and it is projected that by the year 2010, when the population will have increased to 400,000,000, most will be living in cities. Even today one half of the population is concentrated in only one percent of the country's total area. In Canada it is estimated that 79 percent of the total population will be urban by 1980. The Netherlands, already densely populated, anticipates a 75 percent increase by the end of the century.

In Germany the urban population comes to just over 50 percent of the total population, but the pressure on the cities is creating problems of urban integration similar to those in more heavily urbanized countries. In Yugoslavia, where, before the Second World War, 75 percent of the population engaged in agriculture, today close to 50 percent are congregated in cities and towns. The population of Austrian cities has doubled over the last century. In Hong Kong, urban density goes as high as 200,000 persons per square mile, perhaps the highest in the world.

The changes brought about by urbanization cause severe stresses both for the community and for the individual. Housing shortages, due both to war and to the influx from rural areas, are chronic in most major cities. Poverty becomes concentrated in areas of deteriorating housing, whether in the ancient cities of Europe or in the United States. In the United States, current informed estimates place the production of slums at a higher rate than the production of houses, with more people now living in slums than on farms.

From the standpoint of social and welfare services, urbanization has perhaps its most profound impact on the structure of family institutions. The old traditions and values of the original family unit disintegrate. Family functions, roles, and expectations change. Technological development greatly reduces the importance of the family as an autonomous economic and social unit. Conflicts of cultural values emerge between grandparents, parents, and children. The home ceases to function to the same degree as a center for its members.

As social workers we hold the responsibility for insuring that the same skills, genius, and creative drive that have gone into brick-and-mortar progress throughout the world, into the building of bridges, highways, and tunnels, and indeed into smashing the atom and making flights into space, must and do now go into planning with people for their own social needs. Only in this way can our cities reflect viable functional modes of productive living rather than struggles for survival against despair, hopelessness, and frustration. Children then will not be walled off from grass and sky and adults need not be faced with a monotonous routine which, at best, becomes a matter of mere existing—and without much choice.

Man in the urban complex has more than just physiological needs—the needs for food, clothing, and shelter. He also has psychological needs—the needs for attention, affection, status, and a feeling that he is making a contribution to his community.

At one time a man was adequate if he simply provided a roof over the heads of his family and could give his children a piece of candy from time to time. To be able to perform these simple acts was sufficient to obtain physiological and psychological satisfaction and to provide him with status in the community.

Today the bulk of the world population may still be largely rural and agrarian, but the human flooding of the cities is occurring everywhere, and in the technologically advanced countries the flood threatens to leave the countryside increasingly barren of people. In the recent past, when the population was more generally dispersed, it was a fairly simple matter to find a job adequate to one's needs and to acquire all the status necessary to one's sense of well-being. If others elsewhere were doing a better job, the agrarian man did not know about it. It was not brought forcibly to his attention, and as a result, his criteria for measuring his adequacy were pretty much limited by the boundaries of his personal observation.

But then two things happened. First, opportunities for work in the rural community began to dry up through technological change and industrialization, so that man found himself increasingly limited in satisfying his own primordial needs, physiological and psychological. Second, and coupled with the first, was the advance in the communications media, which meant that his growing sense of inadequacy was further reinforced by the vision of those outside his immediate community who were doing what he was doing, but doing it more elaborately.

And so with the drying up of opportunities for work in the agrarian setting, urban society emerged, not because the individual man really wanted to live in such close proximity with other men, but because in order to fulfill his role as a provider he responded to the magnetic pull of the cityscape.

In many ways, of course, urban society offers great opportunities. It offers heightened opportunities in employment, in education, in cultural enrichment, in the modern conveniences of transportation and sanitation. It offers entertainment in unheard-of abundance in the sports arenas, in the museums, in theaters, movie houses, and concert halls, and at home before the television set, but it also has very real disadvantages. Living at close quarters with other people, individual man finds life more impersonal, more competitive, more formal. Individual man finds himself hardly a name unless, in the vernacular, he is a "name."

Living in the city demands more in terms of skills and of sophistication, and so man, newly transplanted within the urban complex, faces, and feels, alienation, a sense of rejection and loneliness, which makes even more painful the vision of those who are more affluent than he in the affluent society he sees all about him. Among the numerical majority, it is he who drives the chauffeured Cadillac, not he who is driven in it; it is he who lives in the railroad flat and is the doorman in the luxury building, witnessing the wealth of men who are, in fact, doing just what he is doing in relation to their families, but doing it within a much higher system of rewards; and he either reacts with hostility by concluding that he is being exploited by the forces that are making others affluent, or he is diminished in his own self-estimation and says to himself, "I'm a failure." Such self-devaluation carries over into his role as a husband and a father and into his concept of his own status and dignity.

The institutions in which he once got status, the lodge, the school, the church—by whatever names they are known in different societies—do not play the same role in urban society that they do in an agrarian community. In most urban societies, status attaches to the country club, the chamber of commerce, the business and professional organizations; and the man at the bottom of the pyramid belongs to none of these. And this fact is world-wide, whatever may be the precise institutions.

In this process, very important things are lost sight of, things like integrity and neighborliness. Such characteristics do not "pay off" in the same way that they did in the agrarian society, and the failure to transplant these values into urban society leads to the sense of alienation I am talking about and to the hostility I am talking about. Is it possible that the alienation and the hostility develop to the point where the individual finds it hard to live with himself?

He becomes anxious and then he becomes apathetic. Anxiety is what he feels during the first week and the first month as a stranger in urban society, as a stranger in a new, impersonal, formal setting where he is nameless and faceless and confronted by the need to identify man amongst the faceless society of men. What he experiences is the converse of community.

Under the burden of anxiety, individual man becomes apathetic, overwhelmed, withdrawn. Because he does not want to acknowledge that he himself is inadequate in a new setting, he must cite power bigger than himself, and what he says to himself and the community is, "I don't care"; "I don't want to succeed anyhow"; "You can't beat the system"; "You can't fight City Hall. Apathy is hopelessness, powerlessness, and the forgetting of the most important fact, the fact that money is not power, that status is not power, that color can never be power, that the greatest power is to be right. And if one is right and believes in that right, one can get power. The Negro cause in America today is right, and that is why it upsets those who refuse to accept change.

The danger lies in hostility and alienation. Hostility results in coups and revolutions; either violent revolutions, like the riots in the Negro ghettos of the United States, or the bloodless coups that have upset many a political apple cart. Under the impetus of alienation, the individual prefers to be hated rather than ignored. Tolstoy once said that "the greatest crime against men is not to deny him what he wants, but to keep him from even wanting."

The question is how, given all the factors that make up reality, we can build into urban society the human institutions which will provide that experience of community. The problem is how to make the urban environment human and humane, how to make the geographical entity in which so many people reside livable, how to guarantee that people do not live as part of an amorphous mass, as impersonal cogs in the urban complex where the size and formality and the impersonal quality of the urban setting tend to deprive the individual man of his sense of identity.

Technology itself is not the enemy. It has the potential, the beginnings of which we already see in the countries with the most highly developed technologies, to contribute to the realization of a persistent human vision: to enlarge the capacities of man, and to extend his control over his environment. Where technology has changed the productive process, its fruits have been visible in higher standards of living. The meaning of technology is not only that it produces more goods, but that in reducing their cost it provides the solid foundation for creating social equality among groups.

In addition, the superior education required by a highly developed technology should mean a great deal to the life enrichment of the individual. It means not only that he is equipped for the job market, but that he is able to enjoy more fully other aspects of life. What we need now is a greater educational input for greater productive output in the future, a formula with many ramifications for the personal enrichment of the individual and for the ability of the individual to make creative use of increasing leisure time.

Technology alone is not the answer. There is a widely held belief in the United States, derived largely from experience in military and space technology, that few tasks are beyond our capability if we but concentrate enough money and manpower upon them. And yet our unmet human and community needs are vast, and despite the contributions of technology to higher standards of living for economic and political reasons, we have not yet evolved solutions to the monotony and drudgery of many work processes and to the routinization of life off the job.

Much of man's battle today is against the dehumanizing side effects of industrialization and technology. It is obvious that we cannot go back to preindustrial methods of production, to hand labor; so the question is how, in modern, urban, technological society, we can give dignity *to* work, provide dignity *in* work, and beyond that, meet the needs of individuals for recognition in the community, for opportunity for leadership, and for growth of a sense of total community. The problem is how to dignify and humanize what tends to be routine and mechanized, both on and off the job.

Some solutions are potentially to be found *on* the job. No one disputes that to the greatest possible extent work should be pleasurable and meaningful, and the time is past due for the recognition that machines can now be designed to serve the needs of those who operate them. In such a creative synthesis of human and productive needs we can achieve not only more efficient production but also more satisfactory personal development. Today it is possible to view jobs as broad entities in which the human personality must be considered as vital a component as the nonhuman mechanism.

In the relatively near future, in what some are already referring to as "postindustrial society," we may be happy to see a man go through two or three cycles of retraining or of new careers because of the continuing need for new skills to keep abreast of new technologies and new intellectual techniques. We should explore the possibility of a new system whereby individuals could continue the education they need to learn new skills. When industry, for example, is forced to lay off employees temporarily, firms should be encouraged to use these "intermissions" as training and study periods; the cost of this time, perhaps, could be borne cooperatively by government and industry.

In highly technological societies, we also have the new benefits of leisure time to consider. In the future, leisure time will surely take a greater number of forms: periodic lengthy vacations; more holidays; sabbatical leaves to provide opportunities for extended physical rest, personal reappraisal, retraining, and additional education; earlier retirement, including "phased" retirement which permits gradual reduction in the length of the workday and work-week some years before actual retirement; and a simple reduction in the number of working hours. Again, the higher degree of education that technological society requires of the individual should contribute greatly to his creative use of increasing leisure time.

Adaptability to such changes is perhaps one of our greatest needs, and it should be the effort of government, industry, labor, and all the social agencies to adopt those measures which will help achieve that adaptability and permit the life of the individual man within technological urban society to be lived at its most fruitful.

We must explore every avenue to the creative adaptation of individuals. It has frequently occurred to me, for example, that we have never permitted mediocre artists to make a living in society, although mediocrity has never been much of an obstacle to earning at least a modest living in most other fields. In music, art, and sculpture, however, we have restricted the financial rewards to the experts, and the modest practitioner has had to make his living in some other way. As a world society we ought to see the wisdom of allowing fully for the creative outlet even if the artist is less than a Michelangelo.

Too many teachers are frustrated artists and bad teachers. I am afraid too many social workers are frustrated musicians and poets. It might prove to be more effective social planning to provide channels in which these people could make their living more rewarding and productive for all.

Flexibility is eminently desirable in society, and a flexible society should reflect the full range of our diversities as individuals. There is great value in diversity; everyone has something to contribute to our world society.

In 1965 I was in Africa with a group of American businessmen. They took me along, I suppose, to establish credibility, and I went because I was curious to see if American business could invest somewhere in Africa other than South Africa or Rhodesia. When we landed at our first stop and I saw all the people who surround airplanes when they land—the men who wheel up the stairs and the men who swarm around a plane—my impulse was to ask how they got their jobs, to congratulate them on their FEPC; and then I realized where I was. This was the first time I had ever seen these jobs performed by Negroes.

On the next flight, I was settled in my seat prior to take-off—and the crew came aboard. This just goes to show that though I have spent a lifetime in civil rights, even *I* can be brainwashed. When I saw that the pilot was black, I had a momentary qualm—even I, who have been saying for years that given the opportunity, the Negro can achieve as well as his white brother. I still had a lingering sensation when we left the ground, but take-off was perfect and so was touchdown at the end of the flight.

While we were in transit the pilot spoke over the intercom. He spoke in the most beautiful Oxford English, and the most beautiful cultivated French. He delivered a lecture on the history and the geography and the economics of the country we passed over. He was nothing like the frustrated radio announcers we get from coast to coast in America. And I thought, "What a waste." We have let talents go undeveloped throughout our history simply because of the inability to ignore the color of a man's skin. If we developed such talent, we might have a cure by now for the common cold, a cure for cancer.

When we met with local government officials, I found the same thing. They knew their subjects. They were beautifully articulate. All I could think of was the waste of talent here and that no world can afford such waste.

Culture grows out of both affluence and deprivation. There is no such thing as a culturally *denied* person. People may be culturally deprived, even in the gilded ghettos of a Westchester or a Park Avenue, but everyone has a culture. There is something positive in all cultures, and perhaps the greatest sense of community comes in the recognition by the individual that he has something to offer and a positive contribution to make. Perhaps it is a question of dignity.

Let me illustrate. This spring, 6,000 Negroes marched in a parade of the 369th Veterans Association up Fifth Avenue in New York City. Of this number, about 4,000 were young Harlem children. As group after group of children came abreast of the reviewing stand each went into its turn on an order from a squad leader and performed elaborate broken-order drill with no further commands. The difficulties of the drills proved that these children were not uneducable. And when they got to the end of the parade route at 87th Street, after a forty-block march, they wanted to march all the way to, and through, Harlem to 141st Street. Given a role to play, a responsibility to discharge, a model to live up to, a direction in which to march, our children in the Negro ghettos of America and the millions of disadvantaged children throughout the world are neither uneducable nor lazy. In the main, they are poor, and poverty is the enemy which spawns all other problems and undermines personal dignity in urban society throughout the world today.

All the institutions within our various societies must gird themselves for the battle necessary to solve the problems of poverty. Government, industry, and labor have their roles to play. Our educational systems have massive roles to play in training people for personally productive and rewarding roles. Our churches and religious institutions must play critical roles in the world-wide war against poverty. Perhaps most important of all are the critical roles that those of us who are engaged in social work must play.

Our goals, as I said earlier, lie perhaps for the first time within theoretical reach. The social worker is a prime civilizing force, and I hope I have made plain by now that the test of civilization lies in the relationship of individual man to his brother. Only through his relationship to his brother can the individual man relate positively to his environment. Technology has made the world a neighborhood; we must make it a brotherhood, for we shall all live together as brothers or die together as fools.

The challenge, then, to the social worker, in whatever corner of the world he practices his profession, is to bring to bear upon the tragic human problems which cry out for relief the great resources of conviction, know-how, and material wherewithal now available in world society—resources which throughout the world today all too often are directed toward mankind's destruction rather than his ascension.

Even where poverty is at its greatest, even where the density of population dazes the mind, real possibilities for solution have been demonstrated. I cannot fail to be deeply impressed by the need for all of us to study carefully the experiences of other countries.

I am impressed, for example, by the fact that while the urban density of the Hong Kong population goes as high as 200,000 persons per square mile and 5,000 persons per acre, and that while the bulk of the population is unaccustomed to living in an urban community, yet neither riots nor pestilence rage.

I am impressed by the fact that although the wage level is still low, there has been an increase of 82 percent in average wage rates paid by major industries in the period from 1958 to August, 1966, accompanied by only a 14 percent rise in the cost of living.

I am further impressed by the fact that Hong Kong's enterprising population is virtually her only natural resource. There is no tariff wall to shelter the inefficient, yet there is relatively full employment.

These are facts that bear close examination and study by those who are concerned with urban problems, whether in the United States or elsewhere.

Although I have several times referred to the Negro problem in America I should not like to leave false notions. There is a race problem in America mainly because the American Negro, as he should, compares his status to that of other Americans—not to other nationalities of whatever color, for by that standard, he would be relatively much better off than most of the world's population.

I would also state from my observations throughout the world that few countries have resolved the issue of diversity, whether it be of class, tribe, race, or religion. Some countries, like Rhodesia and South Africa, have brutally postponed it by a policy of apartheid, others, by virtual extermination and rigid immigration quotas.

Finally, I would emphasize that peace goes beyond the absence of war, and meaningful human relations reflect a great deal more than the absence of conflict. They mirror the presence of justice and equal opportunity. It is the ending of inequities and the closing of the gap between the "have" and the "have nots." Freedom above all must mean the freedom to fight for freedom, to dissent, to protest, to differ publicly with those in power. In many countries throughout the world this right and this freedom do not exist, and what appears on the surface as harmonious calm in such a callous and repressive atmosphere is but the prelude to tragic holocaust. President Kennedy said in his Alliance for Progress speech: "If peaceful evolution is impossible, violent revolution is inevitable." As an American social worker I am conscious and proud that there is freedom in America to fight for freedom. Hopefully, because of this freedom we may some day provide the model of creative diversity where apathy, anxiety, and alienation because of ethnic prejudice or poverty will disappear. This is my dream for America. It is my dream for the world.

Whatever the precise diagnosis of our ills, however, it is the social worker today who must lead the way. It is the social worker who must challenge all responsible people to understand that sometimes the cruelest tragedy is the day-to-day accumulation of small indignities that a human being suffers in deprivation. It is the social worker who must force world society to recognize that people die inwardly from being nameless and faceless, from not having roots in the community, from not having identity of self, and from having to react endlessly to a thousand small, uncaring acts. When this happens, we are all participants. We are all accessories to the crime. In the paraphrase of an ancient statesman, "I prefer the error of enthusiasm to the indifference of wisdom."

In a world society where, for most of our history, we have succumbed to an excess of professionalism and technology, materialism and theoretical concepts, we must, in order to redress the balance, succumb to an excess of feeling, of courage, of caring, and of decency. I believe the time is ripe. The problems are begging for solution, and I believe that our profession is now mature and secure enough to lead in this effort; for more than the victim is at stake. A society that would call itself civilized is also at stake.

Strengthening Human Relationships

JANE M. HOEY

MEMBER, PERMANENT COMMITTEE, ICSW

I AM deeply appreciative of the great honor the officers of the International Conference of Social Work have conferred upon me in presenting me with the René Sand Award. Dr. Sand was deeply concerned about the welfare of mankind and was one of the most distinguished world leaders in medicine and social welfare of his time. He was Secretary General of the League of Red Cross Societies. For many years, he promoted humanitarian causes of the League of Nations and was one of the leading experts who laid the foundation for the World Health Organization. He founded the International Conference of Social Work and the International Committee of Schools of Social Work.

With deep humility and honest pleasure I accept the René Sand Award, not for myself as an individual, but for that small band of dedicated social workers around the world who have labored together for more than twenty years to make René Sand's dream of an international social work fellowship come true. Among this group I wish to give recognition to Ruth Williams, our honored and loved Executive Secretary, who has, through the force of her personality and ability, made the ICSW the effective forum that it is today. The group has been the instrument through which we have vastly expanded our international exchange of knowledge and skills and our person-to-person communication. The group has diligently supported and promoted the social welfare programs of the United Nations. And the attendance here and at previous meetings of the Conference attests to the group's devotion to building on the foundations that René Sand laid down.

A René Sand tradition is now firmly established, and as we continue to strengthen our international social work organizations, both public and voluntary, our arms stretched across the oceans in all directions will form a network of collaboration and achievement for the welfare of humanity.

Sixteen years ago, when I stood before this assembly, we were concerned primarily with a continuation of our quest for a cross-cultural unity as a profession, or, if you will, for a common basis of social work practice. We were trying to identify shared concerns and agreements about social work functions, professional values, and techniques. Just as the social work profession was deeply involved at that time in its psychiatric phase, so also were the 1950 Conference and my paper attuned to mutuality of effort in the provision of direct services to individuals. Over the intervening years, great progress has been made in recognizing together the universality of traditional social work values and the similarity of social work functions around the world. A conference sponsored by the United States Council on Social Work Education at the East-West Center in Hawaii in early 1966 reached essential agreement that social work practice, in its infinite variety, finds expression in one form or another in every cultural setting. The conference concluded, however, that social work methods in any setting are always in a process of evolution to adjust to changing cultural values, economic development, new knowledge, complexities of society, and social change.[1]

A decade and a half ago, at the Vth International Conference of Social Work, it was enough to refer in passing, and almost as an afterthought, to the importance of social policy and its political implications, the inseparability of social and economic problems, and the role of social work in social change.

Today, as Barbara Ward points out with such eloquence, we cannot avoid the fact that we live in a catastrophically revolutionary age, changing our ways of life, our ways of looking at things—changing everything out of recognition and changing it fast. She suggests that we are living with four major revolutions at once: the revolution of equality; of progress and potentiality for material change; of increasing population; and of the application of science and reason to all forms of living. The revolution of equality, she asserts, has its roots in the rule of law and in the

---

[1] Eileen Younghusband, "Intercultural Aspects of Social Work," *Journal of Education for Social Work*, II, No. 1 (1966), 59–65.

vision of souls all equal in the sight of a just God—an equality which is "innate, metaphysical, and independent of the vanities of class, race, or culture." [2] If this concept of equality were implanted in the soil of society, it would mean a society ruled by love and not by force. We social workers have an important role in establishing programs to deal with these changes that "blindly, blunderingly, with immense impact and immense confusion . . . are remaking the face of the earth." [3] It is urgent that social workers unite in an aggressive, world-wide assault on poverty. We must make clear in our national and international associations that the pursuit of self-interest is not the only criterion of socially desirable action to relieve poverty. We must help our statesmen to slough off complacency about social conditions. We must find a set of realizable short-term and long-range goals and a general strategy for the next twenty years whereby our abundant world resources are brought into play to reduce poverty. There is no reason why a rededication of ourselves to this great task is not possible. We have the knowledge, we have the resources, and we have the moral stamina inherent in our profession to take on this giant undertaking.

Perhaps you might challenge me by asking: What, indeed, have we been doing all our professional lives if not working to improve conditions of living? I would have to respond that we may have been too much preoccupied with methodology, specialization, and professional standards. This absorption has meant that social workers and social welfare organizations have not assumed a major role in policy-making bodies; and as a result, I would stress, public social policy too often is being formulated on the advice of economists, businessmen, journalists, or physicians. Especially are we missing from the councils where planning takes place to design programs to reduce, and at length eliminate, the pervasive and conflict-provoking problem of poverty.

It is obvious that hungry, sick, and ill-housed people who are engaged in unsavory occupations and lack a feeling of self-worth are more and more a threat to national and international stability. As social workers we cannot limit our efforts to relieving, for a

[2] Barbara Ward, *The Rich Nations and the Poor Nations* (New York: W. W. Norton and Co., Inc., 1962), p. 18.
[3] *Ibid.*, pp. 137–38.

relatively few individuals, the results of society's inhumanity; on the contrary, we must also involve ourselves deeply in the effects of economic and social deprivation on society as a whole. Traditional methods of intervention in income maintenance, such as social insurance and public assistance, are being challenged, and we are asked to prove that they do or do not achieve our goals. As individuals and through our social welfare organizations we must participate fully and effectively with representatives of many disciplines in analyzing and evaluating our national social and economic systems and in strengthening old, discarding ineffective, and formulating new programs which reflect the values of our profession. In this dialogue it is crucial that social workers inject their philosophy of love and respect for their fellow man and their belief that individuals are beings of infinite worth. Our economic and social programs will respect human dignity when they make it possible for the individual to be himself, to work out his own problems, and to make up his own mind. All men have equal rights. This does not mean that every person should have the same education or that he must have the same beliefs and act in the same way that others do. It does mean that the personality and individuality of each man, woman, and child should be respected.

At the risk of being accused of oversimplification I want to share with you the thoughts that have been going through my mind about some ways in which social workers the world over might instigate, support, and follow through measures to reduce poverty —measures that are both innovative and oriented to professional values. I believe that these ideas are practical and could come to fruition internationally and in any country where social work is gaining acceptance.

My first proposal has to do with three international voluntary organizations—the International Conference of Social Work, the International Association of Schools of Social Work, and the International Federation of Social Workers. I recommend that they become one organization with divisions or sections as needed; possibly beginning with a divison of professional standards and practice, a division of education and training, and a division of international communications through this forum and other exchanges of information. Such a union would have numerous advantages, not the least of which would be a solution to the problem of financing. One organization with one secretariat is more efficient; more important, one organization could relate itself to national social work organizations in such a way as to arrange for an adequate and consistent source of funds. Also, one organization, working with national organizations, could plan for, and bring about, the involvement of more social workers in concern for international social issues and the program of the international organization. One organization would present one point of view in relations with the United Nations, with governments, and with national social welfare groups. It could more effectively seek solutions to the overwhelming scarcity of manpower. It would assure program coordination, prevent duplication, and avoid conflict of interest. Such a unified and strongly supported organization could be the focal point for stimulating and leading a global attack on poverty. What better monument could be erected to that great humanitarian, Dr. René Sand, than to report in 1978 at the fiftieth anniversary of the ICSW that the organization he founded had been a significant instrument in reducing poverty around the world?

Second, I believe that, in each of our countries, social work must speak officially with one voice. This, it seems to me, means the establishment of one national, voluntary association of social work, which, of course, might have many subdivisions. One association representing all of social work could guide and stimulate a well-rounded program of research and fact-gathering essential to analyzing social problems and to reaching agreement on professional goals. The organization could develop position statements proposing programs and modifications of programs designed to achieve professional goals. Operating in this way such an organization would soon establish its right to be heard and to be taken as a respected equal into the highest-level policy deliberations.

As a major function, such an organization should promote the idea of a national economic and social council, which I shall discuss later.

Social workers participating actively in the program of a national social work association can more effectively influence social and economic change than is possible if they act as individuals. A national organization pulls the profession together in support of an agreed-on program and gives its members the tools with which to take individual action. I hasten to add that this is true if the members of the organization are urged and helped to participate in program formulation and thus become knowledgeable about, and supportive of, organizational objectives and methods. Many countries already have one or more social work or social welfare associations.

Through their national association, social workers could exert important influence in the high councils of our countries. To do this is not easy but it is possible and what is more, it is pleasurable and satisfying. I can say this with assurance because I have spent most of my adult life working with all kinds of people—lawyers, physicians, economists, legislators—in influencing legislation and I have loved every minute of it. I would say that first we must develop a genuine respect for our own knowledge and ability. We must shed our timidity and self-doubt. Even though we wish we knew more, we must esteem ourselves for what we do know— and we know a great deal. We cannot influence other professions unless we approach them secure in the discipline and authority of our professional competence. Conversely, we must acknowledge our need for help from other disciplines in improving social measures and we should reach out to them in a spirit of trust and cooperation.

Social workers often hestitate to enter the political arena. They seem to believe that they will lose prestige, or sacrifice a measure of professional integrity. This need not be so, because the game of politics can be played fairly, honorably, and intellectually; and more than a few politicians share social work's goals and values in large measure. But to be effective politically we must learn the rules of the game and abide by them just as we must learn the ways of our own profession.

May I suggest, too, that a strong national association of social work in each country might well become the official arm of the unified international organization I have proposed: informing its membership about international issues, activities, programs, and forums; offering sound financial support to the international organization through its own budget; and involving many of its members in meaningful participation in the work of the international organization. The international organization could be strengthened by relating itself at the national level to a strong organization representing social work rather than by relying on independent national committees of the international organization.

Third, I suggest that, in every country, small or large, highly sophisticated or unsophisticated socially, economically, and administratively, we should consider the establishment of an economic and social council. Such a council would be composed of economic and social scientists, tax experts, public administrators, and specialists in social welfare. This council would be charged with responsibility for guiding and advising on public economic and social policy. For example, the council would seek to understand the factors that create poverty and prevent its elimination, and to find ways of providing a minimum standard of living for everyone. It would answer our question as to what is a decent standard of living. To carry out this responsibility effectively the council would examine the characteristics of the poor in order to come closer to understanding the kinds of programs the country should invest in. The council would investigate the causes of poverty and try to attack the roots of the problem. In an effort to select those which are most effective, specialists would join together in weighing the contributions of various intervention strategies designed to reduce poverty. The economists and their values would influence social policy and social programs; the social workers and their values affect economic planning and decision-making. Together, the economists and the social workers would find consensus on a unified social and economic program that is rational, politically feasible, and sufficiently oriented to the values of each.

If we listen to Rein and Miller, such a council would consider six intervention strategies in the exploration of policy issues and deployment of resources:

1. Modifying the environment and enriching the quality of life by programs to improve health and housing and by a variety of social services, such as day care, homemaker services, and family life education

2. Improving occupational capabilities through schooling, vocational training, and employment services

3. Redistributing income through nonmarket means, such as social insurance, public assistance, and children's allowances

4. Increasing the power of the poor and their participation in community life

5. Changing the economic system through measures such as a minimum wage and promotion of full employment

6. Rehabilitating people by means of guidance, counseling, casework, or psychoanalysis.[4]

Rein and Miller go further to suggest six goals of poverty reduction: social decency; equality; mobility; social participation; social stability; and economic stability and growth. The first four, I believe, might be considered vital elements in individual freedom and justice, and all six as factors contributing to a stable, developing, and peaceful world.

These national councils would not only deal with national problems but would bring their influence to bear on each nation's foreign policy. Through the council's efforts, foreign policies around the world might well be modified to give major emphasis to developmental planning aimed at balanced economic and social growth, including economic programs with a social impact and social programs designed to further economic advancement. The councils might promote the assignment of social welfare specialists in the foreign service and as delegates and advisers at the United Nations. Perhaps even more important, such councils might have a salutary influence on the social and economic functioning of the United Nations and on the expansion and further improvement of the social welfare programs of that organization. Such a worldwide partnership of economists and social workers could revitalize our dream of peace and justice and freedom on earth.

A fourth suggestion relates to broadening and strengthening social work education in every country. If you have responded to my plea for a world-wide attack on poverty and if you concur that we must think in terms of unified programs of economic and social development, then it logically follows that we must adapt the content and methods of social work education to these objectives. Perhaps we should consider educating two distinct kinds of social

4 Martin Rein and S. M. Miller, "Poverty, Policy, and Purpose: the Dilemmas of Choice," in Leonard H. Goodman, ed., *Economic Progress and Social Welfare* (New York: Columbia University Press, 1966), pp. 20–64.

worker: the social strategist and the social practitioner. The former would devote himself to changing society better to serve the individual. His education would prepare him to be a social planner, a social administrator, a social researcher, a social organizer, a social worker educator, and to participate in the formulation of social and economic policies. The latter would help the individual to live and grow to his maximum capacity and with more satisfactions in our crowded, complex, impersonal, and stressful society. His education would prepare him to be a case technician, a social caseworker, a social group worker, a case therapist, a supervisor, a consultant, a social work educator, and to staff a variety of social utilities, such as day care centers, meals-on-wheels, information and referral centers, homemaker services, social institutions, and so forth.

This idea is based fundamentally on a conviction that the profession of social work should be inclusive rather than exclusive, as it is today in some countries. By this I mean that we should invite into our membership and include in our activities, on the one hand, all the personnel in social agencies and institutions who work directly with people (houseparents, case technicians, homemakers, and attendants in institutions for delinquents) and, on the other hand, administrators, planners, organizers, social researchers (regional planners, prison administrators, and public welfare officials). This concept of our profession is designed to spread our influence and to make our voice more effective in a wide range of social and economic programing. Such a profession would be jolted out of its middle-of-the-road conservatism, and it would lead social work education into a convulsive reorientation.[5]

In fact, this concept of a profession carries with it a responsibility to revolutionize education for all persons who are employed in social work. For, as we amalgamate all these groups, we must at the same time identify the nature of the educational programs which will prepare them for the duties and responsibilities of their work. This inevitably leads to an educational program that ranges from vocational training at the secondary school or postsecondary school level through social welfare sequences at the undergraduate uni-

5 Lowell Iberg, "Undergraduate Social Welfare Education—Some Community Considerations," *Public Welfare*, XXIV (1966), 203–7, 252.

versity level and, at least in some countries, to advanced degrees at the master's and doctoral level.

Much of this structure of education exists today in one country or another, although the entire continuum may not appear in any one country. But my concern is with the content and methods of learning and teaching within this structure or in any new structure which may be devised. It is my belief that every person doing a social work job, at whatever level, should have an educational experience in which he is helped to assimilate social work values and to understand and accept social work goals. He should know how these values and goals influence the performance of his own functions. And each student should be required to observe and involve himself emotionally and intellectually in considering the problems of slums and ghettos, and of living and dying on too little income.

Education for social strategists should include knowledge of economics, social systems, adminstrative processes, research, community development and environment, and social engineering epidemiology.[6] Such students would have field work experience in administering social organizations and institutions, in serving legislative committees, in regional planning organizations, in urban renewal planning, in serving social policy committees of the professional organization, in writing policy for a large social agency, in agricultural and labor organizations, in conducting research for public agencies, and in working with policy, research, and advisory institutes on economic, educational, and social problems.

Social practitioners, especially those who are being educated at the university level, would be introduced to social policy issues and problems and would be helped to develop a sense of responsibility for personal and professional participation in the shaping of public policy, with emphasis on the reduction of poverty.

Katherine Kendall has suggested that social work education must adapt to changing times when she says:

A dialogue without end must be initiated now within the profession, within our universities, and in our communities, to spread the word that social work education is entering a new era and to command sup-

6 Walter L. Kindelsperger, "Responsible Entry into the Profession—Some Current Issues," *Journal of Education for Social Work*, II, No. 1 (1966), 41–51,

port for ambitious new goals—goals that will embrace: responsibility for education and training to meet the full range of social work manpower needs; responsibility to match all considerations of quantity with the highest quality of learning; responsibility to work toward new alignments among schools of social work, social agencies, the behavioral and social science fields, and allied professions, with innovations leading to continuous renewal of the field of practice and educational arrangements for it.[7]

I believe with Robert Theobald that:

All the inhabitants of the world must be able to subscribe to a single set of beliefs. Each country at the present time has its own values, and it would be impossible to alter them drastically without destroying both the individual and society. The values of the world community can therefore be based only on the factor or factors that are common to all men.[8]

The Preamble to the United Nations Charter defines these common values, and it is well today to remind ourselves of them:

To save succeeding generations from the scourge of war, which twice in our lifetime has brought untold sorrow to mankind, and to reaffirm faith in fundamental human rights, in the dignity and worth of the human person, in the equal rights of men and women and of nations large and small, and to establish conditions under which justice and respect for the obligations arising from treaties and other sources of international law can be maintained, and to promote social progress and better standards of life in larger freedom.

I want to thank you here and social workers everywhere who have enriched my life. With some of you I have deep and abiding ties of friendship which I cherish. Many of you are dear to me because, in our cooperative endeavors, we have enjoyed the pleasures of success and suffered together the pains of failure or temporary frustration. I feel inexpressibly blessed because I have had the opportunity to know, to respect, and to learn from you, and to win your affection and recognition. But, in a sense, we are all blessed by our mutual dedication to social justice and by the strength we draw from each other as we pursue our efforts to open the doors to a life of dignity and self-respect for all.

[7] Katherine A. Kendall, "Choices to Be Made in Social Work Education," in *Social Work Practice, 1966* (New York: Columbia University Press, 1966), p. 116.
[8] Robert Theobald, *The Rich and the Poor* (New York: Mentor, 1960).

Problems of Future Urban Development

LUCIEN MEHL

MAÎTRE DE REQUÊTES AU CONSEIL D'ETAT
PRÉSIDENT DE L'ECOLE TECHNIQUE DES
SURINTENDANTES D'USINES ET
DES SERVICES SOCIAUX, FRANCE

WE ARE called upon to prophesy, in the primary sense of the word, about the future of the city. One might decide that such an undertaking is foolhardy or, at the very least, ambitious, and that it runs the risk of being aleatory or even fallacious in its results. Nevertheless, it is necessary if one wishes to act pertinently and effectively to prepare for the future.

The prospective method.—Most decisions and activities in the realm of town planning and, more generally, those which are carried out in order to promote urban civilization have irreversible, long-lasting, and often delayed effects. Often the goal itself is distant or long-term. Today human activity is turned toward the future, and investment, both material and intellectual, plays a dominant role.

It can be said that in order to master our physical, biological, and social environment we take detours. The Austrian economist Boehm-Bawerk has noted that investment is a detour in the process of production. But education, professional training, administration, and social welfare activities are also detours which enable us to circumvent the obstacles to attaining our goals. If, moreover, we consider the abstract, multidimensional space of the state of nature and of the decision-action which is put into it, it then appears that in making these detours we are actually following the shortest route.

Therefore, in an environment undergoing rapid change, in a world in the process of becoming, we have to calculate the future of the environment when we make a decision which will have long-lasting or distant consequences; otherwise, the results of the action run the risk of being inadequate in the middle or long run. This study should take into account not only the probable consequences of spontaneous evolution, notably the strong tendencies of the socioeconomic system, but also the probable effects of our present or future actions by which we manifest our will to master this very evolution.

In France, we call the methodology which is applicable to actions with delayed effects the "prospective," a name given to it by its originator, Gaston Berger. The name is not important, however. It is the idea which counts and the way of acting which it promotes. Any politician or planner uses the prospective method in a more or less systematic fashion—or at least he should use it.

The prospective method is a highly synthetic one which tends to utilize the intellectual tools offered by economic forecasting, econometrics, operational research, and, of course, the applied social sciences. It was tried for the first time in France in the elaboration of the Vth Plan, which is definitely a middle-range plan (1966–70) but which was conceived with more distant goals in mind, as described in "Guidelines for 1985."

Nevertheless, the prospective method is not a planner's panacea. This discipline still has a large number of theoretical and practical problems, and it does not enable us to read the future in a kind of sorcerer's mirror. It only suggests a totality of future data which should constitute the main thread of the society of tomorrow. If it results in a picture, it is one that is more abstract than representational.

The epistemological problem.—When the prospective method becomes a tool of the applied social sciences, it naturally encounters the same difficulties and the same obstacles as do these disciplines themselves, which legitimately claim the rank of authentic sciences. The main obstacle is the fact that until only recently the ways and means of classical science, as it was constituted in the nineteenth century, were of little help in the social field. They scarcely enabled us to construct adequate models of human organization and institutions and their actual operation.

Classical science successfully studied two categories of systems of the physical world: (1) the determined systems, containing a small number of linked variables; (2) the aleatory systems with their large number of factors weakly interconnected.

Unfortunately for the researcher, biological and social systems have a great many more factors and variables than do the simple systems of classical physics, and yet they are weaker than the systems studied in thermodynamics. The factors and variables are strongly interdependent; moreover, the system is partly determined, partly aleatory, and sometimes even completely uncertain. It is often extremely difficult if not impossible to point out the precise connections or correlations, even of a statistical nature, which are presumed to exist.

What, then, is to be done? Of course, one could try to use the determined and aleatory models in any case. The determined model is satisfactory for certain simple or simplified hypotheses. The aleatory model gives good results in demography, for example. But for many problems, and particularly for studying the operation and structure of organizations, especially the dynamics of urban complexes, the social sciences are, so to speak, between two chairs.

Or rather they were. For it seems to me that the theory of information and communication and the theory of systems promise to be of some help in the field of social sciences, both pure and applied.

I am not speaking of information in the sense that Shannon uses it—abstract and quantified information which excludes the notion of meaning. In social questions it would seem that one cannot do without the idea of the meaning of a piece of information. One is less interested in the amount of information which one can transmit through a channel than with its scope, its origin, and its effect. I would say, therefore, that information is that which modifies the behavior of a system (institutions, groups, or individuals) without essentially altering its structure.

Thus understood, the idea of information is even more basic to the social field than it is to biology. In effect, society can be regarded as a series of information-receiving centers, linked by a network through which this information circulates. In the social field, the theory of communication must be completed by a theory of regulation, of social control in the broad sense.

Social systems are complex, purposive systems comprising directive bodies and directed bodies, the operating bodies. All complex, purposive systems—mechanical, biological, and social—are subject to mixed control: preregulation, highly centralized, which takes the form of orders and instructions, plans and programs; coregulation, decentralized, which is also self-regulation assured by a constellation of secondary centers; postregulation (feedback), partly centralized, which permits the refining and correcting of the preregulation and the disciplining of the coregulation. This triple control, observable in biological systems, is the rule in social and, notably, economic systems.

Classical economic theory undoubtedly emphasizes coregulation, that is to say, controls which come from the decisions of entrepreneurs and the mechanisms of the market. But, in fact, in all countries the government and public agencies intervene in economic and social life by preregulation (legislation, plan) or by postregulation (corrective measures). In the socialist countries it is certainly preregulation which preponderates, in the form of generalized planning. However, one can observe a tendency toward the decentralization of economic decisions, while at the same time substitutes are found for the market and profit. Finally, postregulation, methodical and no longer improvised, tends to develop.

Social control, in so far as it is institutional, is assured by this triple regulation which permits the association of efficiency of action with economy in the reception of information.

With regard to physical planning, the phenomenon of triple regulation is evident. The spontaneous coregulation of urban growth has had to be disciplined by town and physical planning. However, this preregulation cannot be rigid in a changing world with partly unpredictable developments, thus the importance of postregulatory adaptations in this field. The planning of urban development, like that of economic and social development in general, must be flexible, not only to preserve freedom but also to guarantee efficiency.

The theory of triple regulation leads us to a completely pragmatic attitude in the face of a complex system. It is agreed that it is not necessary to understand a complex system analytically in order to master it. One constructs an approximate model and does the best one can. Constitutions, legislation, plans, and programs are models of society and of human activity. They are imperfect but they serve. Jurists have known it for a long time: we do not know what man is, we do not know what society is, but that does not keep us from practicing law, with any means at hand.

THE URBAN ENVIRONMENT

The first problem which we encounter is that of the physical planning of urban areas. We must also raise questions about the situation of man in the heart of the city.

Physical planning.—Before exploring the future, I propose a backward look, a flash back.

The "prospective" cannot reveal our destiny, nor is the retrospective examination an analytic description of the past. I am suggesting only that we meditate a moment on the meaning of the urban phenomenon in pre-industrial civilization in order to draw a lesson for the future. The "prospective" is interested in the explanation of past data, in the relations which exist between those data: the understanding of these relations might permit us to infer, starting from new social conditions, the spontaneous consequences to expect, as well as the actions to be taken, keeping in mind our goals. One could say that it is a question of extending the method of variations.

In pre-industrial civilization cities constituted accumulation points of geographic space and social fabric in the midst of an essentially rural civilization. More precisely, setting aside the problems of security and defense which do not interest us directly, cities were primarily centers for the exchange of materials and information, the knots in the network of social communication, just as they are today. Although the city may be a consumer, it is a purveyor of information; it is the seat of power from which orders emanate; or, if you prefer, it is from the city that the preregulation messages come. The city is also the environment in which culture flourishes, intellect breathes, and innovation appears for better or for worse. The city is thus trade in goods and trade in ideas. It is communication.

The country, on the other hand, was the physical and biological base of society in pre-industrial civilization. The largest part of the population was scattered there, and it was there that earthly nourishment was produced. Whereas the city unleashes change, the country is an element of social stability.

That explains why in pre-industrial civilization basic ethical values were of rural origin. These values were constituted when civilization passed from an economy based on hunting and fruit-picking to a rural civilization, which was as important a change then as urbanization is today. The power of the rural phenomenon at that time, despite its rather slow development, corresponds to a veritable mutation in the history of humanity, and explains why our values, symbols, and even our vocabulary are impregnated with ruralism: the role of bread and wine in Christianity, the flock, the pastor; *"agir,* from *ago,"* to push the cows ahead of you; *pecuniary,* from *pecunia,* money, originally head of cattle, and so forth.

In pre-industrial society communication was difficult on the technical as well as on the psychological level. The transport of goods, like the transport of information, was laborious and slow. It is understandable, therefore, that an actual market had to exist as a collecting point for the goods offered, and that the various centers of public and private decision-making had to be topographically close to one another. This implied a dense urban fabric, a system of contiguous buildings and houses. The density of the urban woof can explained mainly by the slavery of communication.

At the dawn of the industrial revolution, the means of transporting goods and sending information had hardly improved, with the result that to the categories "market cities" and "administrative cities" was added "industrial cities"; and the older cities were often surrounded by a crown of factories. Here again, it was a question of communication: there had to be proximity between the centers of decision-making, the organs of production and the residential areas.

Today the slavery of communication is much less restricting. We don't need a market in order to function. It is sufficient to concentrate the information about products and prices in an agreed-upon place which is ready to diffuse it. The concentration of the decision-making and operational bodies of a business or a service may still be desirable under certain circumstances, but it is no longer a necessity. It has therefore become possible to knit an urban fabric with larger stitches, further apart, without endangering the functional efficiency of the city—on the condition, of course, that there is a general structure and hierarchy, which implies that in certain areas, centers, or points the density will be great enough to satisfy various technical or psychological needs.

If this conception of the city has become possible, it is also not only desirable, but necessary; for in our old metropolitan areas made of too-dense fabric, communication, the principal function of the city, has paradoxically become difficult and at times impossible. Automobiles and buses circulate with difficulty. Pedestrian movement has become a trial. Leisure time is consumed by comings and goings, waits and fatigue. Finally, the citizen of the megalopolis has little opportunity to communicate and to grow. He is often even more isolated than he would be in a rural environment, without having the advantages of the latter. Of course, a flood of information breaks upon him, but too much information is sometimes the same as none at all, because he does not have the leisure to receive and assimilate it.

I believe that in trying to sketch the structure of the city of tomorrow, the theory of information is of some help to us, because structure, order, and information are related concepts. Let us consider, for example, the requirement to drive on the right side of the road. In the flow of traffic, a unity of information has been introduced. A considerable increase in order results. On the social plane it would also appear that a restraint (drive to the right) creates freedom (of movement). This is fundamental: it is wrong to believe that a moral or judicial restraint necessarily reduces freedom. This is, I believe, a good argument in favor of urban planning and of planning in general.

Let us continue to apply the theory. In order to inject information into the urban system, that is to say, order, efficiency, and freedom, we must, among other solutions, differentiate the channels of communication, and especially the channels of material communication. From this comes the idea which has just begun to be put into practice, of separating the flow of vehicular transportation from pedestrian traffic, principally by using the third dimension but also be separating interurban routes from local roads while at the same time providing for the necessary interconnections and exchanges. In other words, the goal is to arrive at a communications network which is structured and hierarchized in the three dimensions of space.

The developing countries have a great opportunity in city planning; for the developed countries provide many examples of what not to do. These are the best kind of examples; they enable one to avoid certain errors, and to make others. But at least the leaders of developing countries know that something different must be tried. And if they fail, the errors will at least be excusable and original.

There is the matter of the optimum size of agglomerations. Sometimes a maximum figure of 100,000 to 500,000 inhabitants is mentioned. I, for one, have some doubts about the value of such figures. Everything depends first on the functions of the city and the economic and cultural impact it should have. It is obvious, for example, that for a capital city with world-wide impact "the critical mass" would be large. I believe it is now recognized that the growth of metropolises, in so far as it has unfavorable consequences, must be slowed; but to block growth, which would be very difficult to do, would be harmful. Everything depends also on the structure of the city. A well-structured city, diverse in its unity, can easily accommodate more than a million inhabitants. In the same way, the optimal size of satellite towns depends on the size of the metropolis to which they are connected. If one wants the towns to induce a slowdown in the growth of the metropolis, they must reach a certain size.

One can ask whether the proposed figures will have any meaning tomorrow, given the spread of urbanization and the appearance of urban regions in most of the developed countries.

What man came to look for in the city, what he will continue to seek in the future, is freedom, freedom of choice. On that everyone is in agreement. It is doubtful that the citizen has always found it, but that is the goal. If the function of the city is communication, its ultimate purpose is freedom.

It is not just a question of freedom to choose a job, a home, friends, amusements, but also to have a possibility for autonomy and growth. In a rural society the individual is bound by powerful and strict social restraints. In the city one can live in a sort of anonymity which, if it were absolute and final, would of course be deplorable. But in the city a man can construct and recreate himself in the etymological sense of the word. However, since the axiological framework is less rigid, there is a danger that apathetic attitudes or even asocial behavior will show up. The loosening of family and social restraints and the disappearance of diffuse control are not without danger, for they are necessary to order and structure behavior. The freest human activity requires restraints, order. Urban civilization must define its general norms of behavior, a function formerly assumed by the rural environment.

These norms are in the process of being established despite the prognostications of the pessimists. If from now on "the family" is reduced to two generations, and if the second generation makes good use of its power of "answering back," family ties will remain strong. Equality of the sexes has also failed to shake the family. It has been said that we are headed for a society without fathers (that is to say, a society without a mythical image of the father). But it is the social image of the father in a rural society which is disappearing, after having been degraded. In certain respects rural society, particularly in certain countries of Western Europe, is in trouble, or even disarray, shaken to its technical, demographic, economic, and cultural foundations. Very often the father of a rural family no longer has anything in common with the "paterfamilias," lord and master. The older children generally refuse to continue working on the farm under the father's direction because he refuses to innovate, and his authority is contested.

As for urban society, it can no longer be a society where the authority of the father, and of leaders conceived in his image, dominates, and even less a society governed by old people. In a traditional society the mission of the father and the elders was to transmit knowledge. Such a function is more difficult to carry out in a world experiencing rapid technological, economic, and social changes. Often the father learns from his son. Moreover, the fact that women have increasing accessibility to various professions, and even to the most important posts, has abolished another male monopoly.

But it would not be correct to say that the image of the father is being destroyed. It is simply different, and the father shares responsibilities with the mother. All psychologists stress the importance of the combined influence of both sexes on the formation of a balanced personality in the child. Within the family group it seems that for a long time still the mother will assume the stabilizing function and the father that of innovation. But it is true that his role is becoming difficult because he must compete with his own children once they have reached adolescence.

Family structure and relationships are in any case modified, as are in general all social relationships which are based less on unconditional authority than on compliance or more or less tacit consent. Nevertheless, urban civilization must define, at least implicitly, its basic values and norms of behavior. Like parents within a family group, it must guarantee the function of innovation and, at the same time, safeguard balance and stability.

New values appear in the heart of an urban civilization. It is founded on organic solidarity, while at the same time it permits individualism and invites tolerance. In so far as it is a technical and administrative civilization, it requires from its members precision, exactness, knowledge, a sense of adaptation, and, even more, a sense of responsibility. It is important that the economic and social system enable everyone to meet these requirements and be remunerated for his trouble.

PROBLEMS OF SOCIAL ECONOMICS

A general question which cannot be avoided is that of equality, envisaged not from the legal or formal point of view but in its real content. The rural community is a highly structured society, slow to change, where information, small in quantity, circulates poorly. The distance between social strata is great, with the result that inequality is accepted after a fashion. In the city, equality is desired all the more because it seems possible. The example of the Scandinavian countries proves, moreover, that a situation close to equality can appear with prosperity.

Progress toward the least inequality.—In the present state of our social structures and our knowledge of social mechanisms, equality, even limited to income, seems to me to be unrealizable. There cannot be equality, for example, when suitable knowledge and training cannot be given to all those who deserve them. Undoubtedly, it will be necessary to arrive at that point, but it is a matter of an intellectual investment whose results will be postponed.

Even more important is the question of knowing whether absolute equality is possible and desirable. There is obviously no doubt in regard to legal equality and equality of opportunity. But it remains to be seen whether inequality of aptitudes and talents is of a nature to justify, on the ethical plane, inequality of status and, particulary, of income. This idea is certainly not appealing. I am inclined to think, nevertheless, that in the interests of society as a whole an inequality based on talents and held within reasonable limits is desirable because it encourages the assumption of risks implicit in human activities, the development of innovation, and, consequently, technical, economic, and social progress.

In any case, even in the socialist countries a certain inequality of status exists. More generally, it is acknowledged that in order to attain certain social goals rapidly and efficiently, the objective of production must precede the objective of distribution, so long as a minimum level of income and possibilites is maintained. Nevertheless, it is obviously unacceptable that luxury should walk alongside misery.

Not long ago one could still hope that economic growth would spontaneously reduce inequality of social conditions, at least in so far as the distribution of income was concerned. There is still some truth in this idea. As a general rule, developed societies are more egalitarian than underdeveloped societies. This is not a question of morality; for men are neither better nor more just in a developed society. But scarcity is less intense—scarcity of goods and services, scarcity of high professional qualifications—with the result that the inequality which derives from the existence of "scarcity rents" is less evident there, because the factors that generate these rents are less easily found. I do not want to abuse generalizations, but I believe that the economic and social history of humanity is that of the struggle against scarcity. And scarcity is the mother of inequality.

Although it is true that economic growth is a powerful equalizing factor in an industrial, urban, and administrative society, it is still true that inequality increases relatively and becomes insupportable for untrained or poorly trained workers, the aged, the handicapped, and the maladjusted. They cannot take an active and fruitful part in the economic game, especially in a capitalistic system, even one tempered with interventionism. The market mechanisms turn against them, not to mention inflation, which is too often the price of growth, since we will undoubtedly have to wait a long time for the golden age of expansion in stability.

How can we avoid these regrettable consequences? Redistribution by means of progressive income taxes, social security, social assistance, and housing allowances is indispensable. But it is insufficient. Let us suppose that by a miracle it would be possible through redistribution to bring about equality of income. Inequality, like the phoenix, would rise from the ashes, due to the lack of education and training of the beneficiaries.

It follows, then, especially since our resources are limited, that public funds derived from fiscal appropriations, or private funds spent spontaneously by the more fortunate, should be assigned in large part to education, training, social investments, and activities that encourage social progress rather than to individual distribution, if we want to accelerate the march toward the least inequality in an urban society.

We have here a problem of social control which is of the greatest importance, one which the market mechanisms and the spontaneous growth of the economy cannot solve. There was perhaps a time when one could hope that general prosperity and social justice would flow from the self-regulation of economic phenomena. Today we can no longer sing economic harmonies and the credo of *laissez faire*.

Social control should, at least in part, be centralized. While admitting, as certain classical economists believed, that society, and especially the economic system, behaves like a servocontrol mechanism, it is wrong to affirm that a servocontrol mechanism is always stable and efficient and consequently untouchable. Theory and experience have shown that it can get out of order, and that it is necessary, therefore, to watch over it and sometimes intervene in its operation.

Urban planning.—We are now paying heavily for our lack of foresight in the field of urban growth. Perhaps by not interfering we thought we were defending the principles of economic liberalism, but this is an illusion. It is easy to observe that the spontaneous control mechanisms described by the classical economists functioned effectively only for an industrial economy. On this point it must be recognized that the liberal system achieved a startling success. The prosperity and power of the United States are probably the best proof.

On the other hand, the system has never been satisfactory in a rural economy, and in all countries, including the Federal Republic of Germany and the United States, the public authorities intervene in this field. In any case, the market mechanisms cannot function except where there is a true market. This statement, despite its tautological aspect, merits some development. Not only do the data coming from the market relate to incipient and current situations, and consequently are of little help in making decisions with long-range effects, but, in addition, there remains a whole series of goods and services which are not negotiated, or are poorly negotiated, on a market; for example, the infrastructure needed for economic life, health, education, and everything involved in public order and social solidarity.

Many classical economists recognized and accepted public intervention in these fields. It is evident that physical planning, a rational urban framework, and the harmonious development of the city cannot be assured by the market mechanisms. Let us not pretend to give reign in matters of urban growth to mechanisms which the classical theoreticians did not describe as relevant to it. One misunderstands the theory of liberal economics if one insists on applying it to phenomena which do not fit within its scope, which were either expressly excluded by the authors themselves or were not foreseen by them. Because it is these mechanisms which are largely responsible for our present disorder.

It is true that urban concentration, the increase in the density of economic space, may involve the least cost for the entrepreneur. But from the point of view of the interests of the community, one must add to the cost of doing business the increasing cost of public services in an overly dense urban space. Still, one will arrive at an incomplete result, because one must add what it costs from the health, welfare, and cultural points of view.

Construction, remodeling, and development of our cities require public intervention. But in order to preserve liberty, it is necessary that democratic procedures be adopted and that participation be increased.

Housing.—In regard to the financial problem experienced by the less-favored segments of the population, the market mechanisms by themselves have been shown to be powerless. But it must be recognized that government intervention has not always been felicitous. The worst solution is the freezing of rents at too low a level. The promoters cease to construct and the landlords to maintain. The real estate patrimony of the nation deteriorates, and finally the measure turns against those whom it was supposed to benefit. One finds nothing to rent, or one pays heavily, on the fringes of the law, for sordid lodgings.

Nevertheless, the market mechanisms have their merits. The market prices are indicators of scarcity and permit an optimal allocation of resources. They cannot be arbitrarily fixed by the public authorities without running the risk of waste and deterioration. This is a matter of general economic principle. In the socialist countries they are now trying objectively to determine terms of trade and to put into practice true costs and prices.

Two solutions to the problem of financing the rental of social housing were conceivable, and they have both been adopted, but tardily, as is pointed out in the national reports. In any case, the experiences of the past are a lesson for the future.

The first solution is a socialist solution, let us say one of municipal socialism: the local communities construct middle-income housing either directly or through intermediaries. This implies that the resources are found and that fiscal appropriations combined with the fact that the poorest pay a lower rent, at the market price, result in a social redistribution.

The second solution, instead of creating a socialist enclave in the midst of a liberal economic system, consists of turning to profit the market mechanisms themselves: the less fortunate are paid a housing allowance. In this way the effective demand is increased.

As I have said, these two solutions are often combined, and analogous measures can be taken to enable people to own property. It thus seems that one can turn the market mechanisms to social ends. It is what is called *Soziale Markwirtschaft,* which also presupposes a large fiscal appropriation. This explains why in a country with a liberal economy, like the Federal Republic of Germany, the fiscal pressure is equal to that observed in France, or about 23 percent of the gross national product. It is the same in the United States.

Bottlenecks and waiting.—One waits a great deal in urban society: at the post office and social security windows, at traffic lights, on the telephone, and sometimes for a hospital bed or for lodgings. Urban society is a congested society. One has to reserve a seat for all major trips and for the theater, wait in line at the movies. Waiting is even more irritating because, more than space, time is our most precious possession. This is probably because one of the rare things of which we are sure is that this commodity has been severely rationed despite medical progress.

Bottlenecks and waiting therefore constitute an economic and social problem of urban civilization and one which is a popular subject of protestations and debate, not always, I am afraid, based on rational grounds. Of course one can multiply the ticket windows, but then it is the ticket vendor who awaits the client, and during that time he will cost the community money. One can construct roads and turnpikes so that citizens can take trips on Sunday, but during the week the country might be overequipped with highways, and this again would represent an excessive cost to the community while the equipment awaits the user.

Urban civilization therefore has need for some organization in this field. Activities and leisure time must be desynchronized to some extent. The problem is complex. But it is technically soluble, thanks to methods of operational research, and socially also. Self-regulation works poorly. Measures must be taken by the public authorities after appropriate consultations with the groups concerned and in cooperation with the trade unions and with the help of social workers.

In order to preserve liberty, authority must ultimately emanate from the people and there must be participation.

ADMINISTRATION OF LARGE CONCENTRATIONS

To physical planning must correspond administrative planning, which poses the problem of revising the boundaries of self-governing communities and public service districts. Decentralization and participation must be promoted.

Remodeling administrative structures.—It is obvious that the present boundaries and structures of communities, cities, even counties, provinces, departments or states (of federations), which were defined and fixed during the pre-industrial era, no longer correspond to the current distribution of men and activities in an urban civilization. Of course, self-governing communities are strongly opposed to change. They recall their history and their rights and protest any attempt at regrouping or restructuring, which they see as an attack on their autonomy and on local liberties. Nevertheless, even in countries where the tradition of self-government has remained strong, their so-called "autonomy" has, in fact, been greatly reduced.

Entities, especially in the country, which are too small and which have been partially emptied by the rural exodus and redistribution of activities, which are deprived of their resources and nourished by central government subsidies, have only a veneer of independence. The situation is less artificial in the cities, but boundaries have often become inadequate, which poses difficult coordination problems with regard to common services. Local taxes, in so far as they are linked to industrial and commercial activity, do not bring in enough revenue in the "dormitory" communities, hence the need for the complex equalizing measures taken by the central government.

Remodeling and regrouping are therefore indispensable, and that is a job for the future. A great deal can be learned from experiences of the present and those of the recent past.

Although it may become necessary to abolish "microcommunities" by merging them, it would be an error to abolish middle-sized communities of 1,000 to 5,000 inhabitants; the lower limit could be even lower in certain countries, depending upon physical geography especially. These communities constitute viable sociological and administrative units. Their existence reinforces the administrative network of the country and encourages contact between the administration and the people. But the smallest of these communities cannot provide all administrative services and all social and cultural subsidies. Therefore, they should form federations in order to create larger units capable of providing common services which can only be operated efficiently at a certain level.

Federation between the main city and the peripheral communities is also essential, and sometimes interurban or interregional coordination becomes necessary. In other words, an organic hierarchy of communities must be arrived at, with the jurisdiction of each one rationally defined.

However, with certain exceptions, it is neither possible nor desirable to proceed with such changes by authoritarian means, even if approved by the legislature. Public opinion must be prepared, econometric and sociometric studies made, and competent councils and organizations invited to discuss the plans or even to submit proposals or counterproposals. In this case the central government appears to be playing more the role of initiator, arbiter, and counselor than of coercive authority.

It would also be a good idea, at least in certain countries, to redistribute tasks and responsibilities among the various decentralized echelons of governments (from national or federal to the small community), because the present situation is often needlessly complex and irrational, if not confusing.

Finally, the legislature should provide the new entities with their own resources, sufficient to promote true autonomy, because the central government really takes the lion's share by monopolizing high-revenue taxes. A local tax on salaries would be one suitable solution and a good basis for local taxation, especially for cities where industry and commerce are not well developed.

Administrative decentralization.—It is necessary to promote a true administrative decentralization in the broad sense, somehow to increase the jurisdiction of local governments at various levels, and to deconcentrate central or federal administration by giving wider jurisdiction to local officials. Of course, centralization is justified for a certain number of administrative activities, for the establishment of certain plans, projects, or programs, and for the exercise of certain controls. But politico-administrative bodies have a natural tendency toward hypercentralization.

If one wants to struggle against this tendency, one must study the causes of the phenomenon. Explanations based on moral judgments of a reproving nature must be completely swept away: to see in hypercentralization a lack of imagination, to attribute it to laziness, distrust, or thirst for power on the part of officials, seems both incorrect and useless. But it must also be recognized that the objective causes are difficult to discover.

It seems that governmental and administrative hypercentralization arises from the difficulty of defining the over-all goal and even the sectoral goals of social systems. The purpose of a biological system can be defined relatively clearly and objectively, even if it is made up of a number of components: survival, reproduction of the species, increasing independence in relation to the environment. Moreover, the biological organism constitutes a totality, its elements not having any partial goals of their own. But, contrary to what has been suggested by the organistic theories, social systems, whether or not they show similarities with biological systems with regard to regulation, are not assimilable to them when it comes to goals.

On the one hand, social systems show a plurality and competition of goals. Individual objectives, as well as those of various groups, come into conflict with general social aims. And at the same time, individual goals are recognized, in certain respects and within certain limits, as values for the entire society. Because if society is not just a simple juxtaposition of individuals and groups, its ultimate goal is or should be the development of each man as a human being.

On the other hand, individual or social goals are basically heterogenous: they have names—welfare, liberty, security, culture—but no numerical value, no precise rule, and no legal standard can furnish the common denominator or, more generally, the scale of values. It follows, therefore, that the directive body delegates its authority with difficulty and tends to take it back. Because, although deconcentration consists of setting the objectives for subordinate bodies and then letting them act freely within the framework of the law, these objectives resist a formal definition with operational scope. So the central authority controls, transfers, or takes back, hoping to do better because it thinks it has the scale of values, or at least is more capable of hierarchizing objectives, combining them, and establishing the necessary priorities and arbitrations, than of transmitting directives concerning the operations themselves.

While admitting that this is true, the remedy is often worse than the disease, that is, the imperfect achievement of the goal. The information channels are choked up, as are the points for receiving information at the central level. This is the bureaucratic perversion. Moreover, the reaction of the bureaucratic system is generally poorly adjusted. It only knows how to attract business or secrete formalism. For example, faced with a partial failure of its system of standards, it formulates other more exigent and complex ones instead of making corrections based on its errors. In cybernetic terms, a bureaucratic system is a system for running an institution where the postregulation or feedback is defective.

If this explanation is correct, it is then possible to suggest a remedy. The formulation of values, goals, objectives, and paths of action must be improved, especially in the social field where the common denominator of money cannot serve the purpose of working out decisions that it does in economic life.

Of course, decisions on social questions can only come from the chief executive or an assembly; from men and not from electronic calculators. However, it is possible to clarify goals and criteria, define courses of action and the values which they question. In other words, above the techniques of operational research, econometrics, sociometrics, and administrative organization we must institute a new applied social science which could be called axiology, teleology, praxeology, as you wish. Here also, the name is of little importance. Moreover, the use of this discipline would not be limited to basic decisions but would apply to more modest and concrete choices, such as the location of a hospital or the creation of a social center.

The second remedy is the amelioration of the postregulation of administrative systems. First it is necessary to amend, recreate, and strengthen the feedback within administrative systems: it is a question of administrative organization; outside, also, it is the problem of participation. This is one of the new aspects of the role of social work and social welfare.

Participation.—I am concerned here with participation related to the elaboration, making, and execution of decisions by the government. It should be encouraged, but with some discernment: everybody cannot participate in everything.

Just as a division of labor is necessary in production, a certain division of fields of interest is necessary in questions of participation, for reasons of efficiency. Even more important, participation in a representative democracy should not result in the substitution of unqualified organizations or informal groups for the elected authorities and the officials duly appointed by them. It is indeed a principle that no minority group can arrogate to itself the exercise of power which belongs to the people as a whole and is most often exercised through the intermediary of its legal representatives.

If this idea is sometimes lost sight of, it is perhaps because urban administrative structures are inadequate and authority is distant. But besides the appropriateness of remodeling these structures, it is also necessary, especially in large cities, to decentralize administration, creating district municipalities, and perhaps also administrative committees at the neighborhood level. Of course, that will not be sufficient. It could be suggested, then, that elected consultative bodies be developed to study various types of questions posed by the administration of the city, that coordination between governmental agencies and voluntary associations be strengthened, and that certain decisions be submitted for public consultation or even for referendum. Many other solutions to the problems could be proposed, but if participation is to be stimulated and encouraged it must also be organized, with the help of social work.

SOCIAL WORK AND SOCIAL WELFARE

Neglected needs.—Social work should respond to two basic needs which run the risk of being neglected in an industrial, urban, and administrative society where production and distribution are regulated, for reasons of efficiency, by a system of preestablished measures and ensured by necessarily specialized bodies with highly centralized direction. In other words, in such a society the formal channels of communication are essentially vertical and the flow of descending, that is to say, restrictive information, is denser than the flow in the other direction, as I have mentioned. The neglected needs, then, are those which relate to taking into consideration the global and unique personality of the individual, which is only considered by a part of society, notably the administrative machinery, through a series of sectoral approaches.

Moreover, in a society which avoids bureaucratic deviations with difficulty, postregulation, as we have seen, is insufficient and feedback operates poorly. The situation can be judged acceptable if the programs are executed without major upsets, in conformance with the plans, and if the individuals concerned respond well enough to the standards defined by the bureaucratic system. But errors and deviations, poorly corrected, are generators of blocking and tensions which run the risk of growing cumulatively.

The role of social work.—Social work should therefore help individuals and groups to fulfill their obligations and take advantage of their rights in an administrative society. This does not mean that social workers must transform themselves into fiscal or legal advisers and liaison agents with the administration or private associations. Each citizen who has a complex legal or technical problem to solve should obviously seek out the appropriate specialist.

The role of the social worker is to understand the situation of an individual or group in trouble as a whole, to perceive the connection between the different problems faced by his client, to help him define choices and priorities, and, if necessary, to draw the attention of competent agencies to the peculiarities of such and such a case, and to unravel situations which seem inextricable to the specialized services. By reestablishing horizontal communication through informal channels, by enriching the ascending flow of information, at the same time filtering it to eliminate extraneous information, the social worker will participate in the successful operation of urban administration. He will then be elevated to the ranks of the regulators of the city.

We must expect change, accept it, and even ensure it; that is, imagine and invent in the social sphere.

If imagination is our imperative on the technical level, we can be rather optimistic on this point and have confidence in the inventive genius of the human species. But the world of the future also has its moral requirements. In particular, the virtue of tolerance must be practiced even more, and in this area we have less motive for self-congratulation. I well understand that we are offered numerous temptations, in the changes which assail us, the challenges met, and the menaces of tomorrow, to judge and condemn one by one the aged, the younger generation, neighbors, technicians, technocrats, officials, bureaucrats, and, of course, politicians. But without either disavowing our ideas or giving way, I think it is necessary to understand the role and problems of each and our differences and our oppositions.

Norbert Wiener, the first cyberneticist, who was also a philosopher of sorts, hoped that we would develop in ourselves the virtue of knowing how to understand (*savoir-comprendre*), judged more precious than knowing how to do (*savoir-faire*).

It is our job to construct a constellation of vast human communities open to communication. Then perhaps the Garden of Eden will flourish in the Kingdom of Earth.

Mental Health Aspects of Urban Life [1]

T. ADEOYE LAMBO

PROFESSOR OF PSYCHIATRY AND HEAD OF
DEPARTMENT OF PSYCHIATRY AND NEUROLOGY
UNIVERSITY OF IBADAN, NIGERIA

MY FAMILIARITY with, and intimate experience of, the problem of the mental health aspects of urban life is based on my work in Africa. Our long-standing research in a domiciliary-based therapeutic community at Aro, Abeokuta, and in the surrounding villages, combined with an intensive sociodemographic study of selected populations on the periphery of Abeokuta town, has led to insights into the sociopsychological problems of rural development, into the factors underlying motivation toward cultural change, into the social determinants of mental health, and into the problems associated with transition from rural to urban society.

Urban development is a subject which calls for a critical examination not only of the nature of man but also of the subtleties and ramifications of his social relations with others in well-defined environmental situations. Urban settings, according to our experience in developing countries, are becoming less and less supportive and more and more limiting in their promotion of human well-being in a nonmaterial sense.

Cities may be regarded, to some extent, as centers from which the idea of "progress" spreads. The relationship between man and man, on the one hand, and man and his city, on the other, is a topic of such immense complexity that there is no single method available for comprehending it. Medical science has in recent times started to study man within his social framework and man as an indivisible whole, but it is impossible to grasp the whole truth about him. The parameters are large, many of our traditional research instruments are inappropriate, and the concepts and the-

1 Albert Deutsch Memorial Lecture.

ories of many of the disciplines dealing with human problems are vague and incomplete.

The subject of urban development and its implications also has many facets about which no one man can claim all knowledge. It lies on the frontiers of the various disciplines of behavioral science, whose experts share a lively but parochial interest in many of the problems, most of which tend to be explored in isolation—not invariably without bias or preconceived ideas, but nearly always with inspiration, imagination, and, quite often, overenthusiasm.

Urban settlements are as old as human civilization. Lewis Mumford has said that "at the dawn of history, the city is already a mature form." [2] In dealing with the mental health aspects of the problem I must necessarily touch upon social, psychological, and health aspects of urbanism. In doing so I shall refer to certain essential features of African urban communities, such as density of settlement; unstable population, ethnic heterogeneity; demographic disproportion, especially in respect to age and sex structure; and economic differentiation, which gives rise to new forms of occupational and social differentiation. The rapid growth of towns in Africa and other developing countries, associated in the main with labor migration, has had adverse repercussions and ugly consequences for the mental health of many individuals.

In many advanced countries, men are so engrossed in their various occupations, in amassing wealth, or in struggling merely to maintain themselves, in altering their environment, in building for the future, and in rushing hither and thither, that they have no time left to wonder what it is all about and, perhaps much more important, how the rest of humanity survives the stresses of life.

Until recently there has been an excuse for this failure on the part of so-called "civilized" man to inquire into the why and wherefore of his existence. The prosperity that followed the Industrial Revolution, the triumphant progress of science, man's impressive conquest of the external world, are but a few of the achievements that created an omnipotent feeling of optimism. Man had always thought that he was marching forward to a glori-

---

[2] Lewis Mumford, *The City in History: Its Origin, Its Transformations, and Its Prospects* (New York: Harcourt, Brace, and World, 1961), p. 4.

ous future, and to the Golden Age portrayed in some of H. G. Wells's earlier books. So, with the fate of man assured, what need was there for him to interrupt his labors in order to inquire about his habitat? Speed was the keynote of success, and those who moved fastest and crammed the most activities into each fleeting hour would arrive first. There was no time to think.

But disillusionment has come, and we begin to doubt whether material prosperity is necessarily synonymous with successful living. The so-called "affluent" societies, which once considered their civilizations to be the standard by which other civilizations should be measured, now have a high suicide rate, rising crime incidence, juvenile delinquency, alcoholism, venereal disease, drug addiction, pollution of food, air, and water—and now many developing countries find that they must contend with the same problems. We are discovering that much is wrong with the urban social structure that we have inherited. Hitherto we have had confidence that educational possibilities, cultural wealth, and the social amenities associated with urban development would produce wonders in changing man, but in practically every developing country we find a decrease rather than an increase in the intellectual and moral standards of urban society.

HUMAN RELATIONS IN URBAN SETTLEMENTS

Many have pointed to the paucity of urban studies in Africa. The age-old problem of methodology has once again been the major factor militating against them. The apparent complexity of social phenomena frequently bespeaks a lack of theoretical concepts available for their analysis. It has been observed that "it is possible that this apparent complexity of social phenomena in African urban areas is due simply to the fact that we do not as yet have the perspective with which to view these phenomena and to bring them into focus." Mitchell (1963), writing on theoretical orientations in African urban studies, pointed to the extent to which urban studies are a neglected aspect of African anthropology.

In spite of these methodological and conceptual difficulties we have succeeded in collecting useful information on the social and cultural aspects of the new urban communities in Nigeria and have, for example, examined critically the nature of the relationship between a man and his family in urban areas. Although we now have some knowledge of the various factors involved in social pressures which may have disturbing effects on the mental health and happiness of individuals, it has been difficult to investigate the nature of interpersonal relations without reference to a vast underlying system of mutual human expectations embodied in complicated social roles.

In examining the mental health problems associated with urban social stresses in developing countries, we have attempted, through the method of evaluating case-by-case evidence, to isolate for study a cross section of the major problems. We have taken account of the new social forces which are engendered in developing towns of Africa and which tend to threaten mental health, especially those forces which operate at the level of day-to-day interaction. We have discovered that the effective range of individual social interaction in town is considerably narrowed. Although social relationships in tribal areas are more likely to be multilateral, they are, nevertheless, easier to understand than those in the towns. In town, according to our observation, the social fields are wider and interlocking, the networks ramified, roles and social situations confusing and misleading—all this tends to narrow the effective range of the individual's social participation.

An individual who moves from a tribal area to a town often finds that he must adopt new customs and habits if he is to function effectively and participate in urban institutions and structures. As Southall [3] puts it, "the switch of action patterns from the rural to the urban set of objectives is as rapid as the migrant's journey to town." In many parts of Africa the greatest hazard facing this group of people is mental illness. Psychosomatic and neurotic disorders have been the main clinical problems encountered in association with sociocultural situations which force a change in norms under the collective impact of urban situations. While most of the data on this phenomenon have been derived from direct observation in social situations, it has been possible to use case studies to gain further insights into the processes involved.

One of the most potentially explosive, disruptive, and frustrating situations in urban social settings is the often tenuous and

[3] A. W. Southall, *Social Change in Modern Africa* (London, 1961).

peripheral social position of many individuals in a network of artificially created social structures. This tends to lead to progressive social isolation and ill-defined interpersonal relationships. In some of these potentially disruptive situations social and cultural revolution often take place through the creation of social institutions which bridge the gap between the old and the new.

INSTITUTIONS AND ASSOCIATIONS

There is an increasing interest in the study of the role of various types of associations and institutions in urban settings as a form of mental health resource. Many voluntary associations constitute relatively enduring patterns of interaction in which the norms are defined in terms of the role expectations of others in the association or interact in terms of the institution. Thus Little [4] and Banton [5] describe voluntary associations of various types in West African towns as "adaptive institutions" which help a new arrival to absorb the norms of urban behavior and to build up around himself through them a network of supportive relationships. These community organizations provide the opportunity for group work, case-finding, counseling and leadership, and rehabilitation.

In our recent study of industrial workers in Nigeria we discovered that those migrant workers who availed themselves of these new institutions and associations used them as a powerful buffer or safety valve against mental health hazards. Many programs of prevention have sought the solution within a cultural framework in which the "age-old threats of sickness, ignorance, unemployment, squalor and want may be held at an acceptable level, partly by reducing their incidence and partly by increasing the personal and social resources of those who must cope with them."

I shall refer later to a particular group of children known as "lost children"—children disowned by their parents in town—who, with all the makings of future juvenile delinquents, have on their own initiative sought to create something of a substitute family by joining others like themselves. Thus certain dance groups afford a front for what are really mutual aid associations which in many

[4] K. Little, "The Role of Voluntary Associations in West African Urbanization," *American Anthropologist*, LIX (1957), 579.
[5] M. Banton, *West African City: a Study of Tribal Life in Freetown* (London: Oxford University Press, 1957).

cases fulfill the role abdicated by the families (teaching a trade, assisting newlyweds, and so forth). These associations are becoming increasingly numerous in West African towns and are known in French-speaking African countries as "Goumbes."

SOCIAL CHANGE, URBAN DEVELOPMENT, AND MENTAL HEALTH

Even in the nineteenth century there was awareness of the frequent relationship between the problems associated with social change and the incidence of mental ill-health; Esquirol in France and Maudsley in England both testified to this fact at a time when Europe was undergoing the many social changes brought about by industrialization.

To summarize the important social aspects of urbanization as we see these problems in Africa, there are practical problems of living in towns that are undergoing rapid expansion with little or no infrastructure. Housing shortages, the formation of shanty towns, lack of public services, and of sanitation are constant features. Of course we should not omit the social, psychological, and emotional problems of work and employment, underemployment in urban areas, worker-employer relations, labor turnover and interoccupational mobility.

In Africa scarcely a year passes in which the social conditions of life, the modes of conduct, the very habits and amusements of the people, are not subtly and yet surely altered. We stand bewildered at the shattering of what we had considered the most firmly established assumptions concerning the African family structure. Day after day we treat people from rural areas whose emotional structure renders them unfit to survive the discipline and rigors of urban life. Economic imperatives and missionary zeal have spread many new ideas and institutions; institutions of learning, for example, from primary schools to universities are found all over the continent. To accelerate the pace of production, industries are springing up and new techniques are constantly being introduced. In the wake of these developments, human resources are unnecessarily wasted.

Many developing countries present unique facilities for ideal studies and experimentation. In many places urban studies have been accompanied by parallel studies of associated rural environment. A comparative study of juvenile delinquency in new urban areas and in older African towns has been carried out in Nigeria. We have also developed many model programs in mental health and have consequently learned the great lesson that if health programs are to be effective they should ideally be related to other aspects of community development.

In 1961 Leighton and Lambo joined forces to carry out field studies of the prevalence of mental illness in contrasting Nigerian communities. Only in this way could we determine and delineate the role of sociocultural factors in the epidemiology of many medicosocial and mental health problems. It is only thus that we can understand the concept of stress and the community resources which could be used to prevent psychosocial problems. It was a joint international effort to develop instruments for good case-finding cross-culturally.

The problems of "detribalization," integration into the new society and maintenance of existing social structures, and the transfer of tribal values and institutions are additional human and social factors of urbanization. The institution of the family under urban conditions, marriage, the position of women, the status of children, and delinquency and antisocial behavior, not excluding religious and political structures, have also been critically but inadequately examined by us.

Many accounts of the psychological consequences of the phenomena of urbanization have described the urban outlook, ethics, and personality as depersonalized, emotionally shallow and atomized, unstable, self-critical, time-obsessed and coordinated, subject to sudden shifts in mode and fashion, "otherdirected," and so forth. We are, however, concerned in many of our studies with the major consequences to mental health of stresses of urban social life.

One of our main research activities has been to study in detail the reactions of individuals in changing situations—African students in Lagos; unstable migrant workers in Ibadan; aging old ladies living for the first time in an African city; illiterate but intelligent young traders trying to enter the cosmopolitan economy in Accra—irrespective of whether these changes were spontaneous within the group or due to outside influence.

In selecting our case studies, we have laid particular emphasis on some of the problems most commonly encountered in the adaptation of people to the challenges and stresses arising from varying degrees of social disruption consequent upon rapid development, transition from one kind of community to another, and from the unadulterated, almost Utopian, simplicity of rural surroundings to a more highly organized and complex system of life, sexual relations, and social orientations. We have discovered that as the migrant moves from his village to the town not only does the risk of illness increase but he is beset by poverty, social disorientation, and disastrous changes in family life.

The multiplying stresses and strains imposed by development are manifesting themselves in increasing signs of social breakdown; the number of psychiatric patients rises; juvenile delinquency and prostitution flourish; drug addiction spreads in the country as well as in the towns; political crises and conflicts between groups escalate, resulting in wastage of human resources. Many of these are not fringe problems but rather are central to the question of achieving orderly social, political, and economic development.

After many years of evaluating case-by-case evidence in Nigeria, it is now appreciated that the mental health aspects of industrialization, urbanization, and social change have an almost imperceptible wide range leading to anxiety and insecurity. This is due to certain unhealthy social processes, such as massive population shifts, the creation in the cities of artificial satellite communities leading to social alienation of individuals, loosening of primary institutions, confusion of role and relationships, and disorganization of a well-established value system.

There are pressing mental health problems in Africa, of which the most urgent are:

1. Field workers all over Africa and Asia and in many developing countries have reported a rising incidence of delinquency in urban areas, especially among unemployed youth. In Kinshasa (Leopoldville) in 1963 over 100,000 people under twenty-five years of age were unemployed; many more had no regular jobs, and some had only marginal occupations. In Kenya, where 60

percent of the population is estimated to be under twenty-one years of age, unemployment is chronic rather than cyclical and is basically due to economic underdevelopment.

In Nigeria the growing number of unemployed has been attributed to some imbalance among the forces at work. Social (including demographic) and educational changes have grown out of proportion to economic growth.

Quite apart from the purely economic causes, "there is general acceptance . . . that traditional forms and means of social control of juvenile behavior through the family and the tribe have either broken down completely or are quite ineffective in exerting any influence in the new situation of increased geographical and social mobility, urbanization, industrialization and formal school education."

2. Drug addiction, prostitution, alcoholism, and crimes of various kinds have reached such dimensions in many of these countries that they deserve special attention. The incidence of these variants of mental ill-health has risen considerably in many urban areas. In one African country, factors contributing to such medicosocial problems are said to be due to "lack of parental control due to breakdown of tribal discipline" and "insecurity which has its roots in the disruption of family life."

The social, economic, and mental health implications of the high prevalence of unemployment in many African cities where countless young people are completely out of touch with any form of useful occupation have been referred to in many of our studies of social pathology in Africa.

3. Case studies have pointed out the growing and pressing problems of families in urban centers, and efforts have been made to study their formation, origin, composition, social functions, value systems, and other potent cultural characteristics. In this respect, very urgent and of overriding importance is the complex undertaking of thorough evaluation of social policy, social planning, and social action at national levels in relation to human problems. Today, we are witnessing situations of obvious conflict within the families. For example, the changing role of women in urban areas in order to meet new economic demands is creating unresolved problems; the transfer of economic prerogatives to the young has

rendered incongruous the traditional role of the elders as the wielders of executive power.

There are many factors in the urban environment which affect the stability and character of African marriage. The status of women in Africa alters considerably once they live in a town. The union between men and women in towns produces children whose status varies with the circumstances. If both parents belong to the same ethnic group, there is no problem. If the ties of father and mother with their respective ethnic groups are very loose, there is no problem either. But where there is a union between ethnic groups of widely differing culture, the status of the children is not so simple. For instance, in certain West African countries, such as Ghana and the Ivory Coast, it can happen that the father belongs to a patriarchal and patrilineal society (savannah origin) and the mother to a matriarchal and matrilineal society (western coastal zone). In such a case, according to the custom of the father's clan, the child's upbringing is vested in the father; according to the mother's custom, the rights are vested in the mother. Since these unions are frequently short-lived, their terminations involve attempts by both parents to gain possession of the child (child-"stealing"). But very often, faced with the impossibility of resolving the conflict, the families of both parents wash their hands of responsibility for the child. He remains in the town and, while the family continues to maintain him in the material sense, he receives neither the affection nor the education he needs; he is a child "born among strangers," a foundling almost, a "lost child."

4. Endemic diseases and other infections are rampant. They tend to become aggravated by under- and malnutrition and are not infrequently associated with some degree of mental health impairment. Malaria, the enteroparasitic group, and tuberculosis are the diseases most commonly encountered in the African cities. Because of bad planning and density of population human health and growth are invariably endangered. Although well-intentioned, city planning and urban renewal in many developing countries do not seem to have benefited from the mistakes of the advanced countries. They lack foresight, and efforts are often uncoordinated. Vital statistics, especially the causes of morbidity, in large cities in developing countries resemble those of the typical Western indus-

trial nations in some respects as life expectancy lengthens. To some degree, mortality increases rather than decreases in certain urban centers.

5. Severe maladjustment, psychoneurosis, schizophrenia, and other psychoses are now commonly met among the younger members of the population and mostly in urban areas. Young migrant workers, students, and the economically deprived are the most vulnerable. The mental health hazards facing the unstable, unskilled, and underemployed migrant labor force are many.

In 1962, describing a new psychiatric syndrome, malignant anxiety, in urbanized or semiurbanized Africans undergoing the stress of social and cultural change, I wrote:

New medico-social problems in Africa have given rise to various abnormal reactions in individuals in relation to a changing society. Twentynine patients with such reactions have been studied in detail. . . . In many of these patients criminal behaviour of an aggressive type was preceded by, or associated with, manifest anxiety of a severe degree.

In examining the clinical and sociocultural aspects of this condition, I pointed out that malignant anxiety was found to have developed under the impact of social and emotional difficulties. Many contemporary social situations in Africa are almost unique and constitute a natural laboratory for the study of many complex behavioral phenomena resulting from stress-producing situations.

I cannot pretend to have covered all the mental health hazards which threaten the social life and happiness of individuals in urban centers. I have concentrated on certain areas which are of direct interest to me and on others which have some interest for social and psychological theory. As a behavioral scientist one is concerned with the behavior of individuals acting within the framework of a situation determined by political, administrative, demographic, economic, and other exogenous determinants.

Special programs are needed to deal with the stresses of urban life. Let me emphasize that many developing countries lack the array of services found in other countries; even the extent and influence of public and social services, such as education, welfare services, and so forth, are admittedly disproportionate to the effort involved in creating and running them. The reason is not far to seek: they are often badly organized, highly bureaucratic, and designed as though for a European or North American society. On the other hand, other resources can be tapped; for example, the spontaneous organizations and associations referred to earlier are proving of tremendous value in meeting new demands.

Better coordination is needed between many experts and workers in the fields of welfare, education, public health, planning, economics, and architecture, to mention a few, in order to obtain maximum advantage. Continuous dialogue between these disciplines and the sharing of knowledge and skills should lead to substantial improvement in human health and growth. Total ecological approach is essential.

The training of workers in developing countries is important if we are to cope with the problems of urban life. It is necessary to have a source of local expertise and it is equally necessary to diversify the form and nature of training—at both professional and nonprofessional levels—in order to adjust to the ever increasing needs of individuals and the community.

Lastly, in the light of our experience in Africa, it would seem important to enlist the active participation of the community. Such participation and involvement increase the effectiveness of programs designed to help the individual and the community.

Special programs should be flexible and broad to accommodate the changing patterns of our expanding urban areas, the changing needs of the people, and to promote more effective use of social and community resources and better coordination of efforts. Some goals and ideals must be set within the sociocultural framework.

We live in an age of crisis. We are surrounded by crises—political, economic, social, and many others—including the grotesque expansion of cities. However, if we judge from historical experience, continuing expansion and development will always present some hazard to health, including mental health, as will all activities of life. It is the responsibility of our profession not only to minimize these hazards and to increase the supports which can avert or mitigate breakdowns but also to foster in the individual the power to preserve the internal stability which, as Claude Bernard observed long ago, is the condition of free and independent life.

DISCUSSION: IMPLICATIONS FOR SERVICES

LOUIS MILLER, M.D.

DIRECTOR OF MENTAL HEALTH SERVICES
MINISTRY OF HEALTH, ISRAEL

THE CITIES of the world are growing at a tremendous pace, compelling both long-established and new populations into changed modes of life. Change in social life indubitably changes people. It changes their personality and behavior, the way they grow up and grow old, their response to, and tolerance of, their social environment. Social events may play a part in determining the type and degree of physical illness an individual may suffer. They certainly determine, as our studies in Israel have confirmed, the type and degree of mental disorder or deviation that beset him.

Dr. Lambo sets out some of the theory and experience in practice of the effects of the large, industrialized city on the individual. He contributes especially from the point of view of the cities and cultures of Africa. Dr. Lambo lays a special emphasis on the processes which occur in people who migrate into cities from rural societies and traditional cultures.

Migration into the city has no doubt been a fact of history. However, cities have burgeoned especially since the Industrial Revolution and do so still on the basis of the economic differentials that lie between the rural and urban societies. At times cities grow as a result of immigration. This was the case of Israel. Cities in Israel swelled in size after mass immigration both of sophisticated Western people and of semiurbanized and rural Jews from the Islamic countries of North Africa and the Near East. Many of the problems which Dr. Lambo mentions as resulting from rural immigration have occurred.

The sociocultural and personal changes that befall those from traditional cultures who move into the city seem to be fairly clear. They generally include a more or less total disruption of the traditional organization of the group. Changes in the structure, roles, relationships, and functioning of the family also take place. Structural changes in the group and in the family are inevitable because of the different economic organization of the city. Survival demands changes in personal, individual identity, role, and function from the moment of arrival in the city.

The economic pulls of the city break up the traditional institutionalized social forms and patterns of behavior which once were the vehicles for the values of the group. The city does not allow traditional or even clear-cut relations. It demands that each individual make a personal choice of his own social, economic, and personal relations and destiny. Because of this the group migrating to the city may lose almost all its age-old functions. The family is attenuated and is deprived in great degree of many of its tasks, such as the education of, and decisions about, its members. In the city, the family is obliged to pass these tasks on to the services and authorities of city society. So the individual finds himself in a group and a family which are breaking down and have not yet been replaced by new relationships. The greatest mental health threats are to the very young and the aged.

It is not surprising, therefore, that enormous personal casualties occur when a rural-traditional group moves into the city. In the first generation appear problems of employment, and poverty due to lack of skills, resources, and tactical knowledge. Older people, particularly, are at a disadvantage. Unadaptable and unskilled, they soon lose their place and value and are liable to depression and confusion. Children have learning difficulties at school because of the lack of sophisticated intellectual stimulation in the family and their own cultural difficulty in adjusting to an abstract curriculum. Role changes in the family, especially between son and father, lead to conflict. This combined with failure at school seems to be among the basic causes of the widespread poor social attitudes and delinquency of the youth.

The families continue to be large in spite of economic and personal failures. Emotional transactions and adjustments among members of the family and between them and society are replaced by direct expressions of hostility and bitterness. The family is often incapable of handling the least material problem and becomes dependent on the maze of city services which it is ill equipped to understand or employ.

The failure of rural people to change in the city results in the establishment of a cultureless, dense "clot," the slum, within the body of the city. This is joined by the failures, the "downwardly mobile," from other apparently more successful groups. Some escape to the middle-class cultures, but for many there seems to be an irreversible break with their former culture and their extrusion into limbo. However, for some groups, where the former social organization is grimly maintained, or for those who came from situations where social change has already been inherent, the worst threat may be only temporary or may be avoided. This we believe has been the case in some instances in Israel and in the United States.

Westernized city society finds great difficulty in approaching the threat of, or the problem of, the socioeconomic breakdown of its inmigrant groups. Its welfare, education, health, and psychiatric services are attuned to individual assistance for clients who are capable of helping themselves and capable of employing the services with conscious and constructive drive and initiative. On the whole, therefore, many services are used inadequately by those who most need them. Modern services are not really "social" and do not tend to attack "social" causes but deal almost exclusively with the individual handicap, losing sight of its social causes. Agencies do not, on the whole, educate the community to make the best use of their services.

Modern society itself has no social machinery to deal with massive human problems. It does what it can through employment and housing programs, schooling, care services, and recreation. Since such services do not work with the essential general causes of the individual problems they are more often than not ineffective and frustrated. It was the realization of this fact that spurred the reorganization of psychiatric services in the world movement of community psychiatry. Community psychiatry tries to invoke the aid of all services and of the community itself in attacking the fundamental social causes which give rise to psychiatric disability in many individuals.

It would seem logical, and it is borne out by experience, that all urban programs of an economic or welfare nature should be underpinned by social programs which are concerned with the political reintegration and sociological support of the groups in social change. These are the goals of community organization. Programs for community organization strive to stimulate the threatened group, or one already in social breakdown, to participate in social change, to employ its own initiative, to create new socially directed groupings and leadership for meeting mutual needs and to find mutual support. Community action of this sort is the only method which holds out the least glimmer of hope for subserving social integrity and mental health in the most severe cases. And it must be applied immediately with the arrival of the group.

The challenge to the social, care, and educational services is great. Will they be able to face the fact that their tasks are often created by forces which go beyond the immediate problem of the client? And if they do see the social determinants and problems which bring their clients to them, will they be ready to adjust their goals to those needs? The solution of the individual problem which results from social forces in itself often requires the cooperative endeavor of agencies and specialists. It may require a change in the roles of agencies and professions which conflicts with their traditions. Multiproblem individuals and families require comprehensive care programs and often a mobility of identity and self-image on the part of the agency.

The crucial question, however, for all services and resources must be: What may we with our specialized knowledge contribute to the solution of the general community problem? Because of the magnitude of social problems this demand can be challenging and confusing as well. Furthermore, for an agency's effort to contribute to a community organization program often means an uncomfortable intrusion of clientele and community into the affairs, government, policy, and workings of the agency. There is, however, no escaping the conclusion that, while it should be subject to constant evaluation, community organization seems to be the only approach which holds any promise for people threatened by social breakdown. Its effectiveness depends on making possible for groups the opportunity for effective self-decision and responsbiility in the social and political fields and responsibility even for the nature and employment of their own services.

One cannot here discuss the problems of the more successful and affluent, those who are able to fly to the suburbs to avoid the deadened core and declassed areas of the city. From people in the suburbs the city through its tense, machine-like quality exacts high personality tolls by limiting the depth of relationships in the family and community.

Most public welfare and care services were designed for the poor. The affluent are expected to purchase their services privately. These private services are more often than not ineffectual in approaching the problems of the family or of the community in a cooperative way. It is high time that social planning and community action methods be sought for the affluent as well.

What Are the Social Priorities for the Modern City and How Do We Achieve Them?

ELIZABETH WICKENDEN

CONSULTANT ON PUBLIC SOCIAL POLICY TO THE
NATIONAL SOCIAL WELFARE ASSEMBLY
UNITED STATES

WHO AM I, or, for that matter, what superqualifications have any of us, to set priorities for our fellow man and then tell him how he should go about achieving them? I fear we are trapped within the very stereotype most often—at least in this country—assigned to social work by its unfriendly critics. This is the alleged excess of righteous naïveté and relentless zeal with which we are said to undertake the "improvement," according to our own lights, of all about us—people, places, and social institutions. Of course I realize that at home the rest of you are undoubtedly awesome social architects, indispensable to potentates, tycoons, and village leaders alike. But here in socially underdeveloped America we are (despite the ever hopeful rhetoric of our professional literature) still struggling to find a foothold, let alone an established "professional role."

So too must I, your guide of the moment, struggle to locate a few hummocks of solid ground from which we may safely and modestly view the scene. At best we can look from our own experience at the shortcomings of the society within which we work in terms of the needs and aspirations of those people and communities we serve and suggest some possible remedies in the light of that experience.

One starting point is certain: contemporary man is at once irresistibly drawn to his cities and greatly alarmed by some of the products of that attraction. We start with a real ambivalence. For the very person who most loudly deplores the effects of overcrowding—slums, congestion, enclaves of disadvantage, disorientation, and alienation—will react with shocked dismay to any suggestion that he personally might be better off back on the farm, or in the village or provincial town from which he or his forebears very likely came. And even those who remain behind to till the soil and distribute or process its products are increasingly aware of the attractions of urban life; so that urban values and urban ambitions more and more color his aspirations. Thus the city has become not simply a place to which larger and larger numbers of people are drawn; it is also the source of values and patterns of living that for better or worse shape the lives of us all. We live in an urbanized society in which the goals of those who dwell in large cities, small towns, and rural areas are essentially the same, even though the barriers to achieving them may differ with community size. Gone are the days when large numbers of people lived self-contained lives within a village or tribal culture exclusively governed by isolated reality or tradition. The city and its values are a fact of modern life, and no amount of nostalgia for the "good old days" can contribute to the solution of its problems.

Nor were the "good old days" so good as in our reverse arrogance we sometimes assume. (By "reverse arrogance" I mean the assumption that our own problems are the worst ever to afflict mankind, just as we assume that our generation has made the greatest strides.) I was interested to learn that Julius Caesar was obliged by reason of otherwise unmanageable congestion to bar central Rome to daytime chariot traffic. Ancient Rome too had its one-family-to-a-room high-rise tenements, its restless youth, and trouble maintaining a balance with its hinterland. Even in more ancient times the magnetic attractions of the city overran its capacity for effective social adaptation. People came with their dreams and their necessities, but sooner or later the city failed them—just as too often our cities do today.

Our contemporary urban problems are compounded by sheer numerical gigantism and by the complexities deriving from modern technology. There are not only many more of us trying to live upon our finite globe, but modern technology—both in the handling of physical phenomena and in its social organization—has made it possible for us to live in ever larger and more concentrated groups. This has created many unprecedented social problems and, in the view of many social scientists, has changed the very character of our lives. But by the same token the technological revolution in all its aspects, including the scientific attitude of mind which is both its source and its product, has immeasurably widened our potential for solving these problems. It is at this point that we social workers—not only professionals but all the millions of allies who share our goals and efforts—can in all modesty take our stand.

For if there is one attitude which characterizes social work in all its myriad particularities throughout the world it is the optimistic belief that problems created by man are soluble by man's effort. We are perpetual searchers for those solutions and by that very persistence of seeking we remove ourselves from the defeatist and determinist forces that contribute to keeping mankind in bondage. But, while this optimistic conviction constitutes the dynamic of social work, it is not enough. We cannot on the basis of belief alone claim the right to be taken seriously as advocates or technicians of change. We have to earn that right by the authenticity of our diagnosis of ills and the practical efficacy of our proposed solutions.

All over the world—and certainly in the United States—social workers are struggling with this problem. For most social workers are engaged in trying to alleviate in various ways the ills and handicaps imposed on particular individuals and groups by a changing social pattern. From the village or urban community worker trying to help people overcome the discouraging disparity between their environment and their aspirations to the caseworker trying to find a home for a child, a hospital bed for an aged sick person, or something to eat for the destitute, the average social worker sees the human cost of social inadequacy. He is essentially a bridge or a link between individuals and social organization.

In this capacity no one knows better than the social worker the cost of sprawling, unguided, maladapted urbanization. Social workers are troubled by the belief that their traditional tasks of alleviation are not enough, that their firsthand knowledge of the social costs of social maladaptations should be made to serve the purpose of creating a better social order. But then arises a very real problem: are the qualities of mind and training that make a good community organizer, a good group leader, a good program administrator, and a good caseworker the same as those that make a good social analyst and a good proposer of solutions?

I doubt if there is anyone who has a definitive answer to that question but I believe that there is a logical link between the two. It is the practicing social worker, more than any other professional in our vast variety of modern functionaries, who knows what people want and what society is failing to provide. Making that knowledge work for better social solutions is as much a part of the job as easing the way in a particular situation. And it is surely the job of some of us to help those practitioners look with analytical eye and an illuminating perspective at the interaction of personal aspirations and social situation.

This is what I think we must finally come down to when we talk about "social priorities." What were people looking for or from what were they escaping that they came in such vast numbers to brave the hazards of modern city living and now have our cities let them down? Of course, the best way to find this out is by firsthand contact, but since I am not a practitioner at this level I will have to hazard a few speculations and a possible way of looking at these problems which you may easily demolish by the superior weight of experience.

In the first place, it goes without saying that not all city dwellers are inmigrants. As each city-born generation comes along it finds in familiar city streets and neighbors the sense of belonging which holds people to what they know. They are even inclined to find a threat in newcomers, especially those with alien ways, and may cling fiercely to the accustomed security of their own tight-knit, small community. Yet it seems to me useful for analytical purposes to talk of what people seek in city living whether the choice was made by their forebears or by themselves.

Moreover, in recent times, as cities have grown, transportation expanded, and old settlers prospered, a new kind of migration has developed—the flight to the suburbs. Here people disappointed by the quality of life in the cities have tried to reconcile the advantages of city employment and cultural opportunities with the comforts and cozy community feeling of small-town living. In so doing they have created new problems both for themselves and for the city they left behind, but a choice was exercised.

It is, in fact, in the concept of choice that the overriding attraction of the city must be found. For it is logical and realistic to assume that the growing concentration of people in a single or interrelated cluster of communities would produce a wider range of choices for individuals in all aspects of their lives: the work they do; the way they live; the goods they consume; the community services available to them; the way they spend their leisure time; the way they express their spiritual and cultural aspirations; the friends they make; and the opportunities they can give their children. When we think of the ideal city of our dreams it is usually spread out like a groaning banquet table in our mind's eye with a plenteous variety for all and something special for everyone.

Alas, how far our cities fall short of fulfilling that promise. Our modern cities have not provided the social setting in which people can make the kind of choices which meet their own profound desires and serve the community well-being as a whole. It is not so much a question of whether a particular society emphasizes the goal of social or individual values but rather that these are essentially interactive so that a social situation which thwarts the individual inevitably invites an antisocial response. The young person who responds to a feeling of exclusion by delinquent or bizarre behavior; the old person who retreats into apathy; the slum dweller who expresses his frustration in crime, addiction, or violence; the middle-income family that flees to the suburb; the older inhabitant who resists the newcomer—all are giving vent in their various ways to the frustrations of cumulative denial, in so far as they are personally concerned, of the promise of city living. Choices have been promised, but the promise remains unfulfilled. This, it seems to me, is the essential difference between the problems that confront our modern urban society as compared with the ancient pattern in which tradition and custom largely governed individual lives within a relatively fixed pattern.

Three particular aspects of city living illustrate this general thesis. First is the denial of choice with respect to employment and income opportunities. Second is the denial of choice with respect to the components of living by reason of urban inadequacies of provision and the pressures toward standardization and conformity. And third is the isolation of the individual from full participation in his community.

In thinking about the failure of economic opportunity in the modern city it is extremely difficult to generalize. Some cities are the focal centers for rich and productive economies while others represent the most concentrated massing of a generalized destitution. The fact that cities must function and take their vitality from a larger national economy and political direction makes the discussion of their problems apart from that larger setting a virtual impossibility. This is one of the reasons that I prefer to talk about an urban society rather than the city as a discrete entity.

Nevertheless, one has only to look around the cities that one knows best to see that lack or inequality of economic opportunity is a major factor in the frustration of urban dwellers. Rarely is there enough for everyone; and many cannot, by reason of poverty or other disadvantage, reach whatever advantages the city has to offer. Opportunity for all is clearly the number one priority.

In thinking about the nature of this opportunity our minds turn inevitably to the common belief and hope that within the large variety of the city each individual will find work that will be suited to his capacities and aspirations and will give him sufficient monetary return so that he can acquire the components of a good life. Some people are voluntarily drawn to the city by its wider range of choice in occupation, while many more find themselves dispossessed from an old occupation and location by changing circumstances. Thus in our own country, for example, a changing pattern of agriculture has driven many farm workers from the land, and these people tend to flock into our cities.

Two different kinds of difficulties may confront these potential workers, but both are derivative from a basic characteristic of city employment: it must for the great mass of people take the form of a job that lies beyond their own capacity of creation. The individual's choice of opportunities is itself the product of social organization. In some instances and situations there are simply not enough jobs available for all those who are attracted to the city. It is obviously impossible here to analyze all the economic limitations or faulty distributions that create this disparity between jobs and workers. In some countries it reflects an absolute lack of resources, while in others the difficulty lies in organization, planning, and confusion of priorities. But even where jobs are sufficient in number, individuals may find themselves barred from them by lack of qualifications or other arbitrary obstacles.

As modern technology moves toward specialization of function, the undereducated find themselves either shut out altogether or else restricted to work of such marginal productivity that they cannot earn a living at the optimum urban standard. Thus we find that a goal or priority of job creation is not by itself enough. It must be accompanied by such a sufficiency of educational opportunity that each individual may qualify for the work that best suits his own temperament and capacities. Nor can we ignore the importance in the development of personal capacity of an adequate variety and supply of health services to assure the full realization of individual potential and vitality, especially in the crucial years of childhood and youth.

But even a constructive policy of job expansion and preparation to fill those jobs does not solve the whole problem. Even in the most industrialized and mechanized society we cannot *all* be computer programers or supereducated professionals. Some of us find the very idea dreary and distasteful. Some of us are not really equipped for this kind of work, even assuming the most ingenious educational system. And some of us—particularly women—must divide our time and energies between paid jobs and other responsibilities. Thus both in the developing countries and in highly industrialized countries like the United States our ingenuity is increasingly challenged so to devise and divide the work of our society that all may be reasonably employed for their own and society's profit. This is especially important to areas of human service like social work; for it is particularly in these activities that the frontier for new kinds of jobs at every level of skill and expertise so clearly lies. Only when we achieve this triple combination of priorities—more jobs, better preparation, and new kinds of jobs —can true freedom of choice in occupation be said to prevail.

Equality of economic opportunity also assumes a recognition that not all persons can be expected to work and that in a wage-dominated economy few people can rely on earnings for their entire lifetime. Thus provision must be made to assure income to those outside the wage economy. In a pre-industrial society this responsibility rests largely with the family, which shares what it has with its young, its sick, and its old. In the urban world this ancient pattern becomes less effective, partly because of our greater reliance on cash income and partly because of the fragmenting impact of city life on family solidarity. Thus modern industrial society finds it necessary to institutionalize the sharing of income with the retired and other nonproducers, typically through some form of social security program. Such income sharing, while a common attribute or ambition of the urban economy, has rarely reached a level where we can view with pride the range of choices it offers to this important segment of our population as consumers. At least in the United States we think we could do much better, both in the adequacy and the level of protection.

Even if we had solved the problems of work and income the city of today fails its inhabitants in another important aspect of their lives. The exercise of choice assumes an adequate supply and a lively variety of activities, benefits, goods, and services among which to choose; a practical estimate of people's needs and priorities together with a cherishing of the differences in tastes, modes of self-expression, and aptitudes that constitute the salt and savor of the human condition. But few cities in the world, even some of the richest and most beautiful approximate this ideal. Inequalities are made glaringly visible in the slums, ghettos, shanty towns, and bidonvilles, the submarginal housing into which are crowded and isolated from the amenities of city living our poor and dispossessed. Other insufficiencies, especially those of essential services, are less physically visible but nonetheless discouraging to the individual and challenging to our own ingenuity. Even in those fortunate communities where a reasonable balance has been achieved between size of population and the essential provisions to meet their needs, the inexorable pressure toward conformity and standardization frustrates our highest aspirations. Even in the most elementary physical setting of our lives—the houses in which we live and the disposition of our public spaces and facilities—we are increasingly pressed into a mold which is at once inadequate to our needs and unsuited to our diverse tastes. (Each time a new sky-scraper or apartment house goes up in New York I look hopefully for some ingenious and lively architectural deviation, but each time the same gigantic icebox thwarts my hopes.) And if this deadly uniformity oppresses those of us with sufficient income to meet our needs, the lack of a varied plenty for those with less is one of the greatest failures of most of our modern cities. Even travel offers little escape. We seem constantly to become more like each other and to sacrifice the lively charm of our differences to an unnecessary and deadening uniformity. (It is perhaps a trivial but nonetheless telling example that I have personally in the last few years heard the same rock-and-roll records on the Bay of Siam, the town square of Spanish Soria, and in the remoter villages of Tur-key.) I do not think it unreasonable that social workers should put adequacy, variety, and individuality in range of choice on their list of priorities, for only in this way can people truly find the identity on which their own sense of secure existence depends.

Whatever the emphasis of our particular political, economic, and social system it seems apparent that some needs can best be met by an individual's own free choice of expenditure in the market place, while the answer to others depends upon community action and socially provided arrangements. The greatest challenge to social planning and ingenuity lies in the accommodation of these two values. But neither the most far-reaching social planning nor the play of market exchange, nor the interaction of the two, can afford to ignore the yearning that lies within the human spirit to express its creativity and individuality in an atmosphere of scope and variety. This too goes high on my list of priorities for the ideal city.

The promise of the city is blocked, too, by a defeating pressure: the atomization of community life and the submerging of the in-dividual in the mass. Here social work is clearly upon its own home territory; for its service jobs are for the most part directly related to the impact of this pressure on individuals in particular situations. In setting priorities for the good urban life it is hard indeed to separate equality and choice of opportunity from the sense and practice of community solidarity, for they are so clearly interactive. But for social workers—however greatly they may interest themselves in the basic questions of production and consumption that affect the quality of living for every individual and family—the problems of social organization and relationship in the modern urban world lie upon their own daily doorstep.

The very existence of social work as a specialized function results from the complexity of urban social relationships. For just as the urban situation has removed most of the functions of production and consumption from the traditional confines of family and village self-containment, so too have many social functions of the family passed to the larger setting of social organization.

Effective social organization, it seems to me, depends even more than that in the economic and political spheres on achieving a reasonable and effective balance between apparently conflicting goals. Let me illustrate this problem of balance in three areas.

Man wants to live in a society which gives him not only a sense of order, security, and continuity but also a sense of forward movement. He wants the security that only large-scale social organization can afford but at the same time he craves the ability to shape at least a part of his own destiny. He wants to belong to the large and massive community while retaining both his privacy and the closeness of immediate personal association. In each case he seeks to reconcile the values of a mass, urban society with his personal values, aspirations, and identity. I do not believe that any of us—whatever the political, economic, or cultural setting within which we function—have yet succeeded in developing the institutional framework that successfully reconciles these values, and this I believe to be a major challenge confronting our profession.

Social workers—by reason of their commitment to the goal of forward movement and their disposition, at least in this country, to focus on individualistic values—have tended to underestimate the great need for people to seek their individual goals within an enveloping framework of security, order, and continuity. Instead of seeking to reconcile the two values they have tended to overlook the one and thereby seek unrealistic channels for the latter. Let me give a few examples.

Juvenile restlessness and rebellion have become almost universal phenomena accompanying modern industrial progress. We rush into the breach with every kind of program to try to channel the energies of youth into socially constructive outlets. I do not in any way disparage the usefulness of these activities, but we have not yet found the way—so well institutionalized in more primitive societies—to give our young people the sense of their incorporation into an ongoing social structure in which they are at once the inheritors of the past and the initiators of the future. Young people need to test themselves in both respects by demonstrating their ability to meet the requirements of the society they have inherited as well as their zeal to improve it.

Among the most tragic victims of our changing society are the growing numbers of old people. Having denied them their former role as guardians and transmitters of ancient culture and family property, we seek to compensate them with pensions and social services but leave them no organic role within the social whole. We prolong their lives through the miracles of modern science and share with them—often on a niggardly scale—the products of our economy. But we exile them from the main stream of social organization and deny them a sense of usefulness by denigrating the social continuity of which they constitute the natural linkage. We deny them what the city has promised, the chance to function as valued individuals within a larger social whole.

Neighborliness, especially neighborly mutual aid, is too often another casualty of modern life. Mobility, impersonality, and dependence on large-scale centralized organizations have apparently taken the heart out of simple friendly associations based on daily confrontation. Many of our efforts to reconstruct or compensate for this lost value seem artifically unrelated to the other facts of modern life. The typical suburb is in many ways more devisive than unifying, barricading small, homogeneous groups against the larger forces of the modern world. Moreover, some of our efforts at urban community organization, especially among the poor and disadvantaged, operate at either a superficial or an unrealistic level, thus running the risk of compounding a sense of disillusionment, isolation, and deprivation. Neither takes sufficient account of the dependence of people on forces that lie beyond the neighborhood boundary.

Since we cannot reverse the course of history and recreate the village, we need to think in terms of a complex of interactive functional communities that can work together to reconstruct the sense of belonging so essential to human well-being. Some of these can operate on a neighborhood basis and some on a wider basis of common interest. We need to distinguish between those social functions that require a wide base of universality—our basic economic system or a universal social security program, for example—and those in which proximity or common interest is a major factor. Again it is not a question of sacrificing the broadly based securities to the neighborly personal interaction. Both are necessary and both are dependent on our capacity for ingenious social organization. But the breadth and scope of this community interaction should be such that no individual is either forgotten when he needs help or denied his participatory role.

Nowhere are the failures of our modern urban society more clearly revealed than in its favorite scapegoat, the family. We are blinded and bedazzled by our reverence for a family pattern which belonged to the days of village, farm, and tribal society but has little relevance for the realities of modern life. Thus the typical urban society simultaneously fails to give the family the kind of supportive help it requires and then blames on its resultant dysfunction all the other ills of its own social disorganization.

Contrary to the common belief that family breakdown and disorganization result from a failure of personal responsibility, I believe that the modern family is so overloaded by responsibilities that could better be carried, or at least shared, by social instrumentalities that it cannot adequately fulfill its central role of individuation: helping the individual develop his fullest potentialities, protecting him from undue social pressures, and serving as a link to the larger community. There are so many examples of this in contemporary American life that I am at a loss to choose among them, but perhaps because I am a woman and a mother I am inclined to consider a woman's dilemma.

An Indian friend, recently escaped from the pressures and supports of the joint family system, commented on the incredibly hard lot of the American mother. Depending on the age and distribution of her children she may work a sixteen-hour day, a seven-day week, and her vacation is more of the same. Any self-respecting trade unionist would be ashamed even to admit the existence of such a schedule. But if she is also poor or her husband cannot find a job, a woman's problems are compounded a thousandfold. She must make do in a poor dwelling, try to supervise her children under the most adverse conditions, find ways to bolster her husband's morale, supplement his earnings if possible, and very likely absorb the weight of the community disapproval for whatever is going wrong.

I feel that creating the community atmosphere and range of services within which the family can flourish is the most urgent challenge posed for social work by the modern city. Children should be born wanted into a community that is geared to their needs. They should live within the warm protection of a supportive family which is, in turn, sustained by a network of supportive community institutions. They should emerge from childhood into the wider ranges and options of youth equipped to take their place in a society which welcomes their eager impatience with the *status quo*. They should find work that gives them scope for their talents, satisfaction with their achievements, and an income sufficient for their needs. They should become, in their turn, supportive parents, creative individuals, and good citizens in a variety of interacting communities. And as they grow older they should be able to find the sense of serenity, achievement, continuity, and merging of individuality in the larger whole that alone makes tolerable the inexorable fact of human mortality.

This is my measure of successful urban adaptation and my concept of the task ahead for social work. I do not see occupational obsolescence as posing an immediate threat to any of us. We still have plenty to do.

Towns within a Town: a Proposal for Greater Athens

P. VASSILIADIS

ARCHITECT, GREECE

MORE AND MORE, city planners are finding it difficult to plan cities, and this is equally true whether the city is a totally new one or one to be renewed or expanded. The growing complexity of modern life imposes demands upon the planner which far exceed his traditional background and understanding. Thus we see a transition taking place in the planning profession, with city planners becoming more and more concerned with all the aspects of urban life.

It has become absolutely necessary for us to know how the citizens live, as well as how they want to live, for I believe that technicians and social scientists can propose solutions for many of the problems arising from urbanization, but it is only with the understanding and cooperation of the citizens themselves that we shall be able to develop the proper conditions for a creative urban life of a high cultural standard. Our role, in other words, is to suggest ways and means; the citizens will create their own city.

In order to cooperate with the citizens, however, we must speak the same language; their education and enlightenment are as necessary as that of the experts. For however well-informed the average citizen may be, it is not likely that he can grasp the city in its entirety. He must be informed about possible goals to be pursued, about the methods available for achieving these goals, and about his true long-run interests.

Thus, our cooperation with those who study the patterns of life of the people, as well as with those who are in contact with the citizens and who discuss with them their needs for a better and more productive life, becomes more urgent with every passing day.

Hence, we see that a one-sided technical approach to urban problems is likely to lead to a dead end. The solution of one problem, such as, for example, traffic circulation, does not constitute a basis for the organization of the city; it does not constitute a basis for the organization of the city; it does not constitute a total planning solution; it cannot give a fully meaningful form to the city or to the lives of the inhabitants. Sometimes, in fact, the technical solution of traffic problems can prove destructive to the town, if it does not make for a proper way of life for its citizens.

As a result, we often find a traffic circulation system inadequate even before it is finished. This is because other factors—social, economic, historical—in the lives of the people in the city, or even in the whole country, do not follow our forecasts and change in a process which is unaccounted for in our technical approach.

What is needed is a more general, over-all view of urban life. Within such a view, the solutions to the separate component problems of the urban system may then be found. Planning should not be a technical operation applied to cities; it should be the total expression of the way of life of the urban dwellers.

At one time, finding this total expression was much easier. Today, however, it is much more difficult for anyone, let alone a technician, to define the ideals of our time. The most we can say is that there seems to be a general tendency to broaden and strengthen the cultural and material base of humanity. We are trying to provide more spiritual and material goods for more people. It is fitting, therefore, that our planning efforts contribute to this trend. We must design our cities for efficiency in producing and distributing goods and services for all the citizens.

We might express our ideas diagrammatically as a pyramid whose base represents the people and whose height represents the standard of goods and services available. In former times this pyramid was highly peaked; the majority of the goods and services of high quality went to a few people. Today, this pyramid is filling out at the base; that is, more people are getting a larger share and variety of the goods and services. The preservation of the height of the pyramid with the simultaneous broadening of the base must be our chief concern.

Although there are many ways to pursue this cultural goal,

planners are trained to think mainly in terms of the structure or form of the city. Thus, one of the directions of our effort is the building up, or strengthening, of the many separate residential communities in the larger city. With the purpose of making more goods and services available throughout the city, we tend to divide the single pyramid into many smaller ones.

Our proposals for the development of the Greater Athens region illustrate these thoughts.

Athens is the most urbane city in all Greece; its goods and services reach a disproportionately higher level, that is, there is greater variety, than those of any other urban center. If we imagine another pyramid, with the base representing the total number of urban centers and the height representing the degree of urbanity, we will see that the region of Athens occupies the central part of the pyramid from peak to base. A conscious effort is being made to increase the urbanity of the country's other urban centers as well as to decongest the Athens region.

Greater Athens contains nearly one quarter of the country's population, and from 50 percent to 70 percent of the economic activities of the country. Consumption of electricity, for example, is 70 percent of the total for Greece.

The high-peaked pyramid form applies to the structure and most of the functions of the metropolitan area. We see that everything is concentrated in the center, where the population density is extremely high. In the twenty-hectare zone at the center the density reaches 600 persons per hectare, while the average is ten to twenty per hectare in some places in the outskirts.

Most of the stores are concentrated in the center of the city. Further emphasizing this phenomenon is the provision for construction of a single building in the center of Athens, to house all the courts in the region. All the buildings of higher education are found in downtown Athens. Likewise, most Athenians, except those in heavy industry, work in the center of the city; very little employment can be found in the outlying areas.

Another factor which reinforces the congestion is that the wealthier classes reside in the central parts of Athens and Piraeus, the harbor. As a result, the largest number of cars is found in the central area, independent of those that come in from the periphery. Thus, the congestion is not only a result of movements to and through the center, it is also a product of the residents themselves.

All these factors demonstrate the monocentric character of Athens. In spite of the fact that there are over sixty administrative districts and communities in the metropolitan area, the Athenians consider themselves to be part of a single undifferentiated urban settlement with—aside from Piraeus—but one functional center.

It is self-evident that this form of planning has serious effects on living conditions. These conditions are unacceptable, both in the central and in the peripheral region, although for opposite reasons. However, it is mostly in the periphery of the city that one observes great lack of organization of space, the result being a lack of organization in the life of the people. Most striking is the lack of space for public services.

The monocentric structure of the city affects people both practically and psychologically. Everything is congested in the center. Roads are terribly congested, and the new roads constantly being built are never sufficient. The people in the periphery feel that they live on the margin of life.

Every year more people pour in from every part of the country and add to the population of metropolitan Athens. Quite often a migrant comes from a village of 200 inhabitants to become a resident of this city of 2,000,000. It is evident that he has to face many serious problems of adjustment, practical as well as psychological. In older times migrants would agglomerate in certain neighborhoods according to their place of origin. The factor of origin linked them together, and the new migrant was helped to adjust to the big city. Now this is changed, and the migrant who enters the disorganized locale of the city cannot adjust himself and loses the balance that nature and the organization of his village had provided.

The disorganization on the fringe region of metropolitan Athens has a direct influence on the upbringing of young people. For the young people, an organized family milieu or an organized school is not enough; they need an organized community within an organized city structure.

Young people's characters are shaped by and reflect the environment in which they live. I believe that the proper type of planning has direct influence on the education of citizens. I believe that an urban structure which has a proper form needs little policing. Planning chaos brings psychological chaos.

Today's people live much of their lives outside their houses, and so the home occupies less space than it did in other epochs, while the amount that we need for education, work, and recreation, as well as for open spaces and circulation, has increased. The proper planning of these spaces and their hierarchical order will help to produce a hierarchy of human values and greater faith in them.

The planning expression of all this is the creation of correctly structured residential units around a center of social, intellectual, commercial, and administrative activity where a great part of the people's social life will be concentrated. Many believe that modern man is less interested in community life than were his forebears and that he has acquired a metropolitan psychology. Perhaps this is true. I believe, however, although I am a technician and not a sociologist, that nothing prevents a man from feeling that he is a member of the metropolis and at the same time a member of a smaller community, just as he belongs both to a family and to the whole world. On the contrary, it provides a rational setting for the organization of society.

In order to improve the conditions of life in the center, as well as at the periphery of the Athens area, we are proposing, as I have said, the creation of residential units adapted to human needs. In this way we hope to free the individual from the anxiety created by the metropolis. We will give him the feeling that he is a member of a community and not simply a statistic. We will encourage him to cooperate for the common good, we will assure a better use of his time and better possibilities for increasing his income.

We propose to divide the region of Greater Athens, the center area and its periphery, into communities and neighborhoods. These communities are envisioned as self-sufficient and fully organized "towns" which will extend urban facilities to as many as possible of the urban dwellers. It is difficult to decide on the size of these towns. As a first approach we are suggesting communities of 200,000 to 300,000 persons, with subdivisions into neighborhoods of 50,000 inhabitants.

We foresee that the Athens region, except for the two central areas of Athens and Piraeus, which will be occupied mainly by the daytime population, will contain fifteen community towns plus one more in the region of heavy industry and the commercial harbor. These we foresee will be developed in their final form in the year 2000, when the Athens population, according to our forecasts, will have grown to 4,000,000.

These communities would have a self-governing administration combined with the present framework of local authorities. They would have as many functions and services for their residents as possible, such as education, light industry, handicrafts, commerce, cultural activities, recreation and entertainment, athletic grounds, and so forth.

Each community would have a large center where an important part of the public services would operate. It would include buildings and spaces for administrative, cultural, and commercial activities as well as green areas and circulation spaces. Thus the residents would be able to take part much more easily in a community life. They would feel that they share the goods and services of urbanity, just as do those who live in the central areas. They would feel proud of their city and would try to develop social activities to a greater degree. One of our goals will be to give each community-town its own character. This should not be difficult since the Athens region offers much topographic variety and many historical sites.

This proposed structure for the Athens metropolitan area would present many advantages, but I feel that the main one would be the influence on the psychology of the residents. Without losing contact with the metropolis they would acquire another point of immediate interest between the home and the metropolis.

We do not foresee strict boundaries between these community-towns, either psychological or material. The people would have to feel free to move from one area to another.

It is our objective to achieve a balance of services between the community towns and the central areas, so that the metropolis would become an organized whole within which the self-sufficient community-towns would function. The circulation system of the entire region would be organized so as to insure easy communication among the various community-towns and the central area, as well as with distant places of work and vacation and recreation sites.

Thus the pyramid that expresses the monocentric city would be converted into a formation of pyramids, and Greater Athens would become a polycentric metropolis. The built-up area and its extensions would be subdivided into more fully developed towns within the town.

I am aware that the concept of towns within a town is not new in the United States. It is possible that it has been considered in other countries too. But the fact that in a country like Greece, with very different potentialities, we have been led quite independently to adopt the same idea in the master plan for Greater Athens proves the value of the concept.

It is important to report that thirty centuries ago the very same area which Greater Athens occupies now was divided into ten demes. These demes had a section within the city, an inland section, and one near the sea. They had a self-sufficient life although they belonged to the city of Athens.

Pausanias tells us that a community is considered to be a city when it has a gymnasium, a theater, and an agora. Thus, today, with important differences in the conditions, we conclude that it is correct to divide the city into smaller cities just like the ancient demes.

It is not a utopian idea that the region of Greater Athens can be redeveloped on the basis of such a structure. We have the practical possibilities for this when we think that the population will double in the next generation. Thus the new residences, the new factories, the new administrative buildings, the new shops, the new schools, and the new theaters along with the renewal of old ones will be more than doubled, and so it is up to us to use this potential for the right kind of redevelopment of Greater Athens.

Many archaic ideas and institutions must undergo basic changes, and this will prove to be a more difficult task than building anew. It will be necessary, for instance, to reform legal procedures in order to decentralize the courts of the region and to avoid creating a central courthouse, a gigantic "Palace of Justice" which would psychologically inspire more awe than trust in justice.

It will not be easy to enlighten the citizens of the region and convince them that short-term interests will, in a few years, turn against them by creating unprofitable and destructive conditions for the lives of their children. We must overcome all the difficulties and all the material and psychological obstacles in order to leave to our children a city worthy of her history and her future. Such a goal justifies any sacrifice.

I think I may say that what holds good for Athens holds good for many other cities as well. It is my belief that with proper planning and the even distribution of urban facilities we can create conditions that will enable citizens to live a better life in prosperity, integrity, and freedom.

Urban Development in Atlanta, Georgia

DUANE W. BECK

EXECUTIVE DIRECTOR, COMMUNITY COUNCIL
OF THE ATLANTA AREA, INC., UNITED STATES

ATLANTA, GEORGIA, has progressed in the last fifteen years from a relatively small community to take its place among the major twenty-five cities in the United States. Atlanta is a city which has been reported on by men such as Floyd Hunter, in *Community Power Structure,* and by M. Kent Jennings, in *Community Influentials.* The city has its chroniclers, and there is some background for understanding what makes Atlanta move.

I am a social worker, and my major concern is improvement of the environment by changing housing, health, and employment conditions and the social system within which the problems exist. My vantage point is that of the Director of the Community Council of the Atlanta Area, Inc. This planning council is independent of the United Appeal in Atlanta but receives some of its funds from that source. We are also funded in part by the city of Atlanta, by Fulton and Gwinnett counties, and by federal and local sources.

The people of Atlanta are characterized by a high sense of pride in their area. This is perhaps best illustrated by a remark made by Ira Reed, who at that time was teaching at Morehouse College: "Atlanta is a place where a nobody can become a somebody."

Atlanta is a five-county, 1700-square-mile, metropolitan area in the northeast Georgia pine forest, on the edge of the Appalachian Mountains. Approximately 1,300,000 people call this area Atlanta when they are away from home, but they tend to be more parochial and specific when they are at home trying to solve local problems. "Home" has forty-four municipal governments within the five counties.

The economy is good, and jobs go begging for the want of skilled people. Over four thousand national firms have located some type of office, plant, or warehouse in the area. Atlanta is the rail hub of the Southeast and the hub of three interstate highways. There are nineteen degree-granting colleges and universities. It is the commercial and banking center for at least eight states. The state capitol and state offices are in downtown Atlanta. The area has a metropolitan planning commission of reputation.

Atlanta is the land made famous by Henry Grady, Sidney Lanier, Joel Chandler Harris, Ralph McGill, Coca-Cola, *Gone with the Wind,* and General Sherman.

The growth in population in Atlanta is around 4 percent per year. Into this area flow young and old, black and white, people who manage industry and business, teach in schools and universities, talk to computers, and those others with inadequate skills, poor education, and large families who come looking for jobs. There are the most sophisticated of families and the least sophisticated; some generously endowed with talent and opportunity and others completely lacking. And each moves into the city according to his means and finds a place according to his ability to pay. Some know exactly what they are going to do, while many have only a hope that this jewel city will have some kind of job and a good life for them.

Atlanta offers much to those with skills, experience, and education—good housing, pleasant neighborhoods, art, culture, beautiful churches, and convenient shopping centers. For those with little education or limited experience, there is not even a welcome wagon. The community service agencies seem to be unaware of their presence until a family ends up on the doorstep of one of the several hundred social agencies. Then, chances are, the tribal ritual of referral commences. Hither and yon goes the family, and only the strongest survive.

Within the city the population is moving—from central city to suburb; from urban renewal project to a potential urban renewal project area. Stability is not yet to be found.

Growth is desired, encouraged, fostered, sought. Growth is good for business and the economy, but not for social welfare programs. Industry comes in looking for skilled labor. Forty-four buildings of unusual architectural design rise from the ruins of buildings that were fifty years old. A new river—a river of automobiles—

flows through the city. The airport has been enlarged with a second runway and ranks third in passenger traffic in the United States. As one traveler in the South said, "If you were on your way to heaven, you would have to go through Atlanta." Atlanta is a natural commercial distribution point for the entire Southeastern United States.

Atlanta is unique in many ways. It is not dependent solely on heavy industry. It is one of the few cities in the United States which was subjected to the ravages of war.

It does not have a large number of ethnic groups. Its population is largely Caucasian and Negro—mostly Protestant—two societies existing side by side with growing communication.

Negroes comprise about 25 percent of the metropolitan area population and 45 percent of the population of the city of Atlanta. About 50 percent of the Negro families have annual incomes of $3,000 or less; about 20 percent of the white families are in this category.

A number of large business firms are owned and managed by Negroes, and Atlanta has the largest formerly all-Negro educational complex in the world.

The slums of Atlanta, unlike those in other cities, are characterized by low density, small-family dwellings.

The metropolitan area spreads over a greater geographical area than in most cities. In 1950 Atlanta was a city of 22 square miles; in 1960, the city contained 122 square miles and was somewhat of a legend in the United States.

What happened? In a moment we shall attempt to understand it a little better.

According to the abstract of the U.S. Committee report for this conference:

It is customary to think of the developmental approach as involving discrete, regular, timed procedures: first goals are established; second, policies, targets and structures are defined . . . third, boundaries are established for deviations from the goals. Finally, there is evaluation, feedback and the cycle is repeated.

I find little evidence of advanced urban planning in the rapid growth of Atlanta. The emphasis is on economic and physical growth. Goals, if defined at all, come after the action. The various systems move at radically different speeds. Growth of the white community exceeds that of the Negro. There is much trial and error. Decisions are made at the top and "sold," or else the powers that be move on what they agree. There is no consensus on the allocation of resources, and some things just happen and permit other movement.

HISTORICAL REVIEW

A key year in the development of Atlanta was 1946.

Atlanta saw the return of many servicemen who were influenced by their experiences in the armed forces throughout the world. Atlanta had a fine political leader, Mayor William B. Hartsfield, who had been in Atlanta politics for over twenty years and held a dream about Atlanta's becoming a leading city of the United States.

Here we must deal with the "Hartsfield legend":

He was imaginative.

He was *not* a planner.

He had influence, was tough, and could influence people.

He seemed to be tireless.

He was a leader, a pusher, a hauler, a mover, and had an acute sense of timing.

He coined concise and meaningful phrases, such as, "People ain't going where there's a mess," and "We're too busy to hate."

He was right so many times.

He created an image of Atlanta by the way he handled desegregation and the national news media which came to Atlanta to report the racial tensions caused by each court decision.

He bypassed the state and went to the federal government on highway construction, airport construction, and urban renewal.

He sought industry and business and brought them to the area.

He had style, and other people and institutions copied him. Today the Hartsfield style is the Atlanta style: "If they want a football team they buy one."

There have been certain significant events in the urban development of Atlanta.

1946 The white Democratic party primary had Negro voters for the first time, and the police insured their right to vote. This led to increased Negro voter registration and a balance-of-power role for the minority group in the political arena.

1947 The freight rates court decision was handed down. Governor Ellis Arnall bypassed the Interstate Commerce Commission and appealed directly to the U.S. Supreme Court to hear a case regarding the differential in freight rates on industrial products which virtually kept the South tied to a rural economy. (Steel manufactured in Pittsburgh, could be bought more cheaply in Atlanta than steel manufactured in Birmingham, less than 150 miles away.) Arnall won, and so did Atlanta.

1949 The Atlanta Region Metropolitan Planning Commission was organized by a special act of legislature.

1952 A plan was offered whereby the city area would be enlarged from 22 square miles to 122 square miles, with services divided between the city of Atlanta and Fulton County. The voters accepted the plan.

1953 City golf courses were integrated. A court decision to sell the parks or integrate forced issues. The parks stayed open.

1954 The Supreme Court decision on public school integration opened the way for an improved public education system.

1958 The Department of Commerce was formed by the state. Economic development commissions were organized throughout the state with the Georgia Power Company.

1959 With the school crisis, Atlanta women's groups influenced economic and political interests in the state and in Atlanta to keep schools open. The public schools did stay open.

1960's The imbalance of power between rural and urban populations in the state legislature was attacked by a group of Atlanta citizens in the courts in an effort to break the county unit system. The system went something like this: Fulton County with 500,000 people had six representatives in the legislature; a medium-sized county had four representatives; and a small county with, say, a population of 1,700, had two representatives. Georgia has 159 counties, mostly small; the system had to be changed. The Atlanta group persevered; by 1962 it succeeded through the federal courts in breaking up the county unit system.

It took another national policy decision to complete the political change. The Supreme Court decisions on reapportionment of the state legislature forced the states to reapportion. Immediately, Atlanta and its environs received a greater share of representation from the legislature. Nineteen hundred and sixty-two was the year in which a Negro from the Atlanta area was elected to the state senate for the first time since the Reconstruction. The political power of Negroes was felt, and in 1965 a second Negro senator was elected as well as nine state legislators.

Growing Negro political power made possible the election of a congressman from the Georgia Fifth District who, because of his base of support, was able to vote for the Civil Rights Act of 1964 on the final vote and stay in office—the first time a white Southern congressman ever voted in favor of a civil rights measure and stayed in office.

Reapportionment also led to the creation of an additional congressional district in the metropolitan Atlanta area. A second liberal-minded congressman was elected in the new Georgia Fourth District. He had spent six terms in the state legislature. He has a deep social conscience, and it was his efforts in the state legislature in 1963 which caused the reorganization of the Department of Family and Children's Services and the creation of a Children's Division of that department—a milestone in social welfare in Georgia.

1961 With the rise of the civil rights movement, demonstrations put pressures on decision-makers.

1964 The federal Civil Rights Act was passed. Conservative groups made concessions to preserve the Atlanta image—"People ain't coming where there's a mess"—and Atlanta leaders believed it.

All cities in Georgia have two major problems: there is no home rule legislation, and the cities must go to the state if changes are to be made in their local operation. Also, an inadequate tax base has created severe barriers in dealing with expensive urban problems. This has caused Atlanta to use funds from the federal government as legislation is passed. National policy has established guidelines and furnished money, and Atlanta has followed in the general direction with funds under the Hill-Burton Act for hospital construction; funds for urban renewal, highway construction, rapid transit, and sewer construction; state planning for the region, under the Mental Health Act; a massive antipoverty program through the Economic Opportunity Act; and assistance through provisions of the Elementary and Secondary Education Act of 1965.

The state has been bypassed or forced to accept enabling legislation permitting Atlanta to participate in these programs and others.

Rise of planning organizations.—The complexity of federal legislation in all fields has helped to bring about an increase in planning and planning structures in the Atlanta area. The following partial list of organizations and their approximate dates of initial activity illustrate the growth:

1947 Atlanta Region Metropolitan Planning Commission
1961 Community Council of the Atlanta Area, Inc.

1963 Educational planning in Atlanta school system
1964 Community Improvement Program (long-range planning for urban renewal)
      Economic Opportunity Atlanta, Inc.
      Metropolitan Council of Governments
1965 Commission on Crime and Juvenile Delinquency
      Metropole (cooperative police activity in area)

A push toward the coordination of programs has come from the federal government and the office of the President. The Region IV Federal Executive Board, made up of heads of the regional offices located in Atlanta, has developed a liaison committee which includes department heads of federal government, two representatives of city government, the Director of the Metropolitan Planning Commission, and the Director of the Community Council.

A number of problems have been given little attention.

The emerging problems of suburban residents have not been solved.

Local intergovernmental warfare and rigid governmental systems are severe barriers to the solution of our social welfare problems. One of the members of the Community Council's Research Department Advisory Committee said: "The solutions to these other problems will not come until the main problem of local governmental cooperation has been dealt with."

Only lightly have we dealt with another very difficult problem—the provision of work opportunities for all members of society. The problem of job training and job development has received a great deal of attention, but the impact is small. Many attitudes must be changed, and the attitudes of the professions which dominate the various services must be modified before there will be a coordinated, comprehensive effort.

We must also alter the attitude of people about their relationship with their central government and find more specific ways to develop new coalitions between the federal government and our private enterprise system.

Growth and some directed change are illustrated by this material, but there is little centralized direction or planning. There is a reluctance to accept planning as an integral part of the development in the Atlanta urban area, but the attitude toward planning is much more favorable than it was three years ago.

Most of the motivation for urban development has come because of the high emphasis and great value placed on the development of a strong economic base. The emphasis on comprehensive planning for our metropolitan area is coming from the federal government. Because the current political leadership of Atlanta is not afraid of assistance, ideas, and directions from national government, Atlanta probably will act in concert with the federal government to develop some kind of comprehensive planning program in the near future.

The problem of housing and relocation of people is basically unsolved. Attempts have been made, but we have a long way to go. The social planners in our community are involved with the city, and they will play a role in the development of a solution, or an attempted solution, of this problem. The Public Housing Act of 1965 has made many new tools available, and it is time the community paid close attention to our deteriorating areas as well as to the slums.

We are lagging in programs to improve the rearing of children.

Education is being handled better, but we are blocked by a shortage of funds from an inadequate local community tax base to support the kind of educational programs which prevent problems.

The whole system of income maintenance must be reorganized. This is as much a federal as a state and local problem. The underlying concepts of public welfare need to be revised by federal legislation, and perhaps we need a new system by which income maintenance is provided.

The amendments to the Social Security Act which provide for Medicare and for the treatment of children are giant steps toward adequate medical care for our population. However, a great deal of work is ahead.

There is need to develop better neighborhood organizations through which the resident can participate in influencing his government. The disadvantaged receive little consideration in urban planning. The politically impotent seldom share equitably in the available resources.

I am impressed by the resemblance of my city to others in the United States. Most economic and political decisions are made at the top and sent out or down. Similarly, most decisions about physical or social programs are made by the planners and financers of these programs and sent out or down by them.

I am also greatly impressed by the amount of "doublethink" emanating from some of the experts in planned community development. At one and the same time they want central control and an expression of consensus of the will of the people. It is difficult to achieve consensus of "the people," and seldom is it truly accomplished. When it is, it generally falls into deadly conflict with the intellectual authoritarianism of the planner. And when a decision is to be made, who speaks for the consensus of the people in the inner sanctum—the planner friend, the planner neutral, or the planner foe? Where is the independent third force which can modify the decision in order to reflect concern for whether the enterprise works or not?

I am troubled by the authoritarian aspect of the "centrally controlled and planned society." A band wagon has been built, and a siren call summons us aboard. Sheer size in the United States has already limited individual choice. I have grave concern about placing further limitations on individual choice, for we should have a rational process for allocating resources to "good" causes. All too often we seem to do the right thing for all the wrong reasons and then are perplexed by the misshapen results.

Public policy is never going to come in bright, shiny, compact packages neatly arranged like rows of corn in Iowa. I for one would like to know more about the actual experience and the success or failure of the comprehensive planning theorists in the practical, social, and physical decision-making.

Until I see more success based on ethical motivation, I am unwilling to trade an old form of authoritarianism for a new one. There is a "human tendency to see every new discovery or insight as the exclusive path to truth," says Corwin Mocine, commenting on the new planning.[2] Promoters always work with a shortage of fact and quite often direct their research to support preconceived conclusions. I would like to see more facts and much more definitive thought about the unplanned consequences of a planned society.

[2] Corwin R. Mocine, "Urban Physical Planning and the New Planning," *Journal of the American Institute of Planners*, XXXII (1966), 234–37.

Social Implications of Advanced Urban Planning and Development

MICHEL DE CHALENDAR

COMPAGNIE FRANÇAISE DES PETROLS, FRANCE

AT THE BEGINNING of this study we are conducting together a few general remarks may be useful in order to give their proper places to some special cases we have been asked to consider.

URBAN DEVELOPMENT

Does *avant-garde* development differ, and will it differ, from the development we have known in the past? With an effort toward simplification let us distinguish three types of urban development: disorderly (anarchical) expansion; supervised expansion; and planned expansion.

Naturally, each city has known more or less disorderly, more or less supervised, more or less planned periods of expansion. Paris at times went through anarchical phases of growing which the kings of France tried to contain and control. Paris also has been able to create perfectly planned sections which are admired by the whole world. However, Paris has suffered from a regrettable, almost anarchical, growth of its suburbs between the two wars. Today it is redressing the balance. Its main plan covers the whole Parisian region, whose unavoidable expansion will be more and more planned.

Cities founded for a special function, military, religious, or political, have often been planned, but the sequence of events has often proved the initial plan too bold. Rare are the examples of a lasting success. Let us offer our praises to the city where we are now, Washington, D.C. It was designed over 150 years ago by a Frenchman who envisioned the splendid progress of the nation which is welcoming us today.

Let us express to our Brazilian friends the wish that the Lth International Conference of Social Work may offer similar praises to Brasilia. But, however enthusiastic an observer may be at the present time, he must refrain from judging prematurely because the urban planner has to take into consideration space and time. The Brazilians' opinion about present social problems born from the creation of a capital would certainly be most enlightening.

Recent years have been very rich in instructive examples. Since we are witnessing the fortunate or unfortunate social consequences of contemporary urban development let us draw lessons from them in order to define the characteristics of *avant-garde* urbanism. Let us take three examples:

1. The workers' city established in the country to cover the needs of one industry or of a group of industries: it includes from 2,000 to 20,000 inhabitants.

2. The great suburban ensemble, that is to say, a town created in its entirety about ten kilometers from a large city in order partly to offset a problem of overpopulation: it houses from 5,000 to 30,000 inhabitants.

3. The new city of at least 30,000 inhabitants: it appears as the satellite of a larger city or it may be completely independent.

These three types of development offer certain differences and certain similarities.

Differences.—There are differences in dimension; in location in relation to the main city; and between the agencies responsible for its creation—industrial firms in the case of a workers' city, public local authorities in the case of the great ensemble. For the latter the authorities act either directly or through public agencies— organizations for medium-cost housing, composite financial groups, cooperative societies, organizations in which in France even the laborers may participate through a contribution of one percent of their salary.

In the case of new cities the initiative may come from higher authorities acting within the framework of national or regional building organizations. In France a study is being made of the possible creation of eight cities in the Parisian region as well as of the planned expansion of eight large provincial cities.

Finally, there are differences according to the objectives pursued and the composition of the population.

A workers' city is built as an annex necessary for production. The inhabitants are active workers only. The social structure will differ for a long time from that of an old city; for there will be no retired persons, very few civil servants, few merchants, and few professional people. Among the workers themselves one will find only the categories required by the type of work done in the local firms.

In the great ensemble one finds a greater variety, but the population has been chosen according to a criterion which keeps it from being composed of evenly balanced groups. Large ensembles are made up of people who have left unsuitable lodgings, thanks to public help granted to them because of their economic or family status. It includes families with young children, but there are no grandmothers, few women alone, and few working adolescents. The result is a lack of human balance: mothers cannot find help; youth feels isolated. Let us add to this the fathers' tiring daily trip to work, the absence of very rich people (or of people too poor to be housed in brand-new buildings), the lack of artisans and artists, the monotony of the architecture.

As a remedy to these defects the *avant-garde* urbanism suggests the erection of new cities complete and well balanced. English and Swedish examples could show what progress may be expected from an urban creation on a large scale—progress due to the multiplication of jobs close to homes assuring more freedom to labor contracts and lessening the inconveniences of daily communication; progress due to the presence of administrative or cultural organizations that bring at the same time better services to the population and a better mixture of social groups.

Resemblances.—There are characteristics common to the workers' city, the great ensemble, and the new city. They are cities of immigrants, a fact which calls for social services specially concerned with welcoming newcomers and helping them to adapt themselves to new living situations. They are cities without a past which have to strive for a collective soul, a condition which calls for a center and buildings with a collective use, a swarming center, a challenge to architects. They are artistically created cities which require a certain amount of imagination and diversity in their design to make them acceptable. And they are cities with a rapid and intentional growth, the development of which depends on a public or private authority necessarily concerned with planning.

PLANNING

Planning is necessary to avoid a disorderly expansion, whose bad consequences are familiar to us. However, planning may be dangerous if it does not have broad and complex objectives and if the planners do not have a respect for freedom.

We have seen in a few examples the faults of a conception on a too limited scale (the workers' city) or of one with a too narrow objective (the great ensemble). Therefore, it is important to plan the objectives themselves as much as possible.

Avoidance of creating a workers' city for only one firm will encourage other industries to settle in the same location. The great ensembles provide local employment. They should not be established by one organization alone nor financed by only one credit system open only to a too homogeneous group. Persons who do not necessarily need to settle there (artisans and older or single persons) should be invited to come.

Let us suppose now that such difficult objectives have been attained. Planners still can fail if they conceive their role as that of absolute monarchs. In order to avoid anarchy they would fall into tyranny.

Urbanists have as their mission to think of the future, to establish public places and services, open green spaces, reserve land for a still undetermined purpose, being careful not to forestall or manage everything beforehand. Being masters, so to speak, of the public domain they will outline in their main plan zones proper for private construction. They will determine, perhaps, the density of construction since this density will have an influence on the system of circulation, but they must leave a great freedom to builders within the space alloted to them. They will strive to encourage many different public and private groups to cooperate in the expansion of the city. They will recognize that urbanism is teamwork where engineers, architects, economists, and sociologists have their part to play. As soon as possible they will invite the inhabitants to participate in making decisions. They are entrusted with the future but they must respect the unforeseen and realize that a city, after all, is not the only material setting that affects the lives of the population.

The inhabitants themselves, this human community, this living organism with its still little known biological laws—this is what makes up a city. Urbanism is an infinitely complex art subject to evolution and having happiness as its aim. If the planners take themselves for gods, on some inescapable day they will be accursed, but if they know how to imitate the Creator in His patience, His humility, His respect of human liberty, going so far as to accept the presence of evil in an imperfect creation, they will deserve to be called gods by their grateful brethren.

The Social Welfare Program of Norway

LILIAN BYE

DIRECTOR, SCHOOL OF SOCIAL WORK
TRONDHEIM, NORWAY

NORWEGIAN SOCIETY is characterized by outstandingly good social legislation. This legislation is based on a profound respect by the people for the law, which grants equal rights to all, protection for all, social opportunity to all—men, women, and children. Today there is universal suffrage for all adult citizens, women as well as men. They have the right to participate in selecting government representatives on community and state levels and to control the legal system which regulates all spheres of social life.

Within the five Scandinavian nations there are many similarities in language and folkways. In over-all planning they have followed essentially the same social welfare program. Nevertheless, in their individual historical development these countries show great variations as well. The concept of the "common man" has more significance in Norway and Iceland than in the other countries for the simple reason that in Norway and Iceland it was the peasantry who for centuries carried the cultural norms and not the titled aristocracy, as in Sweden and Denmark.

It has, as a consequence, been relatively easy in Norway to realize in depth the modern concept of a social welfare state because the ideology of the modern welfare state is basically related to the traditional ideology of the Norwegian democratic peasant economy with its implicit moral norms and societal values. One of the most remarkable features in the old society was the high status and the legal rights of women, married or unmarried, as well as of children.

However, I do not mean to say that a modern welfare state is a "traditional" state even in Norway. I am only trying to point out that the modern welfare state could be introduced with less resistance and political conflict in Norway than in most other countries. In Norway "freedom for all" and "security for all" have been key slogans for eleven centuries.

Today, Norway is one of the strongest modern welfare states in the world. The People's Pension Act, the final law in the social welfare program, is due to be passed this year. This will coordinate and include all the other acts pertaining to social security, namely, those dealing with health insurance, occupational injuries insurance, the war pension scheme, care of disabled persons, rehabilitation insurance, old age insurance, pension plans for special groups, family and child benefits, and so on.

Some time will elapse, however, before the ideology or legal concept of the welfare society will become a social and psychological reality in the practical experience of all people. But there is a feverish activity on behalf of government, legislators, economists, politicians, and professionals in the field of social work to achieve this end. However, it should be expressly pointed out that there is no conflict between the various political parties concerning the welfare program as such. All parties have worked for it, not just the Labor party, which has held the political leadership for the last thirty years.

The social reforms which make the modern welfare state possible began in 1845. The movement has been particularly strong since 1900 and conspicuously forceful since the Second World War.

The characteristic feature of the welfare state is the view that *the need of an individual is* not only a personal need but represents a social problem for which the greater society must stand responsible. The black forecast that a planned economy and extensive social security would create an unfortunate number of "chiselers" and "cheaters" has not proved to be true. That a small percentage of recipients have taken dishonest advantage of the program may be so. There are districts in northern Norway where people in great numbers are said to live on "the Social." But the problem is not that the people are "bad," that they are "cheaters." The problem is extreme poverty, poor schooling, race mixture, and very poor communication because of the geographic location. The problem is therefore not social security but sociological and psychological difficulties of a rather severe kind which must be studied via the social sciences.

I would rather, to the contrary, stress the high general moral norm of the Norwegian people resulting from an inbred feeling of respect for the rights of others. This is not a new development but stems from the traditional roots of democracy in Norway. However, it would be a misconception to assume that the welfare state does not have its shadowy side. We must not forget that the welfare state also is to be considered as an experiment which at all times requires the objective evaluation of the social scientist. His methods of analysis must replace the politician's subjective, one-sided argument which never relates to the whole picture but only to the part—his part.

The social-political development in Norway during recent times must be divided into three periods:

1845-1922

Norway's first Poor Relief Act was passed in 1845. This was the first time that an effort was made to organize and administer aid to the needy on a national basis. It was the first legal recognition of the nation's responsibility toward its weakest citizens, and the provisions of the law were considered very advanced for the time. However, it was during the second half of the nineteenth century that the industrial age reached Norway with an impact which created new sociological problems that needed the attention of political leaders and intervention by government. The nation underwent the difficult transition from a many-century-old agricultural society to a complex industrial civilization.

During the first period of modern social history other laws were passed; for instance, the Industrial Accident Insurance Law, in 1894, is the oldest social security project in Norway. The first general Health Insurance Act was passed in 1909. Since then it has been changed, revised, and broadened many times until it represents the extensive and all-inclusive medicare program of today. The program is functioning without the disadvantages predicted by the United States, for instance.

The philosophy of the public health and medicare programs relates pointedly to the fact that illness is not a "private affair."

Tuberculosis, venereal diseases, and all other contagious diseases concern society as a whole. An afflicted individual is therefore not granted the right to refuse treatment. If such a case is brought to the attention of doctors or other people in the health field, they are by law obliged to report it, and the patient, whoever he may be, is without delay requested by law to appear for treatment. All people, both adults and children, are by law requested to appear at public health stations in every district to have X-rays taken as a measure of prevention against tuberculosis. This disease was rampant in Norway not too long ago. Today the disease is under control, and the sanatoria are standing empty or are being used for other purposes. The same is true of venereal diseases. There are statistically few cases as compared to the incidence in the United States.

Public health measures are also excellent in relation to drugs, which are carefully tested on a long-term basis before being released to the public. On this count Norway is far more conservative than Sweden. This also holds for birth-control measures and abortion, although both are legal in Norway as well as in Sweden.

The most remarkable laws of this early period were the Child Laws of Castberg passed by the Parliament in 1916. These laws attempt to create legal security and an economically decent status and full protection for *all* children including the illegitimate. These laws became internationally known as the "revolutionary way" to deal with illegitimacy. Even the other Scandinavian countries, including Sweden, showed hesitancy in applying such laws in their respective countries. It is in this relation that we see the decidedly great cultural differences in the various Scandinavian countries. The Child Laws of Castberg gave, fifty years ago, equal inheritance rights to all children, even to those born out of wedlock. These children were also given the legal right to the father's name, to the educational standard which was equal to that of the father or to that of the mother, depending on which was the *highest*. The mother was by law requested to name the father of the child. The man named was held responsible, legally and economically, for the child if within a few weeks he could not prove before the court that he was innocent.

If we compare this law to the Law de Napoleon of France, the

Bastardy Laws of England, or the laws of Holland which even now identify the child out of wedlock with his "no-good" mother, we can understand that the Child Laws of Castberg were considered revolutionary by the patriarchal world. The Roman Catholic Church and countries with a titled aristocracy, including Sweden, refuted the laws on the ground that they would prove disastrous to the family as a social institution: every whore and prostitute would produce illegitimate children as their "way of life." This would in turn ruin the man and his "good" wife's familial relationship since the illicit relationship would become publicly known due to the inheritance-right and names-right of the illegitimate child. But once again the gloomy forecasts failed to materialize. After fifty years of experience with the law, the Norwegian family institution has proved to be remarkably stable as compared to the so-called "nuclear family," more popularly called "polygamy by succession," in the United States.

It would be impossible to understand this legislation, however, without an intimate study of the sociological and anthropological history of Norway. This history would clearly indicate that the Norwegian people were not more revolutionary-minded than their neighbors; but their cultural pattern had evolved from a tradition where the women for eleven centuries, through the old Ting system, have had a powerful legal position with regard to inheritance rights in particular. In fact, the old peasant culture showed strikingly matriarchal trends psychologically. The Laws of Castberg could not have been carried through by vote without this aged peasant norm, unique in Norway with its orientation toward the woman and her child. Sweden and Denmark with their landed aristocracy could not accept this law at first. It was only many years later, after it became evident that the Norwegian family still remained intact and that women could think of easier ways of earning money than by producing illegitimate children, that the law was accepted in the other Scandinavian countries.

I have mentioned this particular law in such detail to prove that we cannot fully understand the social development in any country without understanding the historical and sociocultural background which provides the push or the brake toward modern social development through the process of social change.

1935–40

The second phase of accelerated social-political development in Norway is counted from 1935 to 1940. Some of the acts passed at this time were the Health Insurance Act for fishermen in 1936 and the same for seamen in foreign trade the following year. The social insurance projects already established were revised and extended by several laws during this period. An old age pension plan under preparation for several generations became law in 1936. During this year aid to the blind and disabled was established, the first step toward the total disablement pension and rehabilitation program of today.

During 1938 the government passed the Unemployment Insurance Act. All further efforts were finally stopped by the German occupation in 1940.

1945–66

When the Norwegian government again gained control over the country in 1945, long-term planning was resumed, at first by a coalition government and then by the Labor government until 1965. Last year there was a change of government by vote from the socialistic-labor government to a coalition government. The period between 1945 and 1966 has seen an unbelievable development in the social action sphere. A survey by Dorothy Burton Skaardal gives detailed information about the various social insurance schemes and pensions and their administration.[1] Since 1960 social action has continued at a rapid pace, supported by all political parties. There has never been any disruptive action by any party; the debates have only centered on "when," "how," "how much," "how long," and "how far."

The next important point to consider is the sociological and psychological attitude toward poverty, need, illness, old age, housing, and education expressed by the Norwegian people. The original Poor Relief Law of 1845 carried a psychological tone which was common for that time. Poverty was looked upon as a shameful, self-imposed condition. The wealthy felt that the poor should be

[1] Dorothy Burton Skaardal, *Social Insurance in Norway* (Oslo: Norwegian Joint Committee on International Social Policy, 1960).

supported only at a minimum existence level and with a loss of civil rights. In May of 1900, this law was replaced by another poor law, more modern, but still with a stigma of shame attached to it. Finally, the last social welfare act, passed in 1965, did away with any stigma in regard to accepting public welfare in any form, and with no settlement requirement or loss of civil rights. The law makes it clear that all citizens have a right to all social goods, to all social security benefits or pensions in all major crises of life related to birth, health, education, employment, family planning, housing, accidents, and old age. The main aim has been to establish a class-free society with a minimum level of subsistence high enough to guarantee that there will be no loss of self-respect even for those who receive public assistance. In other words, the law established the right of all citizens to participate in the social goods of their country on all levels and in all districts without being exposed to a shameful means test. At last public assistance has been recognized as a right and not as almsgiving in the traditional, dogmatic sense with its sharp demarcation of "class." Norway has illustrated that it is possible to have a society without "the poor" and without "the overprivileged" in an economic sense.

The question now is: Has Norway at last produced the so-called "great society" where social afflictions do not exist? The answer is "No," and the reasons are clear. There is no such thing as a static society, and there are no social problems which remain solved. Through our concept of social change we know that in all societies, ancient or modern, this process has been at work. Our age, due to world wars and massive technical developments, is experiencing a phase of social change of such violence that it makes itself felt in the emotional patterns of people and nations on a world scale.

In Norway the need is now felt for a deeper analysis on three levels related to modern sociological process in the welfare state: (1) the national welfare state; (2) the welfare world; (3) the welfare culture.

Norwegians are trying to implement on the practical level the intention of the law so that it becomes a reality in daily living. This will mean setting up social institutions where they are presently lacking and training personnel for new jobs. The country is now in the throes of this process. New schools of social work are being founded. There are today three schools supported by the government and one private school with government subsidies. All are trying to raise the level of social work practice from that of manipulation of recipients to treatment of persons according to the letter of the recent law. But practice has shown that it will take extensive education for newcomers to the field, as well as reorientation by short-term measures of old public welfare functionaries, before the attitude will change from the old means test to the rights concept and finally to the treatment model of 1965. Deficiencies are felt on all sides, and discouragement is expressed. At the same time, we know it is a transition period, and given time and patience the new law will surely be implemented according to its intention.

However, when we look at the welfare state as it relates to the well-being of all, some of us have asked ourselves one important question: is it possible to go too far in providing people with security? We note that from the old, well-known physical and material needs, our clients have shifted drastically to spiritual and emotional needs of a magnitude we are not prepared to meet, even in the well-organized welfare state. It is becoming evident to many that welfare related to a good economy and equal rights alone is not enough. We see in Norway a nation evolving which is more egocentric, more power-oriented, and less altruistic than the older, poorer society. We are becoming aware of a growing lack of concern for others. All want to have and fewer want to give. There seems to be less evidence of people willing to sacrifice time and effort, less incentive toward participation in community and state planning. This new culture pattern does not produce "cheaters," but young people lacking in initiative and creative ability. It is a combination of the welfare state and modern industrial civilization which so heavily stresses *to have and to use* without being properly balanced with the old concept *to give and make last* that creates this pattern. This development does warrant some socio-psychological investigation and analysis.

As for the welfare state related to international affairs, there seems to be one alarming consequence, namely, the accentuated stress on nationalism. One often hears stated in Norway, particularly by the politicians, that Norway must develop "Norwegian social work," and American-trained social workers have met with criticism because of their "foreign views." This criticism relates particularly to the methodology of casework and group work, which is less understood by the politicians than social action, social administration, and social politics in general. There is as yet little understanding of the fact that the social process expressed through particular problems might be more similar between, for instance, Finnmark with its large Lapp population and Alaska with its native Eskimo population than between Oslo and Karasjok.

Has the time come to reexamine the concept of the welfare state? Do *all* people, even the young, the healthy, and the well-fed, want security at all costs? Or are there other basic needs which must be considered? If the welfare state encourages a nationalistic, ego-centered effort which thereby rocks international relationships, has the welfare state failed? It is in this area that we find confusion as to the real meaning of the welfare state. It is true that it does mean intervention by government action and control in contrast to the free enterprise in a "free-wheeling economy" that is still idealized in the United States. The welfare state in Norway does, nevertheless, represent a "free" society in the deepest sense of the word. Elected citizens sit on all boards and committees and exercise a strong control over all social and economic action. The real drawback is the narrow perspective from which decisions are made by local politicians who are neither sociologically nor psychologically trained. This can only be offset by better education in all social sciences. This is true particularly for students in the social work field. In other words, the fulfillment of the welfare state goes beyond the scope of political and economic consideration alone.

This can be amply illustrated by the development in the social welfare field in the United States and Norway respectively. In the United States strong emphasis has been placed on the individual needs basis, psychologically oriented toward pathology and, consequently, curative methods. The idea was to "cure" the individual and help him adjust better to the society he lived in, taking for granted that the society was "good." Public interference was unwanted, politics were counted as "dirty," and politicians were "yellow." The concepts of Norway, on the other hand, were diametrically opposite. Society needed readjustment, the individual was psychologically sound when society gave him the right opportunity for security, development, and expansion. Consequently, society had to be changed in order to offer each citizen a maximal opportunity. Politicians were needed and trusted and held responsible for the common good. Political appointments carried high status, and politics was "clean."

Today a noticeable change in attitudes has taken place in both countries. In the United States minority groups and the economically underprivileged have made it clear that society may be "ill" or "pathological." Structural changes are necessary, involving law on federal and state levels. Individuals cannot be "cured" so long as the causes for the symptoms of maladjustment rest with society itself. Government action is needed in spite of all talk about a "free" society. Public money must be released through planned action in the interest of all citizens in spite of belief in a "free" economy.

In Norway, on the other hand, it has become unfortunately obvious that even when society is "good," job opportunities favorable, wage levels high, health maximal, education available to all, and the living standard conspicuously affluent, some people are nevertheless sick, youth is maladjusted, children neurotic, old people psychologically unwanted, and international relationships increasingly distrustful.

The conclusion is that neither view is adequate without being complemented by the other. In other words, political science and social science must go hand in hand, and social welfare must provide both progressive social legislation and economic security as well as opportunity for individual treatment based on psychological and sociological insight. It is this view that Norwegian social work supported by the government represents today.

It is my personal conviction that a third factor—social ethics—must be added in our planning before we can speak of a welfare state in a welfare world. We ought to take seriously Gunnar Myrdal's statement that "it is never unimportant how a good thing is motivated." [2] It seems to me that this is the point where all our efforts need to be focused. What is our personal or national motivation in relation to the social welfare field or the welfare state? Does our personal or national motivation rest on a power complex and greed pattern or are we consciously and truly motivated by selfless interests? It is my firm conviction that we must establish an acceptable modern system of social ethics common to all before we dare answer the last question. Great leaders in the sociopsychological field, such as Gordon Allport and Carl Gustav Jung, have testified to the fact that there exists a universal need for a personal religious affiliation. But a modern system of social ethics must go beyond the boundaries of the orthodox, dogmatic limitations of any one of the established church systems resting on national and individualistic cultural patterns. This would make a welfare culture possible, which is the condition for a welfare state in a welfare world. That we will "love" all people is not probable. That God will appear in various forms to the various people according to their need is certain. But that we must come to respect all people regardless of their different cultural patterns is necessary and possible. It can be done, by consciously establishing the needed identification models and by demonstrating their value in our personal lives.

[2] Gunnar Myrdal, *Beyond the Welfare State* (New Haven, Conn.: Yale University Press, 1960).

The Impact of Urbanization on Rural Areas

PART I

J.–B. LANCTOT

CHIEF, COMMUNITY DEVELOPMENT SERVICES
AGRICULTURE AND RURAL DEVELOPMENT
ADMINISTRATION, CANADA

I AM neither a sociologist or a researcher. I am an administrator who, over the years, has participated in action programs aiming to solve problems of migration and rural development and thus I have dealt with problems resulting from the impact of urbanization on rural areas. Within this framework of experience, I shall discuss the subject on a general basis with emphasis on conditions in Canada.

DEFINITIONS

What is meant by "impact" in our present context? Webster defines the word as "an impinging, a striking together, a single instantaneous stroke of a body *in motion* against another body" (italics mine). The material significance of impact is important in terms of land use, transportation, and so on. The ICSW, however, stresses the social significance of urbanization as it affects the attitudes of people, rural patterns of living, and the interrelationships of rural and urban people. In terms of social change, then, urbanization can be considered as a process—a city growing into a metropolis, the "body in motion." This growing metropolis strikes against (has impact on) that other body, the traditional rural areas which are either stationary or are changing more slowly than the cities.

According to Schnore and Peterson, "urbanization is a process of population concentration. . . . concentrations of people can properly be called urban only if the residents spend most of their time in activities that are not directly connected with food production." [1] Urbanization is closely linked with a declining rural population. This process results in large migrations of rural people, with attendant problems of adjustment to social and environmental change. The main problems of adaptation for these people consist of emotional disorders, maladjustments closely associated with urban living. In this context, urbanization presents a major challenge to social workers and to all others who have concern for the welfare of humanity.

HISTORICAL BACKGROUND

Man, it is said, first builds his environment, and then the environment forms man. Throughout history man has lived mainly in rural areas. Even today, notwithstanding a greatly accelerated rate of urbanization, the majority of the world's 3,000,000,000 people are rural dwellers, with deeply rooted traditions.

Cities and metropolitan areas with 500,000 or more people are really a new phenomenon. Only a few, such as Baghdad and Rome, London, Paris, and New York, date back more than a hundred years. Although mankind has doubled in the twentieth century, urban populations multiplied fivefold. Approximately one third of the world's population live in urban centers. By the year 2000, the prediction is, 60 percent of an estimated 6,000,000,000 or 7,000,000,000 people will be urban dwellers.

IMPACT OF CHANGE

In terms of social change, man is only a few generations removed from rural living; he has not yet really adapted to living in a metropolis (for many people, this means living in a slum, in ghettos). Social anonymity in the city can be very frustrating; so nostalgia brings man back to the fringe areas, into suburbia, along highways. Many people leave the slums to settle in fringe areas; some come there directly from farms. For the most part, however, there is a lack of planning, and so shanty towns and "bidonvilles" develop. According to the World Health Organiza-

[1] Leo F. Schnore and Gene B. Peterson, "Urban and Metropolitan Development in the United States and Canada," *The Annals*, CCCXVI (1958), 61.

tion, these planless fringe settlements hold 12 percent of the world population. Most of these people are poverty-stricken to a point below the dignity due a human being. These people are "voiceless," as Abbé Pierre so aptly stated. They need to have opportunity to express themselves, and to be heard by policy-makers where decisions are taken on various levels of government.

These people face the most challenging and pressing social problems as a result of urbanization. It is probable that the behavioral sciences can offer solutions to these deep-seated problems. If not, action research in depth is required.

What about people who live in depressed rural areas? Here, too, serious social problems result from technological change and mechanization. What are the implications of change for social welfare services in rural areas?

Information is lacking on the impact per se of urbanization on rural areas; surveys of commercial significance mainly have so far been conducted in this particular field. This lack of knowledge concerning impact and its effects, whether beneficial or detrimental, imposes on the ICSW an important role of leadership with respect to basic programs of action research. These programs should include the joint participation of all those disciplines concerned with human problems in urban, fringe, and rural areas, including the impact of each on the other. The need for action research, especially in the social sciences, is universal. How will we meet this challenge?

DEVELOPMENT OF CANADA

Canada enjoys a great abundance of waterfalls, many of which are sources of hydroelectric power. Transcontinental railways and feeder branch lines were built over almost a century. Thousands of agrarian settlers cultivated the land. Large investments of American and other foreign and domestic capital developed the mines, the timber, and other resources that abound in Canada. During the Second World War and its aftermath, industrial expansion occurred at a rapid rate. Concurrently, there was a large and continuing exodus from rural areas to the mushrooming urban centers. This influx has created many complex problems of adaptation to change.

Canadian society.—The tensions and strains of many different cultural backgrounds, furthermore, have combined to present a broad spectrum of social problems. These problems are compounded by the fact that a scant population of 20,000,000 people inhabits the second largest country in the world. This population is found along the narrow ribbon of settlement with some 3,000 miles of common frontier with the United States. This fact and the direct impact of mass media communications across the frontier have caused Canadian rural-urban societies to develop much in accordance with American patterns of life.

Canada consists of many basic cultural groups: the Indians and Eskimos, who are truly indigenous; the French; the English; and the new Canadians of many different ethnic origins, most of whom use English as their language of communication. Roughly one third of the total population is English, one third French, and one third new Canadians. Basically, then, Canada is a highly pluralistic society. Each of its component ethnic groups has made an important contribution to the country's patterns of social living and development.

Pioneer economies.—The economy of New France rested on the fur trade, and farming was soon added. The pull of the fur trade, however, weakened family life and made difficult the establishment of stable community life. Later, a shift in the fur trade established Montreal as an urban center.

Against a background of active growth in the lumber industry, there soon emerged an agrarian society in the St. Lawrence Valley. Pioneer settlements were first developed as "seigneuries." Later, small patriarchal family farms became the foundation of the French Canadian rural economy. These farms are still typical, especially in Eastern Canada.

The French Canadian farm families were large, and many had to emigrate in order to make a living. Over the past century, thousands found their way to New England industries; others, to farm lands, West and South. Most came to Montreal, however, and this city became Canada's largest metropolitan area.

The frontier economy of English Upper Canada was established mainly on an agrarian basis, around the influx of Loyalist families who migrated to Canada after the American Revolution. This economy rested on the family and on closely knit neighborhood groups. Industries based on lumbering and mining were developed early, thus forming population centers. Toronto became the main center of financial, industrial, and commercial operations in this fast-growing urbanized society. Off-farm migrants and overseas immigrants have expanded Toronto into Canada's second largest metropolitan area. Much of Canada's industry is established in numerous urban centers, especially in southern Ontario.

In Western Canada, there arose over the last century two distinct economies: one in British Columbia, which included the pull of the Klondike; the other on the prairies, where wheat farming became the main occupation. The building of the Canadian Pacific Railway was a basic factor in both these economies. The British Columbia economy was composed of Britishers, Canadians, and Americans who jostled for advantage in the atmosphere of the Gold Rush and the mining camp. The prairie economy was pioneered by French and English who settled on the land. This economy was expanded at the turn of the twentieth century by the thousands of immigrants of Slavic, Germanic, Scandinavian, and other Nordic stocks. More recently, many industrial centers have been developed in Western Canada, especially in Manitoba and British Columbia.

As they spread across Canada, the pioneers pushed back and replaced the primitive Indian societies based on hunting and fishing. Confined to reserves over the generations, growing numbers of Indians and metis are now finding their way into urban centers. Here, they pose problems of social adaptation and welfare which are of great concern to governments in Canada, especially in provinces where responsibilities in regard to these people are increasing.

The Eskimo society which borders on the Arctic is also undergoing profound economic and social changes as a result of industrialization or urbanization. Problems of health education and adjustment to the patterns of living of the white people, away from the "igloo way of life," are only a few aspects of this evolution.

Urbanization.—Urbanization in Canada has lagged behind that in the United States by some twenty or twenty-five years. The growth of cities was heightened from 1941 to 1951. Even more significant, the pace of urbanization in Canada has quickened most rapidly since 1951.

Labor force.—Industrialization in Canada has favored the rapid growth of an urban working class recruited principally from rural areas. A rural-minded proletariat was thus established. Through the process of change, and the adaptation of workers to social change, guided by a variety of national and international labor unions, this proletariat is gradually raising its levels of knowledge and skills. The impact of this exodus on rural areas is evidenced by the fact that in 1931 the agricultural labor force accounted for 33.1 percent of the country's total labor force, while in 1965 the figure was 9.2 percent.

This trend is expected to become even more pronounced in the near future, especially under the stimulus of a government man-power training and mobility program sanctioned in July, 1966, by the Canadian government. Under this program, government grants and loans are made available to all workers, urban or rural, who decide to train for new occupational skills. Workers who qualify will then be assisted to move into higher-income jobs wherever available in Canada. The basic criterion is an increased income accruing to the worker, who thus becomes better able to discharge his responsibilities to his family and as a citizen.

Trade unions.—As urbanization developed, trade unionism grew in numbers, in effective leadership, and in services performed. First, the Knights of Labor, especially shoemakers, became active back in the 1870s. The Fraternity of Locomotive Engineers helped off-farm migrants in the 1880s. By 1902, labor unionism had grown to a total of 1,038 locals, half of which were in Ontario. As of 1964, 511 national and international labor unions, including directly chartered local unions and independent local organizations, guided action programs for 7,402 locals with a membership of 1,493,173. This total membership represents 29.4 percent of the estimated number of nonagricultural paid workers in Canada.

What impact does trade unionism have on urban-rural relationships? Trade unions enjoy the privileges of collective bargaining, which has had some influence in developing the concept of collective marketing systems in rural areas. Many people are concerned over the number and seriousness of recent strikes. One can sense the urban origins of farm strikes, such as milk dumping and tractor demonstrations.

Housing.—With cities "breaking out at the seams" through immigration, housing has become a major need in Canada. Recent estimates place this need at 300,000 units. Housing was developed mainly as a result of action programs financed by the Central Mortgage and Housing Corporation. Slum-clearance and suburban housing received much attention and financial support. Recently, rural housing, especially in disadvantaged areas, has received more attention from policy-makers. Housing projects, many on a cooperative basis, are bringing modern conveniences to the countryside, thus contributing to higher levels of living. More imaginative planning is needed, however, to reduce costs which are still high for families of modest means. Coupled with the regionalization of industrial development, with the improvement of roads, increasing numbers of industrial workers are building modern homes in rural districts.

Since urbanization is a recent development in Canada, the rural-urban differences of the Canadian people are still quite identifiable. Persons from the patriarchal family farm environment have different motivations, aspirations, and abilities. A recent farm survey established that the level of rural public school education is lower than that in cities. In some provinces, rural young people lag behind their compatriots from other provinces by a generation or so. It seems evident that these areas have received little or no impact from urban centers where education has reached higher levels.

Education.—Education is a provincial responsibility in Canada. Urbanization has improved education or increased opportunities for young people. In urban centers, school facilities, libraries, and laboratories have evolved as institutions enlarged, and programs and curricula have improved. Levels of teachers' competence have been upgraded, though these levels vary from province to province.

I shall make no attempt to focus on any specific aspect of education where urbanization has had a special impact. It is sufficient to indicate that the trend toward elementary school consolidation and regional high schools in rural areas follows the pattern of similar developments in urban centers. The advantages of larger school units in cities have long since been demonstrated. Urban youth have experienced the benefits of a more sophisticated scholastic environment. Relatively few studies have been made in Canada of the effects of impact in this area of concern. It has been established, however, in some instances that lower educational aspiration levels are definitely associated with the rural environment.

Let us look at one province—Quebec. What is known as "social change" in the rest of Canada occurred as a "quiet revolution" in Quebec. Recent developments indicate a definite trend toward regionalization of rural schools, with the benefit of prior experience in urban schools. This program is faced with deep-seated difficulties, however, especially with apathy, the reluctance of local governments to change, and an outdated system of taxation. Regional rural schools are difficult for pupils to reach, and pupils are subjected to long bus rides over bad roads. Parents object to having their youngsters ride for an hour or more each morning and evening on every school day. These objections have a way of finding expression when there is an election.

Social welfare.—Social welfare, too, is a provincial responsibility. However, the federal government is responsible for some programs of national significance, such as unemployment insurance, family allowances, and old age security. Over the past decades it has entered into agreements with all the provinces to assist them in providing basic social assistance measures. A few months ago the Canada Assistance Plan was approved by Parliament. It is, in a nutshell, a general assistance plan which does away with the categorical approach, bringing together the various income-maintenance programs: old age assistance; assistance to the disabled and the blind; and unemployment assistance. This plan, which applies to both urban and rural areas, will also include federal participation in bearing child welfare costs, aid to needy mothers and dependent children, and health care services to public assistance recipients.

Rural areas have benefited greatly from the concepts, the experience, and the actual services of urban welfare programs. They share with them common goals which, generally speaking, are to maintain reasonable standards of health and decent living.

In Canadian rural areas, voluntary welfare services are provided either by urban agencies through branches or field workers, or through independent agencies, some of which are closely related to their urban counterparts in structure and type of work performed.

Public services were heretofore rendered largely by the municipalities or local governments. The present trend is to transfer this responsibility to the provinces, which maintain regional services for one or more municipalities, so that services may be more readily available to the people.

Welfare services, especially social assistance, have had profound repercussions on the rural economies. In some regions, the total social assistance payments from the public treasury are higher than the gross regional product. Social assistance payments in a region of 300,000 people, for example, total more than $100 million as compared with a gross regional product of $72 million.

Another illustration of the impact of urbanization may be found in Newfoundland. This province's population includes fishermen, miners, and farmers, many of whom live on a very low income. Confederation in 1949 brought to Newfoundland numerous social opportunities inherent to an industrialized society, including the federal-provincial income-maintenance program. With some families and individuals, the sudden receipt of so much cash, coupled with their inexperience in budgeting, caused many problems and, in some cases, abuse. This was to be expected. Gradually, however, the benefits of these improved social programs were felt and observed in the form of better health and regular school attendance.

Improved welfare services in rural areas are due mainly to better personnel. Trained social workers and administrators are replacing untrained welfare officers, or even police officers, who were formerly responsible for welfare investigations and the enforcement of regulations. Professional staffs bring to these regions their competence in casework, counseling, planning, and organization.

Welfare services as they are dispensed in urban centers have changed the basic concept of social aid in rural areas. Formerly, rural social problems were dealt with as a family or community matter and were often discussed publicly at town council meetings. This practice has been replaced by casework, applied to problems of individuals within the family or community.

The influence of urban agencies which work through boards of directors has brought about a similar democratic participation of rural leaders. Local rural branches of an urban agency are usually represented by a delegate to the general board. In this case, the principal problem is that of harmonizing the general policies of the agency with the needs of the rural area where both the attitudes and patterns of living differ from those of the urban community. If the local rural agency is autonomous, and, in more ways than one, closer to the community, then its natural leaders, such as the doctor, the agrologist, the president of the local cooperative, the mayor, become members of the board of directors.

The financing of private agencies in Canada rests largely with organizations known as Funds and Councils, the United Appeals. Fund-raising is undertaken annually, amounts received then being allocated to the various agencies which submit to an audit control. This mode of financing requires adaptation to rural areas where urban-inspired publicity methods are not always understood. The budgeting for operational costs, salaries, and so forth, needs interpretation in rural areas where the tradition of voluntary services is strong, and it is customary to accomplish more with less money.

Agriculture.—Agriculture is another provincial responsibility in Canada, although to a lesser extent than education and social welfare. The federal government has distinct roles to perform in research, standards, marketing, trade.

Among the many areas of concern in rural society, agriculture has received the strongest impact from industrialization and urbanization. Agriculture has become the theater of a basic revolution and must adapt to the effects of mechanization, to scientific and technological changes in the production of food and fiber.

Agriculture in Canada, as elsewhere in the world, must become aware that the mass needs of a fast multiplying and urbanized human race will dictate new methods for mass production. New methods must be found to produce more food for the half of humanity now suffering from malnutrition, for a humanity which will more than double during the next thirty-four years. These methods can only come about through scientific and technological research. With respect to the impact of technological changes on people especially, this research must include action research in all the social sciences.

For rural areas, for agricultural and rural nonfarm sections particularly, the last quarter century represents the beginning of a transitional stage in farm operations and in basic concepts of rural life. It is during this period that the full impact of technology was felt in Canada by the farmer and his family.

The impact of the technological revolution has brought about a situation whereby fewer and fewer farmers produce more and more of the country's food and fiber. It was recently estimated roughly that less than 20 percent of the farmers now raise some 80 percent of the food in Canada. A survey of Eastern Canada farms elicited information that some 50 percent of farmers in the study area are redundant; that is, they could leave agriculture "to the benefit of themselves and to the net gain of the remaining farm community and the national economy." [2] Of the 347,000 commercial farms in Canada, "some 200,000 are in a precarious position." [3]

In this new context, the farmer and his family are faced with increasing difficulties in solving their problems of farm-land stewardship. Their security and their healthy and sound family life are threatened. There is now ample evidence in Canada that the small family farm is passé; the large mechanized farm is here to stay. This larger farm, given adequate capital and sound management, still can be a family farm. In the future, the specialized family farm will include single family operators, family partnerships, and corporations.

A new rural economy is in the making. With mechanization on the farms, it is more profitable to employ capital than to employ people. With modern tax policies, machines can be depreciated—this is a gain. On the other hand, workers must be pensioned—this is a loss. Machines are being constantly improved. Workers improve much more slowly, and only through education—this takes time and money. In short, a large family with manpower used to be the principal asset on the farm as a production unit—nowadays, capital is the principal asset.

2 Conference of Agriculture Institute of Canada, Winnipeg, Manitoba, June, 1966.
3 *Financial Post,* July 23, 1966, p. 25.

Because most farmers lack capital and knowledge to improve their farming practices, there is a growing disparity between the "have's" and the "have not's"; there is widespread indigence in many rural areas. Ironically, this situation is found in a sector of the economy where, largely through rural electrification, levels of living improved most rapidly during recent years. Paradoxically, until very recently, surplus food was a problem in agriculture, whilst the farmer and his family suffered more from malnutrition than did his city cousin.

In Canada, as elsewhere, many people, including governments, suggest that increased price-support subsidies are the solution to these problems of low income. They claim that higher prices for agricultural products are the sole basic solution. Although this claim has some validity, experience tends to show that such subsidies merely widen the income gaps. Actually, farmers with both capital and knowledge of new technological farm practices benefit most by price-support subsidies. The vast majority of farmers who lack this knowledge, and especially those who do not even have the basic instruction to develop these new skills, benefit very little from these subsidies. They benefit so little, in fact, that price is a negligible factor in determining their level of living.

One perceives through the news media some indications that the Canadian urban taxpayer, as in other countries, is becoming worried over farm subsidies. It is to be expected that during forthcoming years the increasing political influence of the urbanites may compel the rural areas to adopt other solutions to the ever growing problems of low income. There seems to be increasing support to provide more urban jobs for people who are becoming "surplus" in rural areas and who would gladly give up farming if given a decent alternative. Programs such as I have already mentioned, for instance, to upgrade instruction in rural areas, to train workers in new technological skills, and to increase their mobility do offer such an alternative.

For some farmers in Canada, even as some farmers in France have found, various forms of group action seem to offer an alternative, at least in part. A few timid attempts have been made at group farming where families or kinship groups set up a cooperative or a corporation to operate larger, specialized farm units. In this way, capital investments per unit are reduced, and a more effective economic use is made of farm machinery and the specialized skills of individual group members. Much of the drudgery of farming would thus be eliminated, social amenities improved.

Farm integration is a formula whereby feed manufacturers, packing plants, chain stores, and so on, enter into contracts with farmers to provide both credit and technical guidance if they will produce certain products in exchange for an assured market. Some top cooperative management experts believe that improved marketing facilities are best obtained in this way. In brief, both integration and group action attempt to solve problems of adaptation to change in this age of technological revolution.

In spite of an economy with a gross national product whose growth averages some 6 percent per year, there is widespread indigence in many rural areas. Approximately half a million families live on an annual income under $3,000. This represents almost 42 percent of the rural population, whereas 19 percent of the urban population has an annual income under $3,000. More than 65 percent of rural males have only elementary school education or less. There is a high correlation between education and income in Canada.

Economic and social development.—How is Canada to remedy this situation? Canada has already adopted several legislative measures to combat both rural and urban indigence. These programs are based on assumptions that, notwithstanding attendant social problems, industrialization and urbanization provide a better life.

The most comprehensive new programs to raise rural incomes come under the Agricultural and Rural Development Act (ARDA). With a broad mandate to attack rural problems through resource adjustment and social development programs, ARDA offers a joint federal and provincial program. Adopted in 1961, this act led to the first Federal/Provincial Agreement for the three-year period ending March 31, 1965, which was replaced by a five-year Rural Development Agreement to end on March 31, 1970. Under its terms, $25 million will be shared with the provinces during each of the five years.

The new agreement provides for federal-provincial programs in many areas. ARDA programs comprise research into resource capabilities and development, including the social sciences. Much emphasis is placed on action research in the form of pilot projects implemented within selected areas that have specific potentials for economic development. ARDA programs comprise land-use and farm-adjustment projects, the rehabilitation and reestablishment of certain rural people by the means of effective employment and income opportunities. ARDA provides for a specialized corps of rural development officers who need training in community development and resource adjustment programs. Community development is seen as a process of planned intervention for the solution of socioeconomic problems with the purposeful and active participation and involvement of the people concerned. The new agreement also provides for public information services and for soil and water conservation programs.

This agreement provides for a total approach to resource development through the implementation of comprehensive plans whose terms will be negotiated separately with each province. The federal government has made an initial appropriation of $50 million to which further appropriations may be added as required to implement special plans on the basis of the total approach—in sociological terms, a holistic approach. Such plans, including programs of regional development which may be regarded as a beginning in rural planning, are being developed in close liaison with urban planning and industrial development programs within which action programs now tend to involve secondary urban growth centers as well as metropolitan areas.

The ARDA program is coordinated with other government programs, such as those administered by the Area Development Agency and the Atlantic Development Board. The former aims to foster employment and higher income through industrial expansion in certain areas. The latter administers a fund of $100 million to provide an over-all plan for the economic development of the Atlantic provinces. Special inputs are being made initially to improve the regions infrastructure.

These programs constitute a planned comprehensive approach to regional economic development, including all the various programs with social impact previously mentioned. Thus, it is seen that the Canada Assistance Plan and other health and welfare measures complete this ensemble to make a concerted attack on low income and indigence in rural areas. It is recognized also that many of these measures have been developed and tested under urban conditions.

In brief, the failures of past experience with partial *ad hoc* measures have led specialists to adopt this comprehensive approach. We know now that the solutions to rural problems cannot be found solely within the agricultural sector. We know also that urban-rural cooperation sustains relationships which are beneficial to both cities and countryside. These relationships are essential factors of economic and social growth in modern society. We know that urbanization has an impact on rural areas, even as rural people have affected urban growth. There exists a large body of knowledge on this subject. Even so, we need to know considerably more about the basic human problems which these interrelationships and migrations generate.

Urbanization has impact on rural areas in a number of ways. Firstly, religious values are being questioned more and more, in keeping with the impact of urban concepts of living on the traditional values of individual, family, and community life.

According to Cox, "the rise of urban civilization and the collapse of traditional religion are the two main hallmarks of our era and are closely related movements." [4] This interaction of urbanization and secularization has already been the object of considerable investigation on the part of all denominations. The sessions of Vatican Council II and of the Conference of the World Council of Churches as well as many ancillary meetings, conferences, and seminars have opened avenues of thought pointing to positive action in furthering better understanding and opening channels of communication.

Much remains to be done, however, to bring about the implementation of holistic programs of planned intervention for the solution of socioeconomic problems. New approaches will need be devised, approaches that may overcome religious barriers and cut

[4] Harvey Cox, *The Secular City* (Toronto: Collier-MacMillan Canada Ltd., 1965).

across disciplines, approaches that respect man as a person, treat the family as the solid foundation of human society, and guarantee the basic, inalienable rights of freedom and justice.

These new approaches will need be tested within a great variety of contexts and situations. With reference to indigence, for instance, assuming that the poor, whether in cities or in rural areas, tend to be apathetic and develop a "culture of poverty," we need to learn new methods of approaching these people so that they will become motivated to help themselves and to seek education for themselves and their children.

As a sequel to the foregoing, I suggest briefly special areas of concern for the ICSW to study in some depth.

1. There is an urgent need for applied research in social sciences, particularly for action research in developing approaches to groups of individuals and families in neighborhood and community situations. Research in depth is needed in the behavioral sciences to learn more about the effects of urbanization on rural migrants faced with problems of adaptation to a new and strange urban environment.

2. The trend toward modern industrial development with a regional approach, a trend emphasized by economic planners, is expanding metropolitan areas into a vast megalopolis. Two instances of note are the Atlantic seaboard in the Eastern United States and the Channel seaboard on the West coast of Europe. In Canada, a relatively small megalopolis is developing in the Toronto-Hamilton-Niagara Peninsula area.

This is a fertile field of action for social planners and social workers, one where urban planners should place more emphasis on people. Would it be too idealistic to aim at conserving the spiritual and social values attached to individual homes surrounded by a "spot of earth" large enough for one to commune with nature? Who would deny those who wish to live in high-rise apartments the privilege of enjoying the anonymity and mobility of urban civilization? Perhaps some would choose to have the best of the two worlds by residing where they will be less than an hour's ride from their work and their children will be close to their school—all within their neighborhood community.

3. How can the impact of problems resulting from urbanization

be alleviated? How can the happy experiences be channeled so that they will have a beneficial impact on rural areas not only in countries advanced socially and economically but also in emerging countries around the world?

I hope that these thoughts may lead to further study, the results of which may stimulate action programs to help people adapt to social change in urban and rural communities.

PART II

H. P. VAN ROOSMALEN

INSTITUTE OF SOCIAL STUDIES, THE HAGUE, NETHERLANDS

URBANIZATION is clearly linked with declining rural populations. This is a demographic approach, but Mr. Lanctot indicates many aspects as essential phenomena of urbanization:

1. Demographic features: (*a*) concentration of population; (*b*) functional differentiation
2. Technological characteristics: mechanization of agriculture or the introduction of technology on farms
3. New patterns of organization: trade unions and their functions in rural areas
4. The change in social welfare: (*a*) housing policy; (*b*) introduction of social welfare programs
5. Changes in behavior and social cultural aspects: the significance of religion, and so on.

Urbanization, defined more as a demographic fact, appears to be a social and economic factor of the greatest importance.

The modification of economic resources, of social attitudes and customs, of the social hierarchy, is a phenomenon that accompanies urbanization. These characteristics are essential to any discussion of the impact of urbanization on rural areas. Since the

differences in European countries are so great, I shall confine myself mainly to experience gained in the Netherlands.

Urbanization and social progress.—In his book *Poor and Rich
Countries,* Zimmerman shows—based on an analysis of the situation
in a large number of countries—a very strong interdependency
between economic progress, expressed by the average income per
capita, and the level of professional and functional differentiation
(a main element of urbanization in nearly all definitions), the
level of education, of social amenities, and of consumption. Urbanization is a necessary sequel of progress. When a certain level
of economic progress is attained, urbanization must be accepted as
an essential condition. Perhaps this interdependency is one of the
reasons that urbanization is not only an accepted fact but also a
goal of many policy-makers. Mr. Lanctot shows this in his exposition. Urbanization of rural areas results in higher education,
higher income, and so forth. Mr. Lanctot implies that rural areas
have to become used to a more urban way of life. But what does
this mean?

It seems to mean a more rational attitude of the villagers in
relation to the existing technical and social possibilities, and a
greater openness to accept change.

Urbanization as a way of life appears to be a logical consequence
of development. It is difficult to define "development" exactly,
and almost all authors like to use their own definitions. From the
social point of view, there is one aspect that lies at the root of
development and is also essential for urbanization: the relationship between man and nature and between man and his environment. Development is an effort to make a sharper distinction between a man's personal life and the natural and social forces in his
environment.

The continuity between the forces of nature, environment, and
personal life has been disrupted.

Gradually, society and the individual try to formulate a response to the forces of nature, which had their effect on his life
and which he had to follow. Typical of development is the fact
that man is becoming capable of changing more and more of his
environment. First, man made nature an object of study and a
tool; later, society became a subject of his study and planning; and

subsequently, even the human personality itself. To a certain extent, this can be called a process of "sensitization" of awareness, but also a personal "liberation from dependencies." Urbanization in rural areas seems to create a condition for this attitude. This holds true for society as a whole, but not for every member of society. Perhaps this is due to the internal tension which accompanies the process of urbanization everywhere. The technical means of society as a whole develop and organize themselves much faster than do the individuals themselves and their social relationships. In many areas, therefore, people have to cope with the means and structure of a more technically developed level whilst they are living in another relationship between personality, nature, and social environment.

It has been said that in the future only 5 percent of the population of the world will live in typically rural areas.

Mr. Venstra, a sociologist working for a physical planning agency in the land reclamation projects of the Zuider Zee, forecast that in the future, in that part of Holland, even farmers will prefer to live in an urban environment and will commute to their farms. It must be noted that when Mr. Venstra discussed this with farmers, they were rather offended. "Such a man cannot be a real farmer," was their reaction.

In any case, social policy and social work have to face a problem. The new technical way of living, which expresses a form of freedom from dependency, creates new forms of dependency for many members of society. In the rural areas, particularly, many people find that the range of technical decisions that have to be accepted becomes wider and wider, while the scope of existential decisions in which they have some influence becomes narrower and narrower.

Features of the urbanization process.—The urbanization processes in several European countries show great differences. In *Le Fait urbain en France* Armand Collins notes a clear difference between the urbanization process in France and that in countries such as the Netherlands, Belgium, and Great Britain. The possibilities of a more widespread urbanization (especially with more and smaller urban centers throughout the whole country) are much better in the latter countries than in France.

It must be noted here that the national and regional planning in France is changing this situation.

Kruyt distinguishes several periods of urbanization in the Netherlands after 1880. During the first phase, large cities such as Amsterdam, Rotterdam, and The Hague grew very quickly. During the second phase (1900-1930), these cities continued to grow, but at a much slower rate; the cities with populations above 20,000 (especially those of 100,000) grew more quickly. After the Second World War, even cities with populations above 100,000 grew more slowly than the smaller towns.

Based on the analysis of internal migration figures, it appears that:

The migration stream is changing. Suburbanization, involving the suburbs of the capital itself, has declined, whereas that involving the suburbs of smaller towns and built-up rural areas has increased. Suburbanization is now taking place at a faster pace and in a more effective fashion in the more outlying sectors of the country.[1]

An analysis of migration trends and of the growth of cities in the southern part of our country (Noord-Brabant) shows the same tendency, and Steiginga proves the same for the Netherlands as a whole. With the exception of the more agricultural provinces, the rural areas show a higher population growth (7.1 percent for the period 1954–59) than that of the whole country (6.7 percent for the same period).

In the Netherlands this process is combined with two important elements: a high density of population (365 per U m²) and a high growth rate (in the year 2000, the number of inhabitants is expected to be higher than 20,000,000).[2] Consequently, the impact of urbanization is already felt in almost every village in the rural areas.

Urbanization and social relations in villages.—In the traditional village, the social structure was clear. This means that the methods of farming were known to every farmer, He learned it from his parents. His son could come into the farm and work with the family. His future too was clear.

Family relationships were rather functional. The expression of

---

[1] M. W. Steiginga, "The Urbanization of the Netherlands," *Tijdschrift economic en sociale Geografie,* 55ste Jaargang, 1963.

[2] *Ibid.*

feeling, such as love for children, was influenced very strongly by this relationship.

The position of the farmer in the social structure was well-defined. He understood the whole structure, the whole hierarchy. His position in the hierarchy was understood by him and by all the villagers.

The farmer participated in the village life and in the decisions involving the community. This participation did not mean that all the farmers had a real possibility of strongly influencing the decisions, but even when he did not have an important place in the structure, the individual farmer felt himself a part of it. He understood that the doctor, the priest, and the more wealthy farmer had to make the decisions, and that understanding created a feeling of safety and belonging.

The doctor, the priest, the schoolteacher, and other nonagricultural workers had a real function in the community. Moreover, they were the persons who were held in high esteem and who could influence strongly the values and attitudes essential to the village life.

This structure was determined by, and limited to, the borders of the village. This made it understandable, safe, and secure for the farmer. The position of the farmer and of the villager was clear in this well-defined society.

Essentially, the impact of urbanization widened the distance between the villager and his own environment. It created a more critical attitude in relation to this whole set of structure, culture, values, and attitudes.

In an article in *Het tijdschrift economische en social geografie*,[3] Tonkens describes the changing position of the farmer. In the past the economic progress of the village depended on agriculture. The farmer was the person who could offer work, money, and land. He was the leader of the social hierarchy. The municipal council was a council of farmers. When a community center or a church had to be built, the farmer, who was almost the only person with money, was the financer. He was a member of the church and parish council.

Nowadays, with the impact of urbanization, many commuters

3 Ir. E. Tonkens, "Weerstanden tegen structurele veranderingen op het Nederlandse platteland," *Tijdschrift economic en sociale Geografie,* 55ste Jaargang, 1963.

are not dependent on the farmer for work, and many people do not need land. The industrialization of a region or village is much more important for its economic progress than the development of agriculture. The farmer is now only one of the leaders of the village, and the municipal council is composed of many members, only some of whom are farmers. The rural way of life is now a less agricultural way of life.[4]

In *Social Class in a French Village,* Julian Pitt-Rivers clearly describes the tension existing between the present social function of the French farmer and his position in the rural social structure.

On the other hand, it must be realized that the roots of a more rational organization in the agricultural sphere have long been present in the Netherlands. The cooperative movement and organization of the farming profession created a consciousness among farmers that they needed to cooperate with each other, not only in the same village, but also with farmers of other villages; that they were producing for a wider market. Through this cooperation, the farmers soon transcended the "boundaries" of their villages.

Apart from this change in the position of the farmer, which is naturally accompanied by internal agricultural changes, the differentiation of the labor force has many other aspects. In the Netherlands, purely agricultural villages are now more the exception than the rule.

A clear distinction should be made between the several types of villages. One is the commuters' village, from which residents who were born and grew up there commute to more urban areas. The influence of urbanization is important, but works slowly. The people continue to have the same social relationships, they meet the same friends, visit the same pubs, and go together to the same church. The change in their patterns of life caused by working in industry but living in their own village is slow. The strong relationships such people have with the traditional groups and with their own family impede a rapid urbanization.

Many times, the values of a typical agricultural way of life are

[4] *Ibid.,* p. 270.

combined with, and complemented by, the new working environment and way of life. The case study on the development of Drenthe [5] gives a good example of this trend.

Some small agricultural villages in the Netherlands show another pattern. If only a small number of persons commute, they become a separate group. They leave their families in the morning and come back in the evening. They do not have an opportunity for good conversation during the day. They are really different from the other villagers, and this difference is one of the reasons that they move from the villages to the locality where they work.

Villages which undergo an influx of middle-class commuters change more profoundly. Frequently, these middle-class commuters are not really villagers and do not participate in the community life. The social controls which exist for the villagers do not seem to apply to these people. They have their own social life, distinguished not only from the village life of the worker-commuters but also from the life of the middle-class people in the cities. Sometimes they develop their own network of social relationships within the village, independent of the existing social structure of the village. This is particularly true during the first phase, governed partly by the distance from the city. The rural village is split into groups which have no close relationships with each other.

In some parts of Great Britain an important consequence of this appears to be the growth of a new class consciousness in the villages. A process of polarization has started. The original village inhabitants, even those who now commute to other towns, have not changed so much, but a middle-class group has built up its own regional life; they maintain their relationships with their own friends, they spend their vacations in other parts of the country, or even in foreign countries. Pahl describes this pattern:

The middle-class people come into rural areas in search of a meaningful community and by their presence help to destroy whichever community was there. They simply make the working class aware of

[5] John Higgs, *People in the Countryside* (London: National Council of Social Service, 1966).

national class divisions, thus polarizing the local society. There is not a real social relationship, which can provide a genuine friendship on a basis of equality.[6]

The national report of the United Kingdom states that this holds true only for commuter villages near the large cities and not for the whole rural area.

The position of the priest, the doctor, and the schoolteacher is changing. In a research project in one part of our country it has been observed that commuters and the younger generation already have a different interpretation of their function than that held by the older generation. The older generation likes to discuss matters like education difficulties and vocational training with the doctor, the priest, or the schoolteacher; the younger generation believes that a specialized agency would be more appropriate.

The negative reaction of the church in rural areas in the recent past to urbanization and industrialization is in this context quite understandable. In many rural communities, religion was a main indicator of the way of life. It was an integral part of the whole social structure. Religion contained many typical rural elements in its various expressions. This holds especially true for the hierarchal structure and the relation of priest or minister with the villager.

The greater distance between nature, or social structure, and the person is shown clearly in the strong relationship between the birth rate and the level of urbanization in the rural areas. According to Mrs. J. C. L. Luyten, a sociologist with the provincial physical planning agency in a Catholic province of Noord-Brabant, in the purely rural areas, the birth rate is higher than in commuter villages, industrialized villages, or small towns.

The meaning of participation is changing profoundly. I stated that the scope of technical decisions is becoming wider and wider, and the field of essential decisions narrower and narrower. We have to understand this clearly. Perhaps for many villagers the possibility of having a real role in decisions did not change essentially, but the understanding of the frame of reference of the decision has been lost. It is now less a part of an existing, understandable structure.

6 R. E. Pahl, *Class and Community in English Commuter Village.*

In the Netherlands national report, there is a discussion of the consciously developed regional policy which has tentatively integrated social and economic planning. Here are some of the problems we met at the village level during the implementation of this policy.

There has been a change in family relationships. The authority of the parents now lacks the immediate support of the economic and functional relationships, and this leads to new pedagogical requirements. The difficulties are enlarged by the fact that those who lived in the rural way of life used to have a typical way of expressing their emotions and feelings. Sometimes—I believe for this reason—the social worker found it difficult to execute his function in the rural areas. There is also another reason for this: his training was especially directed to a more differentiated way of emotional expression. So—in case the method was not integrated in the personal structure of the social worker, had not become a personal experience—there was a clash between the social worker and the people in the rural area.

The differentiation in classes is becoming more conscious. The boundaries of the village are not so important now. The consequence is that the function of the priest and of the doctor is changing, but they do not see this change.

An interesting example of this change in hierarchy is perhaps the following experience. In one rural community, group discussions were organized. Some groups were set up according to the social classes: one group of farmers; one of commuters; one of priests, doctors, lawyers, and so forth. There was also one collective group, representing all classes. In the groups containing people of the higher classes, the opinions about the families of farmers, changes of attitudes, and so on, were quite different from those expressed in groups composed only of farmers and commuters. Even more interesting was the fact that the collective groups, whose members came from all the social classes, showed the same result as the group representing the leading class. After the discussion, however, one commuter stated that the results obtained in this group were not reliable, he could not express his opinions in the group because of the existing structural relationship.

The organization of social assistance was difficult sometimes. It showed too much the atmosphere of relief work, which was not in accordance with the growing distinction between functional and private relations.

The urbanization process in the rural areas is hampering not only many forms of community life but also many relations of dependency. The challenge is to accept the new way of life and to develop methods of social policy that can create, perhaps, new forms of community life. Three elements will be essential in this regard: (1) a receptivity to change; (2) a more exact distinction between private and functional life (even between private and public life); and (3) new forms of participation, including a higher form of participation in decisions and, at the same time, a new form of security, such as the old form of participation gave to the villager.

Social Services as Social Utilities

ALFRED J. KAHN

PROFESSOR OF SOCIAL WORK, COLUMBIA UNIVERSITY
SCHOOL OF SOCIAL WORK

OUR SPOTLIGHT is on the urban environment in a world which, while still largely rural in its modes of work and living, knows that it is destined for complete urban dominance. An advanced industrialized society requires somewhat less than 5 percent of its labor force for agriculture. A combination of physical-space realities, industrial advantages in proximity, land-use economics, and consumer preference concentrates the remainder of the population in a pattern of urban-suburban-metropolitan-megalopolitan living.

United States projections place 180,000,000 people in 216 cities in 1985; this was the size of the total population in 1960. Yet as early as 1960, there were 52,000,000 Americans living in only 16 urbanized areas, and 96,000,000 (53 percent of the population) concentrated in 213 urbanized areas covering only 0.7 percent of the country's land.[1]

This degree of urbanization is a product of the past 100 years, and it is a phenomenon to which man has nowhere made adequate institutional adjustment. That the challenge is a world-wide one is suggested in the fact that at conservative estimate "more than half of the world's people will probably be living in cities of 100,000 or more by 1990"; already, of the 250 cities throughout the world with populations of 500,000 or more, nearly half are located in the

---

[1] Kingsley Davis, "The Urbanization of the Human Population," *Scientific American*, special issues: *Cities*, CCIII, No. 3 (1965), 41; Ralph Lazarus, "Surviving the Age of the City," in Committee on Economic Development, *Making American Cities More Livable, Saturday Review*, January 6, 1966, p. 44; Lawrence K. Northwood, *Urban Development in the United States* (New York: U. S. Committee of the International Conference of Social Work, 1966), Ch. 2.

so-called "developing countries." [2] While many of these agglomerations were founded in agricultural and mercantile economies, their continued growth and viability are based on their role in the industrial process. Calcutta, India's metropolitan area of 7,000,000 people, may serve as illustration.[3]

Thus, as we consider conditions for a desirable urban environment we appear at a given moment to be addressing the needs of only a portion of the population—a large portion in industrialized countries and a smaller portion elsewhere. Yet it is the future of almost all people, everywhere, which is at stake.

SOCIAL PLANNING AND URBANIZATION

The modern city cannot fulfill its economic, political, cultural, or social functions unless it constitutes itself as a suitable environment for human existence. Universal experience suggests the need to provide adequately for: distribution of food, materials, and services; water supply and public utilities; sewage disposal; traffic management; public transportation; clean air; postal service; protection against lawlessness; control of crime and delinquency; recreational, cultural, and religious activities; housing; education and socialization; so-called "welfare" and health services.

Our purpose in this listing is to recall that while all these provisions are basic they can be implemented more or less adequately, their costs distributed more or less equitably, and access made more or less universal. Cities or their parts may be—and already have been—hellholes or jewels of civilization.

It has become clear only in recent years that the choices among these alternatives are in significant degree political (in the broadest sense) rather than wholly technical. In fact, it is only recently that we have fully appreciated that all of these are, indeed, arenas for choice and not determined by forces beyond communal influence. Among the variables for decision are the specific service designs—involving many dimensions—as well as priorities for resource and manpower allocation. As this has become more apparent the concept of social planning has expanded to include the

2 Davis, *op. cit.;* Nirmal K. Bose, "Calcutta: a Premature Metropolis," *Cities,* CCIII, No. 3 (1965), 91–102.
3 Bose, *op. cit.,* p. 91.

notion of introducing "socioeconomic and human behavior considerations in the making of decisions by all governmental and private agencies and groups in the community." [4]

To put it simply and directly, the decision about how seriously and in what manner to cope with air pollution or water pollution is only in part a scientific and technical matter; it is also a political matter and a value question. Is this not also true in relation to public transportation or police services? And if these are areas of decision in which human priority, preference, response, and participation have significance, should not one consider how to provide a social planning process which deals with such matters?

I have deliberately chosen illustrations in fields which have seldom been associated with social planning in order to suggest the validity of a new departure and the urgency of the need. Are we prepared, or will we become prepared in the next several years, to educate social workers or other social welfare personnel who are technically competent to join with engineers, economists, transportation experts, and physical planners so as to add to the planning process a human dimension, a preoccupation with what the choices to be made will mean for individual development, family life, neighborhood, and community? Furthermore, are we prepared to give sufficiently high priority to the education of personnel qualified to inspire and facilitate the widespread urban community development through which citizens will express their preferences in these matters and will utilize democratic political machinery to implement their choices?

In short, are we serious in our commitment to contribute significantly to the effort to humanize the urban environment, making it supportive of man's potentialities where it so often appears reflective only of greed and powerlessness?

Ours is, then, a plea for a broad conception of social planning as applied to the city. It is a call for training in social planning and in community development as part of social work education. It is

4 Robert Perlman, "Social Welfare Planning and Physical Planning," *Journal of the American Institute of Planners,* XXXII (1966), 238; also see United Nations, "European Seminar on the Problems and Methods of Social Planning" (Geneva: 1965; mimeographed); *Social Progress through Social Planning—the Role of Social Work,* Proceedings of the XIIth International Conference of Social Work (New York: International Conference of Social Work, 1965), pp. 259–65.

also a prediction that the expansion of social planning may convert such fields as urban transportation from the sole domain of engineering to the province of social services. Now as we turn to a somewhat less debated area, the role of social work in the planning of social services (a segment of social planning), we find it necessary to urge a considerable broadening of vision.

PHILOSOPHY AND POLICY

When New York City participated in the 1965 power failure, which affected a large section of the northeastern United States, people were trapped in elevator shafts and subway tunnels, hospital services were curtailed, traffic signals ceased to operate. I listened for points of view about the causes of the failure and for attribution of blame. Since the crisis was dramatic and the inconvenience and suffering considerable, data accumulated over several weeks. I heard a good deal about overconcentration of utility companies and about the rigidity of bureaucratized organizations. Street-corner philosophers even speculated about the relationship between technological sophistication and the vulnerability to sabotage and conquest. But there were also many things which I did not hear.

What I did not hear is especially pertinent. No one blamed the people in an elevator stalled between the twenty-third and twenty-fourth floors of a skyscraper for not carrying pocket generators, or perhaps pocket parachutes, for just such an emergency. Nor were the people in the subway tunnels told that it served them right for not being accompanied by their own emergency horsepower, or for not at least having pocket flashlights!

These criticisms occurred to no one. Why? Because in some realms we understand modern industrialization, urbanization, and technology and the interdependence which these bring. Man is more potent and powerful but also, in some spheres, far less self-reliant. We protect him and provide for him institutionally, because there is no way for him to manage this new type of environment by himself. The occasional citizen who continues to make the attempt is considered to be an eccentric, or even severely ill. Thus, our society develops its water supply, general electricity systems, roads, the post office, and sewage systems without much concern that it will thereby undermine the moral fiber of its citizens, destroy family life, or even decrease free enterprise. In fact, every schoolboy knows that the automobile industry is one of the pillars of the free-enterprise economy and that the public road system is an essential public subsidy to Detroit.

Public utilities and public services are taken for granted as necessary concomitants to industrialization, urbanization, and technological progress. I here urge upon the social work profession and its allies in social welfare a continuing effort to interpret to the public the notion that there are also essential social utilities which are no less necessary and whose use carried no more stigma than that of public utilities and services.

A social utility is a social invention, a resource or facility, designed to meet a generally experienced need in social living. It is defined as so vital that the broader community suffers from the results of the deprivation faced by an individual. Because of this, the provision is not left to the market economy even though some particularly affluent people may continue to resort to the market.

The conception of social utilities carries the social welfare system beyond the traditional limitations of social services. In many places, social services have been considered as directed to the failures, the maladjusted, and the sick and as consisting only of facilitating and rehabilitative efforts. As the professional literature of recent years has noted repeatedly, the general post First World War social work preoccupation with remedial and therapeutic interventions led to a conceptualization of the profession as serving social welfare programs which came into play only when the normal primary institutions and the forces of the market place had broken down. (This was called a "residual" view of social welfare in the United States report to the 1956 International Conference of Social Work.) Inevitably, social work was seen as a helping, liaison, therapeutic, rehabilitative activity. Its clients were perceived as casualties, failures, victims, deviants in a world of generally self-sufficient and self-sustaining individuals. The assumption was that all social welfare programs and social work services, were basically temporary and transitional.

In recent years another perspective has become known as the institutional view of social welfare.[5] In this view, society takes account of technological and social changes which alter the relationships of man both to primary institutions and to the general social environment. New social "inventions" appear in response to the functional prerequisite of life in this changed social environment, and they are as "normal" in their way, in their relationship to these changed circumstances, as were the primary social institutions of a primitive agricultural economy. Nor are they to be considered temporary or transitional. Social insurance, public housing, services to the aged, day care services, and counseling programs may in this light be seen as social responses to new challenges and circumstances. To stigmatize or penalize the user is no more rational than it would have been to call a nineteenth-century American farmer excessively dependent because of the many ways in which he counted on the other members of his family.

Social services may be interpreted in an institutional context as consisting of programs made available by other than market criteria to assure a basic level of health-education-welfare services, to enhance communal living and individual functioning, to facilitate access to services and institutions generally, and to assist those in difficulty and need.

The emphasis on the notion that some social services are social utilities represents my conviction that community well-being and the success of the economy depend on their existence and my belief that we must organize such utilities so as to make them as accessible and nonstigmatic as the water supply and postal service.

Although vocabularies vary, there is now considerable convergence upon these perceptions and goals. In fact, while talking of "provision according to need," Beatrice Webb apparently used the term "social utilities" at the turn of the century.[6] In a discussion of child welfare issues the British Ingleby Committee recently said that the state should "assist the family in carrying out its proper functions. This should be done in the first instance by the provision of facilities such as housing, health services and educa-

[5] Harold L. Wilensky and Charles N. Lebeaux, *Industrial Society and Social Welfare* (New York: Russell Sage Foundation, 1958), pp. 138–47.

[6] Beatrice Webb, *Our Partnership* (London: Longmans, Green and Co., 1948), p. 149.

tion. Some families will need greater and more specialized help through the welfare services." [7] UNICEF's Bellagio Conference on child welfare planning heard from the secretariat a plea to "break with the traditional belief that a national policy for children should be confined to dealing with the underprivileged and the handicapped. A national programme should cover all children. . . . irrespective of their social class, their place of residence and economic status." [8]

In many countries the concept of social benefits conveys the idea that "all persons meeting certain qualifications such as attainment of a prescribed age and having a certain period of citizenship or residence receive benefits without regard to any previous contributions or taxes paid or demonstration of individual need." [9]

The several sources quoted differ somewhat, perhaps subtly, in emphasis. In fact, it becomes useful in sorting out issues of access, financing, and service delivery to distinguish three types of social services. First, there are the general resources and facilities which I call "social utilities"—something not understood by those who see social services as completely encompassed by case service. Included here are:

1. Services or resources to be used by the individual as he chooses to do so (the park for example): symbolically, at least, such facilities have no doorkeeper.
2. Services or resources available to users by status (the kindergarten or day nursery for children of a given age who have developed normally) : one's status provides the key for opening the door.

Then there are the more traditional case services, needed by a smaller population but also available as a right and removed from poor law stigma and moral taint:

3. Services or resources which become available on the basis of professional judgment or evaluation (the residential treat-

[7] *Report of the Committee on Children and Young Persons* (Ingleby Committee) (London: Her Majesty's Stationery Office, 1960).

[8] Herman D. Stein, ed., *Planning for the Needs of Children in Developing Countries* (New York: United Nations Children's Fund, 1965), pp. 11–12.

[9] Charles Schottland, *The Social Security System of the United States* (New York: Appleton-Century-Crofts, 1963), p. 1.

ment center): an appropriate diagnostic judgment opens the doorway to service.

While these are relatively clear-cut categories, there would by no means be world-wide consensus as to which are social utilities or social resources and which are case services. In many places in the United States, for example, strong forces define day care as a diagnostically assigned service. Some status services for senior citizens, taken for granted in the Scandinavian countries, are unknown or cannot be afforded elsewhere. On the other hand, diagnostic accessibility is a luxury in many poor and developing areas. (The very definition of a status which opens the way to service is created by a public decision: is the aged person to be defined as one who is seventy, sixty-five, or sixty years old?)

Despite this desirable and necessary variation, the emphasis on social utilities, and on diagnostically rendered facilitating and remedial case services as a right, represents a considerable advance. It is one of the prime characteristics of the welfare state under its many euphemisms. In the United States a group of legal scholars has recently developed the doctrine that:

The new expectations progressively brought into existence by the welfare state must be thought of not as privileges to be dispensed unequally or by arbitrary fiat of government officials but as substantial rights in the assertion of which the claimant is entitled to an effective remedy, a fair procedure and a reasoned decision.[10]

Charles Reich suggests that the individual's relationship to these new benefits, entitlements, resources, and facilities be recognized as constituting "the new property," the rights to which can be maintained under law.[11]

While rigorously compiled consumer preference data are limited, Geismar has found that in contrast to planners, consumers place high priority on universally accessible social utilities, to use our term.[12] By the test of usage and response to availability there

10 Harry W. Jones, "The Rule of Law and the Welfare State," *Columbia Law Review*, LVIII, No. 2 (1958), 155.

11 Charles Reich, "The New Property," *Yale Law Journal*, LXXIII, No. 5 (1964), 733–87.

12 Ludwig Geismar and Bruce W. Lagay, "Planners' and Consumers' Priorities of Social Welfare Needs," *Social Work Practice 1965* (New York: Columbia University Press, 1965), pp. 76–93.

would appear to be little doubt about this, despite periodic warnings from conservative political quarters. Public preference is ahead of organizational and professional practice in some sectors of social welfare, sectors which derive secondary gains from an accent on a charity-philanthropy concept of all social welfare and a view of clients, problems, and programs which is best described as "residual."

In the context of world-wide discussion of guaranteed minimum income, improved social insurance, humanized public assistance, there are those who might regard an emphasis on social utilities as a diversion. The argument is increasingly heard that one should assure people enough money and permit them to buy needed services. The market mechanism is cited as an ideal way to engender healthy competition and assure accountability.

While the issue is real and complex, the assumption that an income guarantee makes it unnecessary to plan utilities is, of course, a false one. Most proponents of social utilities, precisely because they appreciate current social realities, favor liberalized income-transfer policies as well. Nonetheless, one must recognize that the issue essentially is: what *mix* of income and utilities is most likely to advance what social objectives? (To round out the picture, one would need to ask what mix of income policy, social utilities, case services, and institutional change would advance what social objectives.) Schorr suggests, if we may paraphrase, that the mix is affected by: (*a*) the significance of the service (can it be left to individual choice?); (*b*) considerations of economy or organizational effectiveness; (*c*) the view of what people are entitled to have; (*d*) complexity (can the family provide the resource, even given access in a market?). We might add: (*e*) the issue of whether the service imposes or depends on public sanction; and (*f*) the question of whether diversity and great variability are to be tolerated or promoted.[13]

Certainly one would not offer social utilities as a substitute for cash and the options it offers, or where the services are a vehicle for discrimination and unwarranted control.

To conceive of social services as made up of resources and facilities available at user initiative or by status rights—what we call

13 Alvin Schorr, *Poor Kids* (New York: Basic Books, publication pending).

social utilities—and of case services available on a diagnostic basis is to recognize that several patterns of financing are available. It is likely that each country will develop its balance among possible sources in a manner most suited to its institutions. Included among the possibilities are general tax revenues, a portion of the earnings of communally owned factories or other enterprises, social insurances, trust funds, user fees, industry, industry-labor contributions, foundations, individual contributions. What is crucial is the mode of access to the service, the guarantee of the right and the definition of the user, not the financial device—unless the device conditions these other factors.

Similarly, while most social utilities will probably be administered as statutory services on a local or central governmental level, they may also be operated by nonstatutory (voluntary) organizations, voluntarily financed or financed by public subsidy or purchase of care. In general, the right is affirmed for a widely needed service, it seems unlikely that coverage will be possible without either public operation or at least public subsidization and standard-setting.

Richard Titmuss reminds us that "universalism in social welfare [free, on-demand services], though a needed prerequisite towards reducing and removing formal barriers of social and economic discrimination, does not by itself solve the problem of how to reach the more-difficult-to-reach." [14] Martin Rein talks of the "creaming" of services by the better situated and more competent users.[15] In short, the decision to convert our social services into social utilities and case services available by right, while a necessary step toward equity and the implementation of social goals, does not per se offer any guarantee of access. One must still face questions about organization for service delivery and staffing of programs.

THE FUNCTIONS OF SOCIAL UTILITIES

A review of services encouraged by directives from the United States Welfare Administration and programs being funded by the

[14] Richard M. Titmuss, "The Role of Redistribution in Social Policy," *Social Security Bulletin*, XXVIII, No. 6 (1965), 19.
[15] Martin Rein, "The Social Service Crisis," *Trans-action*, Vol. I, No. 4 (1964).

Community Action Program under the antipoverty effort provides the following illustrative list. There is some overlapping; the order is random: casework and personal counseling; services to encourage participation in developing and extending community resources; day care; homemakers; foster care for children and adults; literacy training; employment and counseling; training for self-care; information and referral; legal services; auxiliary services, such as baby sitting and shopping assistance; health education; diagnosis of rehabilitation potential; community care and follow-up for hospital dischargees; family financial counseling; low-cost credit services; home-improvement information; housing and home management instruction and service; consumer information and education; child development programs; neighborhood community centers; precollege educational counseling; and library services.

The recent United States emphasis on neighborhood legal services and multiservice centers would probably impress social workers in other countries as innovative and exciting. On the other hand, American practitioners are painfully aware of the almost token nature of our homemaker and home-help services, as contrasted with British or Scandinavian tradition. We are impressed with the programs of cheap family vacations in a number of European countries, which, in turn, may envy our extensive counseling programs.

Yet, one is stuck by the relatively static picture in social utilities. We have been timid. Not enough is happening, if we take as our criterion the fact of massive social change and the range of need for new patterns of social coping. What is more, although the list is long and impressive, it becomes less so as one adds data about caseload totals and geographic coverage. With notable exceptions this is the situation around the world.

What is called for is an escalation in socal invention so as to produce new social services suitable to the present era. The interventive repertoire needs to be enriched to reflect our new philosophies. At the same time, we must rally to achieve support of a sufficient quantitative development. I regard these as social work responsibilities, since our proximity to human need and response to social change is a strategic point from which to develop new

programs; and our access to data about impact and response pre-
pares us to be administrators of service.

Some of the newer possibilities and challenges may be more
clearly perceived though the device of a classification of the several
functions of social utilities and case services. While the categories
are preliminary and tentative they do illustrate the conclusion
that earlier conceptions of social services encompass only a portion
of the whole.

1. *Information, liaison, facilitation, and advocacy.*—The liaison
function has long been recognized as a critical one in social work,
but it was devalued somewhat in the 1950s and early 1960s during
a period of emphasis on therapeutic activities. The recognition
that many services had become "hard to reach," that some services
"disengaged" themselves from the poor, and that, in general,
modern, large, specialized, and bureaucratized institutions inevitably confront complex problems when they seek to render indi-
vidualized and sensitive services have made these functions re-
spectable again.

Renamed as a "social brokerage" or "urban brokerage" service,
the liaison activity has new status and appears in new forms.
Often, in multiservice centers, it is found together with outposts of
many other programs. In the Community Action Program, which
is part of the United States antipoverty war, it includes or is carried on in close partnership with a program of case and policy
advocacy and a broadly conceived community development effort.

There is currently much interest in the British Citizen's Advice
Bureaux (CAB), a widespread service (466 local units at latest
count) which handled more than a million inquiries last year,
accurately and well, and which finds that it may also provide a
useful "window on the man in the street." The emphasis here is
on information, advice, steering, and referral in a stigma-free
atmosphere, open to all groups in society. An "open door" is
achieved by combining expertise with range and avoiding over-
professionalization. CAB may be consulted about subjects ranging from social security benefits to consumer rights in installment
purchases, from landlord-tenant issues to locating a spot for a new
business, from personal problems to application procedures for

educational benefits. CABs distribute information booklets and transportation maps as well.

CABs locally established and locally controlled, but they are supported through information materials, training assistance, and general guides by a central certifying organization. Although CAB is a voluntary service, the bulk of the funding is from local public authorities, under Britain's 1948 local government act. Staffing is both volunteer and professional in a 70:30 ratio. CABs are widely known in Britain, extensively used, and almost taken for granted as a necessary urban amenity. While there are those who would convert CAB to a statutory and professionalized service, very few would think of eliminating the function.

In a recently completed study my colleagues and I concluded that there is considerable need for these functions in American cities. While we adopted and adapted much of the CAB pattern, we found need for variation to accommodate to our own social welfare and general governmental system. We assumed need for a greater case advocacy component in programs here. Because a number of options exist with reference to administration auspices, combinations of functions and staffing, we have outlined several recommended experiments. The strong likelihood that there will be serious follow-up confirms our assessment of the general readiness for this type of social utility.[16]

This emphasis on possible new organizational arrangements for some of these functions does not reflect any intent to deprecate more traditional auspices for facilitating and liaison services. However, it does seem clear that modern cities will be experimenting with new and expanded information, liaison, advocacy, and complaint mechanisms to counteract complexity and depersonalization. The possibilities of group approaches are relatively untapped.

2. *Development provision.*—Facilitating and liaison services are an attempt at a bureaucratized solution to a problem inevitable in bureaucracies. Other social utilities may be concerned with another function, one which grows out of recognition of what family

16 Alfred J. Kahn *et al.*, *Neighborhood Information Centers: a Study and Some Proposals* (New York: Columbia University School of Social Work, 1966).

and other interpersonal relationships become under industrialization and urbanization.

In effect, from the day when it became apparent that the unit family could not do everything related to production, socialization, education and training, cultural enrichment, maintenance of motivation, and facilitation of family formation, the process was under way. What characterizes our present situation is the quantitative change. If we wish to protect some of our core values and to assure intimate primary group experiences and the fruits thereof, we must find other institutional vehicles for some of the functions of the family, the traditional neighborhood, the extended family, the peer group, the religious institution.

The thesis here is simple. Social change creates new prerequisites for adequate socialization and role training in industrial communities. Since these are recognizable as meeting functional requirements of the broader society, they ought to be socially created in the same spirit that earlier societies invented public roads and public education. The user is "citizen," not "client." There is no personal defect implied in the need for the service and no penalty involved in the use. Such social inventions designed to meet the normal needs of people arising from their situations and roles in modern life might be thought of as "developmental provision." Full comprehension of what it means to be mother, adolescent, retired adult, child with only one parent, is a starting point in planning such provision.

Thus day care programs are needed for young children—younger children, in fact, than one would have released from the shelter of the family ten years ago. Or we sustain old people in the community by a diversity of communal provisions ("meals on wheels" and home helps are two illustrations) where the intimate family is no longer available for such support.

This is only a beginning. Consider some of the major life transitions and what primary group institutions once offered, and still seek to offer in many places, so as to assist people through them: entry into elementary school; the beginning of adolescence; the transition to the world of work; the early days of marriage; the period of pregnancy; the early days with a first baby; adjustment to the death of a spouse; retirement; old age. These are normal, everyday, universal experiences, and the institutional efforts to help people meet them represent social wisdom, communal self-interest, not charity or sympathy for victims.

The response ranges from group counseling and education for parents whose children enter school, through organized activities for adolescents—including coffee houses and "hang-outs"—to vocational guidance and counseling services, to family life education and counseling (including group activities for "young marrieds") , down to specialized services for older people.

Day care (or better, child development centers) and home-makers are very high-priority developmental services too often miscast in case-service terms. The former is now experiencing major expansion in the United States under the impetus of Operation Head Start, an antipoverty program. A degree of inventiveness might now be applied to devise a related program to provide the short-term or emergency baby sitter. Is it not time that the city dweller had access to a resource more routinely available and reliable than the teen-age baby sitter or the neighborhood mothers' exchange for a function whose requirements grow out of current living conditions? Is it necessary to spell out the consequences for personal health (parents need rest, change, diversion), involvement in children's education (parents need to attend parent-teacher meetings and adult classes), emotional security (children and parents need to be comfortable about the substitute arrangement for brief periods—shopping, clinic visits—or longer periods which may occur several times a week), deriving from the fact that some mothers never can make secure arrangements for care of their children no matter how urgent the other demands upon them? Facilities can and should be located in parks, in shopping areas, and in conjunction with other major facilities, such as medical centers.

Priorities must vary from place to place. Several sections of the United States could profitably devote resources to new types of family (or adolescent) vacation resources; new opportunities for peer experiences for adolescents, including group trips, cultural-educational activities, camping; and new supports for induction of young people into marital life and help after the birth of their first child (to include information and guidance in furnishing and maintaining an apartment, furniture loans or grants, a practical nurse's aid after a child's birth, consumer information, more adequate family planning information).

All of this is merely illustrative of the challenge and the opportunity. Many new services are certain to emerge as the need grows and the stigma is removed.

3. *Basic educational, health, and housing services.*—This is a mixed category which partakes of developmental provision (education and some public health services) and case services (medical care). It is set apart here to note that the time comes at which some social services become so basic as to merit elaborate institutional underpinnings. At that point one often forgets that they are analytically, at least, part of social welfare.

Education, in particular, was recognized as a basic social utility so early and is given such high priority everywhere that it is often omitted in United States social service listings. This is less often the case in the developing countries where the health, education, and welfare categories are defined as the parts comprising the total social welfare system. Health is enjoying much the same recognition despite complications inherent in the professional ideologies of physicians.

All welfare societies (perhaps a better term than "welfare state") guarantee minima in these fields, but one notes the rapid raising of the level of guarantee as society's demands upon the individual are matched by resources for expansion of services.

For reasons too complex to summarize here, much of the provision of housing and housing-related services for middle and low-income people has been removed from the market place (or the market has been considerably controlled). The variations are greater than in health and education, and the extent of current provision is far less comprehensive. It is not yet possible to specify the boundaries of programs, major solutions to the market-nonmarket balance, relation of other services to the provision of dwelling space, and so on. Here, nonetheless, is a field in the midst of development and expansion, for the modern state recognizes that city man must have an adequate family dwelling as the center of his life activities.

4. *Recreational and cultural opportunity.*—Much in these realms remains in the market place; but modern societies continue to expand these functions through direct public operation and partial or complete subsidy. Sometimes the cultural or recreational program has the function of developmental provision, as in the instance of some pioneering recreational activities for senior citizens or those cultural programs which speed up the socialization of "closed-out" groups. At other times the function is directly and plainly pleasure, enhancement, and the fostering of creativity. A society's dreams and desire to enrich the lives of its citizens—with no ulterior ends in view—are also a legitimate basis for social utilities.

5. *Help, therapy, and rehabilitation as case services by right.*— Case-oriented social services remain urgent in a world of considerable personal pathology, breakdown, and problems. Social workers have developed their most refined skills in this field; some people, in fact, see social work only as a clinical profession. There are even places where social workers are not considered competent to administer the facilitating and therapeutic social services which they render.

Our long recognition as direct-service practitioners and the general community acceptance of the validity of these services do not permit us to mark time, however. While devoting energies to the development of the more generally needed facilities and resources we must continue to cope with manpower problems, inadequate expansion of many kinds of counseling and treatment programs, and large-scale failures in services to specified client groups.

Special energies and creativity have gone of late into experimentation with group and family-focused, in contrast with individual, service. While expanding community care resources and undertaking to go further along this line, we have become less fearful of group care, even for children, if it is well organized. There is significant new recognition of the secondary prevention impact of emergency and crisis services.[17] Much could be done to locate case-finding competence and emergency aid at points

17 Howard Parad, ed., *Crisis Intervention* (New York: Family Service Association of America, 1965).

where individuals are met in the important transition between life's developmental stages. Useful demonstrations of such crisis service have been carried out in day care centers, abortion clinics, and medical social work departments, for example.

PACKAGING, ADMINISTRATION, AND PRIORITY

This preliminary effort to classify social utilities and case services by function is meant only to outline possibilities and to point to tasks before us. Programs in several of the categories may at times belong together. Indeed, what is developmental provision in one part of the world may be therapeutic elsewhere.

Administrative logic, local practice, and case-finding strategy may suggest certain operational combinations. Thus, information services may usefully include emergency case services as well, whereas developmentally oriented services should often include case-finding and referral resources.

The issue is how the mix affects access and image, while deploying resources efficiently. We have argued in the United States, for example, that it is necessary to separate income maintenance from social service programs if the latter are to develop without traditional "poor law" stigma.[18]

Basic issues of service delivery thus remain to be faced once over-all policy is accepted and a philosophy of social utilities adopted. Universal answers are not likely for communities at various stages of social welfare development, but there does appear to be some convergence on the notion of planning for decentralized service delivery systems while retaining a degree of centralization to implement standards, protect over-all policy, and assure sound use of specialists.

Political, economic, ideological, and cultural differences will probably continue to sustain varied service patterns, yet the urbanization phenomenon also increases the amount of common and even shared experience. Therefore, confronting the poverty of ideas in some domains of social service and the inadequate development of obviously needed services in some places, we may find a degree of encouragement and even excitement in sharing prob-

[18] Alfred J. Kahn, "Social Services in Relation to Income Security: Introductory Notes," *Social Service Review*, XXXIX (1965), 381–89.

lems and experience. World-wide, the field of social welfare has more experience, wisdom, and inventiveness than it commands in any one place. Perhaps together we can create a system of social services fit for a planet now capable of sending a man to the moon and meeting his needs for viable environment while there.

Surely it will be self-defeating for the social work profession to allow itself to be limited to clinical and therapeutic roles, when faced with the *added* (note that one does not suggest *alternative*) responsibility of invention, promotion, and administration of social utilities. We ourselves have discovered and demonstrated to others that clinical competence does not serve a client with desperate need for a basic maintenance resource or service. And we know that social services are needed by everyone. The fact is that new social services are not being made available. The real issue is whether the social work perspective on human need will help shape those services.

In conclusion, and returning to my earlier illustration, I do not know enough about electric power grids to say whether we need emergency power generators in skyscrapers, new safety devices at key points in the interlocking system, or simply more kilowatt capacity. I do know that the man in the street cannot be accompanied by his own horsepower as he enters the subway. Social workers have significant knowledge about life in the modern world. Let us stop waiting for power failures.

New Trends in Client Participation in Urban Development

I. A VIEW FROM THE UNITED STATES

BERNARD M. SHIFFMAN

DIRECTOR, PROGRAM DEVELOPMENT AND TRAINING
COMMUNITY PROGRESS, INC., NEW HAVEN, CONN.

MOST of the discussions and seminars in which I have participated that dealt with the question of client participation in urban development never seemed to get to the central issues. Whether it is due to our "urbanist" ignorance or our fear of the "client," we tend to participate in parallel conversations, and with the best of intentions we neither define which citizens we are interested in involving or at what level. Nor do we clarify the urban issues which "they" could help the community identify and solve. Participants in these discussions have usually had different experiences and operated on a variety of assumptions and hypotheses.

My perspective, only a little modified by recent conversations with Algerian, German, English, and Australian visitors—and by my Canadian birth and education—is that of a citizen social worker in the United States who struggled with but accepted the conventional wisdom of the 1940s and 1950s. Sociological studies and doctoral dissertations piled up the evidence that low-income, poorly educated people, members of minority groups—namely, low-income Negroes—did not belong to social organizations, did not join political parties, did not vote, did not feel that they belonged, and did not participate in the little or big decisions which affected all of us, both new and old American citizens. By inference, all others were educated, trained, employed, belonged to churches, fraternal clubs, political parties, participated in the urban and political decision-making process, or at least the decisions which were made—where to put a public housing project, or a new highway, or a new school, or what to do about family planning—were made with their reactions in mind. Neither truism was true!

The conventional wisdom was based on valid observations of the results of the interlocking systems of irrelevant education, biased employment practices, inadequate housing, poor health services, inequality in opportunities, and prejudice, and hardly ever was the evidence of the causative factors explaining "why they didn't participate" presented. As a result, most of the citizens of the United States, including the social welfare specialists, believed that "the underdeveloped people" were apathetic, uninterested, and had no desire to share in the community's affairs. As cities became larger, human problems more complex, helping professions more specialized, solutions more sophisticated, the prophetic projection that more and more people did not care to participate in urban development was fulfilled. Overly specialized institutions and professions carried on the thinking and planning activities of the city. In the main, the managerial expert with full time to devote to his special area of competence and his segment of the activity controlled all phases of urban development, bringing in the "informed" citizenry for sanctioning purposes and only rarely as the base for social policy formulation.

Lewis Mumford once said:

The chief function of the city is to convert power into form, energy into culture, dead matter into the living symbols of art, biological reproduction into social creativity. The positive functions of the city cannot be performed without creating new institutional arrangements, capable of coping with the vast energies modern man now commands.[1]

This was and remains the central problem for people in cities. In the United States, we have swung in a century or two from the unmanageable town-meeting form which involved many to the managerial-expert bureaucracy which involves few, without finding the appropriate institutional arrangements capable of coping with the changes in the urban complex. Nor have we been more successful in the humanitarian field of social work. As a matter of

1 Lewis Mumford, *The City in History* (New York: Harcourt, Brace, & World, Inc., 1961), p. 571.

fact, in the brief history of social work, it began with the concept that the advantaged should do for the disadvantaged and that beneficiaries should not even participate in solving their personal problems. . . . With the enlightenment which flowed from Sigmund Freud and John Dewey, the theme for client involvement was established, but the notion that clients themselves should be encouraged to take action on their own behalf, to picket offices, organize politically, support candidates or legislation, demand new institutional arrangements to cope with their view of urban problems, was revolutionary and is currently causing psychosomatic illness for all parties engaged in the political-welfare power struggle.

In the United States, the ambivalence to the idea of client participation, which is intellectually acceptable, can only be understood if one understands that in this country the freedom to speak is tempered in action by not "too freely"; freedom to participate is conditioned by "appropriately"; the right for all to share in decision-making is with "some reservations." We Americans are conservative, unreformed humanitarians who struggle with our ambivalences. Putting it another way, how does the established leadership, whether political, social, or educational, lead and encourage citizen involvement which ultimately will direct its energies against that same sponsoring leadership or its conservative programs? This, then, is another question: How, and by whom, can the clients be organized, supported, and strengthened to act on their own behalf in solving urban problems and not become an instrument of the controlling "in-group"—city hall, planning councils—or the dissident out-group whatever the source of their leadership?

I have no answer to this dilemma or to the question of what are the appropriate institutional arrangements to handle our urban developmental problems. There are no simple, single answers. I do believe that we must give up, if with some pain, our conventional wisdom about clients, about decision-making, and about expert knowledge. "There are no experts in moral issues," says Charles Frankel, and most of our urban problems, such as the distribution of health services, are moral problems. Economic or material poverty in the United States is not a production problem, it is a distribution problem—it is a moral issue.

Too few lay citizens in any of our economic class groups have been involved in the public dialogues which identify the problems or involved in community activity which makes adjustments or finds solutions to these problems. The manner in which the economically disadvantaged people participate or fail to participate in community development is a special case of the universal phenomenon. In the last five years, in the United States of America, a little more attention and concern have been given to involvement of the poor as a direct result of enlightened welfare legislation, the civil rights movement, and a worsening state of affairs in the worn-out urban centers of Cleveland, Cicero, Harlem, and the South Side of Chicago.

I believe this is a shortsighted position unless we give equal attention to involving the rest of the community. But let us examine four ways in which clients have been involved in urban development and the recent trends.

1. *As consumers of services.*—As a consumer the citizen may use a service or, if he has a choice, he may reject the service. When he bands together with others informally to reject the service, he can modify or eliminate it, or create new services, provided the managers are sensitive to the necessity for adjustment. For example, the manner in which clients have used the emergency departments of hospitals has resulted in a reorganization of medical services in many hospitals.

While this is the oldest form of involvement and is often misread by the actionists as apathy, some of the current trends include: more formalized consumer activity, which has resulted in the organization of credit unions for the low-incomers; buying clubs of a cooperative nature (traditionally developed by university-oriented, middle-class groups) to mitigate the problem that the poor pay more and get less; school boycotts to bring attention either to the poor quality of education for the poor or to the lack of integration; and group visits to the legislature to give the "consumer's view" of the law. This last type of activity is most often stimulated by an outside organization or group and is rarely self-generated. While very effective, it represents only potential political power since clients or consumers of service are difficult to organize for a variety of reasons, one of which is the fear of reprisal while another has been the failure to support leadership for a consumers' lobby.

2. *As citizens, taxpayers, or voluntary contributors.*—The "poor" client or beneficiary of services traditionally has been discouraged from voting or from participating in community affairs. While he was an indirect taxpayer, his interests were rarely considered in tax laws, programs, or services, and although proportionately he may have contributed his "fair share" to voluntary organizations seeking financial support, he was rarely given access to decision-making regarding policy, programs, or services. The combination of civil rights activities and a new concern for the legal, constitutional rights of all citizens has mushroomed voter registration and developed new action organizations. Since social welfare activity has become a vital part of the formal political process, the newly recruited and special-group-organized voter is in a position to make local officials more responsive to what could be the "swing vote."

Another trend is the increased effort to organize welfare clients and those eligible for public welfare as a protest lobby group which, exercising their legal rights, might even destroy the existing bureaucratic system in order to obtain a type of guaranteed family income. Again, an elite leadership group is utilizing the self-interest of consumers to gain a goal from which they believe all would benefit. In the United States, in the past year, welfare clients have instituted a national organization which seeks to function as a poor people's lobby, working for a guaranteed annual income and using political power, picketing, conferences, and sit-ins. This is a most significant trend which is producing severe ambivalence, especially since there has been some talk of organizing welfare clients in unions. The autonomous (?) organizations of the poor have refocused attention on the question: What are the inalienable rights of American citizens?

3. *As employees.*—In the United States, the community development programs, as they grew larger in the expanding urban

universe, were selected, influenced, and tended to project the ideas of the staff and the managers of the service, recruited, with the workers, from the upper-middle-class, highly mobile, better-educated segment of society. This tended to exclude the people for whom social welfare programs were planned. In the physical planning of cities, on the other hand, the middle-class, organized business and citizen groups whose self-interest was involved made sure they were represented and participated on both staff and policy levels. They were there and they protected their interests—which, in my opinion, accounts for the failures in public housing and slum clearance.

Through the 1964 antipoverty legislation, a new trend has been initiated. People from the low-income group have been recruited and trained, and are now employees of the community action agency. As employees, they can to some degree determine the nature, the quality, and the method of delivering the services which are being planned. Antipoverty legislation is currently being processed; if passed, it will greatly widen the use of low-income or client participants in public service employment. Entry jobs complete with training programs are being planned so that public and private agencies which work in the public interest may be adequately staffed. This is a trend which will grow, first because of its intrinsic value, and second because it is the only way the new positions needed in the service field can be adequately staffed. A valid method of involving clients in urban development, it poses the question of how free can the former neighborhood leader be when he is acting as a staff member of the "establishment."

4. *As members of advisory groups and policy decision-making boards.*—Most of our organizations operate with either advisory groups or boards of directors. These devices usually provide community sanction for the activity. If they are advisory, and the service is in the public sector, they function as community sounding boards and feedback devices and interpret the agencies' program to the community while bringing reactions, needs, and concerns to the enterprise so that programs can be undertaken by the administration at will. The management powers of boards of directors are legislated by law or are included in the articles of incorporation.

Unlike the advisory board, the directors usually have the authority to employ the chief executive and hold fiscal control over the budget. In a few of the membership-type social agencies, members actually serve on boards or advisory committees. In most instances, the community agencies or organizations, governmental or voluntary, involved in community development in the United States recruit prestigious or wealthy citizens to serve on these groups. Infrequently, an "ordinary citizen" is recruited and serves as much as a symbol as he does as a member in an unfamiliar atmosphere. In the main, we have failed to develop consumer participation in either voluntary or public systems.

The antipoverty program in its vigorous experimental period, before 1966, initiated the concept that "the poor" must have a real share in policy-making and sit with voting power on the community action boards of directors. After making a vigorous step in the right direction, if not in a reasonable fashion, and after only one year of attempting "instantaneous citizen involvement on a policy level," which did not work, and as a result of political attacks by worried mayors and frightened city political machines, the Office of Economic Opportunity retreated to safer ground: first, to "reasonable representation"; and second, to "pulling the financial rug out of the community action program." In spite of this retreat, the American urban development system will not be able to return to "excluding clients as usual."

In recent years there has been an extension of the community or neighborhood council format in which citizens band together, usually to improve the neighborhood, to "fight downtown" or City Hall. These have rarely been mass movements, but rather the enlightened elite of a neighborhood who attempt to draw in people on specific issues or who give the illusion of power by claiming to speak for the community. In the United States, with increased segregation along class, educational, religious, and racial lines, the neighborhoods which need these citizen councils most have the least experience, skill, or leadership to organize themselves.

Official response to the power of the organized—or the illusion of the organized—has encouraged the development of new organizations, or disorganizations, many of which do not know how to use the community machinery or structures to get attention for their "solutions" to the urban problems. This results in and will increasingly create chaos in the streets.

Two additional trends should be noted. After a lapse of many years, the public welfare departments in a number of states have recognized that client advisory groups can do much to help administrators and managers operate a more efficient and effective program. In New York City, a staff is being recruited and trained for this new function. Staff are too often surprised at the untapped skills that clients bring to bear on problems and their desire and willingness to assist the department improve its services. In addition, some of the more daring agencies have recruited clients to serve as consultants on new services as well as to function as trainers in staff development programs.

The real question becomes one of value and goals. Noticeably lacking in the antipoverty programs—and therefore they failed to accomplish what they might have—was the ability to specify the intended outcome, which leads one to select the types of involvement that have the maximum possibility of succeeding. Specifying the objectives of client involvement is rarely done. The nature of the problem which has been selected for attention is another critical factor which needs careful analysis before formulas for deciding who should be involved in decision-making can be established.

The pressing urban problems or issues in urban development depend on one's values and frame of reference. Each time I am forced to enumerate them, I arrive at the same list:

1. Our involvement in war is the most pressing international, national, and urban development problem. In effect, it determines and limits our commitment to social reform. All other programs or services are retarded by this social and economic waste. At what level do we involve client beneficiaries in this urban problem?

2. Another series of urban problems seem to worsen the more we work at them; housing; transportation and traffic; water supply; air pollution; and education. The need for a universal liberal education has never been more acute than now as we are working for universal suffrage, yet we are concentrating currently on raising the quality of, and including in, a technical and vocational

education, and not on improving the quality of life. At what levels and in what manner can we involve clients in these major issues?

3. One of the chief urban and rural development problems is the inability to distribute income with social justice. In the United States, blessed with an affluent economy, it is a moral issue and no longer a problem of production. Who deals with moral and value issues in an oganized society, especially when there are no experts on moral issues?

4. Poverty, in style of life as well as in financial resources, is another urban problem. The director of the Office of Economic Opportunity has projected a date by which economic poverty can be eliminated. Little attention has been given to the quality of living. Who should be involved?

5. The large urban complex with big governmental units, big business, big churches, big social organizations, larger hospitals, huge welfare departments—with every indication that they will get bigger—presents the problem of the need to decentralize authority, power, and decision-making.

6. It is my conviction that no one problem can be pulled out of the urban knot and given priority but that the problems of urban living are all part of the same cloth, requiring coordination at the top planning level and integration of all human services at the neighborhood level. How, then, do we involve clients in this process?

Instantaneous client participation is only a beginning. The real involvement of the client is a long, slow process. Providing the chance to meet and talk, either through election or selection, does not guarantee involvement. It is only a first step. There is no single solution to the city's problems. Client participation is not a panacea; nor is it a guarantee that it will make the work of government or agencies easier. Nor should it be seen as a substitute for the professional urban worker's continued responsibility for pressing for social justice through legislative and cultural reforms, for adapting and modifying the organizations through which people are helped. In all probability, involving people will make work harder, more frustrating, slower. But it may be the "critical" way to a real "pay-off," and the "people" do represent the largest reservoir of unused resources for community development.

II. A VIEW FROM SOUTHERN ITALY

ALBINO SACCO

HEAD OF SOCIAL ACTIVITIES SERVICE INSTITUTE
FOR THE DEVELOPMENT OF SOCIAL BUILDING, ROME

THE PROBLEM of southern Italy is due for the most part to geographical conditions (mountainous or hilly areas with few plainlands suitable for agriculture, and those few isolated from one another) and to historical factors (after the fall of the Roman Empire, and with the end of the unity of the Mediterranean world, southern Italy remained completely peripheral vis-à-vis Europe).

Since the unification of Italy in 1860, the causes of depression in the South were investigated by many scholars and attributed, in turn, to historical, geographical, and psychological factors, but the political and legislative measures taken to relieve the depression, dealing only with partial aspects of the problem, did not produce concrete results. The disequilibrium between North and South progressively increased.

Indeed, the political unity of the nation favored the northern areas, already more advantageously situated than the predominantly agricultural South because of the greater availability of liquid capital resources, the ease of communication both internally and with the rest of Europe, and the more abundant supply of labor educationally equipped to acquire the vocational training so necessary in an era of rapid industrial development.

For these reasons, and others, prior to the Second World War there existed northern Italy, characterized by a rich and intensive agriculture and industry of considerable dimensions, alongside southern Italy, with little industry, a fundamentally poor and only slightly diversified, extensive agriculture, and with large, private, landed estates and numerous small holdings.

This persisting lack of balance, is an enormous problem for

Italy, especially when it is considered that more than one third (18,000,000) of the entire population lives in the South. The problem of southern Italy was first confronted globally and systematically in the immediate postwar period when, with the fascist regime fallen, the efforts of the Resistance movement, the liberation of the country, and the constitution of the republic established the conditions in which a drive could be made to clear away long-standing injustices and to achieve, through the development of the more depressed areas, a higher level of social justice.

The first move toward developing southern Italy in the postwar period came from the people themselves, and was revolutionary in character. This popular movement took the form of the occupation of land by peasants and was followed by land-reform measures which considerably reduced large estate ownership, leading to the widespread distribution of small and medium-sized farms, organization of agricultural cooperatives, and so forth. Agricultural reform has without doubt contributed to the economic and social development of southern Italy, although by itself it could not resolve the complex problem of a vast, densely populated area in which there was manifest disparity between the potentialities of agricultural resources and population.

The first global public intervention was undertaken by the Cassa per il Mezzogiorno (Southern Italy Development Fund). Established in 1950, this is a public agency whose function is to coordinate and stimulate economic development. The purpose of the Cassa is to supplement "ordinary" government intervention with "special" interventions, financed from vast appropriations voted by government legislation for the development of southern Italy, whose precise objective was to eliminate the disequilibrium between social and income levels in the South and those in the rest of the country.

The Cassa operates in the public works sector (roads, port facilities, water supply, school building), provides grants to industry, agriculture, and tourism, and promotes vocational training, social, and educational project. In addition, the state has undertaken commitments of an entrepreneur nature in the South, providing large volumes of investment capital through the Industrial Reconstruction Institute for the establishment of large-scale industrial projects.

The approach to the development of southern Italy has, however, undergone a process of continuous evolution in the past twenty years, passing through at least two phases. In the first phase the approach was essentially one of "aid." In the face of the serious depression and the scarcity of local resources, the development initiatives were intended to raise living standards so far as possible, establishing a network of infrastructures throughout the area which, together with special incentives, would encourage the free flow of investment capital from the North for productive projects. This phase may be defined as one of "external intervention."

In the second phase, the approach was based on a more clearly defined appreciation of the scope of the problem and of the fact that something more than widespread interventions and incentives was necessary to set in motion a self-propulsive mechanism. It was therefore considered advantageous to concentrate the provision of infrastructures, incentives, and public investment in a few districts ("development poles") in which the potential was greater, by virtue of their geographical location, ease of communication, social traditions, relative availability of resources, and existing industrial plants. From these poles, it was hoped, development would spread throughout the rest of the area.

With the site of the poles determined and with the consequent organization of "Consortia" for the industrialization areas and nuclei, local enterprise began for the first time to assume a primary role in the development policy for southern Italy. The Consortia, set up by local authorities and business interests, were entrusted with the management of the areas and nuclei and with planning economic and town development. This phase may be described as one of "multiple (external and internal) intervention."

In the light of the experience and the results obtained from the policy adopted for the development of southern Italy in the last five years, the following seem to be the more immediate requirements:

1. It is necessary to accelerate the devolution to local public and private bodies of responsibility for the development process

in their areas, extending their field of responsibility to ordinary government intervention, experimenting and creating new and more efficient channels of participation.

2. Close coordination is necessary between special (development) intervention and ordinary intervention, and between the development of southern Italy and that of the country as a whole. That is to say, global planning is required, at both the national and local level, of all interventions in all sectors.

Social work, which has expanded considerably in Italy since 1946, has from the very beginning been particularly committed to the South, not only to welfare activity but also to stimulation of social and cultural development, to the encouragement of participation in development initiatives originating outside the area, and to the promotion and support of initiatives undertaken independently. In particular, public and private bodies operating in southern Italy have extensively adopted the methodology of community development, defined as "the process of creating conditions of economic and social progress of the entire community, with its active participation, and with maximum reliance on its own initiative." [1] In the various situations in which this methodology has been applied, the professional social worker has been engaged directly with the client (individual, group, or community) as the one principally responsible, among a mixed team of specialists, for the process of participation, understood as the personal involvement of individuals and groups in local community development.

Another important aspect of the role of the social services, and one which is also valuable from the viewpoint of client participation, is the social worker's function of observing and reporting the human and social problems and needs of the community and of its individual members and of advising specialists regarding the precise approach to these problems. Sociologists admit that the recent growth in the social sciences and social research in Italy is without doubt due to this effort by social workers to identify and report problems.

[1] *Social Progress through Community Development* (United Nations, 1955), Chap. I.

Social workers have played a particular role as "promoters of participation" in three instances especially.

Agricultural reform areas.—The reform agencies, after an initial phase characterized by measures and projects of a purely "welfare" nature, subsequently adopted a policy aimed at encouraging individuals and communities to set in motion a process of autonomous community development, involving not only the economic aspects but also those concerned with the social life of the new communities. These objectives are pursued by a wide range of social service personnel among whom the social worker plays the most important role.

The Abruzzo pilot scheme.—In 1957 UNRRA-CASA, in collaboration with CEPAS [2] and under the auspices of UNESCO, carried out a community development scheme covering twelve mountain communes in Abruzzo. The object was to demonstrate:

1. That existing legislation contemplated assistance that was sometimes not even applied for, and sometimes badly utilized
2. That the existing institutions should be recognized, supported, and, in certain cases, reviewed and recognized, but only when maximum effort is made to contribute to their efficiency
3. That the effectiveness and permanence of results achieved vary inversely with the amount of effort originating outside the area
4. That the precise awareness of the situation by the population concerned is a most important step toward relief of a depressed condition; and that the problems of depressed areas can only be resolved by those affected, especially when the population although afflicted, is not completely overwhelmed by these problems
5. That action carried out with recognition of these factors has a natural "spread" potential.

The working plan was based entirely on the presumption that the program would provide for the gradual participation of the

[2] Centro di Educazione Professionale per Assistenti Sociali (Center for the Vocational Training of Social Workers), Rome.

community, after it had been provided with appropriate informational and social stimuli, especially by the social worker. The latter role was divided into three different functions: group organization; advice concerning welfare organizations; source of information for other social service personnel.

OEEC-AEP scheme in Sardinia.—The area covered by this scheme (177,000 hectares; 110,000 inhabitants; 41 communes) may be considered as typical of the Mediterranean basin as regards the mountainous nature of the country with its irrigable plains, variable climate, predominance of a subsistence-based family agriculture, inadequate food and health facilities. A development scheme was studied by the European Productivity Agency of OEEC and then implemented by a committee of Italian and international agencies.

The scheme was carried out by a specially constituted body, comprising a director, seven section heads, and some seventy assistants who were economists, agricultural experts, social workers, and sociologists. The work was divided into three sectors:

(*a*) Agriculture, with informational services regarding agriculture and rural domestic economy; (*b*) education and social work, including adult education, vocational training, information and audiovisual aids, and social services; (*c*) craft industries and small businesses.

The scheme was therefore fairly wide in scope, with the main objective that of helping the population to break the vicious circle of a completely enclosed family economy; skeptical of any offer of outside assistance.

One limitation of these experiences is that they are fragmentary in character and have slight relevance to the important social, economic, and town-planning problems which are still presented by the development of an area as vast as southern Italy. On the other hand, the limitations should be considered in the context of the conception of the development of southern Italy dominant at the time when these schemes were carried out, when discussion of the interrelationships of the various levels of planning (local, district, regional, national) and of the various sectors of planning (economic, town-planning, social) was not as advanced as it is today in Italy.

A recent planning scheme at the district level carried out by ISES [3] in Calabria is an interesting example of the new trends in client participation in development. An area of Calabria comprising 28 communes (for an aggregate of 80,000 inhabitants) asked ISES to conduct a study for a social, economic, and town-planning development program. The study was made by a large group of the Institute's specialists (social workers, sociologists, economists, town-planning experts) with the active participation of the local government authorities of all the communes concerned.[4]

Economic and social conditions in the Soverato District may be considered typical of those in most of southern Italy. An area without exceptional development prospects, the district nevertheless has some real prospects of improvement in agricultural production, the possibility of more tourism, and some hope of establishing industrial projects on a modest scale.

The working assumptions for the Soverato District program allowed for a good measure of social initiative. They provided that the implementation of the economic and town-planning development program should be accompanied by planned intervention—together with, and in addition to, administrative, economic, and town-planning intervention—intended to mobilize the conscious participation of the population in its formulation, direction, and operation.

In order to give an inkling of the task involved it may be helpful to present a synthesis of the social and cultural develop-

[3] The Istituto per lo Sviluppo dell'Edilizia Sociale (Institute for the Development of Social Building) is a public statutory institute set up in 1963 as a result of the reconstitution of UNRRA-CASAS. Since 1946 intensive work has been done by ISES in social building and social services; in the first phase the objectives were the reconstruction and reorganization of the rural areas most badly damaged during the Second World War; subsequently, new formulas were applied in the social services and in social, economic, and town-planning programs, especially in the depressed areas of the South. ISES, whose most significant achievements have taken place in the rural areas of southern Italy, has always maintained, ahead of official town-planning thinking, that the "rural area-urban area" dichotomy can be overcome by an integrated concept of an urban-rural "continuum" which contemplates the diffusion of the essential features of urban, cultural, and social life.

[4] The study was published by ISES under the title *Il Comprensorio di Soverato* (Experimental and Methodological Contribution to Planning in Southern Italy) by La Nuova Italia, Florence, in 1965.

ment program for the district, seen as an essential part of a planning process, and of the practical working techniques, some of which postulate the specialist services of the social worker. In general, the objectives are to achieve:

a) The transition from an archaic, rural, social structure to an integrated, modern, rural and industrial social structure

b) The organic development of the district's economy, social life, and town-planning structure

c) The control by the population of the dynamics of development, with "control" being understood as direct intervention in the systematic formulation of program, an understanding of development legislation, and executive participation in operation of the program.

In order to attain these ends the necessity was perceived of programing the gradual transformation of those aspects of social life that could hinder the development process, and the gradual orientation of those aspects which were considered to be favorable to achievement of the objectives. Specific objectives were established:

1. In order to remove the characteristic passive and fatalistic, and therefore irrational, attitude of the individual to the sources of production: (*a*) productive association; (*b*) rationalization of cultivation, and mechanization; (*c*) technical training in agriculture suitable for all who work on the land

2. In order to counter traditionalism and the lack of confidence: (*a*) increase in, and more equitable distribution of, income; (*b*) higher educational levels for all generations; (*c*) increased efficiency of the social security institutions

3. In order to remove the reactionary attitude and to modify the ambivalent attitude toward authority (charismatic concept of authority, personalistic and private interpretation of the function of government, and so on: (*a*) eradication of the existing "occult" power of the hegemonic classes, and open war on preferential treatment; (*b*) strengthening of electoral and representational arrangements; (*c*) encouragement of local activity of political parties and national organizations

4. In order to remove exclusive and antiassociative attitudes of the individual, due largely to the concept of the family as the only social entity capable of affording protection: (*a*) introduction of the individual to the notion of belonging to the community; (*b*) introduction of women into the extra-family social context; (*c*) stimulation of the active interest of the clergy in the development program

5. In order to guide the dominant value of individualism toward socialization so that it may contribute to direct participation in the civic development of the social environment; selection of local people for the leadership of political and business organizations.

In order to achieve each objective there were then defined the necessary instruments, some of which were new institutionalized forms of participation: a democratically constituted committee to increase cooperative activity; an elected executive committee to manage public investment projects. Other instruments relate to technical or financial initiatives formulated to influence the social and cultural life of the population; a special agricultural credit system to assist collective associations; adoption of priority criteria for public investment in education, with special regard to technical and industrial schools; building of hospitals, day nurseries, sports centers. Still other instruments concern direct initiatives in social education, largely entrusted to the professional social worker: civic education centers for adults and young people; social centers; welfare institutions. Lastly, there are instruments relating to social services, also entrusted principally to social workers but not performed within the context of formal structures: women's committees to study family problems, the education of young children, the work of women in and outside the home; social service specialist activity to stimulate the interest of the individual in the program; promotion of group and community activity to solve problems of common interest.

The experience gained by Italy, like that gleaned in other countries, has demonstrated that an integrated approach to regional problems and to economic policy measures is not alone sufficient for launching a development process or for sustaining one already

under way. Social action as an integral part of the program and
of its implementation is also necessary in order to overcome the
inertia of populations—inertia which all too often is created by
the paternalistic character of intervention formulated externally
and which is often limited to sectors that do not take into account
the choices and initiatives of individuals and communities. Social
action is also required to offset the shortage of entrepreneurs and
the inadequacies of local authorities, both so often characteristic of underdeveloped areas.

Modern social sciences and advanced public intervention
policies, in fact, attribute their growing importance to the effects
of interaction between the various aspects of the social environment. At the same time, the human factor, in the broadest sense
of the term, is reassessed, in that any action for increasing production, public utilities, consumption, does not achieve satisfactory results without the active participation of the population
and without an adequate understanding and control of the in-
dividual-environmental dynamics associated with this participation.

The criteria of a policy based on incentives, by which it is
intended to stimulate free enterprise on the part of producers,
have little effect in communities where the economic, social, and
cultural conditions are not at a level which can guarantee an
adequate response to the incentives.

A planning policy that is intended to raise the minimum levels
capable of allowing an effective freedom of productive enterprise
must program certain fundamental initial choices. If this policy
does not have the assent of the population, the development
programs would be carried out by means of technocratic measures which, formulated outside the environment in which the
social development is to occur, would not actively influence the
social-subjective factor, thus failing in one of its principal objectives and becoming precisely a policy of coercion, setting in
motion processes beyond control.

The activity of social workers, which is guided among others
by the principle of the "participation of the client in the therapy,"
must perforce attempt to apply this principle in the context of the
planned development of depressed areas.

III. A VIEW FROM A DEVELOPING COUNTRY

ALI AKBAR

LECTURER, COLLEGE OF SOCIAL WELFARE AND
RESEARCH CENTER, DACCA UNIVERSITY
DACCA, EAST PAKISTAN

THE CONCEPT of participation is not new. As an enabling process, social work has always been concerned with helping the client to help himself. But the characteristic methods of organization and administration of the social services were such that the principle of "beggars should not be choosers" was implicit in most of them. Those who were in need of social services were regarded as a separate class, and had no direct influence on their organization or administration. The gap between recipients and providers of services was clear and distinct.

But the old dichotomy is difficult to maintain today. A great many social services are now provided under the auspices of government as a right. The most classic illustration of this trend is the provision of a minimal income to citizens through contributory social insurance rather than through poor relief.

The concern today in the Western countries is with measures designed to offer enlarged opportunities to the beneficiaries of services to participate in the organization and guidance of these services. In a young country such as mine, Pakistan, an even more fundamental concern is with measures to allow the collaboration of all citizens in building a satisfying and harmonious community life for all. If the enlargement of opportunities of one group is preceived as the curtailment of the opportunities of another, there will inevitably be tensions. Participation, in the final analysis, implies sharing of power, power to make policy and to make decisions for either the allocation or the reorganization of resources, and this cannot be done without mutual understanding and cooperation if tensions and social disharmony are to be avoided.

When the vast majority of the citizens, as in most underdeveloped countries, are beneficiaries of services, the term "citizen participation" is perhaps more significant and meaningful than "client participation." The principle of participation becomes a focus of concern when a section of the citizens expresses a lack of confidence in the established institutions of the society because of a feeling of nonrepresentation in the decision-making. Even when there is not dissatisfaction, participation provides a method to mobilize popular support and cooperation to achieve a national goal.

In advanced Western countries, especially in the United States, it is now being realized that without the active cooperation of the target population, program goals are difficult to achieve. It is gradually being accepted that for the realization of program goals, as well as for the promotion of social harmony, there should be adequate linkage and consistent communication between the beneficiaries and the organizers of services. This is sought through "maximum feasible participation" by the beneficiaries of services in policy-making, in program planning, and even in administration.[1] The principle of participation is regarded as a desirable social goal as well as a tool to further program goals.

In the underdeveloped countries, especially in the region from which I come, interest in client participation stems from the urgent need to mobilize popular support and contributions to economic and social development efforts in order to establish a self-sustaining economy. Most of these countries are very poor, but their governments have accepted the responsibility, "within the organization and resources of each country," to provide for the basic economic and social well-being of the people. Most governments have undertaken long-range plans for economic and social development; consequently, the major programs are, directly or indirectly, sponsored and administered by the government. The voluntary sector, though significant, is very limited in its over-all impact. In advanced countries citizen participation occurs through a variety of organizations, many of them nongovernmental. In underdeveloped countries, citizen participation has to be encour-

1 Perhaps the provision of client participation in the Community Action Program of the antipoverty program in the United States is a representative reflection of this new trend.

aged and promoted through collaboration of citizens in government-sponsored programs and programs of self-help. Thus the Second Five-Year Plan of Pakistan asserts:

An immense responsibility rests upon the leadership in the Government to show the way, to demonstrate faith and confidence, and to fashion the public service into an effective instrument for assisting the people in all walks of life to make their own contribution to the country's development.[2]

Since most programs of social development in these countries are directed toward helping people adjust to changing social and economic conditions and inducing them to accept new ideas and practices, it is of prime importance that people have the proper understanding of the purposes of these programs and are motivated to achieve the goals of the programs. Most governmental programs attempt to provide for participation of people as one way of eliciting their cooperation and contribution.

Governments have moved forward "democratic decentralization" as one way of encouraging and promoting participation. Not only have the local governmental institutions been endowed with considerable power and autonomy, but they are also increasingly being used as agencies to communicate with people and to secure their cooperation with, and contribution to, national development programs. The notable examples of this trend are the basic democracies of Pakistan and the Panchyet Raj of India. Through community development and other socioeconomic projects, the governments are attempting to mobilize resources on a self-help basis to improve the lot of the people.

Within this general trend, the theme "client participation in urban development" acquires a new significance, especially for the underdeveloped countries, where the process of urbanization is very rapid and its impact on the social and economic organization of the society is much more drastic and far-reaching.

We can view urban development as a response to urbanization, an apparently inevitable consequence of industrialization. Urban development seeks, through various measures, to create a satisfying community life and social harmony for the city dwellers. The fun-

[2] Government of Pakistan, *The Second Five Year Plan* (Karachi: Planning Commission, Government of Pakistan, 1960), p. 105.

damental problem is comprehensive planning of the physical environment and the organization of social life to provide adequate housing, public utilities and social services, slum clearance, and so forth. Client participation in relation to these programs should be understood in the broader sense as citizen participation, that is, the exertion of influence on the organization and administration of services and activities through a variety of channels.

We must bear in mind the nature and magnitude of the problems which are characteristic of urban development, and the institutional and organizational framework within which they are handled. My own experience is limited to Pakistan, and especially to her Eastern wing.

URBAN DEVELOPMENT IN PAKISTAN

Pakistan is still predominantly rural,[3] but the process of urbanization is very rapid. During 1951-61 the urban population increased by 56.4 percent; in some cities, the population doubled during this period. While in 1951, there were only 282 urban localities—cities and towns with more than 5,000 inhabitants—there were 393 in 1961. This rapid growth is expected to continue as industrialization and economic development continue.

An important feature is the great increase of population in the larger cities and the appearance of several new towns and industrial centers. Some satellite towns have been specially built for the rehabilitation of refugees and displaced persons. Within cities, growth takes place both by making more effective use of land and by spreading outward toward the rural areas. Usually the old parts of the city, with narrow streets, congested houses, unsanitary and unhygienic living conditions, are bypassed during this process. Redevelopment of these parts is deemed to be too expensive.

The growth of cities is accelerated by the heavy migration of rural people, many of whom cannot bring their families. Many city dwellers do not identify with the city as their real home; they look to it as a place to earn a living, and expect ultimately to return to their villages. While the trend among the higher- and

[3] Only 7 percent of the population in East Pakistan and 22 percent in West Pakistan lived in urban areas in 1965. There are about 70 cities with a population of 25,000 and over in a country of 112,000,000 people. Only two cities, both in the West wing, have more than a million people.

middle-income groups is to build houses in cities, in most communities they have not yet been able to build stable, integrated neighborhoods. A large section of the city is occupied by housing estates for government or semigovernment officials, many of whom are very mobile. There is also a significant number of shelterless persons, a floating population, who build their makeshift huts on vacant land or on the periphery of the city. By natural selection as well as by planning, different parts of a city tend to be occupied by different social classes. Social segregation is more visible and distinct in our cities than it is in the rural areas.

The rapid growth is creating overwhelming difficulties in providing even minimum housing, public utilities, roads, and communication to the city dwellers. The problems are so severe and the resources are so limited that most programs of urban development have to be included as part of the long-range national development plan. The Third Five-Year Plan in Pakistan estimated that the minimum requirement for urban dwellings during 1965-70 would be 1,550,00 units, but it did not expect to meet more than 50 percent of these urgent needs. Under such severely limiting conditions, the determination of priorities and the phasing of programs have necessitated painful decisions on the allocation of resources.

Urban development and citizen participation.—For urban development, a city can hardly be regarded as an autonomous unit, the concern only of its occupants. The city serves, in addition to its residents, the people of a whole region. A city is usually the administrative headquarters of a district or a subdivision, and provides educational and health facilities for a region. Much of what is done for the city is often decided by national or provincial authorities. The major public utilities are organized by departments of the provincial government. The residents have no direct influence on the policies or organization of these services. Their influence is expressed through their elected representatives in the legislature, who determine over-all policies and provide a legal and financial framework for their operation.

The government has introduced the system of basic democracies in order to furnish local forums to influence decisions, to insure "territorial priority" to national plans, to insure official responsiveness to popular demand, and to associate people in program planning at different levels. This system includes tiers of councils at successive levels, composed of the representatives of the people and of the government departments. The smallest unit, a town committee, serves from 1,000 to 1,500 people, an indication of the grass-roots character of the system. The councils are designed not to be "instruments for obtaining consent" for decisions taken at the national or provincial headquarters, but to be agencies for planning which originate at the grass roots. Nevertheless, in spite of the best intentions, the effectiveness of popular representation is limited by the responsiveness of individual administrative officials. The councils tend to become advisory bodies under these circumstances.

Another new trend is toward opening public relations units in governmental departments in order to foster communication and make people aware of the purposes of various national development programs.

Local government and citizen participation.—The unit of the city government is the municipality, established as an agent of the provincial government, with limited responsibilities and functions. Its resources are limited, often dependent on provincial grants. Many of its functions, such as water supply, sewerage, road construction and maintenance, are also fulfilled by departments of the provincial government or by separate autonomous bodies which operate on a larger scale. Its impact is therefore limited.

Since members of the municipality are elected, municipal government is often the monopoly of the politicians. Prominent citizens and business leaders usually do not directly participate in municipal activities. The marginal city dwellers, the transients, seldom take an active interest in city government. The problems of the poor are acute, and their experience with the municipality is such that they do not expect much from it. Some politically strong or organized groups may bring pressure to bear on the municipality through an agitational approach, but in general there is a perceptible lack of the kind of citizen involvement needed to make the municipality really effective. Although the system of basic democracies has broadened the base of local participation and has created enthusiasm for long-range local planning through liberal grants channeled through the works program, its impact so far as creating a keen and alert urban citizenry is concerned, is still inadequate. Apathy and indifference, coupled with the unstable and transitory nature of human relationships in urban areas, make it very difficult to carry on organized local efforts.

Physical planning and citizen participation.—In the absence of local or regional planning, the rapid process of urbanization has resulted in the haphazard growth of cities and slums. Now all big cities have an improvement trust or other autonomous development bodies. Several cities have master plans, but in the absence of up-to-date laws for city and regional planning, the status of these plans is not clear.

The main functions of the improvement trust are comprehensive city planning, development and allocation of land, and slum clearance. In spite of an apparent systematic approach, lack of foresight and inexperience often create unexpected problems. Problems of parking space, traffic control, drainage, and so forth, are frequently the unplanned consequences of planned development. Another kind of problem stems from lack of coordination between units of several departments. The improvement trust is purely a physical planning agency. There is no agency for over-all coordination and planning of all agencies of urban development.

The improvement trust has wide powers to acquire lands for redevelopment and reallocation. The first target of redevelopment is usually the ouskirts of the city where slums grow, and therefore the victims of redevelopment are the poor slum dwellers. Lands are acquired and compensation paid, but frequently the residents do not move out without resistance. The housing shortage is so acute and land values so exorbitant that residents try to hold on until forcibly dispossessed. Pathetic scenes of police evicting people from their homes are not uncommon.

Who are these evictees? Some of them are, of course, owners of acquired property. They are usually given alternative lands. But the alternative land may be unsuitable or the temptation of cash may be such that some of these former home owners will become part of the floating population. Many of the evictees are renters or unauthorized occupants on the already acquired land. They are refugees or rural migrants. They are day laborers, hawkers, ricksha pullers, beggars. They do not have the resources, even with modest government assistance, to improve the locality in conformity with the value of the land and the over-all city development plan.

There is no citizen involvement in this type of city planning. But what might be "feasible participation" in such a situation? How can the national plan and the interest of the residents be reconciled? The local residents cannot be involved directly in policy-making or program development at the national level. Participation during the execution of the project tends to be a psychological device for getting acceptance and thereby legitimation of a program which would uproot them from their homes and neighborhood. The question of participation is relevant at the point of reallocation, to reduce the hardships and difficulties of the residents affected by the project. But resources are so limited that there is practically no worthwhile reallocation plan. Everywhere there is a waiting list—for alternative land, for public housing, for resettlement. As a result, the improvement trust usually relies on the law of acquisition. Even for the reallocation of developed land, the demand is so great that frequently the choice is made by lottery to avoid making any decision at all.

Urban community development and citizen participation.—In almost all towns there are government-sponsored urban community development projects. A project serves communities of fifteen to twenty thousand people. Two social workers and from three to five auxiliary workers are assigned by the provincial directorate of social welfare to help people operate much-needed social services on a self-help basis. The workers, with modest development funds, concentrate on obtaining the participation of the people in assessment of needs, mobilization of resources, and organization of services. Within each project there are a number of voluntary agencies in the fields of recreation, health, adult literacy, vocational training, and social education. A project council is formed with representatives of these agencies, prominent citizens, and members of the basic democracies. The council serves as the planning and coordinating body for the project area in relation to its social welfare needs.

The major objective of urban community development is to

enable residents to create an integrated community at the neigh-boorhood level through mutual cooperation in self-help programs, and to prevent further deterioration of the physical environment and of social life. It seeks to foster a sense of civic responsibility and neighborliness. It also provides a forum for communication and opportunities for the growth of leadership. The major impact of this joint collaboration has been to give the residents a sense of belonging in an alien urban environment, away from close relatives and the integrated neighborhood of a rural area. Through participation in mutual self-help programs and the activities of local agencies, people develop an awareness and confidence in urban living.

But these programs, especially in slum areas, only touch the marginal aspects of the problems confronted by the poor. The poor are preoccupied with the overwhelming problems of earning a living, and these programs are apt to be of little significance to them. In order to offer incentives for participation, several programs, such as cottage craft centers, sewing clubs, vocational training centers, and so on, are organized in urban community development projects to emphasize the economic benefits of these programs.

Problems and prospects of citizen participation.—We can see that the general trend is toward the acceptance of citizen participation as a desirable democratic value, and also as a means to further program goals. There are various forms: direct participation in policy-making and program development, usually at the local level; participation through representation, usually at the national level; and participation in mutual self-help programs, usually at the neighborhood level in the urban community development projects. Participation, to be feasible and meaningful, has to be related to the appropriate level of decision-making and to the particular type of program at issue. All programs do not affect all citizens alike, and participation is relevant only for people who experience the effects of programs. Futhermore, there are different aspects of programs, each having a different impact on different groups of people.

The program of slum clearance, to take a most striking example, adversely affects the poor, at least in the short run, but is necessary to achieve a national goal. The problem therefore arises as to how to reconcile sectional interests with national interests, proximate goals with long-range goals. Attention must be given to minimizing the hardships of those who are obliged to sacrifice their present self-interest. This requires provision of alternative resources to replace so far as possible those that have been lost. It requires also developing acceptance by the group adversely affected. The acceptance may be obtained through persuasion or through alternative rewards. But Pakistan has very limited resources, and the alternative rewards are frequently inadequate. People may receive only an increased potential for social mobility because of the expansion of economic opportunities as their alternative reward.

So long as there is no feeling of alienation and helplessness, so long as there is no system to blame for poverty and deprivation, and so long as there are opportunities for advancement, participation in higher-level decision-making does not become an issue. But to avoid passive acceptance of circumstances and to mobilize people's support and cooperation, participation has to be promoted and encouraged. This requires training and experience, and these in turn can be acquired only as there are opportunities for participation. Such opportunities are now being provided through the basic democracies and on a very much smaller scale through urban and rural community development projects. The government has promised to enlarge the power of these grass-roots planning organizations as they acquire experience and confidence.

Another difficulty in realizing the goal of citizen participation is that of enlarging the scope for participation and improving the competence of the people in participation. The government may genuinely desire wider popular support and cooperation, but the existing social structure and values may prove to be serious obstacles. Simply decentralizing is not adequate. Decentralization may increase the aggregate inequality in the exercise of power, thereby making participation more difficult. Equality comes through sharing of power and opportunities. This requires organization and education of citizens, and development of initiative and leadership. This will be a gradual process in Pakistan. At present, major reliance must be placed on the benevolence of the bureaucracy, which is also the enlightened section of the country.

Social Planning and Urban Development

WILBUR J. COHEN

UNDERSECRETARY, U.S. DEPARTMENT OF
HEALTH, EDUCATION, AND WELFARE

THE PROBLEMS of urban living and the need for planning are not of recent origin. Social problems existed when man established his first city. In fact, according to Webster's *Dictionary*, the word "urban" may have originated out of the term "a palisade of hurdles." Times have not changed much. The term is still appropriately descriptive of most urban areas.

Nevertheless, people all over the world, in ever larger numbers, are choosing to live in "a palisade of hurdles" rather than in the rural areas that have historically been the home of the great majority of the people of all countries. Regardless of the economic development of a particular country, whether it is highly advanced, underdeveloped, or somewhere in between, growing urbanization and the problems that come with it are part of the national scene.

World-wide, this trend will markedly increase in the next decade. As industrialization soars to new levels—as it is doing in every country in the world—people migrate to the urban areas to meet the manpower needs of the cities that house the industries. Moreover, because of the startling advances in agricultural productivity, people are encouraged to move from rural areas for the very simple reason that they are no longer necessary to the agricultural process.

The problems that have come with urbanization are not only going to be with us for a while, they are going to become more complex. As a result, it is urgent not only that we accelerate our attempts to solve those problems that now exist, but also that we plan now for the prevention of as many future problems as we can.

Neither task can be lightly undertaken. The urbanization of the world's population is only one phase of a very complex mix of drastic and accelerating changes in the way we live. Simultaneously, new discoveries and inventions that affect the very roots of our existence come forth in increasing numbers.

It goes without saying that the very changes that now characterize our lives, and will continue to characterize them, make social planning even more difficult. For how does one plan for the future when there is no way of knowing exactly what it will hold?

How, for instance, could the designers of some of our older cities have ever dreamed of today's needs for streets, highways, and parking lots to accommodate the automobile? How could social planners—if there had been any around—have even imagined the impact the automobile has had on the way we live, on family relationships, on community structure, and the difficulties, as well as the benefits, it has engendered?

How could the urban planners of a time as late as the 1930s foresee today's need for air fields to handle the huge, swift jets that link our cities and our countries?

Today, a huge megalopolis, a consolidated urban area spreading for hundreds of miles, forms almost before we know it and brings with it new problems about which we have little knowledge and even less understanding.

Like it or not, the social problems of today and of tomorrow flow from, and are affected by, the material change that is so very much a part of our life and yet is neither quite under our control nor subject to accurate prediction. This change not only demands new ways of meeting new conditions, it also requires (and this is perhaps more difficult) that our society discard many of its old ways, no matter how comfortable they seem, if they are no longer effective.

Surprisingly enough, a high level of national affluence, an abundance of material wealth, does not seem to guarantee, by itself, a lack of urban social ills, nor is wealth alone the cure-all for social problems.

Most developing countries are in the beginning or early phases of the rural-to-urban movement. Even though they are experiencing population increases and migrations from country to city, these countries have one big advantage: they can plan their urban areas in the light of today's known factors and benefit from the mistakes more advanced countries made at the same stage of development.

In effect, the task of the emerging countries is one of building; the task in the already industrialized and urbanized countries is one of rebuilding and rearranging, of updating existing urban arrangements.

President Johnson has alerted this nation to the gigantic task that is before us in the closing years of this century. On March 2, 1965, the President sent to the Congress an historic special message on "The Problems and Future of the Central City and Its Suburbs," with recommendations for legislative improvements. Considering the physical condition of our cities, the expected growth in population, and the trend toward greater urbanization, the President warned that we must build one new house or building in this country during the next forty years for every one that now exists. In other words, we must duplicate what we have now, and at the same time replace and repair much of what already stands. *We must do in 40 years what we have done in the past 400 years.*

This means that our sprawling metropolitan complexes, with their crowded conditions, traffic jams from morning till night, spreading slum areas, water shortages, inadequate waste-disposal facilities, contaminated air, and general obsolescence, will have to accommodate a great many more people than they now do.

With his eyes firmly on the future of this nation, and thus on the future of our cities, President Johnson has recommended substantial increases in federal support and assistance available to states and communities to improve our urban areas and upgrade urban life. We are beginning to work with the cities and the states to develop rapid mass transportation systems, new approaches to urban renewal, improved and expanded health facilities, better educational facilities, more adequate highway systems, and other needed changes and improvements in the make-up of our cities.

But the ultimate measure of an urban area is not the form or nature of its physical structure, but the quality of the life of the people who live there. Pericles in his famous funeral oration took pride in the fact that Athens was "no workaday city only" but that it provided "so many recreations for the spirit" and that the city dwellers were "lovers of beauty without extravagance, and lovers

of wisdom without unmanliness." Using these standards, a great
many of our cities are failing in their function. In city after city,
full opportunity to get the maximum benefit of urban living is
completely missing, or is withheld from many. The quality of
urban life is not what it could be and should be. Not by design,
but by neglect, cities have become environments more suitable for
the automobile than for man, adequate for the needs of neither.

How, then, can we help make our cities more satisfactory places
in which to live?

As social workers and persons concerned about social welfare we
are concerned about the individual, the family, the community. It
is our responsibility and our contribution to think about the
"wholeness" of each man and the interrelatedness of his wants,
needs, and aspirations. To do this there must be a mechanism to
bring together for some common action those concerned with
physical facilities, employment, income, education, medical care,
transportation, recreation, and culture. For social workers and
persons in social welfare this means working closely with engineers, economists, architects, city planners, sociologists, educators,
members of the health professions, and politicians—learning to
talk and work with professions whose backgrounds and emphases
differ from each other and from their own.

Urban planning cannot be conducted satisfactorily by one profession or one group alone. It is not only a multidisciplinary activity; it is both a professional and a political undertaking. It
involves working with the community power structure and encouraging it to undertake some social and economic changes faster than
it would do otherwise. It involves maximum feasible participation
of the people who are affected by social change, and this means
both the poor and the rich, the professional and the politician, the
urban and the suburban dweller.

To accomplish this objective our schools of social work must
work much more closely with schools of architecture, public
health, education, and other units in the university. Institutes for
the study of urban problems are being established in some of our
universities. Social work education must enter into these studies,
enable faculty to incorporate into the curriculum new concepts
and experience, assign students to field work in the broad areas of

urban planning, and take a more active role in all phases of urban planning.

Social workers, for instance, should take a vital interest in the trend toward new towns and new cities which has taken place in a number of European countries and is beginning here also. Essentially, a new town is one that is built from the ground up on what was previously sparsely settled land, and is planned in detail *from the very beginning* to include everything necessary to the people who will live there. An integral part of the planning process is done by anthropologists, psychologists, sociologists, the health professions, transportation experts, and other members of what might be called a "human engineering" team. It is the responsibility of these experts to make sure the city is designed in such a way that the needs of people in every age group and at all income levels are met in an environment that is functionally effective, attractive, pleasant, and comfortable.

As a result, the populations of the new towns are not necessarily grouped according to income. Adequate housing for those with low incomes as well as high is spread throughout the community so that all will have ready access to the many services and facilities essential to an independent and full life within a city. New cities, therefore, provide the opportunity to plan away the possibilities of slums developing, of ghettos being created, of social ills being concentrated in any one particular area. Opportunity can be built *in*, and social and economic isolation can be planned *out*.

We must apply these same techniques to our existing cities. What we can do is to concentrate on large contiguous areas of the run-down portions of older cities and rebuild them, community by community; not just as huge housing complexes or industrial compounds or commercial enclaves, but as total, comprehensive communities that offer housing, jobs, educational opportunities, social services, and recreational outlets to people who will then want to work, play, and *live* there.

New towns and new communities within old towns seem to be one way to develop the immense amount of new urban areas that will be needed to accommodate the population we expect to have in the future.

Social workers should also become concerned with the tendencies to build retirement villages apart from the broader community. I cannot help but think it unwise to congregate the children of all middle- and upper-income families in the suburbs and all the retired people in a separate village or community. To me this is but another form of segregation. The intermixing of the generations is one of the stimulating features of a healthy society.

The essence of my thesis is that facilities and services should be planned together. All too often the planning for factories, housing, and schools has overlooked the necessity to plan at the same time for the social and health services needed to help meet the human problems which arise when large numbers of people live closely together.

We are going through one of the most tremendous and most significant periods of social change in our nation. It is a period of vast new opportunities for social workers, educators, the health professions, and young people who seek new and challenging opportunities for service. In the past five and a half years under the leadership of President Kennedy and President Johnson, there have been more than a hundred significant pieces of domestic legislation, enacted by the Congress and approved by the President, to deal more effectively with problems of housing, transportation, health, welfare, education, social security, beautification, poverty, civil rights, children and youth, senior citizens, and the handicapped.

We are trying out many new ideas and new methods.

We have, in the past two years, inaugurated an attack on poverty with the objective of eliminating it from our country.

We have been experimenting in hundreds of cities with community action programs under the antipoverty legislation.

We have inaugurated a highly successful Head Start program across the country for the education of several hundred thousands of deprived youngsters aged three to six.

We have organized new programs of legal services for the poor.

We have started VISTA to bring volunteers into domestic programs comparable to our international Peace Corps.

We are starting a National Teacher Corps to bring new teachers and new skills into the heart of the cities.

We have just completed the first year of a program of aid to education in thousands of school districts with high concentrations of low-income families.

We have been expanding a program that provides school and library books in every city and town.

We are creating new community mental health centers in hundreds of places with the hope of cutting in half the number of people confined to large mental hospitals.

We have started a rent supplement program to enable low- and moderate-income families to obtain better housing.

We have established the Jobs Corps and a Neighborhood Youth Corps to train youth, established a work-study program to enable youth to continue in college, and created an adult literacy program to wipe out illiteracy.

We have just completed the first sixty days of our Medicare insurance program for 19,000,000 of our aged citizens in a most successful manner, contrary to the dire predictions of many who said we could not do it. But we did!

We have inaugurated a policy of making family planning services available and will be starting a series of regional conferences to make these policies known to all concerned.

We have started a Medicaid program in cooperation with the states to enable every child and youth under twenty-one whose parents have insufficient income to obtain high-quality medical services.

These programs and many others I could cite are under way now. But we know that much more needs to be done.

Additional proposals are under study for consideration of the Congress in 1967.

The President has asked us to improve social security benefits for the aged, the disabled, the widows and orphans.

He has asked us to prepare a comprehensive program to improve child health, including dental and eye care for young children.

He has asked us to prepare an expanded program for the education and training of the handicapped.

We are studying how to make sure that every large community has the social welfare services it needs in an emergency.

We are considering how to extend incentives to work in our welfare programs and to expand training for employment.

We are considering ways to expand the number of neighborhood health and social service centers in the heart of the big cities so that services can be brought quickly and directly to the people in a less fragmented manner.

We are trying to find means to modernize outmoded hospitals in the urban centers and to develop medical social service units in every health facility so that the social, economic, and other needs of the patient and his family will be served.

We are considering how to build more and better convalescent and nursing homes.

To accomplish all these objectives we must train competent staff to handle the variety of jobs to be done. We have a serious shortage of social workers, teachers, nurses, physicians, dentists, librarians, counselors, and many other professionals.

We live in a troubled environment. And troubles are compounded by the problems neglected by past generations and deepened by the vast changes being made daily in our lives, our work, and our relationships to our fellow man. These problems will not vanish overnight—or even over a decade. But we have begun to deal more effectively with them in recent months and we will do more to resolve them as time goes on.

I believe that the final outcome of greater investments in health, in education, in social security, and in social services will be to offer each individual a greater freedom of choice of what he may do with his life. And this is a freedom of choice that must extend to all people throughout their lives and give greater meaning to their lives. Society must be truly open. There should be no restriction on a person's opportunity for education and training, or on his occupational choice because he is a member of a minority group or because of sex, race, place of birth, or residence.

The freedom to choose the size and spacing of one's family must become a reality for the poor as well as for the affluent. And this choice has important implications in terms of maternal health, infant mortality, dependency, and the education and training of women. With childbearing and child rearing completed by many women while they still have many active years ahead, the possibilities of their resuming interrupted careers, beginning new ones, or contributing to meaningful volunteer activities provides a new dimension of choice for their lives.

Increased freedom of choice will contribute to, and be reinforced by strengthening the role of the family, strengthening parental responsibility, continuing education, and carrying out civic obligations. It will require a social structure that is at once more diversified and more interdependent—a more truly pluralistic society. More choices for every individual mean an awesome responsibility, requiring a great degree of education and self-discipline. Diversity and interdependence must be buttressed by intelligent cooperation between all groups in the community.

Freedom of choice must be available to all. It must embrace those sometimes forgotten people whom social workers have been serving so faithfully these many years with inadequate finances and personnel. Making this freedom of choice a reality is truly the challenge that we face in the decade ahead.

Some will call the picture I have painted a visionary one. Others may say it is a real possibility but question the effect it will have on incentives and initiative, on work and morals. It is true that even if the goals I have outlined were attained, all our problems would not be eliminated: as long as there are human beings, there will also be problems.

The problems we face call for an educated and adaptable society and a growing, dynamic, healthy economy. We are presented with a challenge and with great opportunities.

Now is a wonderful time to be alive, to work, to think, to write, to speak, and to seek and strive for new and imaginative ways to make a new and better world. Like all great ideas, this notion of opportunity and choice is as yet only imperfectly realized in the institutions and in the social structure, but the foundations have been laid. So we go forward with renewed determination to set and to reach new goals for all the peoples of the world.

The Paradoxes of Urbanization and Regional Development

GERALD HODGE

ASSOCIATE PROFESSOR
DIVISION OF TOWN AND REGIONAL PLANNING
UNIVERSITY OF TORONTO, CANADA

REGIONAL DEVELOPMENT is absorbing more and more of our discussion about economic development, in the rich countries and the poor. Conferences were held almost monthly in the past year by economists, public administrators, and now social workers. City and regional planners tend to be somewhat smug about this new concentration on regional development, for they have been saying for many years that it is just as important *where* resources are allocated as *which* resources are allocated.

But it is not enough for planners to know that their message about the importance of the spatial dimension of economic development has been getting through. It also means that we should now be ready with constructive suggestions and not just more polemics. Indeed, some of the more thoughtful planners are presently trying to remedy this situation.

However, the more we probe this problem of regional development the more the paradoxes appear. While national programs in the past did not pay much attention to place or space in their plans and, therefore, showed inconsistencies between their objectives and their results, it is still another thing to make the higher degree of spatial integration which we preach into successful development. To know that the futures of urban areas and rural areas are intertwined is one thing; to formulate a functioning system of urban centers and rural areas in which the centers are not too large and costly to operate, too antisocial, and do not attract too many migrants from rural areas, thus depleting the latter of their human resources, is still another task.

To repeat, there are many paradoxes. For example, millions throughout the world are attracted to the large cities even though they often find there living conditions which are considered repulsive by planners and other bureaucrats; there is little evidence that large cities are becoming less efficient to operate, and attempts to redress the balance by encouraging the growth of small centers in underdeveloped regions often encourages more development in large centers. Thus, I see no alternative but to be equivocal about the problem of counteracting the effects of overcentralization and urban concentration. But it may be helpful to illuminate some of these paradoxes and, in this way, start to see our way out of them.

Paradox 1. Metropolitan growth without diminishing returns. —It is frequently argued that the growth of large cities is increasingly uneconomical. Yet the continued growth of even the largest metropolitan regions in the world—Mexico City, New York, London, Paris, Montreal, Moscow—is a gross contradiction of this proposition. The evidence indicates that the expected diminishing marginal returns have not set in. This is not to deny that there may be massive social costs associated with further agglomerations of population in metropolitan areas. But, by and large, net private costs have risen at a much slower rate than net social costs.[1]

The reason for the continued growth of cities as commercial centers was outlined in the work of John Marshall. He noted long ago that industries generate external economies. That is, when an industry locates at a certain point it makes it easier for others to follow suit: labor skills can be developed and workers interchanged; services and supplies can be organized to serve more and more firms; and local markets develop among the industries. Isard has elaborated this point further with his concept of juxtaposition economies.[2] These economies come about not only because of the linkages between the firms but because of the relationships between the individual firm and the urban area in which it locates. Examples of these economies are relatively easy to identify. Among them are: savings on public utilities that have been

[1] Roger Dehem, "Concepts of Regional Planning," Institute of Public Administration of Canada, Winnipeg, 1965.

[2] Walter Isard *et al., Methods of Regional Analysis* (New York: John Wiley, 1960), pp. 404–9.

installed for general usage; ease of access to business and financial services; administrative economies due to the easy communication among many different kinds of firms and government agencies, since a large city is often a major seat of government; and savings on the cost of such things as housing, since in a large city a well-developed local market for such items will usually exist. Once a large center emerges, a national market for goods produced in the industrial sector will come to be focused upon it. This, in turn, will lead to further investment in market-oriented industries and services, and cumulative growth will be set in motion.

It is also difficult to argue that the existence of large cities with many marginally employed people is direct evidence of over-urbanization. Even though there may be a concentration of workers in excess of steady employment one must recognize that marginal employment in construction, trades, and personal services is generally more productive than are alternative occupations in agriculture. Long-term unemployment in urban areas is generally held at very low levels in most countries, and the workers' small wages are compensated for by the fact that more members of the family are able to work and contribute to family incomes. John Friedmann points up this paradox in a slightly different way: "The higher the rate of investment in a city, the greater will be its share of marginal population." As he points out, this does not support the thesis that overpopulation is a symptom of over-growth. "On the contrary," he goes on to say, "the rapid influx of migrants may be regarded as a healthy sign and, despite the serious social dislocation it creates, moves in the direction by which the society transforms itself into an image of a modern and productive nation." [3]

Even from the point of view of public amenities the large urban center operates at decreasing average costs, at least up to a point. Every new investment for supplementary employment seems to reduce the average cost of services. This is true whether we talk about the water and sewage services, transportation, air- and water-pollution control, or schools.

If, in fact, there is a point of diminishing returns for social and

[3] John Friedmann, "The Phenomenon of Urbanization in Latin America" (Cambridge, Mass., 1964; mimeographed).

private gains in a large city it has not been reached. Continued metropolitan growth must be regarded as one of the prime facts of modern civilization.

Paradox 2. "Voting with the Feet."—Both pro-city and anticity advocates must acknowledge that the continued growth of large cities indicates that millions of rural people choose to work and raise their families in urban areas. Granted, the conditions they find there may be repulsive and inhuman from our point of view, but they are often no worse than those they leave behind. A number of studies have shown that the movement from rural areas and small towns is made on the expectation that opportunities to make a livelihood in the city will be greater.[4] The desire for work and for better incomes, for educational opportunities, and for a sense of independence are the reasons most frequently given. Even though they may find that their future takes them no further than the low-wage urban mass, their judgment that life will be decisively better in an urban situation commits them to be permanent residents of the city.

Depending upon the country, between 40 percent and 70 percent of recent urban growth is a result of rural migration. The depopulation of both rich and poor rural regions is a striking feature of present-day settlement patterns. In the prosperous Canadian prairies, for example, rural population loss in both absolute and relative terms has been going on for about thirty years, with a net out-migration rate of about 20 per thousand of population. There are similar figures for the depressed regions of eastern Ontario and the Maritime Provinces.

In other words, many rural people are choosing to live in cities —in almost all countries, under almost all types of institutional arrangements, even when conscious efforts have been made to stem the flow.[5] The fact that millions of urban-bound migrants do not see the city as an unfavorable environment may well explain the generally cautious efforts of most national governments to halt

[4] Philip M. Hauser, ed., *Urbanization in Latin America* (New York: Columbia University Press, 1961), is a good example.

[5] The Soviet Union made concerted attempts in this direction, but to little avail. See R. J. Osborn and T. A. Reiner, "Soviet City Planning," *Journal of the American Institute of Planners,* XXVIII (1962), 239–50.

large city growth. The feeling that the large urban center possibly
does have something to offer in the way of productivity and cultural and social advancement for the nation seems to restrain
them. If people are "voting with their feet," maybe what they are
voting for is worthwhile.

Paradox 3. The "invisible" slums.—The critics of urban expansion usually cite the dreadful living conditions that most people
endure in large cities as the prime reason for limiting urban
growth. The solutions offered are smaller cities and the use of local
materials and labor to provide a better environment. One need
only look at the slums in smaller centers and those in rural areas to
know whether conditions can ever be much better. The supporter
of urban expansion is in a no stronger position regarding environments for people in large cities. His solution is a combination
of "filtering down" housing from higher income levels (but the
differences in income are so vast between the few that have decent
housing and all others that this is inconceivable), public housing
schemes, self-help housing, and plans for neat, contour-street
neighborhoods.

Both supporters and critics of large cities, in their own ways,
ignore slum settlements. Because slum settlements are often officially "invisible," they may not be eligible for improvement programs. Even where their existence is acknowledged, slum conditions are not accorded much importance. (Have you ever seen them
recorded as such on a planner's land-use map?) At best, slum conditions are treated as inadequate housing conditions, which, as
most social workers know, is a great oversimplification of the basic
problems that beget slum settlements.

The essence of this paradox is that we do not recognize slum
settlements—bidonvilles, favelas, campesinos—as a feature of the
urban pattern that, unfortunately, will have to endure for some
decades to come. Slum settlements provide a class of housing, no
matter how inadequate, for people of very low income levels.
These conditions will not be substantially improved until income
levels for most urban people are higher. Yet the slum represents
the first foothold of the rural migrant in the city, the place from
which he sets about satisfying his desire to achieve, the space upon

which he lavishes much of his income in a desire to improve it.[6] Unless there can be an immediate elimination of slum conditions, they ought to be recognized as a semipermanent fact of modern urban development and made more amenable.

Paradox 4. Regional development strengthens the metropolis. —One of the strongest sectors of support for regional development comes from those who seek to divert a significant portion of growth from large cities in order to distribute more equitably the benefits of economic growth to other regions and/or to prevent a continued build-up of unsavory living conditions in the metropolis. A program for regional development does not, however, mean that pressure will be taken off the metropolis even though that may be its objective. The opposite may come to pass; for the metropolis has emerged because it has a high degree of efficiency in carrying out the tasks associated with economic development. It creates external economies and thus attracts industry and services; it encourages specialization and diversification of labor skills; it reduces outlays for transportation; it acts as a principal domestic market; and so on. A program aimed at encouraging growth elsewhere must, paradoxically, not diminish the very qualities that give prominence to the metropolis.

The capital, the labor skills, the sophisticated services, the markets provided by the metropolis, the linkages to the rest of the world, are all needed to initiate growth in peripheral regions. This is particularly true in depressed regions, but it is also important in regions that have their own growth potential. The latter may be able to develop their own urban systems more quickly than depressed areas and thus reduce their dependence upon the metropolis. But no matter what the growth potential of a region, the metropolis must participate in energizing it.

This means that the metropolis will grow too. For example, it has been said of Canadian visions of developing far northern regions that to put only 250,000 people into the north means adding another million people to the gateway cities of the south (Mont-

6 The work of Hagen and McClelland has shown how strong the "desire to achieve is and how significant it is in economic development." See Everett E. Hagen, *On the Theory of Social Change* (Homewood, Ill.: Dorsey, 1962); and David C. McClelland, *The Achieving Society* (Princeton, N.J.: Van Nostrand, 1961).

real, Winnipeg, Edmonton, Vancouver). Just to help unlock the
known resources of this northern region and to develop even ten
centers of 25,000 people each in this virtually unpopulated area
will require massive support in the form of transportation, commercial services, public administration, special equipment to suit
the northern environment, and so on. The various southern
metropolises are the only sources of this support. This situation
can be replicated across the world, from the opening up of the
Guayana region of Venezuela to the transmigration schemes of
Indonesia.

In other words, regional development means a "payoff" of a
substantial kind for the existing metropolis. It will achieve even
greater scale and urbanization economies, thus sustaining its position and even achieving more growth. The expansion of the metropolis to service the peripheral regions will attract more migrants
and capital. While regional development may decrease or hold
steady the proportion of wealth and population in the metropolis,
its growth in absolute terms will still be substantial, as witness
New York or a dozen other cities. Such growth is not calculated to
reduce big-city slums, traffic congestion, or air pollution.

Paradox 5. Poor urban systems in poor regions.—A high degree
of concentration of population in a single center may lead to the
neglect of development in peripheral regions. Despite all the
problems associated with big-city growth, a large center will possess its own momentum for growth and self-adjusting mechanisms
for change which make it easier to direct attention there rather
than to peripheral areas. The alternative, according to many, is to
develop "growth poles" at strategically located urban centers in
outlying regions. Considerable industrial development would be
promoted in these centers which would spread money and jobs to
the surrounding region. In this way, a more balanced distribution
of cities could be instituted through which the impulses of economic and social change could be transmitted and regional resources could be mobilized for better over-all growth.

The institution of such a concept depends, of course, on appropriate government action in choosing growth centers. This is
much easier said than done, especially in depressed regions. For

the latter regions will often possess an underdeveloped urban system, thereby providing little basis for selecting one or more "growth poles." Their urban systems will tend to be characterized by a large number of small centers of similar size and development operating more or less independently within their local hinterlands. There will not be, as there usually is in an advanced regional economy, a regular hierarchy of centers interconnected by efficient transportation and communications and, in turn, connected to other regions and other countries. It therefore becomes extremely difficult to select appropriate growth centers in poor regions.[7]

Even if centers in poorly developed regions can be selected, it is difficult to make them into growth centers. Such centers are in their present state because, often, they possess no natural locational advantages for resources, transportation, or markets which would attract industrial growth. They may be situated in what a recent Canadian study calls the "economic shadow" of already developed large centers and be able to offer no comparable advantages of industry.[8] Moreover, urban centers in such regions tend to possess structural features which conflct with a rapid transition to growth. Another Canadian study in the generally depressed eastern Ontario region showed that centers in the poorest areas have a very low level of physical development, a preponderance of persons sixty-five years of age and older, and an adult population with low educational attainments.[9] None of these attributes augurs well for programs of improvement. In combination, they would prove staggering. At the very least, the gestation period on programs designed to change the situation would be long.

Paradox 6. The decline of industry in postindustrial society.—It has long been contended that the key to successful regional development lies in the dispersal of industrial development. In this way it is hoped to diversify employment opportunities in regions dom-

[7] Gerald Hodge, "Urban Systems and Regional Policy," *Canadian Public Administration*, June, 1966.

[8] D. Michael Ray, *Market Potential and Economic Shadow*, Research Paper in Geography, No. 101 (Chicago: University of Chicago, Department of Geography, 1965).

[9] Gerald Hodge, *The Identification of "Growth Poles" in Eastern Ontario*, a Report to the Ontario Department of Economics and Development, August, 1966.

inated by agriculture or some other natural resource development, to create an export base for the region, to make higher incomes available to many, and to engender positive attitudes toward modernization. Industrial dispersal is still the key in most underdeveloped countries; it is progressively less valid in countries already in or fast approaching the phase of postindustrial development.

In the United States and in several countries of northwest Europe there has occurred a significant leveling off of both the number and the proportion of workers employed in manufacturing.[10] In the United States this trend goes back a decade. In general, it portends less industrial development to go around to all regions and makes even more difficult the task of attracting industry to regions with few advantages. It has, of course, been questioned whether local initiative can be of much use in attracting industry away from established locales. But, more important, the real growth in postindustrial society is in the tertiary (retailing and wholesaling) and quaternary (education, research, recreation) service sectors, which are inherently urban-based.

Despite the pressure of major problems and paradoxes, the physical planner, like the social worker, cannot long avoid having to offer solutions, or at least alternatives. Theoretically, there is a variety of alternatives for the spatial organization of activities—concentration of effort on a single large center, a few major centers, a network of cities and towns, or on some combination of these. But there are two major difficulties with trying to implement any one of the theoretical alternatives. On the one hand, because of meager financial and manpower resources most of the alternatives are not open. On the other hand, a host of problems presses for immediate solutions. Any strategy for improvement will have to allow immediate problems to be tackled while holding open the possibility of bringing into existence a new spatial pattern of urbanization.

We have already implied that it is necessary to make slums "visible." Friedmann suggests that the immediate problem be responded

10 Jean Gottman, *Megalopolis* (New York: Twentieth Century Fund, Inc., 1961); John Friedmann, "Regional Development in Post-industrial Society," *Journal of the American Institute of Planners,* XXX (1964), 84–90.

to by supplying the slums with: (1) basic services to sustain normal family life under crowded conditions—water, sewerage, garbage collection, clinics, road maintenance; (2) basic services necessary for encouraging rapid upward social mobility—primary and secondary schools, kindergartens, vocational training centers; and (3) basic services to develop a healthy community life—playgrounds, communal halls, churches, and local administration.[11] The extension of these services is of critical importance in treating slums as integral parts of the city and in creating a decent environment for millions. Programs of this sort should be carried out in such a way that costs and impacts can be monitored and valid assessments made of the program's efficacy.

Few people, planners included, have dared confront the prospects for the dimensions of urbanization in the future. Richard Meier is one of the few, and his efforts at answering the question of how big a city can comfortably be are imposing. In particular, his hypotheses for Madras, India, in the year 2050, wherein a population of 80,000,000 might be expected to reside, call for a full use of our stock of technology and simultaneous innovations in social organization.[12] Water supplies and traffic movement proved to be the most critical issues; but the former has a solution in the process for extracting energy from sea water and producing distilled water as a by-product, while the latter has a simple solution in a rental system for bicycle-type vehicles available at each terminal of a rapid transit network. Already known technology concerning food and fuel production, construction techniques, and manufacturing industries can be employed to develop very large cities that are no less inconvenient than New York and London are today. Will we have the courage to pick up Meier's challenge?

These two examples of alleviating slum conditions and the design of very large cities cover the pragmatic and the hypothetical in a strategy for improvement. Connecting these and other facets to the decision-making process will have to be a number of tactics

---

[11] Friedmann, "The Phenomenon of Urbanization in Latin America."
[12] Richard L. Meier, "Relations of Technology to the Design of Very Large Cities," in Roy Turner, ed., *India's Urban Future* (Berkeley: University of California Press, 1962), pp. 299–326.

which will undoubtedly include the following concepts. Lloyd Rodwin has proposed "concentrated decentralization," [13] in which regional centers are promoted to acquire essential transportation, minimum overhead facilities, and necessary intelligence mechanisms. Such centers could come to compete with the existing metropolis, transform the cultural pattern of the region, and even help the primate cities cope with the impending tide of migrants. On this last point, Thomas Reiner speculates about how effective regional centers can be in stemming migration to the metropolis.[14] He sees them acting as stepping stones between country and city and, maybe more important, as places of transition from traditional society to modern urban society. This role might be exploited effectively.

In the final analysis, all this discussion rests on the question of people: not on the upper or middle classes—they have the wherewithal to take care of themselves. Not even on the working classes; but most surely on the lower classes. A fully developed approach to social planning, or "guided mobility planning" as Herbert Gans calls it,[15] is ultimately needed. Physical planners must divest themselves of some of their more cherished notions, such as the neighborhood concept, and social workers must take more of a goal-oriented approach than a pathological one. If such a professional synthesis comes about, we may be well on our way to counteracting the ill-effects of urbanization within a regional framework.

[13] Lloyd Rodwin, "Metropolitan Policy for Developing Areas," *Daedalus,* XC (1961), 132–46.

[14] Thomas A. Reiner, "Comment," in *Papers and Proceedings,* 1st Far East Conference of the Regional Science Association, Vol. I (1963).

[15] Herbert Gans, "Cities as Places to Live and Work: How Much Improvement?" Conference of the American Institute of Planning, 1962.

Reports on Research

I. WORKING MOTHERS AND FAMILY LIFE

K. N. GEORGE

DIRECTOR, MADRAS SCHOOL OF SOCIAL WORK

INDIA

THE STUDY of working mothers and the effect of their employment on family life sponsored by the Welfare Administration, U. S. Department of Health, Education, and Welfare, was carried out by the Madras School of Social Work.

Because of time limitations, the study was confined to middle-class, white-collar working mothers within the income range of Rs. 100 to Rs. 500 ($14-$67). The total number of working mothers in Madras City who fulfilled these conditions was around six thousand, and the sample was 15 percent of the population.

In order to ascertain whether problems faced by the working mothers were exclusively the effects of their employment, it was felt that a comparison of the family of the working mother with that of a nonworking mother would be necessary. Owing to limitations of time and resources, however, it was not feasible to conduct this comparative study on a large scale. Fifty families falling within the range of those who came under the study were chosen from about two hundred families in various parts of the city.

To have a complete picture of the impact of the employment of the mothers on family life, it was decided to interview at least fifty husbands of working mothers. These were chosen at random from families in which the youngest child was five years old or less. Husbands of nonworking mothers were also interviewed.

It is evident that there is an increasing tendency among mothers to take jobs outside their homes. The proportion of working mothers to the total number of women in the working force is roughly one to two. Eighty-seven percent of the mothers gave, as might be expected, economic reasons for having taken employment, and the remaining 13 percent, noneconomic reasons.

It is contended that the effect on the family of a mother's employment is likely to be more adverse when she works under severe economic duress. In such an event, a woman might be compelled to accept mediocre arrangements for the children and the household in her absence, whereas a mother who is under no pressing economic need but works for other reasons will have the means to make proper and satisfactory arrangements. It should be conceded that it is equally probable that the home might be subjected to no less effects if the mother were non-employed, that is, if there were no additional source of income although the family badly needed it. Under such circumstances the mother's employment would not be an unqualified evil, but perhaps only the lesser of two evils. Thus it will be seen that it is very difficult to make a generalization regarding the relationship between the reasons for a mother's employment and the effect of her employment on family life.

When one examines the effect of a mother's employment on family life, one must perhaps give the greatest importance to the most obviously tangible result which employment yields, that is, additional income.

The importance of the mother's wages in raising the economic position of the family can be assessed by the fact that nearly 64 percent of the husbands who estimated their own economic position without the mother's income as "can't make ends meet" described their changed position in the light of the wives' additional income as "enough to get along," and about 10 percent as even "comfortable." Nearly half the husbands who in their own self-estimate had originally only "enough to get along" called themselves "comfortable" or "well-to-do" with the extra income that their wives added to the family coffers; 60 percent of those who described themselves as "comfortable" with their own income alone estimated themselves as "well-to-do" in view of family income augmented by their wives' earnings.

On the average, the mother's income amounted to 67 percent of the husband's and 41 percent of the total family income. The economic benefits to the family derived from the mother's income must be high when we consider the fact that the average monthly income of the fathers in these families was around R.300/-, which by itself could barely assure a hand-to-mouth living, judged by standards in Madras City.

Another measure of the financial benefit is the fact that 64 percent of the husbands were prepared to have their wives quit the labor force only if there were a sufficient rise in their own income; and for this nearly 88 percent required the increase to be between 50 percent and 100 percent or even more.

What are the problems or difficulties that the employment of mothers, while yielding rich economic dividends to their families, impose?

It should be mentioned at the outset that the traditional pattern of family living is in many ways immensely beneficial to working mothers. It is common in India for an aged or widowed parent to live with the son's or daughter's family, or for a poor relation to live with another's family and help in household tasks while being supported in return.

Sixty-six percent of the working mothers in our sample have reported the availability of a relative to help them with child care and home management. In a majority of the families (52 percent) where the youngest child is less than five years old it was found that the help of relatives was voluntarily sought. Twenty-seven percent of the mothers had servants; about 7 percent had neither relatives nor servants to help with household tasks. A highly significant association was found to exist between the age of the youngest child and the type of supportive services relied upon. As the age of the youngest child increases, they tend to rely more on servants, or on no help at all, than on relatives, who seem to be the type of assistance most frequently sought by working mothers whose youngest child is quite small.

Working mothers expressed the greatest dissatisfaction in regard to nursing sick children. The percentage was high in families in which there were only servants or no supportive services at all (27 percent and 22 percent respectively) and low where there were supportive relatives (10 percent). The other causes of dissatisfaction were, in descending order of importance: ill-treatment (9 percent); bad company (8 percent); poor discipline (4 percent); truancy (4 percent); irregular feeding (3 percent); and accidents (3 percent). Here too, more concern was expressed in families that had no supportive relatives than in those that did.

Thus the significance of having relatives in the home is very evident. Nearly 50 percent of the employed mothers and over 60 percent of their husbands preferred to live in a joint family because of the ready assistance with household tasks available. A slightly smaller percentage of nonworking mothers expressed a similar preference.

In our study, the category of joint families included not only those in which assistance was at hand from relatives permanently residing with them, but also some unitary families where the working mother received help in child care and household tasks from relatives, her own or her husband's, who lived apart, either sharing a portion of the same house or residing a short distance away. In a number of cases, these mothers left their young child or children in the home of such relatives while they were working.

The pressure on the time that the mother has to perform her duties in the home directly results from her full-time employment. In India the housewife is expected to perform all the major home tasks, and it is not customary for the husband to help much. Hence, it should not be surprising that 53 percent of the working mothers said they did the bulk of the household work, which is only 4 percent less than reported by the nonworking mothers. Also, it was found that the proportion of working mothers who spent from three to six hours and more in household work was greater than that of nonworking mothers by nearly 5 percent and 6 percent respectively. Making allowance for an incorrect estimate of the time involved in housework that could result from the fact that working mothers have to crowd their activities into their limited time, and allowing for an eagerness to present the socially acceptable image of a conscientious mother, it is abundantly clear that in most cases the amount of work that a working mother must do is not considerably less than what a nonworking mother has to do.

An analysis of the performance of child care duties in the homes of working mothers revealed that the mothers bore the brunt, their participation being 69 percent, with relatives 15 percent, husbands 10 percent, and servants 6 percent. Such data indicate that neither the presence of relatives and servants nor the participation of husbands in household tasks reduces to any appreciable extent the burden of housework placed on the working mothers.

It was found that the proportion of mothers having four or more children was greater in the nonworking group by 4 percent, although the difference was not highly significant statistically. However, this is an area which we feel requires further inquiry before anything conclusive can be said. Nevertheless, we may tentatively venture to say that there were at least two indications of a trend toward smaller families among working mothers in Madras City. First, only about 10 percent of the mothers in our sample who are thirty-four years of age or below have more than three children, and nearly 78 percent of those over thirty-five years of age have only three children or fewer. Second, the age of the youngest child of 52 percent of those in the sample is three years or over. This is very significant when read with the fact that about 71 percent of the mothers in our sample are less than thirty-five years of age.

Incidentally, the frequency of abnormal pregnancies (abortion, stillbirth, and so forth) was greater in the group of nonworking mothers by 7 percent. Again, the association was not statistically significant.

About 18 percent of the working mothers, those having a child ten years of age and over, felt that the education of their children was affected by their employment. Many attributed this to the lack of supervision and a few mentioned the additional responsibility placed on these children to help the mother in child care and household work. Thirty-six percent of the husbands agreed on the adverse effects of the mothers' employment on the education of the children.

On the whole, 42 percent of the working mothers and 62 percent of their husbands referred to child care as the area of highest concern. While 50 percent of the husbands agreed that a mother who is employed full-time outside the home cannot do full justice to her role as wife, 64 percent said the same about her role as mother. Although a good number of mothers as well as fathers in "mother-employed" families expressed misgivings about proper care of their children, apparently this concern was no deterrent to the willingness of the mothers to continue working.

Forty-four percent of the husbands of working mothers agreed that there is a more satisfactory relationship and a better adjustment between husband and wife when the mother is not employed. It is interesting to note that 40 percent of the husbands of nonworking mothers agreed with the antithetical statement that there is a more satisfactory relationship between husband and wife in families in which the mother *is* employed. Thus we see that almost an equal number in each group suspect the possibility of a better marital harmony in a situation different from their own. This must be taken as indicative that employment of the mother need not affect marital harmony.

There are chances of conflicts if the husband is positively against the wife being employed. Fifty-six percent of the husbands said that they were "always favorable" to their wives' employment; 42 percent said "sometimes"; and only 2 percent, "never." Asked whether they liked to have their wives continue working, 12 percent said "no." All these stated that they were only "sometimes" favorable to the employment of wives. However, none of them said that employment of mothers was thoroughly undesirable; 4 percent even opined that it was thoroughly desirable. And none of them wanted his wife to stop working immediately, but only in the event of a sufficient rise in his own income. The reason given by the majority was that they felt home management and care of children suffered as a result of employment of wives.

About 33 percent of the working mothers expected a favorable attitude from the husband toward their continuance in the job if the husband's own income were to rise sufficiently; this was proved very nearly correct by the husband's own reaction. Nevertheless, nearly 73 percent of the mothers were willing to continue working even after a sufficient rise in their husband's income. At first this difference in attitude between husband and wife may suggest a source of potential conflict in their relationship. However, the remoteness of a problem of this nature can be estimated by the fact that the possibility of a sufficient rise in income in the next five years was found to exist in the case of only 4 percent of the husbands.

In answer to another question, 10 percent of the husbands assessed the employment of mothers as "thoroughly undesirable, but can be inevitable"; 44 percent, as "somewhat undesirable"; and 46 percent as "thoroughly desirable." This, read with the fact that 86 percent of them agreed that "it is much better for a family to face the absence of a mother because of her employment than to live in economic inadequacy" goes to prove that while difficulties can and do arise when the mother goes to work, most fathers feel that for the ultimate well-being of the family it is much better for the mother to work than not to.

As regards the problems of the husband that may result from his wife's employment, no one referred to any serious difficulty.

In general, working mothers seem to make a fairly satisfactory adjustment to the strain imposed by their dual roles, although the pressures on their time and energies are very great. In the absence of inexpensive day nurseries and crèches, a majority of them have to rely on relatives or servants to take care of their children. This dependence, although not quite uncommon in the West, is more marked in India where the joint family has been the traditional pattern of family life. However, we do not find the working mothers associated so much with the joint family in its traditional sense (two or more brothers living with their parents, spouses, and children under the same roof and sharing a common cooking fire), as with an extended family organization where, usually, only a single relative lives with the unitary kin group. While the unitary family does not seem to mind the curtailment of its privacy that results from such an arrangement, still it does not lose its identity completely as in the case of the traditional joint family.

The only area on which a considerable proportion of mothers as well as fathers have misgivings or concern is child care. It is reasonable to assume that in many cases their concern stems not so much from the actual presence of serious problems but from the fact that they are not yet completely free from the influence of the traditional thinking that the mother's presence in the home at all times is imperative. A sense of guilt, however vague, can inspire doubts about the desirability and consequences of one's act even though there may be nothing, or only very little, in the actual situation to warrant them.

Social progress always proceeds at an unequal pace. There is no reason why lack of social adjustment and change or prejudice and tradition should stand in the way of a mother's employment being beneficial to all concerned. Social, economic, and public policies should aim at striking a proper balance between increased productivity and the social goal of contentment. Working mothers should be viewed not only as employees but also as housewives, and social efforts should be directed toward enabling them to discharge their dual roles equitably. This implies provision of public services, such as inexpensive crèches, nursery schools, and midday meals for children at school. Changes in attitudes are no less important. An increased participation of the husbands of working mothers in home and child care and better planning on the part of mothers in the organization of their house and office work should ease their burden considerably.

Changes in these directions are inevitable, but a greater awareness of their need is necessary before such changes necessitated by the changing roles of women in the Indian society can occur.

II. RESEARCH IN GERMANY

ARNO KOSMALE

GERMAN ASSOCIATION FOR PUBLIC AND PRIVATE WELFARE

BY "RESEARCH" we mean research work on the question of, or at least in the field of, "urban development." I make this distinction because quite a lot of research work is being done which is useful and valuable for urban development but which is not necessarily urban development research.

For example, all communities, states, and the Federal Republic herself, that is, the Central Government of Germany, have a large quantity of statistics on many different questions of interest, such as housing, labor, delinquency, and social services. This material is of great value, but it is a question of definition whether we can count general, nonspecified statistics as research work or not.

Many university institutes, like those in Hamburg, Kiel, and Berlin, and some scientific agencies, such as the Agrar-Soziale-Gesellschaft in Göttingen, the Deutsches Jugendinstitut in Munich, and the Deutscher Verein für öffentliche und private Fürsorge in Frankfort, carry out research on special questions. The results they achieve furnish valuable material for those who deal with urban development, although the research itself does not fall under the heading of urban development.

In the last two years research was done on the problem of the mother in German society. It has been published in two big volumes, and at least a third will soon follow. Now, within this research are a lot of questions and answers that deal with urban development problems, such as the horizontal movement of families and working and living conditions in urban and suburban areas, and so on.

Another research project, conducted by a university institute about three years ago, dealt with the living conditions of old people in the city of Cologne. One of the objectives was to find out how elderly people live in urban areas and the kind of service necessary to meet their needs. Again many questions of special interest for urban development were involved, but again this was not urban development research.

In other words, there is a lot of research done, but: (a) very often it is separated and even isolated; (b) there is a lack of coordination in research work; (c) although the results of such research are useful and valuable for urban development questions, most of the work is not specially directed to that problem.

On the other hand, some university institutes have specialized in social planning, social development, and social actions as a whole. Two of these are the Soziolographisches Institut der Johann Wolfgang Goethe Universität, Frankfort, and the Sozial-Forschungsstelle an der Universität Münster in Dortmund. These two institutes, one could say, hold the key position in general *Sozialforschung*.

Research work in this field faces several problems:

1. It must be concerned with a broad scale of highly different objectives. *Sozialforschung* deals with economic problems, housing, industrialization, traffic, and so forth.

2. *Sozialforschung* deals with the needs of human beings and the means to respond; that is, with actions and reactions of man and, generally speaking, with psychological social problems.

3. *Sozialforschung* also takes into account questions of administration and organization.

I once read that three components make up science: (*a*) measurement of facts; (*b*) classification; (*c*) determination of proper relationships. One can say that it is easy to measure facts; it is more difficult to classify and set up categories; and it is most difficult to find the proper relationship between different facts within different categories. These are, I believe, the problems that *Sozialforschung* has to face. In research on urban development we need all three factors and we need them at the same time and for the same goal.

For historical reasons, our universities have a strict faculty system with strong border lines between. This means in practice that research work is separated, isolated, noncoordinated, directed to special aspects of a problem, and very seldom to the question that is to be solved as a whole. In a situation like this one has to overcome the biggest lack and one has to reach close cooperation and coordination. University institutes like the two mentioned coordinate a great deal by using different materials and also by using research teams consisting of members from different faculties.

Although it must be repeated that there is a lack of cooperation and coordination there are reasons for optimism. The needs of practitioners strongly demand cooperation and coordination of science, and science, I must also say, is willing to follow this demand. I could give some examples of recent research work where medical scientists, sociologists, experts on city planning, economists, and others worked together, shared their results, and thus tried to solve problems.

The question is raised now and then as to who should be responsible for coordination and cooperation. My feeling is that universities should be made responsible for pure scientific research. They have the power to establish nonfaculty institutes and coordinate the work that is done. Responsibility for utility research should be put on the person or the body for whom the research work is done, whether it is the city, the state, or somebody else.

III. FOUR SOCIAL WELFARE PROGRAMS

IN ISRAEL

JONA M. ROSENFELD

PAUL BAERWALD SCHOOL OF SOCIAL WORK
HEBREW UNIVERSITY OF JERUSALEM
JERUSALEM, ISRAEL

IN THIS PRESENTATION I shall report on part of a study of social services from the users' point of view, carried out by Abraham Doron and myself at the Paul Baerwald School of Social Work of the Hebrew University of Jerusalem. The study was financed by the International Office of the Welfare Administration, U. S. Department of Health, Education, and Welfare. It is a first study relating to our wider interest in the delivery of social welfare services to particular "populations-at-risk." By this we mean those who should constitute the beneficiaries of the actual or desirable social service network rather than just those who are served in practice.

It is my belief that the task of the social welfare researcher is not only to conduct the research competently, but also to insure that its results will reach and benefit people both within his own country and beyond it. The opportunity to communicate about research in an international forum may contribute toward encouraging the emerging nations and new communities to grasp the opportunity to do better than the established nations and communities have done rather than to "muddle through." Nations and communities which start out today can take hold of so-called "hard" facts, based on systematic studies carried out nationally and internationally which are thus transmittible and universal in nature. In planning for welfare services and in conceiving of emerging social service needs, the new nations need not confine themselves to "soft" facts, based on the lessons of practical experience—however important—which by their nature are unique and exclusive.

The study deals with two issues which are theoretically and practically relevant to social welfare planning, to social welfare policy, and thus to the lives of people in urban industrial society. The first issue, the macrocosmic one, is whether there is a possible sequence or progression in which the range of social welfare programs is used by people according to their level of integration into industrial or, if you wish, urban society. The second issue, related to the first and the more microcosmic of the two, concerns itself with barriers to the delivery of the social services in a truly equal or egalitarian way. By "delivery of service" I refer to the manner in which the services are perceived and used rather than to the manner in which they are conceived or offered. "Egalitarian" services are accessible to all and used by those who need them most rather than by those who best know how to use them.

Planners of social welfare services in any heterogeneous community are bound to be concerned both with the possible sequence in which welfare services are used by different consumer groups and with how these services may be delivered so that they are indeed used by those for whom they are ostensibly intended. The same issues seem to be of more than theoretical interest for social welfare planners, policy-makers, and social workers who deliver the service in countries or communities which do not have a fully developed network of social services. For one thing, these countries or communities have more freedom in their planning and policy-making because they have less to undo. In addition, they might be interested in assessing priorities for introducing alternative social welfare programs into a growing, developing society. With all the uncertainties involved in social planning, planners in most of these developing societies can be certain of one phenomenon: they will have to provide services which cater to the needs of masses of people moving into an industrial society, services which will be needed for a long time to come. Indeed, this study proceeded on the assumption that there is a link, not yet fully explored or known, between the movement of people into urban industrial society and the kinds of services which facilitate their movement from one stage to the next. If this is correct, it behooves social planners to provide not only services which help people cope with their current stage, but those which prepare them for moving into the next one as well. This coping and this preparation can presumably be facilitated by appropriate social welfare services.

A rational basis for determining the proper sequence of social services and for maximizing the accessibility of available services is not easily found. One is handicapped by the relative dearth of studies on consumer behavior in the field of social welfare. Another handicap is the apparently inevitable social distance between those who conceive of and deliver social services and those who will or might use these services to their advantage. Social welfare planners and practitioners do not usually belong to the same "group" as the consumers do. In addition, the planners cannot easily plan services for consumers or clients who have not sought them. Yet, in the absence of more objective criteria, planners and practitioners resort for guidance to their experiences with clients who *have* sought their services, and these experiences may be inappropriate for clients whom they have not known. In view of these predicaments, it seems to me that social welfare research can be of practical assistance to social welfare planners by providing a rational basis for social policy. In a modest way, this research on the relationship between use of welfare services and levels of integration into industrial society attempts to do just this.

In our study we tried to discover in what manner the degree of an individual's integration into industrial society is associated with his use of four social welfare programs. For that purpose we interviewed a random sample of 116 men between the ages of twenty-five and thirty in the course of their regular reporting for Army Reserve duties. We asked them, first, questions concerning their degree of integration into the life of an industrial society; and secondly, questions on their current use of, and acquaintance with, four social service programs—medical services for treating the common cold, dental care, adult education facilities, and workmen's injury insurance. For these latter questions we tallied only the use of services for which an actual need was established.[1]

On the basis of answers to the questions on integration, we defined an individual's integration into industrial society by three scales of participation and by indices of integration. The scales turned out to be independent of each other, whereas the indices were not. Two of the scales refer to behavioral phenomena, one to the degree of informed political behavior and the other to time consciousness. In addition, we selected one attitudinal scale which refers to the individual's traditionalism in family relations. The three indices of integration refer to the number of years in the country, the level of education, and the occupational status of each respondent.

To assess the relationship between integration into the life of an industrial society and the use of, and acquaintance with, the social welfare services, respectively, we computed the correlations between them. We correlated the respondents' use of each of the four social service programs and their acquaintance with the operations of each program, respectively with each of the three scales of participation and with each of the three indices of integration, respectively. In total, we computed forty-eight correlations: twenty-four between use of services and the scales and indices and twenty-four between acquaintance with services and the scales and indices. Of the twenty-four correlations between each of the six indicators of integration and the use of the four service programs, nine were statistically significant beyond the .05 level. Of the twenty-

[1] I shall not refer here to our attempts to measure the users' capacity to evaluate the services used and the appropriateness of the use made.

four correlations between each of the same six indicators and acquaintance with the service programs, only four were significant beyond the .05 level.

There are two findings of this analysis which in terms of their content are relevant for our discussion here. They are based on the particular measures we selected and limited, of course, by the nature of this single sample.

First, we have learned that acquaintance with a service program —knowing how it operates—is little related to integration. In other words, integration does not, apparently, coincide with greater familiarity with the operations of a service program.

Second, we have learned that individuals who are *not* integrated into industrial society tend to use medical services more than the integrated do. The integrated, in turn, tend to use adult education facilities and dental services more than do the nonintegrated. This finding demonstrates something which seems to me to be of more general interest, namely, that integration into an industrial society is indeed a relevant variable for understanding the *uses* made of social welfare services.

These are the highlights of a number of findings which cannot be reported here. To the stock-in-trade question, "So what?" it may be well, for the moment, to acknowledge rather than ignore the methodological limitations of this exploratory study so as to give examples of the kinds of conclusions that can be drawn on the basis of the findings which bear on the two social policy issues raised earlier.

If indeed there is a progression in the use of social services by levels of integration, and if indeed the low-integrated use health services before they use adult education facilities, the social welfare planner who plans services for a community in the process of integrating people into industrial society knows what to expect from consumers on the periphery. Such knowledge may help either to provide what the consumers expect or, if the planner so wishes, to counteract this tendency. He may choose to counteract it in order to promote the use of adult education facilities when he considers that more conducive to integration than the use of health services, or when there exists a relative oversupply of health services and an undersupply of adult education facilities, as is the case in Israel today.

Moreover, if such a planner were seeking to promote use of adult education or dental care facilities by the nonintegrated, there are two kinds of findings which might help him to do so. His first priority would not be to increase their acquaintance with the service programs but rather to modify the actual delivery system of the two services. Secondly, on the basis of the findings on the scales of participation and indices of integration, he could identify those who do not use these services. He would know, for example, that those who do not participate in the political life, who are less well educated, and who have lower occupational status—to take but three dimensions of these measures—use adult education and dental care facilities less frequently than those who are newcomers or those who are traditional in their attitude to their family. In his attempts to promote use of these services, therefore, the social planner would direct his attention to those with the former characteristics rather than to those with the latter.

It scarcely needs mentioning that only an unwise social welfare policy planner would base his hopefully rational decisions on this one study. But perhaps this study may encourage similar researches which, if carried out in several different countries, may indeed generate theories and theory-based experiments. Whatever these might contribute to the welfare or well-being of one community, one city, or one nation, in the final analysis it is a different and transcendent well-being which gives social welfare research its special promise and urgency—the well-being of individuals.

Demographic Factors in Urban Development

MILOS MACURA

POPULATION DIVISION, UNITED NATIONS

THE IMPORTANCE of demographic factors in urban development is widely recognized in modern technical literature. There is broad agreement that population is a vital component of urbanization. But there is also considerable disagreement on whether the growth of urban population, especially in less developed regions, is too rapid. The flows of population from rural to urban areas, and the urban development as a whole, become, in this respect, a matter of controversy.[1] This controversy is perhaps due more to the lack of information on the growth and structural changes of population in both urban and rural areas than to the differing opinions on urbanization as a progressive developmental process.

The recency of urbanization in its modern forms, as well as the relative newness of demographic research in general and of urban research in particular, contributes to this lack of knowledge. On the other hand, the complexity of demographic trends in relation to spatial and urban phenomena precludes the use of simple research techniques.[2] The reluctance to adopt a standard definition of an "urban" area and an "urban" population is perhaps a small indicator of the methodological problems which are being faced in demographic urban research.

---

[1] "Whether consciously or not, American social scientists tend to reject industrial urbanization as an ideal for these transitional societies; instead they favor the development of moderate-size towns with handicraft industries and the preservation of many rural traditions. The fact that social scientists who hold to 'democratic' ideals should implicitly oppose extensive industrial urbanization is somewhat ironical, for recent research supports the hypothesis that democracy flourishes most vigorously within advanced industrial-urban societies." See G. Sjoberg, "Cities in Developing and in Industrial Societies: a Cross-cultural Analysis," in P. M. Hauser and L. F. Schnore, eds., *The Study of Urbanization* (New York: John Wiley, 1965), p. 222.

[2] See K. Davis, "Foreword: Urban Research and Its Significance," in J. P. Gibbs, ed., *Urban Research Methods* (New York: Van Nostrand Co., 1961), pp. xiii–xix.

It should be pointed out, however, that the great variety of forms in which urbanization takes place discourages the standardization of methods and techniques for the urban study of demographic changes. Traditional rural-urban differences in various spheres, including the demographic, are being accompanied by new differences that emerge both in industrialized and in less developed countries. New features of urban organization and life change former urban concepts and add to the complexity of current stages in urbanization. Considering the world as a whole, it seems, therefore, that the distance between an urban area and a rural one is much greater than it was a century ago during the early expansion of urbanization. It seems also that the variety of forms of urban and rural settlement is greater than it was, in spite of the equalization of living conditions in urban and rural areas which seems to take place in some regions.

A simplified model of the growth of urban population which made provisions for natural increase in population and inmigration from rural areas is no longer valid. Migration patterns are more elaborate and include, in addition to migration from rural to urban areas, the migration within the urban stratum and the effects of urban transformation of nonurban localities that occur as a consequence of changes in demographic, economic, and social characteristics.

Urban development, considered as a complex process in which there is an interplay of many components, including the demographic, differs from region to region according to the variations in its scope, its intensity, and its characteristics. For example, the physical integration of cities, suburbs, and neighboring rural areas in highly urbanized regions as a spontaneous process is different from a planned, decentralized urbanization through construction of new towns or satellite cities. Urbanization also takes place through the development of transport facilities and the reorganization of the space with its economic and social functions. The equalization of housing, transport, and living conditions, which tends to reduce the differences between rural and urban areas, and the deterioration of urban settlements because of economic or psychological reasons, or other specific features of urban development, should also be recognized. It seems that in many economically developed regions the traditional differences between urban and rural regions tend to disappear while new differences within the rural area emerge.

On the other hand, it seems that in many less developed regions the differences between urban and rural and also the differences within the urban areas gain in importance.[3] The growing pressure on agricultural resources and on rural settlements as a consequence of the rapid growth of population contributes to the problems already existing in the rural economy. The slow transfer of population to nonagricultural industries, which is far from being efficient and successful in reducing the rural overpopulation, adds to the problems of urban areas. The rapid growth of unhealthy and overcrowded settlements with inadequate facilities and heavy unemployment cannot improve the living conditions in towns and cities. The slow development of nonagricultural industries and their concentration in our cities add to the centralization of population; they discourage the construction of new urban centers and their rational distribution over the nation.

All these trends have to be taken into consideration, of course, when we study the demographic component of urban development at the world level. But the national peculiarities of urban growth do not necessarily have to be in harmony with world generalizations. If they were properly considered according to the national definition of urban population, the following statistics would give a rough idea of the regional differences in urban development.[4] Around 1960 the percentage of urban population of European countries varied between 80 (Netherlands), 78 (United Kingdom), and 23 (Portugal). With the exception of Japan, with 63 percent of urban population, and Singapore and Hong Kong, levels of urbanization in Asia were much lower and ranged from 43 percent (Malaya) to 3 percent (Nepal). Even lower were the levels of urbanization south of the Sahara: Ghana and Senegal about 23 percent and Uganda about 5 percent of urban population. In the Americas the levels of urbanization are lower than in

---

3 Sjoberg, *op. cit.*, pp. 216–35.

4 *Demographic Yearbook*, 1962, 1963, 1964 (New York: United Nations); see also table and definitions in 5, in the Annex.

Europe, primarily due to the lower urban development in Latin America; they varied from 70 percent (USA and Canada) and 67 percent (Venezuela and Chile) to 23 percent (Honduras).

National figures confirm in broad terms the general thinking on urban development by continents. Perhaps they also provide a satisfactory basis for national studies of urbanization by allowing for specific features of urban characteristics and by meeting the national criteria of "urban." But the exclusively national consideration of "urban" does not satisfy comparability requirements needed for international analysis. A thorough examination of definitions used, for example, in European countries indicates that countries with similar levels and characteristics of urbanization publish statistics which give the impression that these levels and characteristics are entirely dissimilar. The differences, statistically speaking, are even greater on a world level. Finally, there are many regions for which there are no statistics on urban population.

With the aim of overcoming these difficulties, Davis and Hertz suggested fifteen years ago [5] that a standard of 20,000 population be used to differentiate between "noncity" and "city" population. This standard has also been accepted in a preliminary United Nations study dealing with the levels of urbanization [6] and in a United Nations study of world urbanization trends from 1920 to 1960 which is now in process. Though the standard suffered from many deficiencies, well known to experts in urban research, it was considered a convenient criterion in view of the unavailability and nonuniformity of statistical data. The following discussion will be based on estimated trends of total and urban population, using the 20,000 standard, and the arbitrary nature of the delimitation of urban and rural populations must therefore be kept in mind.

The preliminary estimates of total population and of population in places of 20,000 and over, and those with less than 20,000, are still subject to revision by the Population Division of the United Nations. As indicators of orders of magnitudes and of trends, however, they seem to be quite satisfactory. Some impor-

[5] K. Davis and H. Hertz, "The World Distribution of Urbanization," *Bulletin of the International Statistical Institute*, XXXIII, Part 4 (1951), 228–30.

[6] *World Survey of Urban Population Growth* (document prepared for the thirteenth session of the Population Commission, 1965).

tant conclusions concerning urbanization trends in the world and in its developed and less developed regions may arise from these estimates. There is a strong feeling that they will not change with the revision of the estimates.

Between 1920 and 1960 the world population increased by 1.6 times (from 1,860,000,000 to 2,994,000,000); the population in localities with 20,000 and over tripled (from 253,000,000 to 752,000,000). The growth of both total population and population in localities of 20,000 and over in the developed regions was substantially smaller than in less developed regions. In the developed regions, total population increased by less than 1.5 times (from 672,000,000 to 977,000,000), and population in cities of 20,000 and over by 2.3 times (from 185,000,000 to 433,000,000), while the corresponding increases in less developed regions were 1.7 times for the total population (from 1,188,000,000 to 2,017,000,000), and 4.7 times in localities with 20,000 and more people (from 68,000,000 to 319,000,000).

The world's population is still predominantly rural.[7] It was estimated in 1960 that about 75 percent of the population continued to live in places of less than 20,000 (in 1920 it was 86 percent). In the developed regions this population made up 56 percent (73 percent in 1920), while in the less developed regions it was 84 percent (compared to 94 percent in 1920). World population remains predominantly rural because of the predominantly rural nature of its reproduction. Of the absolute increase of 478,000,000 from 1950 to 1960, about 221,000,000 was the increase of population in urban areas, and about 257,000,000 was the increase of population in localities of less than 20,000. The bulk of the latter increase took place in the less developed regions.

In view of the rapid growth of urban population in less developed regions and their very rural character, further clarification is needed regarding the volume and relations between the two segments. Along with the rapid growth of the decennial increment of total population in less developed regions (from 123,000,000 to 359,000,000) there was a rapid growth in the portions of that increment attributed to cities with populations of 20,000 and over

[7] Davis and Hertz, *op. cit.*, pp. 227–28.

(from 26,000,000 to 118,000,000). About one fifth of the decennial increment was the city portions in the 1920s, one fourth in the 1930s, more than one third in the 1940s, and somewhat less than one third in the 1950s. But in spite of their growing attracting ability, cities were not in a position to absorb the entire natural increase in population of the less developed regions. A growing part of that increase, in absolute terms, continued to accumulate in localities with population of less than 20,000 (from 97,000,000 to 241,000,000). It should be noticed that the accumulation of noncity population was 2.5 times larger in 1950–60 than in 1920–30.

Rates of growth of city population varied during the last forty years due to many reasons.

Annual Rates of Growth of Population

Locality and Population	1920–30	1930–40	1940–50	1950–60
World				
20,000 and over	2.63	2.67	2.20	3.54
Under 20,000	0.80	0.72	0.59	1.22
Total	1.07	1.05	0.91	1.75
Developed regions				
20,000 and over	2.38	2.20	1.27	2.75
Under 20,000	0.73	0.11	–0.04	0.30
Total	1.21	0.80	0.44	1.31
Less developed regions				
20,000 and over	3.29	3.69	4.06	4.73
Under 20,000	0.83	0.97	0.83	1.54
Total	0.99	1.19	1.17	1.98

The single reason which contributed most to the fluctuations was the growth rate of the total population. It is evident that during the past forty years urbanization trends were generally higher wherever the rates of natural increase were higher. The effects of the Second World War are also visible, particularly in the developed regions where many countries suffered heavy population losses. The final balance, however, resulted in a negative trend in localities under 20,000. It is difficult to determine whether and to what extent the high rate of growth of city populations from 1950 to 1960 was due to postwar compensation factors, particularly since many events have taken place during the same period with stimulating effects on urbanization in less developed regions.

Over the last twenty years migration between the less developed and the more developed regions of the world was, demographically, almost negligible. Changing trends of population growth are therefore to be viewed primarily as a consequence of the changing patterns of reproduction of the population, with an emphasis on declining mortality, particularly in the less developed regions. While the average birth rate in the less developed regions in 1920–30 was approximately 40–45 and remained around 40 in 1950–60, the mortality rate fell from 30–35 to about 19 over the same period, with a resulting increase in the rate of natural growth of population from 10 to 21 per 1,000. Respective changes in the vital rates in developed regions were: for birth, from 30 to 22; for mortality, from 17 to 10; and for the rate of natural growth, from 13 to 12 per 1,000.[8]

There is no satisfactory evidence on the reproduction differentials in urban and rural areas in the less developed regions. Some statistical evidence suggests that both fertility and mortality may be higher in rural areas than in urban, but that there is a somewhat higher rate of natural increase in urban areas.[9] It also suggests that the differences in the rate of natural increase may tend to diminish. Assume now, only for the purpose of estimating the

[8] *World Population Prospects as Assessed in 1963* (United Nations publication),
[9] M. A. El-Badry, "Trends in the Components of Population Growth in the Arab Countries of the Middle East: a Survey of Present Information," in *Demography* (Chicago: Population Association of America, 1965), II, 140. El-Badry suggests the following adjusted crude birth and death rates for urban and rural areas in the United Arab Republic:

	1934		1959	
	Urban	*Rural*	*Urban*	*Rural*
Birth	44.4	49.1	44.1	45.2
Death	29.5	36.0	17.8	19.4
Growth	14.9	13.1	26.3	25.8

See also "Demographic Aspects of Urbanization in the ECAFE Region" (prepared by the Population Branch, Bureau of Social Affairs, United Nations), in *Urbanization in Asia and the Far East*, Tension and Technology series (Calcutta: UNESCO, 1957), 100–106; "Demographic Aspects of Urbanization in Latin America" (prepared by the Population Branch, Bureau of Social Affairs, United Nations), in P. M. Hauser, ed., *Urbanization in Latin America*, Technology and Society series (Liége: UNESCO, 1961), pp. 102–7.

net rural-urban migration, that the rate of natural increase in 1950–60 was equal in the rural and urban areas of less-developed countries. Then, the net inmigration in cities of 20,000 and over may be estimated as over the decennial natural increase of the city population, corresponding to almost one fourth of the decennial natural increase of the noncity population. In other words, the net transfer estimate corresponds to almost one fourth of the natural increase of noncity population. In the developed countries, however, the bulk of the natural increase used to settle in the cities: out of a population increase of 119,000,000 in the developed regions during the same period, only 16,000,000 was, in fact, an increase in population living in localities with less than 20,000 people.

Further research on future urbanization trends, based on the estimates prepared by John Grauman for the United Nations Urbanization Seminar,[10] has not changed our earlier impressions of rapid urban developments. While the average rate of growth of world population between 1960 and 1980 will be higher than that between 1950 and 1960, the rate of growth of city population is expected to be lower. But the absolute decennial increase in city population may be about 40 percent greater, due basically to the very rapid growth of the total population. In the developed regions not more than 10 percent of the increment in population is expected to settle in localities with population of less than 20,000. This will bring their city population in 1980 to 52 percent. In the less developed regions more than 60 percent of the increase may remain in small localities. Thus, in 1980 the ratio of city to total population would not exceed 24 percent in those regions. It means that, according to the present assumption, future development may be even more discouraging than the development in the recent past.

To generalize, it seems that the developed regions of the world are entering a stage in which their populations will tend to reach some kind of demographic maturity characterized by the predominance of industrial and urban elements. Increasing agricultural

[10] "World Urbanization Trends, 1920–1960: an Interim Report on Work in Progress at the United Nations Population Division," document prepared for the United Nations Urbanization Seminar, Pittsburgh, 1966.

productivity offers in these circumstances an opportunity for massive employment of labor in the nonagricultural sector, the growth and diversification of which call for additional employment in spite of higher productivity. Spatial distribution of population, either in cities or in suburbs and urbanized villages, is, therefore, not a mere function of patterns of production but a result of either spontaneous or organized efforts to meet the changing requirements of work and living. The growth of population is increasingly under human control, with more complex backgrounds affecting the reproductive behavior of people. Urban population seems gradually to lose its mainly quantitative aspects, with an emphasis on quality and values. Obviously, all this is not a nonconflicting process; but the problems which arise are much greater in other than demographic spheres.

The basic problems of urban transformation of populations of the less developed regions seem to be primarily in their national economies [11] and in the rapid growth of their population. The recent growth of urban population of 4.7 percent per annum in these regions was hardly surpassed by the rate of growth of the nonagricultural sector of their economies. The rate of growth of rural population of over 1.5 percent was generally either equal to, or only slightly lower than, that of agricultural production. In

[11] "It is probably true to say that Asia is over-urbanized in relation to its degree of economic development. At comparable levels of urbanization, the developed countries of today had a correspondingly greater proportion of their labour force engaged in non-agricultural occupations. In that sense, Asia can be said to be relatively over-urbanized. The pace of urbanization, especially in the last decade, has far exceeded the growth rate of economies of Asia." See P. M. Hauser, "Summary Report of the General Rapporteur," *Urbanization in Asia and the Far East*, p. 9.

"La société urbaine est profondément différente de la société rurale. Plus exactement, elle cherche son organisation spécifique, au milieu d'hésitations et de tâtonnements, qui comportent de lourds gaspillages de valeurs humaines. Avant même que se constitue une société, il faut que se forme une population capable d'assurer son propre renouvellement de génération en génération. Or, les conditions d'attraction de population dans les villes industrielles distinctes des villes marchandes et administratives anciennes ou des centres de spéculation coloniale, sont peu favorables, au début du moins, à la constitution d'une population stable capable d'évoluer par ses propres ressources. Les sociétés industrielles, et en particulier les sociétés minières, se sont préoccupées longtemps de se procurer une main-d'oeuvre jeune sans se soucier de créer réellement une population." See P. George, *Questions de géographie de la population*, travaux et Documents, Cahier no. 34 (Paris: Institut national d'études démographiques, 1959), p. 177.

such circumstances there is not much chance for improvement, and no choice can be made for more productive work and better living. Economically nonjustified migration to cities, which often takes place in less developed regions, does not help either the individual or the nation. It seems to be mainly an escape from the physical or social overpopulation in the countryside. This is one of the reasons why changes in the reproduction patterns of the population lag behind the pace of urbanization and why the structures of population insistently maintain their early shapes.

Urban Development Implications for Training Social Work Personnel

ELLEN WINSTON

COMMISSIONER OF WELFARE, U.S. DEPARTMENT OF
HEALTH, EDUCATION, AND WELFARE

IT IS most appropriate that the meetings of the ICSW should be focused on urbanization, with its many complexities and its implications for the field of social welfare. No other trend since the Industrial Revolution has so sharply etched the needs of people with the blade of change. And it is within the framework of change that social work education must examine itself to see how well our instructional programs are meeting the challenge of the times—and how ready we are to anticipate the requirements of the future.

This readiness applies to the world community as a whole, not merely to the highly developed nations. For wherever we turn, we are all viewing the costly, tragic effects of explosive social problems —problems which have multiplied in our cities far more rapidly than our social structure has expanded to prevent or control them.

Everywhere, the ideological and technological revolutions of the present decade have caused major areas of human activity to be altered. Political relationships and boundaries have shifted. Cultural attitudes, standards of conduct, and established ways of living are being transformed—sometimes shattered.

We seek a higher quality of life for all people. Yet, even in the United States, despite economic abundance, we find many of the same anxieties, the same social pressures, that are found among the nations of Southeast Asia, of Africa, of Latin America. The degrees of stress differ, of course. But by our standards, and despite our resources, in my country in 1966 there are 34,000,000 people who are poor,[1] and several million others whose low financial resources bring them perilously close to the brink of poverty.

[1] Social Security Administration, Department of Health, Education, and Welfare, determination of poverty-income level at $3,100 per annum for a family of four.

In the United States, the Welfare Administration has major responsibility to give leadership to improve social conditions. Thus, we are concerned, for a variety of reasons, with the direction in which social work education is heading.

The International Office in the Welfare Administration works closely with the Agency for International Development, the United Nations, and the Organization of American States to expand training opportunities for social workers around the world, especially in the developing countries. More than a thousand social welfare workers from other countries come to our office every year on study or observation tours financed by their own countries, by United Nations and other fellowships, or by other types of educational grants. The International Office works with the schools of social work in this country and with public and private welfare agencies to arrange programs that will help these students and observers to absorb the best of our concepts and methods and find appropriate ways to adapt them to the needs of their own people.

Without question, we learn as much from these knowledgeable visitors as we are able to teach. These visiting students are helping our schools of social work and our welfare agencies to develop a more global viewpoint and to become more alert to apply the knowledge that other countries have acquired through their own progress or struggles toward more effective social development.

While we hope that the number of visiting students will continue to expand, we are more and more aware of the growing number and vitality of schools of social work in other countries. We think it urgent that the capabilities for training be enlarged in every country so that the skills and knowledge acquired will be directly related to the setting in which practice is to be carried out. Thus, the training of social work personnel must involve both the values of the individual country and those of other countries that have a contribution to make.

On the home front, the Welfare Administration's mandate to administer extensive federal social legislation charges us to be concerned not only with the numbers of qualified social workers available for public welfare services but also with the extent to which their education is relevant to the social problems of our times, which constantly become more complex.

The most severe of these problems are festering in our big cities. During the past year they have come to a head with riots, sit-ins, protest marches, picket lines, and other physical demonstrations of the frustrations of hundreds of thousands of citizens who are dissatisfied with the quality of life they currently experience.

The fact is—and we know it—that the United States today faces a crisis in its cities, and the crisis is one of social disintegration. Decent housing, better schools, improved health, more job opportunities, adequate financial assistance for those who are too old, too young, or too disabled to work, a broad gamut of supportive social services—these are both immediate needs and long-range goals which challenge our patience and tax our skills to the utmost. But the problem of the city is also a problem of the human spirit which schools of social work may not ignore, for it is at the heart of the social ferment now effecting so many changes in social work practice.

Let me give you a few facts about urbanization as it is occurring in the United States.

In 1960, our total population was 180,000,000, of whom 70 percent lived in metropolitan areas, in our cities and their immediate environs.

By the year 2000, we can expect that 74 percent of our estimated 330,000,000 population will be residents of standard metropolitan areas. In fact, already some 400,000 people are moving to major central cities every year—most of them from depressed and rural areas where they are unable to earn a satisfactory living or enjoy the opportunities of our contemporary society.

We should be constructing 2,000,000 new dwelling units a year to serve our expanding population. During 1965 our building rate was 1,500,000 units a year—25 percent behind what is needed for basic minimum housing—and the rate is even lower in 1966. Adequate housing thus has become one of the most critical problems of the city dweller.

For the person with low income, for the person who migrates from nonurban areas to the city and is also poor, there is little chance to obtain housing anywhere other than in run-down buildings in already neglected neighborhoods where sanitary and service facilities may be inadequate or, sometimes, nonexistent.

In city after city in this country and around the world, the inner city, the old city, is already or is fast becoming a slum, inhabited by racial minority groups or other impoverished families. The tenants pay high prices for food and exorbitant rents. There are not enough playgrounds, swimming pools, or other public resources for recreation. Schools, hospitals, and clinics are crowded, and in many communities the facilities are outmoded or even totally lacking.

Public transportation is inadequate and costly. How does one get a job outside the ghetto when he cannot afford the daily bus or tramfare—or does not know what life is like outside his own neighborhood?

Consequently, we find social isolation and extremely limited opportunity, not to mention lack of incentive, for personal development and education, or for other steps toward social improvement. As we all know, the poor have no monopoly on these conditions, for not only millions of people on marginal incomes but others as well are being drawn into the same web. It is a question of degree of destitution.

The initiative and leadership to prevent as well as to correct these societal failures wherever they exist must come in large part from the social work profession. To do the job, the practitioner will have to be a reformer as well as a professional, concerned as much with the social environment as with the individual personality, and the school of social work may have to sacrifice traditionalism in curriculum content to make room for attention to social action.

TASKS FOR SOCIAL WORK EDUCATION

As I see it, there are two broad tasks which our educational systems must prepare the social worker to perform in today's developing urban society around the world.

One of these tasks is essentially therapeutic in that it serves those who need help in finding, have been unable to find, or have lost, a role in life that is satisfying to themselves and to society.

Casework, group work, the staffing of special services and facilities—such as mental health clinics, day care programs, and homemaker services—and, undoubtedly, new techniques which will be developed, are tools for this task.

The whole focus is upon the casualties among us, on helping them to find a place in the main stream of society when that is possible or, at the least, to attain whatever measure of self-fulfillment and self-sufficiency they have the potential to reach.

I include *prevention* of individual and social problems as an important therapeutic function. For, in the majority of cases, social pathology can be avoided, or minimized, by early recognition of the signs and symptoms. Prevention of family breakdown, prevention of desertion, prevention of child neglect—these require expert diagnostic skills as well as the ability to treat smoldering problems before they burst into fire, and the school of social work must provide its students with the tools to do the job. I cannot emphasize this too strongly; for the level of social development any nation achieves depends in substantial measure upon the number and kinds of social problems it is willing to tolerate.

Just as we take certain public health precautions to assure that our population is protected from the transmittal of diseases, so must we see that our populations are protected from social hazards that disrupt families and create lost generations of youth and of the aged. The settlement house concept is extremely important to this effort, and the United States can profit by the experience of Denmark and of other highly advanced Western European countries. With modernized versions of the settlement house, I believe we can reverse the present trend of providing fragmented social services from headquarters that are distant from the people who need their services.

Neighborhood social service centers.—I would like to see centers located in the heart of every poverty sector so that a wide variety of services would be readily accessible. In terms of my country, these centers could include offices in which public welfare workers would interview applicants and recipients of public aid, would provide casework and group work services as needed. They could include or be next door to certain types of health clinics. The centers could also provide education and constructive recreation projects for the elderly, day care programs for children, a base for homemakers and other direct-service staff. The patterns, but not the objectives, would of course differ country by country.

One of the most effective ways to motivate people to take advantage of comprehensive, coordinated services is to see that, geographically, the services are close to each other and close to those who need them. You will be hearing more and more about one-stop centers in the United States—one of the innovative devices we in Washington are encouraging as a means of enabling our welfare agencies to be more adequately responsive to the welfare needs of each community.

Just this summer, for example, the New York City Department of Welfare opened its first Satellite Neighborhood Service Center. Located in West Harlem, a section of the city with an extremely high incidence of poverty and its attendant unrest and discontent, the center is the first of several to be opened in New York. It is, in effect, a miniature welfare department set up in the heart of a deprived neighborhood and geared to serve its specific needs. It will not only be concerned with the financial needs of the residents but will furnish guidance and counseling services and information on other sources of help in the city and how to apply to them.

Satellite centers, by whatever name, can become a tremendously useful tool in our efforts to repersonalize services to city dwellers. We expect that they will function as a cooperating and coordinating force with local groups and agencies toward more effective community planning and services. They offer an excellent laboratory where therapeutic skills may be developed and practiced, and I hope that our schools of social work will utilize them fully when planning field experiences for their students. The objective of these centers is just as applicable to a large city in any other country as to one in our own land.

Social statesmanship.—The second major task for social welfare is the achievement of "social statesmanship." This is the ability to help make changes and adjustments in our present social structure which take account of the demographic, economic, social, and other forces which have so altered the nature of our world.

Through social statesmanship we must find ways to keep the human and personal touch in our mobile and urbanized society. We must find ways, as people move from a rural to city setting, to see that they are not lost in the concrete jungle, that needy sick people are more than clinic numbers to the physicians and nurses who take care of them, that children of the slums get as much personal attention and have as highly trained schoolteachers as children in more affluent neighborhoods. We must find ways to assure that children and families in all income groups receive the services that will help them function effectively and happily.

New and enlarged responsibilities have been given to public welfare in this country by a veritable flood of important social legislation over the past few years. At the same time, this means new and broader responsibility for our training facilities. To fulfill the intent of the new legislation, we must have not only large numbers of social workers interested in public service but also practitioners whose education has been soundly based in economics, the tax structure, and the principles behind government procedures and programs. In many cities, the social worker must also possess the social statesmanship to work with city managers and planners, with industry, civic groups, and other citizens concerned with administrative changes and improvements. Yet, there is no denying that the social work profession is ill-prepared either numerically or in competence for this role.

SHORTAGE OF MANPOWER

The manpower shortage is acute in virtually every social welfare agency, but it is particularly acute in our public welfare agencies. Last year, for example, a departmental task force on social work education and manpower estimated that by 1970 public welfare agencies in the United States would require almost 50,000 more workers for public assistance programs and over 38,000 additional workers to specialize in services to children.

Almost 40 percent of all counties in the United States, containing about 15 percent of the total child population, do not have any full-time professional public child welfare workers. In the counties which do have such workers, the ratio is one worker per 10,000 children!

We need 10,500 more social workers for new federally aided community mental health programs as well as mental hospitals and other facilities for the mentally ill—6,000 more to staff hospitals, clinics, and other medical facilities.

Add to these figures many special programs, such as those serving the elderly, and we find more than 100,000 opportunities for qualified social workers.

Stimulus to social work training.—The Welfare Administration is trying to meet this crisis by making an increasingly heavy investment in social work training. On the one hand, it seeks to help schools of social work to expand their facilities and to enlarge the number of student traineeships through financial grants. On the other hand, it strengthens in-service training for agency personnel.

Whatever the country, training of social work personnel must include study for some in special schools, training for many in connection with their day-to-day jobs.

Early this year, President Johnson issued an appeal to all Americans to make their summer months especially productive. In support of the President's program, the Welfare Administration urged state welfare agencies to use existing federal authority to finance summer programs for faculty members of graduate schools of social work. By means of demonstration project grants, the states could add professional assistance to agency staffs to relieve the summer shortage of skilled public welfare personnel. As a result, 121 faculty members from 31 schools of social work have been employed in 34 projects in 27 state public welfare agencies. These university people have gained valuable experiences to take back to their classrooms. At the same time, I feel certain, the public welfare staffs have also profited by their association with forward-looking faculty members already deeply involved in course content related to social work practice in large urban areas.

We have also brought two doctoral students into the Welfare Administration for the summer where they have been getting first-hand experience in program development as well as in our total spectrum of welfare services and the problems of administering them from the national level.

More and more, the states give summer employment to college students. Working as aides to caseworkers, they obtain valuable insights into the problems and needs of families in trouble. This trend to offer summer experience to college students is accelerating and is proving to be useful in recruiting many of the students upon their graduation from college.

Innovative graduate and undergraduate programs.—Innovative approaches to graduate education are essential, and in the United States the Council on Social Work Education as well as the Welfare Administration is encouraging experimentation. The new sequence in social welfare administration at the School of Social Work of the University of Pittsburgh is a case in point. Here a graduate school is departing from the traditional approach in that this two-year program is focused on administration. It has a different sequence of courses as well as different course content. Field work placements have been made in public welfare agencies and in other settings. Since the caliber of public welfare programs is so directly related to the caliber of the administrator, the importance of this focus can hardly be overemphasized. Such innovative changes as this need to be more widespread.

It is encouraging also to note that some of our schools are looking critically at curriculum content to see what can be done to align it more precisely with social development. Several are experimenting with ways to shorten professional training. No matter how rapidly we accelerate training programs, however, it would be unrealistic to expect that we can provide the two-year course of graduate social work training traditional in this country to all the men and women who are needed now, let alone those who will be needed in the immediate future.

Since it is clear that, for a long period ahead, undergraduate education will be the limit of formal education for the majority of caseworkers, it is vital that more attention be given to undergraduate sequences and more study be made of what should be included in undergraduate social welfare programs. We know that content on social welfare can and should be added within the liberal arts program. To the extent that we strengthen the potentials of undergraduate education, we will recruit more knowledgeable young people into social work; and we will be able to join the other professions that gain strength and prestige from their requirements for preprofessional preparation. Moreover, we need more high-caliber recruits. It seems clear that a good undergraduate social welfare program with stiff intellectual requirements can help to attract the more competent students. This is one of the areas in which we have much to learn from other countries, where training is largely focused on the college as contrasted with the graduate level.

In-service training needs.—The role which agency in-service training fulfills in the continuum of social work education is being increasingly emphasized. It is well-recognized that workers of all types need to have more knowledge and to develop more skills after they are employed in a social welfare agency. Also, practitioners who will not be applicants for graduate education in social work need more content and greater skills than they now possess or will acquire without special programs.

There are likely to be many experiments in agency in-service training of six to nine months' duration, giving workers the opportunity to learn new skills. It is important for many reasons that there be collaboration between school faculty and agency staff development personnel in conducting such agency in-service training. Effective and sound educational methods must be used, and the training must reflect the best of our social work values and philosophy. There needs to be consistency in the assumptions that underlie social work education, whether they evolve in schools of social work through curriculum policy or in agency in-service training. Because theory contributes to practice and practice to theory, the vital interrelationships between schools and agencies must be kept open and dynamic, each learning from the other, each reacting quickly to changing concepts and changing needs.

Utilization of personnel.—If we are to meet present and future needs, and if we are to assure the full participation of the social work profession in our efforts to eliminate poverty and dependency, we must give greater attention to approaches which are more rapid and far-reaching than the traditional relationships of social worker to client. We must find better ways of providing services to people in groups. We must prepare social workers for leadership in community planning and community action. We must have administrators who know how to break down jobs so that they can be performed by persons with varying skills, and we must become more adept at teaching those skills quickly. The range of qualifications required—from subprofessional to doctoral—is far wider today than ever before in our history. In this connection, we should not overlook the practical values inherent in the employment of nonprofessional, indigenous workers recruited from the very clients the welfare agency serves.

If we are to help lift an isolated, depressed segment of the population out of poverty, one of the first tasks is to meet the immediate and pressing needs seen by these groups themselves. Properly trained and supervised, the indigenous worker can bridge the communications gap between the professional worker at one economic and cultural level and the client at another. At the same time, this nonprofessional can release valuable professional time for counseling and other services by assuming many of the routine functions essential to the operation of the welfare agency.

We need to remind ourselves, at times, that social development is not only inventive planning to achieve broad ideals and goals, it is also attention to demands of everyday living—things as simple as teaching a mother how to care for her baby, how to keep her household tidy, and how to organize the seemingly overwhelming number of daily duties. Nonprofessional workers can help clients in this manner, and with such other problems as repairing dilapidated homes, planning a more nourishing diet without spending more money for food, or purchasing clothing wisely in relation to the family budget.

Another important role for the indigenous worker is to help clients find and effectively use community services, encourage them to participate in community planning activities, to organize or serve on committees representing neighborhood interests, or better to understand the responsibilities of citizenship.

The indigenous, nonprofessional worker also is able to perform many other necessary functions in the welfare agency, such as the numerous mechanical, clerical, and maintenance services of typing, filing, mimeographing, cleaning, repairing. Since these services are essential to the operation of any business office, the experience the worker gains in the agency often leads to his employment in another setting. At a slightly different level, indigenous personnel with appropriate educational background can be trained as homemaker aides, day care service aides, or health aides.

In all the nonprofessional roles, the indigenous worker as a paid employee is a symbol to the group from which he has been drawn that the welfare agency really wants to help them and that others can succeed just as well as he can. Moreover, this group offers a potential manpower resource which cannot be ignored in face of the increasing caseloads of social agencies everywhere.

The use of indigenous, nonprofessional workers, however, is not without problems and has not as yet won full acceptance in this country. First of all, they have to be trained. It may not necessarily be the responsibility of social work education to provide the training directly. Nevertheless, schools of social work should see that their graduates are prepared to do so when they enter active practice as professional social workers. Further, our schools must convey to their students a strong sense of conviction about the importance of full use of workers whose skills are inferior to their own. Without that conviction, they are unable to involve the indigenous worker successfully and positively in the program and goals of the agency, nor can they plan activities which he is able to share, supervise him, or help him to find rewards in serving as a member of a helping team in his own community.

This brings me to the fact that we lack satisfactory measures of social service effectiveness for personnel at all levels, not merely the nonprofessional. It is not nearly enough to talk about what people do or what they ought to do. We also should be able to specify what they accomplish.

The simpler the task, the easier it is to measure its effectiveness. When we get into the more sophisticated aspects of social service, the subtler roles of the social worker, it becomes increasingly difficult to establish precise measurements of the results. This is an additional challenge which I feel certain the schools of social work will be willing to accept.

There will always be major emphasis upon the highly trained social worker who provides counseling services to a very limited caseload. But there is now a much broader role which the profession should be prepared to fill. The challenge for social work education is to find large-scale methods of applying its body of professional knowledge to the vastly enlarged scope of practice which confronts us today, and this includes research designs to enable us to evaluate the effectiveness of that practice.

One further development has exciting implications for public welfare in the United States and, consequently, for social work education. On June 29 of this year, the Advisory Council on Public Welfare submitted to the Secretary of Health, Education, and Welfare a detailed report of its two-year study of federally aided public welfare programs. The study includes testimony from almost 350 persons from 47 states and represents the views of welfare, health, civic, religious, education, labor, and business organizations, and social welfare.

The Council has recommended sweeping changes. For example, the twelve-member group has concluded that there should be a federal minimum standard for financial aid to the poor which all states would have to meet in order to continue to receive federal aid. The Council also has proposed the elimination of special public assistance programs (Old Age Assistance, Aid to the Blind, Aid to the Permanently and Totally Disabled, and Aid to Families with Dependent Children) and that a single, comprehensive program be substituted in which *need* would be the only criterion for eligibility. At present, many needy people are being deprived of aid because they do not fit into any of the special categories.

The Council also made these other important recommendations:

1. Establishment of a full range of social services in public welfare agencies which are to be available as a matter of right at all times and in convenient locations to all who need them, regardless of their financial status
2. Development of a method to assure legal representation for all who feel they have cause for complaint against decisions made by a public welfare agency, and provision to pay the cost of such legal representation
3. A positive program for informing recipients and applicants of their rights to assistance and services through public welfare, using all appropriate means of communication
4. Prompt extension of coverage and liberalization of benefits under the social insurance programs
5. A greatly expanded social welfare research effort commensurate in size and scope with the national annual expenditures for public welfare services
6. Increased support from the Welfare Administration to ex-

pand all phases of recruitment, education, and training for social welfare personnel at all levels of practice—preprofessional, professional, and advanced

Should these dramatic changes in public welfare policies become effective at some future date, there will indeed be a revolution in social welfare practice in our private agencies as well as in public welfare. Even now, the possibilities are being carefully studied by civic leaders as well as by professional social workers around the nation.

The recommendations of the Council should have a profound effect on our schools of social work. For, if this is the direction we can expect social work practice to take—or even a mere hint of it—social work education can afford to lose no time in making the necessary adjustments.

Universally, we are all facing similar pressures, similar anxieties, and similar aspirations to upgrade the quality of life for all as society around the world becomes more and more urbanized. We must work together to assure innovations in social work education, broadly defined, in all countries which will anticipate the innovations in social planning needed to keep social welfare programs attuned to the broad scope of social development, to the changing nature of our times.

I. IN EUROPE AND AFRICA

JEAN ILIOVICI

CHIEF, SOCIAL WELFARE SERVICES SECTION
BUREAU OF SOCIAL AFFAIRS, UNITED NATIONS

IT IS, of course, a difficult task to discuss matters related to urban development since the circumstances prevailing in Africa and in Europe are so diverse. There might be some merit, however, in using these two widely contrasting examples to show the extent to which the challenge presented by urban development to social welfare workers and social welfare educators differs from one country to another and from one region to another.

Let us consider first the level of urbanization, that is, the proportion of the total population living in towns of 20,000 inhabitants or more. This level has reached only 10 percent in Africa, whereas it is four times higher in Europe. On the other hand, the rate of urbanization is much higher in Africa, where the proportion of urban dwellers has increased by approximately two thirds during the decade 1950–60 versus less than one fifth in Europe. With a few exceptions, the rapidly growing African cities have a very high preponderance of men. Africa is therefore far from a stable urbanization, where not only male workers but also their families have satisfactorily settled. The situation is radically different in Europe, where there are more women than men in practically all cities. The high proportion of adults of working age in the cities is a feature common to Africa and Europe. Urban areas, consequently, have a smaller ratio of economically dependent people than elsewhere; but one must not forget that the African migrant worker often keeps close links with his family in the countryside and has therefore more dependents than the data would suggest.

The implications of urban development for social welfare cannot be derived from demographic trends alone. They also largely depend on related policies formulated at the local or national level. Such policies may take a variety of forms, from a limited attack on the most urgent problems created by the settlement of migrants in the fringe areas of cities to comprehensive town planning and broad, regional development schemes. Large-scale, concerted plans of action are still lacking in most African countries, whereas European countries are faced with urbanization problems of more manageable dimensions and have more resources at their disposal to tackle the situation. Urbanization trends and urbanization policies both influence the shaping of social welfare programs. Social welfare workers must be prepared to staff these programs effectively; ideally, they must also be prepared to play a role in the formulation of national policies related to urbanization.

Social problems which are associated with urbanization and with which social welfare programs are concerned may be usefully classified under three headings: (1) those that arise from the inherent nature of the urban environment and mode of life; (2) those that arise from a simple transfer, through migration, of rural problems (poverty, illiteracy, unemployment) to urban areas where they become more conspicuous; and (3) problems that arise from the process of growth and change under rapid urbanization (those created in cities by sheer increase in physical numbers and by the difficulties of transition from rural, traditional to modern, urban life).

I need not elaborate on the socioeconomic features of urban life, whether they are associated with the predominance of a market economy, the high proportion of wage earners, employment of women, or with the nuclear family pattern and the number of individuals who must be taken care of partially or totally outside the family. Another relevant feature of modern urban life is the existence of a complex network of social services and facilities, for the full use of which appropriate guidance is required. These aspects of urban development are by far the most important in Europe, and the implication for social welfare programs is the continuing emphasis on counseling activities and on a variety of preventive and remedial services which have been called the "social utilities" required by modern urban life.

By contrast, what strikes the observer of the African scene is the importance of the second group of problems, those that the migrants bring with them. Those social welfare activities with a strong educational component which are often part of rural development programs need to be extended to cities when urban life appears more or less as an extension of life in the rural areas. But this alone is not enough. Social welfare programs have a major role to play in assisting in the transition from traditional to modern life of the masses of population involved in a process of rapid urbanization. Constructive activities aimed at creating new community structures are of special importance, focusing to a large extent on those elements of the population—women and youth—

who should become not the main *victims* but, on the contrary, the main *agents* of social change.

The implications of urban development for social welfare training may be seen in what has just been said of the changing emphases in social welfare programs. It is a major responsibility for social welfare educators to assist in the assessment of short- and long-term, qualitative and quantitative manpower needs. The rate and pattern of urbanization in which the country is engaged are certainly among the most important factors to be taken into account. In particular, the social impact of urbanization is much greater than might appear, considering the proportion of the population that is urban—this in view of the concentration of social problems and needs in the cities, of the demographic trends, and of the way in which migratory movements affect even those who remain in the rural areas. The adaptation of training programs must be based on job analyses, referring not only to the changing tasks of social welfare workers but also to the higher level of division of labor and increasing specialization brought about by the industrialization and urbanization processes.

Lastly, it should be among the objectives of training programs to prepare social welfare personnel to play an active part in the formulation of urbanization policies. In the short history of many African states, there are, fortunately, outstanding examples of effective urban planning—sometimes within the broader framework of regional development. On the other hand, costly mistakes have been made. Ill-conceived housing policies have resulted in the overcrowding and rapid deterioration of new dwellings. In other cases, housing for various income groups is segregated, and the social aspects of communal life totally ignored; or slum-clearance schemes have resulted in destroying well-integrated communities without substituting anything comparable. Those are clear instances where the kind of knowledge and experience that social welfare personnel might have brought to the planning agen-

II. IN LATIN AMERICA

VIRGINIA A. PARAISO

SOCIAL AFFAIRS OFFICER, ECONOMIC COMMISSION
FOR LATIN AMERICA OF THE UNITED NATIONS

URBANIZATION in Latin America can be summed up as a complex of three related but entirely different processes of population concentration, modernization of traditional urban patterns, and diffusion of urban patterns throughout the whole society.

Population concentration derives from high rates of population growth and redistribution. Present growth rates rank among the highest in the world. While rural natural increase rates (that is, the excess of births over deaths) are higher than urban, urban rates remain high. Internal migration from the rural and smaller urban centers to the big cities is characteristic of the region. If the trend in big-cityward movement during the last two decades continues, nearly three fourths of the regional population will be urban by 1980, and 90,000,000 out of 375,000,000 people will be living in cities of more than a million each.

Accelerated city growth is accompanied by progressive introduction, assimilation, and reinterpretation of contemporary urban characteristics by traditional urban societies, in the larger as well as in the smaller cities. Modernization is manifest in the changing forms of organization of work and production, distribution and consumption of goods and services, dimensions of social relations and social interaction, and patterns of cultural symbols, values, norms, and institutions.

Three principal factors facilitate the diffusion of urban sociocultural patterns to even the remote rural areas. These are mass production of the tangible and intangible contents of culture that are quickly displacing family production; improved means of transportation, especially bus service, that makes mobility possible for a large number; and mass media communication, in particular the transistor radio. Under urban influence, the aspirations and felt needs of people in rural areas and small provincial cities become increasingly more difficult to satisfy locally. Attitudes toward established authority, patterns of familial roles, and intergroup and personal relations and forms of organization and activities are all undergoing changes.

While there are wide variations among countries in terms of modernization and urbanization, cultural homogeneity or heterogeneity of the population, and the size of the population and territory—which in the small Central American and Caribbean countries give the process somewhat different characteristics and limitations—the features that distinguish urbanization in the larger and more rapidly changing countries include:

1. Persistence of important traditional urban cultures dominating rural majorities
2. Very rapid modernization of the main urban centers under the impact of the economic and cultural dominance of Western Europe and North America
3. Simultaneous flooding of these large centers by migration from more traditional provincial cities, small towns, and rural areas
4. Consequent unevenness of urban development in all senses, in which the most modern forms of economic activity, consumer demands, standards of social services, and so on, confront enormous masses of population that relate themselves to modern forms only marginally.

The pressures on social work training to assimilate itself imitatively with the modern is very strong. One might say that the implication of urbanization for social work training is that social workers need to be trained in the techniques that have evolved in the so-called "advanced" urban societies. A little reflection however, will show that this answer is not only platitudinous but misleading.

Under the conditions of rapid urbanization in the multiple sense we have indicated, one can assume that the majority of the population of Latin America has problems of adaptation, of socialization, and of acquisition of new skills to which the techniques of social work should be relevant. Conservatively, this number could well be half of a regional population of 250,000,000 growing by nearly 3 percent annually, with the most acute needs concentrated in cities of 1,000,000 to 5,000,000, with their numbers increasing by 5 percent each year or so. Further, this rapid concentration in the big cities dramatizes the contrasts in levels of living among the social classes and the need for expanded social services with the corresponding complement of trained personnel for the marginal groups. For example, Santiago, Chile, has 2,500,000 inhabitants in one conglomeration. In the strict sense of the term, about 20 percent (and in a broader interpretation, half) of the population can be considered marginal. Assuming that each social worker can work with a thousand persons through social groups and local organizations, it would take 1,250 workers to serve this part of Santiago's population alone. At present, some 700 professionals are concentrated in Santiago, the majority of whom work in hospitals, clinics, and programs dedicated to special problems of adjustment. The deficit according to such a standard now is 50 percent, increasing by 5 percent annually. The total capacity of the schools of social work exceeds 200 graduates a year by a narrow margin. In Santiago this increment would be much lower because not all graduates go into practice, not all those who practice do so in Santiago, and the loss of workers with longer service is also high in view of generous retirement plans and pressures to stop working because of family responsibilities. Moreover, if present employment trends continue, the great majority of graduates will go into specialized programs having little or no relevance to the needs of the marginal population.

This situation is common to all the countries, with variations only in degree. Venezuela, for example, estimates its present need at 3,000 social workers, yet there are only 84 professionally trained social workers, some of whom are not actively engaged in practice. The only school at a professional level graduates an average of 60 annually, a number utterly insufficient to meet the rising need, to say nothing of the large deficit that now exists. One might therefore conclude that many more social workers should be trained. No doubt, but this conclusion does not take us very far. The possibilities of expanding *effective* training are limited by: (*a*) the continuing confusion as to the specific purposes and emphases of training: (*b*) the impossibility of preparing large numbers of qualified teachers in a short time; (*c*) the absorptive capacity of institutions that employ social workers; and (*d*) the ability and willingness of governments to allocate much larger resources to the training and employment of social workers.

A closer look at what social workers are presently doing outside the more specialized clinics for problem children and the handicapped shows that a good part of their time is spent in activities that do not require professional training. Many such tasks consist of finding a hospital bed for a sick person, filling in routine administrative forms required of applicants for benefits or service, measuring and handing out relief, taking down general individual and family data, making inventories of community resources, and so on. On the other hand, social workers are also sometimes assigned responsibilities for which present social work education provides no training—teaching social work, doing research in social welfare, planning and administering national programs, for example. The question, therefore, is not just what number should be trained, but what numbers for that purposes. For urban, rural, industrial, medical, school, or other settings? For public or voluntary programs, generic or specialized? These are issues that social work education must give attention to now.

The present functions of social workers indicate that there are at least three levels of responsibility: nonprofessional, professional, and specialized professional. An undifferentiated training that does not correspond to the levels of responsibility is both wasteful and ineffective. For Latin America, three types of training program are needed: (*a*) a program to train a large number of direct-service personnel, quickly and at a relatively low cost, in the use of basic techniques of working with people within the framework of social work perspective, approach, and value orientation; (*b*) a university-level training to prepare a smaller number of professionals for supervisory and executive functions at the social agency level; and (c) advanced training for a core of highly competent professionals for planning and administering social welfare programs at the national level, for training functions in social work, and for scientific research in social welfare.

The modern elements of Latin America's population constitute the new dominant classes. Their members have multiple links with social welfare. They constitute the organized public opinion that supports the programs and dictates their content; they pay for them through voluntary contributions and taxes; and they staff them. Naturally, the programs respond to their "modern" interpretation of welfare. The masses to whom social welfare services are directed, representing unstable mixtures of traditional urban and rural culture patterns, are far from modern. Struggling to gain a foothold in a still evolving urban society, they are handicapped economically, socially, culturally, and politically in their efforts to relate satisfactorily to a rapidly changing environment. Society itself does not offer adequate support to this transition from the traditional to the modern in terms of levels of living, social organization, or democratic processes. Under such circumstances, training emphases based on the concepts and techniques of highly industrialized societies now taught in the schools of social work become open to question. These imported models are premised on the provision of facilities, services, and opportunities for self-advancement, self-help, self-determination, and participation. In environments where such provisions are lacking, practice based on an education in such concepts and techniques necessarily suffers limitations and distortions. "Acculturation" and reinterpretation of imported concepts and techniques, original formulations rooted in national and regional experiences, orientation to social change, and flexibility in the application of techniques to varied settings are important issues in Latin American social work education.

It has been pointed out again and again that social work teachers have no specific preparation for teaching. Apart from sporadic courses, perhaps, in general pedagogy, there have been no experiments in training courses for teachers of social work. The relatively low salaries render teaching an unlucrative career. The present financial situation of the schools necessitates the employment on a part-time basis of the majority of social work teachers and reduces the ability of the schools to build up strong, creative, and independent teaching staffs. A combination of these factors frustrates any attempt to train significant numbers of the qualified teachers who are needed if the social work schools are to upgrade the preparation of a larger number of social workers.

Notwithstanding the unsatisfied needs for social welfare services, increases in the number of established positions for social workers are slow. Most social welfare institutions along with other social programs have limited capacity to employ in view of the common instability of the sources of financing and the insufficiency of funds available for the expansion of services and the creation of new ones. At the same time, since most social welfare institutions are modeled after those of highly industrialized and affluent societies, unless they are adapted to local resources and needs the forms of organization and the contents of the services can drain the economy without necessarily resolving the problems effectively. The institutional priorities, norms, and values deriving from the combined influences of the local dominant classes and foreign models rarely coincide with those of the popular masses.

One Latin American social worker has said that the profession is better accepted and accorded a higher status in the smaller cities than in the big ones. The fact is that the social workers' participation in the more recent and broader social programs is limited, and other professions are going more and more into services in which social work techniques are relevant. This, in part, may be due to the inertia of social work in adjusting its methods and its concepts to contemporary society and its needs. Except in a few instances, social work has remained within the bounds of its traditional forms of helping; new responsibilities are in the stage of definition, and there is no clear statement of their content; and social work education has not caught up either in theory or techniques to provide a base for the task of preparing social workers qualified for the requirements of the urbanizing society. Consequently, governments, although recognizing that social workers are needed for certain limited responsibilities, are not willing to allocate much larger resources for the training of more social workers, for the preparation of higher-level professionals whose education must necessarily be more costly, and for the expansion of employment opportunities, especially at the top level of the public service hierarchy.

Thus, the more practically relevant implication of urbanization for social work training seems to be the need to understand better the social processes and to adapt training to urbanization in Latin America rather than to urbanization in New York or London. Social work education in Latin America need not undergo "urbanization." Certainly it must transform itself to fit national and regional conditions and to meet responsibilities that are uniquely Latin American.

III. IN INDIA

N. F. KAIKOBAD

TATA INSTITUTE OF SOCIAL SCIENCES
BOMBAY, INDIA

THE POLICY of urban development in India has for the most part been confined to the physical and economic aspects. The social aspects, in terms of health, education, and welfare, have remained largely outside the strategy of urban development. Though the social service programs have, no doubt, been given a place in successive five-year plans, there is little evidence that they have been connected with the strategy of urban development.

The consequences of this situation are reflected in the training of personnel for social welfare. It may be pointed out that in the absence of an assessment of manpower needs in social welfare, it has been difficult to lay down the categories of personnel or of levels of training.

Training of social welfare personnel began in India in 1936, with the establishment of the first school of social work. On the eve of independence, in the year 1947, there were three schools of social work in the country. Since 1952 the number of schools has increased rapidly, and all but three offer two-year postgraduate programs.

One of the factors contributing to this rapid growth is the linkage of social work with labor welfare and, more recently, with personnel management. This arose from the fact that in the early 1930s the largely unorganized industrial labor groups in India constituted an underprivileged section of the population for whom social services needed to be organized. The first school of social work, the Sir D. J. Tata Graduate School of Social Work, now known as Tata Institute of Social Services, started its work in a labor community, and in the course of time it persuaded the management of a few factories to allow it to work within the factories. The management allowed this privilege on humanitarian grounds. Later, a variety of factors helped to promote social work within industry. The legislation requiring large factories to employ qualified labor welfare officers to look after the welfare facilities for employees created a demand for social work graduates, and a number of schools came into existence to supply this potential market.

While labor welfare continues to be the major field of employment of professional social workers, the situation is less favorable in other areas. No doubt, trained social workers have secured positions in social welfare and rural community development, but this has not happened by any plan or design. The fact that professionally qualified social workers are involved in planning, administering, and evaluating these programs is gratifying, but there is no clear-cut policy on recruitment of trained personnel for social welfare posts.

Trained social workers are also employed in urban areas as administrators of workers' education programs and organizers of community centers, as medical and psychiatric social workers, family planning workers, supervisors of institutions for women and children, probation officers, inspectors of certified schools, and adult education workers. Since we do not have a clear policy as to what positions must be filled by trained social workers and which could be filled by semitrained or auxiliary personnel, invariably one finds that professionally qualified workers are bypassed when the question of filling certain social work positions comes up in the governmental and voluntary organizations. This lack of clarity is also responsible for unrelatedness between the sources of employ- ment and the training institutions. The country has yet to estab- lish a cadre for social workers at the state and national levels. Without this, a close and responsive relationship between the needs of the field and the training facilities will not be assured.

In spite of these limitations, the social work schools have been contributing substantially to the development of new social serv- ices for the urban population. They have been the first to perceive certain needs of the urban population and to provide leadership in meeting these needs. It was these schools that initiated family serv- ice programs for the urban poor and underprivileged by starting family welfare agencies. Similarly, child guidance clinics, school social work programs, counseling services for college students, and demonstration projects in urban community development are but a few examples of the pioneering work of the schools of social work in India. These projects were undertaken primarily to meet the needs of urban communities and also to provide a model for voluntary and governmental agencies to follow. It is gratifying to note that some of them are gradually being adopted by voluntary organizations.

Two recent projects need special mention. The first is the in- troduction of casework service in a few industrial concerns. The second is the draft bill dealing with adoption of children. Inspired by the school-sponsored child welfare agencies, in it is the result of steady efforts behind the scene by professional social workers to evoke the interest of national organizations in the need for such legislation. The Indian Conference of Social Work has been ac- tively associated with this move from its inception. When the adoption bill is passed, the schools of social work can take legiti- mate pride for playing their catalytic role in the field of social action.

Our social work education from the beginning was based on the American model in its approach and in its curriculum organization, obviously because the majority of India's social work educators took their advanced training in the United States. Though the fundamental principles and methods of social work are universally applicable, they have to be adapted and related to a country's specific needs. Under the leadership of the Association of Schools of Social Work, social work educators are reappraising and modifying their curricula. The Association through its annual seminars is promoting a reexamination of the scope and methodology of social work education in India. Gradually, indigenous teaching material is evolving. There is also a growing awareness of the need to promote development programs for teachers.

The Association of Trained Social Workers, an organization for promotion of professional standards, came into being in the last few years. This organization has been striving to promote better public understanding of the social work profession and has actively voiced the need for certain modifications in the curriculum. On the wider front it concerns itself with issues of social policy and with welfare programs.

The Central Social Welfare Board, established in 1953 to support and strengthen voluntary action in social welfare, has helped 6,000 welfare agencies to develop their programs. As many as 30,000 or 40,000 voluntary workers are said to be involved in activities of the agencies that receive financial aid from the Board.

Some years back it was believed that those who operated welfare agencies knew what was best for those whom they set out to serve. This belief no longer goes unchallenged. The leaders of voluntary organizations themselves have realized that they need some orientation training. A number of major national organizations as well as the schools of social work are setting up brief training courses for volunteers in key positions in welfare agencies. The Government of India has given financial support for this program. Similarly, in-service training programs have also been instituted for nontrained, experienced workers in government and voluntary agencies with a view to upgrading existing welfare services. Schools of social work have been involved in organizing these in-service training programs, particularly in the fields of juvenile delinquency, family and child welfare, and urban community development.

So far as urban development is concerned, the programs of housing, family planning, and urban community development are bound to grow considerably in India in the near future. New housing estates will need a functionary, a community welfare organizer to establish better relationships between tenants and housing authorities and to further an harmonious and wholesome community life. Family planning programs will require better equipped, dynamic community educators with zeal and professional competence if we are to win the race of population control. A beginning has already been made with the introduction of urban community development projects for promoting aided self-help programs, particularly in the localities inhabited by lower- and middle-income groups. These three fields offer great challenges and opportunities to the profession to prepare personnel who can handle these programs with skill and insight. The curricula of social work education will have to lay greater emphasis on group work and community organization, for the small social groups in India can play an effective part as instruments of social action and social change. Social welfare personnel in the future will be called upon to encourage group and community action to advance the goals of urban social development. The teaching in social work has given considerable emphasis to such special groups as the poor, the sick, the beggar, the delinquent, and the handicapped, and this will, no doubt, have to continue. However, there is a need to stress the preventive aspect of all these social problems, and trained social workers will have to have greater skill in mobilizing community resources and involving people's participation in self-help programs. They will have to have a better grasp of social planning, social legislation, and social administration.

There is a need to reexamine employment and educational opportunities in the social welfare field. This will probably reveal that properly trained persons are required at various levels, and educational opportunities must be organized to provide them. There is the need for social work persons trained at undergraduate as well as at postgraduate levels to man the expanding welfare programs in urban India.

Highlights of the International Congress of Schools of Social Work

ROBERT A. B. LEAPER

UNIVERSITY COLLEGE OF SWANSEA,
UNITED KINGDOM

THE International Conference of Social Work which meets every two years, has become a very large gathering indeed. This year there were about 2,800 delegates from 74 countries. The ICSW has, in fact, become so large that we are worried about effective participation. However, some of the meetings connected with it, at which professionals concerned with some more limited aspect of social welfare meet and exchange knowledge and opinions, are most valuable. Such a meeting was this year's International Congress of Schools of Social Work (ICSSW). It would be pretentious and impossible to attempt to summarize all the authoritative papers presented by experts at general meetings or all the conclusions reached by the many study groups attended by the 500 participants. One can only give personal impressions and comments on what seem to be the most striking conclusions.

With the general theme of the ICSW in mind—the Congress discussed "Education for Social Responsibility and the Contemporary Role of the Social Work Profession." The first and most striking thing was to reflect that there are now some 450 schools of social work giving some form of professional training to those who will become social workers. Seventeen new schools were admitted to membership this year, making a total of forty-five countries in which professional social work education is now carried on. Moreover, in an opening address, the General Secretary, Dr. Katherine Kendall, of the United States, was able to pay tribute to twenty-six schools which have a history of fifty years or more of professional social work education, and she referred to the pioneers who had started this teaching at the beginning of this century. Collaboration and cooperation through the ICSSW have now reached the point where a full-time and independent secretariat is required, and at the general assembly the President announced immediate plans to take this step. Already a British trust has made a grant toward the cost, with the rather interesting proviso that funds must be raised to a matching extent within two years from other countries, excluding the United States. My first general impression, then, is that social work as a profession is now established internationally and that professional training is now to be taken as a serious preoccupation in most areas of the world.

My second general impression is that collaboration in the various fields of social welfare has become a reality. Social security, industrial welfare, health services, education, care for the handicapped are now established facts; and central government, independent industry, and voluntary organizations are now cooperating far more readily than in the past. Cooperation and moves toward coordination at the national level are now reproduced at the international level.

At such a large international gathering there are two kinds of highlights—those which make an emotional impact because of the occasion and those which give new insights and spur on the participant to rethink his work and its implications. It is difficult to convey the sense of occasions of emotional impact. I shall long remember the end of the closing session of the Congress when all the delegates rose spontaneously to applaud Dame Eileen Younghusband, their president. The delegates' appreciation of her is not without significance. Here is someone who has made a very considerable and distinguished contribution to the training of caseworkers, both in her own country and on the international level. Her chairmanship of the government working party in Britain has resulted in a whole new system of training for social workers outside the universities. Her United Nations report on social work training has had considerable impact in many countries. Yet in her paper to this Congress and in many other pronouncements to it she showed herself very sensitive to new forms of social work, particularly in rapidly developing countries. I do not think it is too fanciful to suppose that it was symbolic of the wish of the delegates to conserve the best of the knowledge and experience gained so far, and yet to adapt it to the world needs for new kinds of social workers, that their president was given such acclaim.

In terms of the subject matter of the Congress there were several highlights, several questions which recurred throughout the discussions:

1. In social work education, and indeed in social work practice as a whole, this seems to be a time for reassessment and reappraisal. In societies where there is certainly more crime, more violence, more maladjustment, less acceptance of the roles which each generation and each group might play in a harmonious society, those who work with people are driven to a careful examination of their functions in society. No one made the elementary error of blaming social workers for the failure to find in so many countries an adjusted and disciplined social life, but many must have felt compelled to restate the function of social work in new terms.

The first paper of the Congress introduced us to this idea. Mr. Gerima, from Ethiopia, spoke of the new needs and the new approaches to social work in Africa. New attitudes are engendered by new political conditions; the changing social and economic conditions of many African countries mean that a restatement of social workers' contribution to society has to be in terms which harmonize with new expectations.

In another lecture Dr. Eileen Blackey, of the United States, quoted the commentary made by Dr. Eugen Pusić of Yugoslavia, on the United Nations program for social and economic development:

Dr. Pusić reminds us that specialized training for social work was first developed in countries with a pronounced individualistic outlook on social problems and a corresponding understanding of social welfare services as a means of helping in the process of individual change and adjustment. . . . These are often transmitted to developing countries as models of social work practice and education to be adopted. The educational task lies in the selection, modification, and reorientation of these contributions in such a way that they advance rather than block the programs needed in the respective countries.

Several points in the secretary's report to the general assembly of the Congress also reflected these new developments. Dr. Kendall described the schools of social work as "moving out of carefree youth into the heavy responsibilities of full adulthood." She reported on a Latin American seminar on social work education in 1965 from which came the decision to launch a Latin American Association of Schools of Social Work; moreover, a seminar on the same lines had taken place in Africa with similar encouraging results. Both these regional activities were welcomed as part of the world-wide quest to adapt the best of past knowledge to the needs of rapidly developing regions. Dr. Kendall also reported on discussions to try to reach agreement on the equivalence of qualifications from one country to another—clear evidence of the need for international exchange both of experience and of personnel.

2. The second main question was the search for the meaning of "social responsibility" in social work education. This was the theme of the meeting, and it is perhaps hardly surprising that so far-ranging a question was by no means settled by the end of the Congress. It was tackled in two ways:

a) How can or should the faculty of a school of social work undertake some kind of involvement in community affairs (other than by their professional task as educators) which would bear witness to their social responsibility?

b) How can the curriculum be reformed, or newly drafted, to include subjects which will give students a better understanding of their responsibilities as influential members of a democratic society when they become professional social workers?

Dr. Herbert Aptekar, of Brandeis University, had prepared some guidelines which raised a large number of questions for the discussion groups on this theme. He reported from a survey made of a large number of social work schools on their interpretation of the term "social responsibility" and concluded that there are many diverse conceptions. At the final session the Rev. Swithun Bowers, of Canada, in summing up the discussions certainly did not conclude the debate but underlined the two points I have mentioned and left the matter open for further consideration. However, there were in some of the plenary sessions points which the discussion groups returned to several times as being most significant. For example, there was Dr. Blackey's point that we are now moving from the residual concept of social work to a more positive and universal concept. Social work is not just concerned with giving relief of one kind or another to those who cannot help themselves, but with helping individuals, groups, and communities to develop themselves toward a higher standard of living and a more fulfilled way of life. In this social workers have to cooperate with economists, planners, and administrators in positive programs. In a memorable analysis of the present tasks of the social work educator Dame Eileen Younghusband said: "If social work students are simply taught to become faithful retriever dogs for administrators, they will hardly fulfill social work's role as a precipitator and shock absorber of social change and its more fundamental role in humanizing social relationships." There was constant reiteration also of the point that social work students will understand their social duties better if they see that by their actions and their preoccupations their professors are themselves involved in working for social reform and social action and are not just talking about it with true academic detachment. This raised the problem of the commitment of educators to particular actions of reform which might identify them with political groups, but in general it seemed a danger that was worth risking.

Social responsibility needs, however, a sound base of knowledge and understanding, and this has implications for curriculum content. Indeed, Father Bowers recalled in his closing address the comment of a social worker from Asia that the first responsibility of the educator is to his students and to their personal development. The content of the curriculum depends, of course, upon the educational level of the students and also upon their subsequent field of action as social workers. Dr. Virginia Paraiso, of the United Nations Economic Commission for Latin America, analyzed the perspective with which the curriculum had to be viewed in Latin America:

Present trends in social work education in Latin America should be envisaged within several wider contexts:
1. Transformations in secondary and higher education as a whole
2. Transformations in the instruments and objectives of social policy
3. Transformations in the social, economic, and political structures.

The particular emphasis given to any subject would therefore depend upon the social, administrative, and political structures and changes of the country and region. However, it was clear that the education of the social worker would have to include some knowledge and understanding of social philosophy, public administration, political science, as well as subjects like psychology, which are more closely related to the methods of his own profession. The problem remained of how to do this without giving merely superficial indoctrination or reducing the quality of the professional training for an exacting job.

3. There was also considerable discussion on the implications for social work practice in a changing world. Here I seemed to detect a note of caution. It has now become commonplace to state that we have given too much attention to individual casework, and that the United States pattern with its psychiatric emphasis is irrelevant to the needs of many other countries. It was also agreed that we have to face the fact of great differences between the concept of social welfare in a free-economy, capitalist society and in a socialist society—or in one like Britain, which is a mixed society. This would necessarily mean a different emphasis in the ways in which social workers can help in society. For example, a complete system of social security, universal in scope and financed by taxation and compulsory contributions from all wage earners, would have an obvious effect on the fields of activity of social workers. However, the Congress emphasized on several occasions that there are certain values implicit in social work practice which are valid whatever the methods employed or the setting in which it is found: respect for the individual, acceptance of clients, confidentiality, a professional attitude toward one's task, and so on.

In many lectures there was a preoccupation with the need to give social work students the means of learning and personal development. Perhaps there has been too much exposition of methods as if they were unquestionable. We are not concerned with turning out well-drilled automata who never question the assumptions of their profession, but fully educated people who know the background and history of social work and are encouraged to be critical and well-informed without falling into the juvenile error of rejecting all the past simply because it is past.

4. The last point is that there are now different levels of training and preparation for social work, and that this was an inevitable development. This, to me, is a remarkably open-minded attitude to find in an international assembly of people who have had to struggle hard for professional recognition. Even today in some countries the role of social work educator is not given its due recognition, and academic purists are in some cases even now apt to sneer at what they call "mere vocational preparation." This criticism does not apparently apply to the very vocational training of doctors, lawyers, and engineers! However, if there is any justification in such criticism, it behooves social work educators to exact the highest academic standards in their courses while at the same time insuring that the content is really pertinent to the needs of social workers, and administrators of the social services. The Congress showed an awareness of the need to train many who have a basic knowledge of social work method in the administration of the social services, which in turn demands an understanding of the processes of political and sociological change. It is important also to leave the way into social work training open for those who are either educated in some other related academic discipline or have practiced social work at a field level and need further training prior to taking on administrative duties. All too often there seems to be a belief in some countries that while the professional social worker can operate at field level, all questions of policy and administration have to be decided by people educated in the more traditional disciplines of the law or the arts—often without any real understanding of social work. Such an attitude was thought to be indefensible, and the implication was that courses giving a critical insight into the history, processes, methods, and assumptions of social work should be found in the social science curricula of universities. On the other hand, if schools of social work exist separately from universities, it is imperative that their connection with the universities be strengthened so that the results of sociological research, for example, will be made available to those responsible

for social work education. All too often there is insufficient inter-change between the various disciplines.

My comments report the viewpoint of one observer and are not in any sense a summary of the conclusions of the Congress. In Washington in 1966 it seemed to me that social work educators from all over the world:

1. Recognized the need for a reassessment of their role and their present methods of social work education
2. Accepted that they and the students whom they prepare for their profession have to be aware of, and involved in, social reform and cannot accept a merely passive role as charitable workers who collect the human mistakes left over from an unjust society
3. Recognized, nevertheless, that there is now a large repository of knowledge about social work and its implications which it would be foolish to ignore
4. Welcomed an expansion and an upgrading of social work education and a closer relationship with those trained in re-lated disciplines.

Techniques and Methods of Coordinating Public and Voluntary Services at the Neighborhood Level

I. IN JAPAN

YUICHI NAKAMURA

PROFESSOR, JAPAN SCHOOL OF SOCIAL WORK

MY MAJOR is social casework. However, casework is and should be *social* casework, which means that it must not be individually oriented but socially oriented. When we say that we provide a casework service, it means that we help a certain person deal with his problem by himself in connection with his environment, including his family, his neighborhood, and the larger community to which he belongs. In this sense I am very much interested in both the client's personality and his environment, including the neighborhood.

When I was asked to discuss this subject, I felt a little bit puzzled. There was in the letter I received from the Secretariat of the ICSW a note that this subject is related to multipurpose centers. However, in Japan we do not use the term "multipurpose center" as such, so I did not understand exactly what it meant. We use such terms as, "community center," "neighborhood center," "settlement," and so on. So let me use just one term, "neighborhood center," to represent those various expressions.

A neighborhood center provides various kinds of services, such as education—or, more exactly, social education and preschool education—health, counseling, homemaking, and so forth. Some neighborhood centers provide a public bath service, a laundry service, a restaurant, a shop that sells daily necessities, all at lower than normal rates. As such, a neighborhood center is, actually, a multipurpose center. However, merely listing these services does not mean very much. It is important to know why they are or should be combined under the name of a neighborhood center. A neighborhood center is not a patchwork of all sorts of services. It must be a center in the sense that it is a kind of medium between the people in the neighborhood and social services provided by various agencies in the larger community. It must help the people make the most of appropriate social services to meet their own needs. But I cannot explore this question, because our main concern must be with the coordination of public and voluntary services.

Here again we encounter a number of theoretical questions. Some neighborhood centers are under voluntary auspices. On the other hand, the number of public neighborhood centers is increasing year by year. And, what is more complicated, some semipublic centers are appearing. When I say "semipublic," I mean a private center that is entirely or partially supported by public funds. Are the services given in a public neighborhood center "public services"? And are the services provided by a private neighborhood center actually "voluntary services"? How about the semipublic centers? I raise these questions not to make the matter clearer in a literal sense but to make us confront the reality.

You may be interested in knowing that in some prefectures or municipalities in Japan there has recently been developing a kind of corporation which is private in form but is almost entirely supported by a prefectural or municipal government. This arrangement has both strengths and weaknesses. From the standpoint of finance, it is stabilized to some extent as compared with a private center which must always face serious financial difficulties. However, we cannot expect a big expansion in its activities because of the slow payment or even the stagnation of the allotted appropriation. What is worse, it sometimes becomes a pool where government officials can find jobs after their retirement. Thus it is most difficult to achieve at the same time both the financial stability of a public agency and the creativity and flexibility of a private agency.

It seems to me that one of the most important aspects to be considered is the question of how to coordinate public and voluntary services provided outside a neighborhood center, such as public assistance, family service, child welfare, medical care, and so on. The coordination of public and voluntary services is carried out primarily by a community council of social welfare which covers a larger area than a neighborhood center; it is not essentially the function of a neighborhood center. However, many communities do not have their own councils of social welfare; or, if they do exist, they are very nominal or so-called "signboard" community councils and not very active in coordinating public and voluntary services. In such cases, neighborhood centers, if any, must assume the function of coordinating various welfare services temporarily but actively. In what way and to what extent? It is very difficult to answer, but I should say that the following matters must be taken into particular consideration:

1. A neighborhood center must be a channel through which the needs of people in the area are interpreted to the larger community. In order to realize this objective it must have a group of multipurpose social workers who are good at a little bit each not only of casework and group work but also of community organization and social research.

2. The center must be keenly aware of the social situation of the neighborhood by trying to obtain firsthand materials through continuous and constructive social research and must analyze and interpret them in relation to the larger communities. In this connection it must have a long-range perspective.

A multipurpose neighborhood center is actually in a strategic position today to evaluate and to coordinate all sorts of public and private services at the neighborhood level through its firsthand knowledge and understanding of the neighborhood, its rapport with the people in the area and with public and private agencies in larger communities (cities, counties, or prefectures), and its function of community organization.

II. IN THE UNITED STATES

ABNER D. SILVERMAN

DIRECTOR, MANAGEMENT DIVISION, U.S. DEPARTMENT
OF HOUSING AND URBAN DEVELOPMENT

THE COORDINATION of social services and the provision of neighborhood centers to improve the general welfare of people living in slum or blighted areas have reached new heights of interest in the United States. This is the direct consequence of the war against poverty which President Johnson and the Congress launched in 1964. The Economic Opportunity Act of 1964, the basic legislation of this program, provides for the funding of community-action agencies to carry out community-action programs. A community-action program mobilizes the resources of the community; provides service and assistance to help eliminate poverty; provides for the maximum feasible participation of the beneficiaries; and is conducted, administered, or coordinated by a public or nonprofit agency.

All the social legislation of this country enacted during the past few years, either in express terms or by direct implication, calls for cooperative and coordinated action. The proposed Housing and Urban Development Act of 1966 has as one of its stated purposes: "to assist cities to coordinate activities aided under existing Federal programs with other public and private actions in order to provide the most effective and economical concentration of Federal, state, local, and private efforts to improve the quality of urban life."

Although everyone favors cooperation and coordination, it is difficult to set up a process by which programs can be made mutually supporting. Programs are tailored to meet specific needs. The programs develop along specialized and fragmented lines, but the beneficiaries of these programs cannot be effectively served in a fragmented fashion.

The difficulties are increased by the variety of ways in which our system of welfare—in its largest sense—operates. Many of our federal programs are permissive rather than mandatory, flow to the communities through the states, and the prevailing levels of income maintenance, health service, and education depend upon the social conscience and financial resources of the state. Certain programs are directly operated by the federal government, while still others, such as the urban renewal and public housing programs, bypass the states and flow directly to local public agencies.

Further, to this body of governmental instrumentalities must be added the large number of national voluntary associations which through local affiliates provide aid and assistance to people in need. These agencies are regulated by their own boards of directors, raise and spend their own money, and have their own objectives.

Finally, there is the very real difficulty of making the services accessible and persuading the intended beneficiaries to utilize them. Obviously, the coordination of social services is not an exercise in the art of administration for its own sake, but an attempt to make more effective the national effort to raise the quality of family life. If the people cannot be reached and helped the efforts are useless.

In this context it may be interesting and perhaps instructive to examine some attempts to coordinate social services for low-income families residing in public housing projects. The housing of low-income families has been part of the nation's welfare program for twenty-eight years. Historically, the Housing Assistance Administration, formerly the Public Housing Administration, has taken the position that its role is to reshape the physical environment of disadvantaged families. The reshaping of their social environment was considered the responsibility of other public and private agencies.

Some housing authorities have undertaken to educate families in the use of equipment and in homemaking practices. Great efforts have been made to secure services for public housing occupants, and especially to use community space for health and welfare outstations.

A survey in 1965 covering 1,150 housing authorities administering 2,295 projects showed that over 19,000 individual program activities were being conducted. These programs, including adult education, health clinics, health services, child care, recreation, library services, safety, youth groups, elderly groups, tenant councils, welfare, and employment, were sponsored predominately by public agencies. Private social service agencies sponsored about 15 percent of the total program; other voluntary organizations, 17 percent; and the tenants, through their own associations, 10 percent. Twenty-seven percent of these programs—of adult education, child care, and employment programs, tutoring, and family welfare services—were considered directly related to the national effort to reduce the effects of poverty and help families to develop their potentials and become more independent economically and socially.

Fifty-eight percent of the projects had indoor community space where various activities were conducted. The on-site or neighborhood location of services is considered essential. This permits doorstep accessibility, a vital element in serving low-class families who are reluctant to leave their familiar neighborhoods, and facilitates encouragement of resident participation. There is evidence that daily contact and communication between a site-based worker and the tenants develops into a trusting relationship, particularly when the residents learn that help is available, is reliable, and involves no loss of pride or dignity. As a result, in many states, the administration of public welfare assistance has been decentralized, and branch offices have been established on low-rent housing projects or in the immediate neighborhood.

Despite the large volume of social service, educational, health, and recreational programs the amount of on-site space is limited, many needed services are not available, many families do not participate in the activities, and the meshing of services into a coordinated, mutually supporting program is for the most part still an ideal rather than an actuality. Therefore, measures were taken to improve the delivery of services, their coordination, and their impact upon the families.

A task force was created in 1962 by Robert C. Weaver, Secretary of the Department of Housing and Urban Development, and Abraham Ribicoff, then Secretary of Health, Education, and Welfare, to test ways in which the joint action of housing, health, welfare, and educational services could be made more effective. The task force undertook to test the means by which the federal social service resources could be combined with state, local, and voluntary agencies so that the thrust of the many separate programs could be polarized and focused on residents in a public housing neighborhood. Four public housing projects were selected for the experiment: one in St. Louis, with a tenant population of some 12,000 people; one in New Haven, Connecticut, with a tenant population of some 3,000; one in Pittsburg, California, with a tenant population of some 1,200; and one in Miami, focused on the problems of the elderly.

We sought a term to describe our intent. We considered "coordination of services" but decided that it was an overused phrase and covered so many different types of working arrangements that it did not fit our purpose. We considered "saturation" and "cooperation" but discarded both and finally called the demonstration projects "concerted services projects."

This was more than an effort to find a new word to describe an old concept. We recognized that there are factors which, apart from the nature of the welfare system itself, inhibit either cooperation or coordination among different bureaucracies, whether public or private: the autonomy of each organization and distrust of any surrender of individual decision-making power which might adversely affect its status as an independent body; different chains of command from the service level to the level of policy decision-making; the necessity to convince each level of the hierarchy of the desirability of joint, supporting action. We recognized that each bureaucracy, public or private, would be concerned with the advancement of its own program and with its own target population; that there were inequalities of funding and that the agencies with relatively greater financial resources would be reluctant to use them for purposes that might not seem immediately pertinent to their primary interest. We recognized that there would be legislative constraints or individual charter restrictions that would militate against a true blending of separate activities into an organized whole.

Nevertheless, we thought we should attempt it, and we did. To achieve this end we established ten criteria for a truly concerted "concerted services project":

1. Full commitments from the governor, the appropriate state departments, the mayor, the local housing authority, and certain local agencies, when the project is launched
2. An advisory and planning body with lay and professional representation
3. An official local coordinator or coordinating body
4. A program comprehensive enough to meet identified needs, and of such kind and quantity as to bring about improvement in social and economic behavior and well-being and some reduction of financial dependency, with services readily accessible, available when needed, and of an adequacy and quality to satisfy the standards of the grant-in-aid agency
5. Cooperative planning to determine the role of each participating agency
6. A system for reaching all families in need of services
7. Family-centered, coordinated delivery of services
8. A real effort in planning, developing, and operating the project to: (*a*) work closely with local community organizations; and (*b*) build within the public housing residents an active sense of community and participation in the project
9. A research component that will assure coordinated evaluation of the various parts of the concerted services project
10. Planning and operation of the project in ways that will assure continuance of the services after the project has been concluded

Needless to say, our ten criteria proved no more inviolate or universally acceptable than have the ten criteria for human conduct handed down to Moses on Mt. Sinai.

Our first experiment was launched in June of 1962, at St. Louis; our last, at Miami in April, 1964. It is too soon to measure results, but we can recognize some of our failures and some of our successes.

We received the full commitment of all the offices and officials named in Criterion 1. But commitment requires more than encouragement and agreement with the goal. It requires waivers of state and local policies and modification of the regulations of participating agencies. Moreover, officials change. At the moment, it would seem that the local housing authority should be the responsible agent which articulates the needs of its tenants. It has a special responsibility to make "concerting" work.

In two cities, the original community-wide structure which enthusiastically pledged support for the ideal of concerted services collapsed, and neither local housing authority took the initiative to reestablish a new structure. Project management policies which irritated tenants were not modified, thus the effort to give the residents a sense of self-worth, dignity, and security was in part frustrated by regulations and procedures which made the tenants feel that they were objects of charity. In one community, the housing authority decided to demolish old buildings so that the site could be used for modern structures. The residents, among whom were some of the leaders of the community, were offered new accommodations ten miles away. The people were outraged. This action seemed to them proof that the project was a hoax. The problem was solved by a change in the schedule for reconstruction. Still, for a short while, it seemed that the effort of many agencies to change the social and physical environment of the community would be irreparably damaged by the well-intentioned but ineptly administered unilateral decision of one participant.

Criteria 2, 3, 5, and 8, which relate to planning, assignment and the coordination of roles, and the development of resident participation, have proved most difficult to achieve. At one project, the coordinating mechanism completely broke down and had to be reactivated by outside intervention; at another, there was confusion between the roles which could be played by lay and professional people working together and those which could only be achieved by professionals alone. Our experience indicates that there must be a coordinating head who understands the difference between coordination and administration. There must be agreement as to the roles to be played by the participants, and there must be an independent resident council which can request the help the residents feel they need rather than what the agencies think they need.

Two planning bodies are required: one at the level at which services are delivered and one at the level of the department or agency heads who assign staff and establish policy and procedures. Autonomous bodies will waive their procedures or adopt new policies only voluntarily and to the extent that they are committed to a common goal; so there is need for a coordinating body at the working level, where differences or conflicts in policy and practice are uncovered, and at the top level, where they can be reconciled and a common policy established. Moreover, the planning bodies must be used. After agreement as to roles, there must be a feedback to the policy-makers of results and problems for their consideration; otherwise, it will cease to be operative and will not be available in crises.

Of all the criteria, Criterion 4 was the easiest to achieve. All the projects had competent designs for a program. What was sadly lacking, however, was adequate and timely funding. As a result, the activities were started in sequence, never in concert, and in some cases there were long delays.

Criterion 6 was very difficult to achieve. Lacking were adequate basic data on the social characteristics of the target families and a mechanism for securing their participation. The employment of indigenous workers as case-finders seemed useful, as did the development of a neighborhood council which not only helped to plan the project but made the community feel that it was their project.

Criterion 7 proved to be difficult, but it was one which all the participating agencies attempted to meet. The difficulty in large measure could be traced to legislative or policy constraints. For example, an excellently staffed family service agency at one of the projects was limited to serving only actual or potential public assistance recipients—somewhat less than half of the target population.

Criterion 9, which calls for a comprehensive research component, was met in only two projects. Thus far there has been no feedback of information which would have bearing on the effectiveness of any existing system of operation or suggest changes in methodology.

It is too soon to judge whether the objective of Criterion 10, the continuation of services, will be achieved. We do know that the participating agencies have been affected by the joint activity, and there is tangible evidence that they have modified their plans and procedures better to serve the families involved.

On balance, it is hard to say whether the results have established any transferable body of experience or methodology. We have learned that the essence of concerted services is cooperative planning. This goes beyond our initial design. The handicaps are many: differences in the quality of the professional staffs of the agencies; different salary schedules; different working hours; different attitudes toward clients. These difficulties are discovered in the operational phase of a concerted activity. They can be resolved only by the decision-makers of the agencies who are committed to the concept that planning is ongoing and continuous.

We have learned that there must be a real effort to build within the target population an active sense of belonging to the community and of participating in the project from the beginning. An independent neighborhood council is invaluable in securing participation, in providing information on the value of services, and in pointing out gaps in the project design.

We know on the negative side:

1. It has not proved possible to fund the programs in a timely fashion.
2. The obstacles to coordination are real, and only deep dedication and acceptance of the common goal can overcome them.
3. The quality of service is very uneven. It is almost impossible to raise the level of individual aspirations when the level of income is less than half of the budgeted family requirement, or when agency policies destroy a family's sense of security.

We know on the positive side:

1. A substantial amount of funds has been channeled into the demonstration projects.
2. There has been an increase in the variety and size of services.
3. There has been impact upon the community at large.

The members of the task force, all senior officers of their respective agencies, have found the benefits arising from knowing each other as persons, learning from each other about their programs, and sharing professional insights so great that they wish to continue the process even after the demonstration is concluded.

Another instrumentality has been developed as a means of waging the war on poverty, namely, the neighborhood multipurpose center. The neighborhood center is not a new invention. A descendant of the "settlements" which grew up in the last years of the nineteenth century in London, it has been carried forward as the settlement house movement in this country ever since. However, it has taken on new aspects. The original concept of the settlement as a place where friendship and understanding might arise between members of different social classes through personal contact and communication, or, as it became in this country, a device whereby the immigrant family might become Americanized and part of the community, has become that of a building in which can be stationed the health, welfare, educational, recreational, and economic services that are needed to help families become socially urbanized and self-dependent.

This concept was given express congressional approval by the Housing and Urban Development Act of 1965, which authorized federal grants toward the cost of providing a neighborhood facility which is: (1) necessary for carrying out a program of health, recreational, social, or similar community service; (2) consistent with comprehensive planning for the development of the community; and (3) available to a significant portion or number of the area's low- or moderate-income residents. The act further directs that priority shall be given to applications for projects that will substantially further community-action programs approved under the Economic Opportunity Act. This statute became law on August 10, 1965; thus far grants have been approved for neighborhood centers in thirteen cities. In addition, the Office of Economic Opportunity has approved as of May, 1966, the funding of neighborhood center program components to a total of nearly $29,750,000.

As of June 7, 1966, identical bills had been introduced in both houses of the Congress to authorize the Secretary of the Department of Health, Education, and Welfare to make grants toward the cost of newly constructed or remodeled community service centers. This program would provide federal assistance to the states for planning and operating community service centers in which would be brought together all the public welfare, public health, mental health, vocational rehabilitation, and related social services. This constitutes further evidence that current thinking in this country believes that coordination of welfare services requires careful continuous planning and a locus where the professionals can work together and be readily available to the public.

There is tangible evidence of the value of placing professionals who represent different disciplines and different bureaucracies in daily contact, especially in dealing with the same target population. Inevitably, working together leads them to understand each other's problems, to respect each other's professional insights, and thus to develop mutual respect and the desire to cooperate.

In one such arrangement in Puerto Rico, four separate agencies of the Commonwealth stationed their workers in a large housing complex. Uniform office hours, salary schedules, and a common director were agreed upon. A central intake was established, and in a short while a new, single operation was created out of four conflicting and duplicating activities.

Even if the neighborhood center does not lead to such program integration, the ease of communication between professional workers, when they are permitted to consult their opposite numbers without going through formal hierarchical channels helps create a desire to reinforce each other's work rather than to proceed independently.

Perhaps a more significant result of using neighborhood centers to effect coordination will come about through use of the facility by the neighborhood residents. Even if the center is conceived of as a type of department store in which each separate commodity is handled by a separate concessionaire, it will be impossible for professionals located there not to be forced to work together, by referral and by consultation. Thus, as clients come for help and as help is extended there will be joint participation, and the basic conditions which create coordination will exist: knowledge of the problem; knowledge of the resources; and ease of communication. Moreover, if the residents also participate in its recreational activities, use of the center will increase, and thus the task of securing neighborhood participation will be facilitated.

There is nothing new in this. Its essence was far more succinctly expressed in the "Younghusband Report," the report of the Working Party on Social Workers prepared for the Ministry of Health in Scotland. Let me quote from Sec. 1104:

> The elements of good teamwork are:
> 1. An administrative structure which facilitates cooperation
> 2. Good working relationships between different departmental officials at the working level
> 3. Regular meetings and discussions at all levels.

It is a simple formula, difficult to apply. It needs communication, conferences, mutual respect, surrender of absolute autonomy, and above all profound dedication and commitment to the common goal of helping people in distress.

It will not happen spontaneously, but the rising expectations of the poor and underprivileged will demand and secure positive responses from the communities in which they live, and community-wide cooperation through coordinated activity in a neighborhood facility is one of the responses that will improve our urban environment.

III. IN THE UNITED KINGDOM

ELIZABETH R. LITTLEJOHN

SECRETARY OF THE STANDING CONFERENCE
OF COUNCILS OF SOCIAL SERVICE
UNITED KINGDOM

THIS is a subject of supreme importance at a time when there is increasing ability to understand and identify social problems, greater skills in social work and social administration, but, unhappily, an almost universal shortage of trained personnel. The degree of sophistication in social services (in their widest sense), of urbanization, of industrialization, and related developments all affects the way in which this subject is approached.

I speak from experience in the United Kingdom, a densely populated country with many large and medium-sized towns, which had its first industrial revolution over 150 years ago and is now faced with the growing pains—quite well advanced—of a second technological revolution. Our social services grew up unplanned, in response to social crises—the drift to rapidly expanding cities in the early nineteenth century; terrible housing conditions; overcrowding; and the consequent aggravation of disease, crime, family breakdown. These evils were tackled with primitive skills and resources, as the need arose, largely by nongovernmental (voluntary) organizations. Later, in the twentieth century, we became more sophisticated and evolved the skills and techniques, usually of a highly specialized kind, now used by social workers. Public health workers, medico-social workers in hospitals, psychiatric social workers, family caseworkers, child care workers, and, of course, social administrators, joined the workers from the voluntary services who had struggled, up to then, often with more good will than professional skill.

But even at that stage social problems were still seen by most people as isolated from one another. For example, a homeless family was thought simply to need a house; a handicapped child, to need medical care. In this way professional services of high quality were developed but were applied only to certain sections of the community. This phase was acceptable so long as poverty was widespread and many people expected to have their social problems ignored anyway—as contrasted with the middle and upper class, who of course did benefit from these skills through private services for which they paid.

The stage which we have reached today is quite different, for the following reasons:

1. There is now general prosperity and a general expectation that efficient social services will be provided universally, whether by governmental or voluntary agencies.

2. Social workers and social administrators have discovered that

their own skills and techniques are inadequate when used in isolation, since most social problems have many aspects not only requiring the help of a number of specialists, but also needing general diagnosis.

3. The physical pattern of the community is more and more important as a factor in the way that social services can best be provided since it affects the mutual accessibility of citizen and social worker.

In the United Kingdom, although hampered by financial difficulties, we have taken a number of steps in the last ten years to meet this new situation. Some of these steps involve government policy and have universal application; some are experiments by local government; and some are undertaken by voluntary bodies. For example, the large mass of social legislation which laid the foundation of the welfare state in the late 1940s included provision for cooperating with, and providing financial help for, voluntary services. In the 1950s we had three years of experience with our postwar social legislation which was more comprehensive than anything before (social insurance; financial assistance for the uninsured; a universal health service; an education service covering primary to adult education; and care of deprived children, to cite the major services only). Already it was becoming evident that in both administrative and human terms these services were too separate and made no provision for coordination between one another or between governmental and voluntary services and left peripheral needs unmet. Because family and children's welfare services are of great importance in any society, the government asked local government authorities to set up coordinating committees consisting of representatives of health, welfare, education, and child care departments and also of the voluntary agencies concerned. This action was permissive, but some authorities organized these services in such a way that the value of a general family service became evident. Some actually built centers where such services could be grouped. At the same time, a few nongovernmental experiments were proceeding, promoted by voluntary organizations. Money was made available by foundations, and some family centers were set up, mainly in new towns or on new municipal housing estates.

Here voluntary bodies, such as casework agencies, marriage guidance councils, and family planning clinics, were housed together. In some areas the governmental child care services and also the probation and welfare services agreed to be included.

This kind of administrative action was later taken by local government in the field of general welfare services also. The experiments just described made more authorities realize that coordination improved the quality, convenience, and acceptability of services and made good use of scarce personnel. As a consequence, local government has tried to group its own services, such as, for instance, the welfare services generally, those for the elderly, and those for the physically handicapped. In addition, in many places nongovernmental services also have been invited to cooperate—and have sometimes taken the initiative. Indeed, for the last ten years actively (and for much longer on a smaller scale) voluntary organizations have been to the forefront in recognizing the need for coordination among themselves and with governmental bodies. The National Council of Social Service and councils of social service locally have been the main nonspecialized organizations concerned with this work. They exist in many urban areas and represent a wide range of voluntary social agencies in the community. They also invite the governmental agencies to be represented. When fully effective these organizations promote joint consultation and, where appropriate, joint action on matters affecting social policy and social problems. They work in partnership with local government.

Of course, these kinds of techniques and methods of coordinating public and voluntary services are still very much in the experimental stage even though there is general agreement on the need for them. There are still plenty of obstacles and problems. For one thing, where there are entrenched and highly developed services in a country like the United Kingdom there is fear that coordination might mean cumbersome machinery and a lowering of professional standards. Then again, the effect of specialized instead of generic training in social work leads to a narrow interpretation of social problems and fear of a threat to professional status, particularly if cooperation with voluntary services is required. Also, the institutional framework normally tends to encourage departmentalism rather than coordination. In the United Kingdom the government is constantly studying ways of remedying this. It must be faced, too, that voluntary agencies can more easily raise money for clearly defined and comprehensible specialized services. Then there is always the factor of personal dedication to a cause (so familiar and so important to all our work) which nevertheless militates against coordination and in favor of specialization.

Yet coordination must come. More integrated services can identify problems earlier and therefore may ultimately reduce social costs. They will also be more convenient and therefore more fully used by the client. They will be based on better use of highly trained personnel in both public and voluntary services, probably with a general social worker providing the basis of the service and using specialist consultants were necessary.

But coordination at government level, supported by legislation, is essential. This can produce an integrated social welfare department or a group of related departments which may well be subdivided to keep the advantages of specialization for consultative purposes and to work on necessarily specialized projects, such as those for the handicapped. This gives the advantage of specialization but lessens the danger of fragmented and isolated services. At governmental level permissiveness is not successful on a wide enough front, and therefore positive policies are needed. Nongovernmental organizations are in a different position. They rely on good will and the enthusiasm of members, and therefore coordination must be permissive. This means that those who work in this field need community organization skills as well as those of casework and group work.

In the last resort, a great deal must obviously depend on the physical circumstances of the community being served. Where multipurpose social service centers are used in the United Kingdom or where more limited centers providing family services are used, or those for the elderly or physically handicapped only, they are usually based on a neighborhood unit. This, however, can mean anything from an estate or small town with a population of 5,000 to one of 50,000 or even more. Little significance seems to attach to making the center very local; in fact, it has some disadvantages. Experience has shown that many people prefer the anonymity of a multipurpose building in the town center to one with more limited grouped services where the client is apt to meet his neighbors. This factor which is more significant in the United Kingdom, which has a fairly complex class structure and where an attempt has been made, not always successfully, to persuade all sections of the community to use the services.

Experience in the United Kingdom suggests that there is, in fact, still considerable doubt whether a multipurpose building provides the most effective method of coordination. It may well be that generic training of social workers, government policies requiring coordination, and nongovernmental bodies, such as councils of social service bringing all agencies and organizations together in consultation, lead in the end to more effective cooperation than does physical proximity.

The United Nations Program
of Regional Development

JULIA J. HENDERSON

DIRECTOR, BUREAU OF SOCIAL AFFAIRS, UNITED NATIONS

I AM particularly happy to discuss the program of regional development, not only because it is new in the program of the United Nations Social Commission (now the Commission for Social Development) since the last meeting of the ICSW in Athens, but also because I am deeply convinced that we cannot solve the problems of urban concentration by focusing on the cities themselves in isolation from the problems of rural development and over-all national development. There is such a high rate of failure in both industrialized and developing countries in solving urban problems, whether housing, employment, or social welfare, that we believe there must be an entirely new approach to the problem.

The United Nations has been giving systematic attention to the urbanization question for a decade. Indeed, our Population Branch, as it analyzed the results of the scattered mid-term censuses around 1955, noted that the rate of urbanization was continuing to accelerate in the developing countries and had leveled off at a very high rate in the industrialized countries.

In the face of these findings, the Social Commission began a gradual shift of emphasis from the overwhelming priority given to rural community development in the first half of the 1950s to a more balanced consideration of rural and urban problems. In 1957 the Report on the World Social Situation, for the first time, was devoted in large part to an analysis of the social problems of urbanization in economically underdeveloped countries. At the same time, a series of regional seminars and surveys was launched in cooperation with UNESCO and the regional economic commissions on the nature and scope of the urbanization problem in each region. These took place in Bangkok (1956), Santiago (1959),

the Mediterranean region (1959), Addis Ababa (1962), and War-
saw (1962), bringing together town planners, engineers, economists, sociologists, and social workers. All these studies and seminars threw considerable light on the problems of moving rural
poverty into the cities; the lag in employment opportunities, in
education and training for urban life; housing and sanitation
problems; and the problems of social disorganization.

Many more specialized activities were already under way, particularly through the Housing, Building, and Planning Branch
and the Social Services Section, as well as through the specialized
agencies concerned with education, health, and nutrition. Help to
scores of developing countries in housing and town planning was
supplemented by specialized meetings to exchange experiences
and develop guidelines for metropolitan planning, regional planning, establishment of new towns, and urban renewal programs.
Even the African countries, with the lowest level of urbanization
of any region, watching their small cities double and triple in
population within a few years of independence gave a high priority in the early 1960s to their technical assistance requests for
advisory services in town planning and to problems connected
with social disorganization, such as institutional care of children
and juvenile delinquency.

This interest in United Nations assistance in specialized areas
led to the attempt, in 1961, to prepare a Program of Concerted
International Action in the Field of Urbanization. This program,
which was adopted by the Economic and Social Council on the
recommendation of the Social Commission in the same year,
analyzed the major problems associated with rapid urbanization:
(1) the inadequate economic base to support increasing urbanization; (2) a lack of adequate community facilities, including physical facilities and public social services; (3) inadequate administrative structure; (4) inadequacy of plans and planning machinery;
and (5) the difficulties of transition to urban life of rural migrants, particularly when the cultural gap between rural and
urban milieu is wide.

A series of cooperative endeavors to tackle each of these problems and specific projects for each region were outlined in the

program. Parallel to these efforts at joint action with the specialized agencies and regional commissions, the United Nations
Technical Assistance Program, and later the Special Fund, showed
marked increases in assistance for housing and physical planning
as well as industrial development—probably the two most critical
problems facing most of the exploding cities. The demand for
help in the social services in urban areas continued to be an important aspect of United Nations activities, including some attention to the applicability of community development techniques in
urban areas. United Nations help in developing family and child
welfare services has expanded, particularly through the joint
projects with UNICEF which have emphasized the training of
child welfare personnel for both urban and rural areas. The operational program in housing and town planning has quadrupled
since 1961, and the industrial program, including attention to
industrial estates, is growing at an even faster pace. Parallel with
the new emphasis on housing and urban planning has been the
increasing emphasis of WHO on environmental sanitation and the
establishment of urban health centers.

In spite of the growth of these activities, the Secretary-General
has had to make pessimistic reports to the Economic and Social
Council at the mid-point in the development decade, concerning
world progress in closing the gap between rich and poor nations
and special difficulties in the fields of urban housing and employment as well as in efforts to raise agricultural productivity to feed
the burgeoning populations.

The effectiveness of the United Nations action in relation to
urbanization is considerably lessened by the difficulties in getting
the countries themselves to attack the problem in a comprehensive
manner. Five or six ministries are generally concerned with urban
problems, complicated in many countries by the relation of central government and municipal authorities, which makes it hard
to obtain even a request for help that is based on an over-all policy
or approach. Two notable exceptions are to be found in requests
for a United Nations urban development mission to Lagos in 1962
and to Singapore in 1963. In response to these requests, missions
were set up covering housing and physical planning, including
urban land problems, transport, sanitary engineering, and eco-

nomic and social problems. Out of these missions we have had further high-priority requests from these cities (through the national governments) to tackle specific problems, such as transport.

In 1965, at the Social Commission, the United States Government introduced a program for research and training in regional development as one of the important and fundamental answers to the urbanization problem. It was argued that it was not enough to help countries assess the nature and scope of their problem or to provide specialized assistance to cope with the population already in overcrowded cities, but that a longer-range effort should be made to divert or slow down the migration to capital cities in favor of newly developing regions in which a new economic base is laid through natural resource development, industrial development, or higher agricultural productivity. It was pointed out that there have been successful experiences in regional development in many parts of the world: the projects in Northeast Brazil and in the Guyana region in Venezuela; in the Aswan region in the United Arab Republic and the Volta River basin in Ghana; in the Nagoya region in Japan and the Galoya region in Ceylon. To these may be added over-all attempts to decentralize economic and social planning to the regional level, as in Yugoslavia, Chile, and Pakistan. To these may be added still other types of programs designed to get better distribution of population as well as to solve some of the problems of metropolitan regions, such as Calcutta. In addition, there had been abundant experience in Europe, in both the East and the West. The Economic and Social Council, on the advice of the Secretary-General, requested that we establish research projects in cooperation with the host countries to examine the relevance of this experience both to the urbanization problem in the countries and to raising the levels of living in the areas concerned. The new program calls for training regional development planning and administrative personnel as well as social development personnel in countries which appear to have the most transferable experience.[1]

In several respects, this program is not a new idea. Our town

[1] See Resources for the Future, Inc., *A Report to the United Nations on a Proposed Research-Training Program* (Baltimore, Md.: Johns Hopkins Press, 1966), contributed by the Foundation as a preliminary study or prospectus for the program.

planners have long been advising governments on the merits of regional development planning from the physical planners' point of view. The European Social Welfare Program has organized seminars in France and in Poland on social problems connected with regional development. Our economists have recommended regional planning as an important subdivision of national economic development planning. The FAO has under its aegis a number of regional agricultural development programs; the Resources and Transport Division have organized a number of groups, seminars, and Special Fund projects connected with comprehensive river valley basin developments; and in 1965 the United Nations Conference for Trade and Development adopted a resolution bearing on the problems of depressed regions within countries.

In other respects, however, the program is new and distinctive and has an important potential for the United Nations and for the governments which participate in the program. I shall discuss several of these points: (1) the integral approach to regional development; (2) the importance of basing the program on practical experience; (3) the relationship between regional development and the urbanization problem; and (4) training of personnel.

1. *Integral approach.*—Certainly one of the main reasons for stepping up our interest in regional development is the possibility it offers for a comprehensive and combined attack on the interrelated economic, social, demographic, and physical aspects of development. We have given a great deal of attention since the beginning of the decade to national development planning. It was only at the beginning of the present decade that we had sufficient ideological agreement on the importance of planning for development that we were able in the United Nations to give national planning a high priority. At the same time, we recognized that even broad and comprehensive plans can also be quite unrealistic and fail to involve the population which they are intended to help. We have therefore continued our efforts to build economic, social, and physical development at the local level, particularly through our community development and social welfare programs.

In the past two or three years we have made a valiant attempt to relate village or community development to national development planning. Many planners have been interested in this as a method for establishing two-way communication between the national governments and the localities. In larger countries particularly, however, it is highly important to provide an intermediate level between the national authorities and the local leaders. We believe that specific efforts to tackle the problems of the region where there are common economic problems as well as cultural ties and common traditions provide a possibility of making this bridge between local and national efforts. We believe that the region is also an appropriate level in many instances for the provision of qualified technical staff which is necessary to supplement the efforts that individual villages and neighborhoods can make for themselves. Whether or not the region represents a state or provincial government or a new administrative authority, the governor of the province or the director of the regional authority offers an important point for coordination of the extension services of national ministries of agriculture, public works, health, education, and social affairs. We do not expect that coordination problems will disappear, but at least we think there is a better chance they will be solved at the regional level than at the national level when the ministries are too large to allow for face-to-face consultations or at the village level where most ministries cannot afford full-time personnel.

We have tried to emphasize the integral nature of the new program in its objectives, in its emphasis on regional planning and administration, and in the methods by which we are developing the program. We established very early an internal collaboration within the United Nations which involved the Bureau of Social Affairs, the Center for Economic Planning and Projections, the Center for Industrial Development, the Resources Division, and the Public Administration Division. Furthermore, we have discussed the program at each stage with our colleagues from the specialized agencies and the regional economic commissions. Finally, we established an advisory committee made up of specialists in regional development drawn from their background as economists, social scientists, and physical planners. We hope, through these methods, to insure that we are looking at regional development as an integral process strengthening those elements which are weakest and training personnel to see all aspects of the question.

2. *Practical experience as a base.*—In the United States we know that the experience of the Tennessee Valley Authority continues to offer an attractive field of study for students, administrators, economists, and social workers from many countries. It was perhaps one of our earliest and most comprehensive attacks on the problems of a poverty stricken region.

Since the beginning of that experiment, however, the idea of regional development has made great progress in the world; particularly since the Second World War the European nations have given special attention to the development of the less-favored regions within their countries. The Dutch Government offers one of the best examples of collaboration of planning organ, ministries, and population in bringing up the level of depressed rural areas. The Italians have worked assiduously through the Cassa der il Mezzogiorno to raise the levels of living in the southern part of their country; Yugoslavia, in the light of its special political and ethnic regions, has made a special effort to raise the poorer areas, such as Macedonia, to the general level of its more highly developed North. Czechoslovakia, Poland, and France are all tackling development planning through the instrument of the region. This rich experience in Europe now offers many opportunities for study and emulation as well as for training personnel for the developing countries.

As I mentioned earlier, every part of the world has had some practical work in regional development. For example, the development of such regions as the Galoya in Ceylon and Nagoya in Japan represent a wide range of experience from a completely rural and plantation area on the one side to a completely industrial and urbanized area on the other. In South America are such outstanding efforts as the Sudene project in the Northeast of Brazil, Guyana in Venezuela, and the Cauca Valley development in Colombia, all attempts to open up new regions for balanced agricultural and industrial development. Even in the African countries, the special authorities for the Volta River basin in

Ghana and the Aswan Province in the United Arab Republic now have some three or four years experience in planning and establishing new economic bases for the development of these regions. From a study of the reports we believe that many of these experiments have been stronger in their economic and technological aspects than in their social development programs, although most of them show increased investment in education and, to a lesser extent, in health services. We believe that one impact which the Social Commission program may have in its studies of the experience in all these countries will be to point out any imbalances of this kind and to help the government find ways and means of giving more balanced attention to social development activities and, in particular, to help them evolve methods that will secure greater popular participation in regional development.

All the governments we have approached with the suggestion that they receive a preparatory mission from the United Nations to help formulate research and training projects in regional development have responded favorably. We believe we will find that at least half of these countries have highly relevant and transferable experience and we will therefore bring in suitable persons from other countries to study this experience.

3. *Regional development and the urbanization problem.*—The third distinctive feature of the program is the attempt to establish a definite relationship between regional development and the problem of overrapid urbanization or overconcentration in one or two cities in the developing countries. While we know that the objective of diverting or slowing down the migration to the capital city or the prime commercial city has been among the stated targets of certain projects, there is as yet no solid evidence that the slowing down has taken place. There are often political as well as economic and social reasons for developing a particular region, and the experience has often not been transferred to other developed regions within the same country for lack of investment capital or an obvious resource base, or the lack of trained personnel to undertake a second or third major project. The result may be simply to drain the most talented and educated people to the new city and region and to leave the overpopulated areas still pushing

their rural poverty-stricken people toward Caracas or São Paulo or Accra. The social scientists still have a basic job to do in giving us the factual basis for policy-making. A few countries are establishing new towns and industrial estates with the specific purpose of achieving a better population distribution as well as dispersion of productive units. It should be rewarding to compare the results of this approach (which has been adopted in Pakistan and Chile, for example) with the results of an all-out effort to develop a particular region such as the Northeast of Brazil or the state of Oaxaca in Mexico.

4. *Training of personnel.*—The program will be distinctive in its emphasis on training personnel for regional planning and administration and personnel for social development within regional programs. As I have noted before, a review of the literature as well as the testimony of experienced regional specialists indicates that the social development aspects of this project are generally weaker than the technological and economic aspects. The types and levels of training, the relationship to schools and institutes for training social welfare and to community development personnel, for example, have yet to be worked out.

This leads me to a brief discussion of some of the major problems we see in launching this new program. The first is probably its lack of precision. Because it is so comprehensive in nature, both officials and planners tend to look at regional development from a particular professional point of view and to neglect certain aspects of it. It is as hard to define what community development was in 1953 and for some of the same reasons. Indeed, we suffer even from the use of the term "regional development" since it means development not only of regions within countries but, in some cases, of subregions of continents, such as the Central American countries or the Magreb in North Africa, while in United Nations parlance it means whole regions, such as Asia and the Far East, Latin America, or Africa. Along with this lack of precision comes the general struggle for leadership among the professions. It is common for the town planners in many countries to see the Ministry of Public Works as the center of such efforts. In other countries, the economists take the lead. In no case do we know of a country in which the Ministry of Social Affairs has been the focal point for regional development, and for this very reason there has been a tendency to give a low priority to social aspects.

The research methods to be used in answering the many problems raised by regional development are still ill-defined, and trained social science research personnel simply do not exist in many countries. In others, they are so absorbed by strictly urban problems or by rural problems or by problems of conflict and tension that the focus on regional development is difficult to find.

Finally, the network of governmental and nongovernmental bodies dealing with the social services is often nonexistent or very weak in these regions. The method for insuring popular participation in the development of these regions is still largely unexplored territory.

It is for all these reasons that we have decided to begin with preparatory missions to the countries which have agreed to participate in the program. The first such mission will visit projects in several African countries. As we establish individual country projects, we trust that the outlines will become sharper and clearer. We will follow this stage very shortly by establishing a special program within the United Nations Research Institute for Social Development. We expect also within a twelve-month period to begin some training activities in a few of the projects. We would like to depend on cooperation with the training institutions and professional societies in the eighteen countries thus far selected.

I am confident that this program offers new possibilities in dealing with problems of urbanization and that it is completely in harmony with the theory and practice we have tried to evolve to promote balanced economic and social development. The will of the governments is clear, but there remains the problem of increasing the number of skilled professional people who will be able to translate these ideas into realities.

The Special Needs of Young Children
in Shantytowns

I. IN BRAZIL

MARIA LUIZA MONIZ DE ARAGAO

PRESIDENT, BRAZILIAN ASSISTANCE LEAGUE

BRAZIL covers about half of the surface of South America. In the Americas it is second in size only to Canada. The great variety of our climate is due to the fact that the country reaches far northward and far southward, and to the fact that the altitude of the different regions varies while the coastline is extremely long. While most of the country enjoys an average temperature higher than 22° centigrade (71.6° Fahrenheit), six states have a subtropical climate similar to that of some European regions, and the equatorial and tropical zone, which covers more than half of the country, is uniformly hot. The rains play an important part in the leveling of the temperature.

A periodic drought, the *Secas do Nordeste,* occurs in the "drought polygon," which covers 10 percent of the surface of the country and lies in the northeastern part of Brazil. The consequences of the drought are so serious that the federal government contributes 3 percent of the income of this region to provide the needed economic and social help.

Compared to other tropical countries, Brazil has achieved the highest cultural level in spite of these difficulties. From the sociological point of view, the population is the geographical expression of a social structure, with its groups, values, and mores. Brazil has a population of 80,000,000 people unevenly distributed through the country. The coastal region and the south are densely populated, while Brazil becomes more and more sparsely settled as one moves north and west. The over-all density of population is nine inhabitants per square kilometer.

The country is divided into six geographical regions (north, northeast, middle north, east, middle west, and south) in which are found the twenty-three states, four territories, and one federal district, which are themselves subdivided into prefectures.

Some parts of Brazil are depopulated because their inhabitants migrate to more economically advanced regions. This phenomenon, called "the hollow frontier," is accompanied by constant internal migrations of which the most important is from the rural areas to the cities. Although the urban population increases three times as fast as the rural population, in 1960 the rural population represented 54 percent of the total.

The over-all increase in population is over 3 percent, a population explosion. It is estimated that in 1970 Brazil will have 96,000,000, of whom 40 percent will be under fourteen years of age.

In the population pyramid the men are on one side, the women on the other. The base represents the youngest group and the top, the oldest group of population. The wide base of the pyramid indicates an extremely young population. Many children are born in Brazil, which is a young country. But, on the other hand, the pyramid is not so high as that of an older country, where people live longer.

In the Brazilian pyramid, the number of women is almost equal to that of the men (49.2 percent and 50.8 percent), and the population is essentially composed of children and adolescents of both sexes. In 1950 42 percent of the people were under fourteen years of age and only 4.2 percent were over fifty. Only 33 percent of the total population are considered as economically productive.

In the south, the density of population is higher, thanks to more developed industries, better transportation, better employment, and a concentration of foreign immigrants, mostly Germans and Italians. It is the most urbanized region of Brazil.

In accordance with the definition of young children established by the Executive Board of UNICEF, only children six years old and younger will be considered here. There are about 13,000,000 children in this age group (15.9 percent of the population) who need special care in order to survive and reach school age under more favorable circumstances.

The most acute problem is that of infant mortality; there are 112 deaths for each thousand births. Even in the big cities, with the exception of Rio de Janeiro and São Paulo, the rate of infant mortality is higher than 100 per thousand. As happens in all underdeveloped areas, Brazil is struggling against transmissible and degenerative diseases. According to official figures, 40 percent of the deaths are caused by transmissible diseases, of which 90 percent are infectious diarrhea, influenza, pneumonia, tuberculosis of the respiratory system, measles, and tetanus.

We are fully aware that health problems are closely related to nutrition, a fact which makes extremely difficult any attempt at systematic classification of diseases. A substantial number of Brazilians suffer from malnutrition, but it is in the northeast that the problem is the most acute. Among the obstacles to implementation of the improvement programs are the ignorance and superstition of parents who cling to ancient taboos attached to certain foods.

Other negative elements are: the low income of a great part of the population; illiteracy, which is now diminishing in the big urban centers; lack of health education; constant migrations; slum housing; and unemployment. Looking for better living conditions, people leave the rural areas for the cities where, most often, they do not find the solution to their problems. Adjustment to the urban environment is extremely important for the future of the newly moved family, and housing conditions are a most important factor in this adjustment. Thus it has been necessary to organize housing projects for the most primitive migrants. These projects, with minimum standards of living conditions, sanitation, health and social education, have had a marked influence on the family life of the migrants.

The *favelas* (shantytowns) are one of the most important factors in the high incidence of infant mortality, juvenile delinquency, disintegration of the family, promiscuity, and so forth. The housing facilities known as *barracos* (barracks) are nothing more than a series of tiny rooms without light, without water, without sanitation, and without drainage for rainwater. They are built out of clay, raw wood, or processed wood. For example, in

Recife in the northeast, 400,000 of the city's 1,006,000 inhabitants live in 120,000 *mocambos* (slums on stilts). According to a study done in 1963 in Rio de Janeiro, the cultural center and formerly the capital of the country, the 210 *favelas* then existing housed 1,068,653 people in 231,440 dwellings.

In spite of the magnitude of the problem, a lot has been done to improve the standard of living: plants to produce powdered milk have been built; housing improvement groups have been active in the areas of the *favelas;* housing facilities have been built. As a result, infant mortality has been reduced as the areas were cleaned up. The number of juvenile delinquents has diminished through the endeavors of social organizations, both public and private, religious institutions, volunteers and help from international organizations.

It is the children up to six years of age who have shown the greatest impact of these efforts. That is the time of life when a child is most dependent, most in need of care, tenderness, and affection, and when he stays home constantly. Consequently, it is the time of life when he suffers most from the problems of his environment. In general, these children are born from non-legalized unions but live with their parents and thus can get an approximation of the benefits of family life.

Others, the offspring of ephemeral unions of immature and irresponsible parents, suffer from birth from the instability of their environment. The mother, left alone to care for the family, must support one, two, three, or more children. At the same time, she cannot look for work because she has no place to leave her children. Such mothers seek help from public or private social agencies.

Usually, the mother will place her children in an institution so that she can take employment as a servant. Those who cannot place their children but need to work hire women whom they pay to care for the children. Thus the youngsters are left in strange hands. Often the mother, freed from her responsibilities, loses the taste for family life and indulges in new affairs, and more and more children are abandoned.

In the state of Guanabara, births have increased by 3.05 percent per year during the last ten years. The number of children increases by 150,000 each year, on the average. Since there are approximately 1,068,653 children who are classified as living a marginal life, we can conclude that 37,500 children are yearly added to the marginal population.

Public and private institutions have tried to face the situation and to establish programs which might offer objective solutions to some of the problems. One of the most recent experiments is the relocation of families in housing which is better from the physical, social, and moral point of view. Several housing projects have been built, which give the tenants the opportunity to have light, water, sewage, and decent sanitary equipment. The units are nicely separated; they have a small vegetable garden and some facilities for small husbandry and can be bought at terms which will fit into the budget of the buyer. The houses are well built and are located near schools, medical centers, social agencies, churches, movie houses, clubs, shopping centers, and public transportation. In such surroundings, children discover a new meaning to everyday life. They have fresh air, medical care, recreation facilities, kindergartens, nursery schools, and elementary schools. Together with these local programs, other types of help are offered such as, for example, help to the mothers who need to support their families. The goal is to avoid placing the children in institutions by supplying work which can be done in the home so that family life is preserved.

The Brazilian authorities have been looking for solutions to the problems of marginalized minors. The juvenile court of São Paulo is conducting an experiment which concerns: the family, through family placement; the problems of antisocial acts, through the creation of a home for minor children; means of social communication, through the Service of Technical Commissions; and abandoned children, through the establishment of a Permanent Watch Service, the Watch House, and the Services of Family Placement.

The Permanent Watch Service took in 10,821 minors in 1964. It is remarkable that only 11 percent of these children were placed in institutions and that all the others could be sent back to their families. Family placement and handling of the child by his own family are encouraged through the grant of financial aid to the families, as long as they do not have adequate means of support. Another interesting experiment is the Watch House, which screens the cases of minors under six years of age from the legal, social, and medical angles for the purposes of adoption.

Under the direct supervision of the Ministry of Health, the National Department of Childhood is concerned with the defense and protection of children. Besides its direct action in the community, the department provides financial and technical assistance to the agencies in charge of protecting mothers, children, and adolescents.

Especially interesting is the plan for the nutrition of infants, pregnant women and nursing mothers, and children of preschool age as part of the agreement between the Brazilian Government and USAID (Food for Peace). Special attention is given to the distribution of powdered milk in a number of areas. In 1965, 20,000 tons of powdered milk were distributed and supplemented by capsules of vitamins A and D. The building of plants to make powdered milk is part of the program. One factory is already in production in the south, and plants in other areas are in the planning stage.

A program of education is necessary, through publications, advertising campaigns, mothers' clubs, and youth clubs, of which there are at present 910. Adequate training of professionals is another part of the program. Scholarships for technicians and auxiliary personnel have been established so that people already in the field can be better prepared and others will be attracted to the work.

A course in health for school children is given for doctors, nurses, dentists, social workers, and teachers. Another course in child care and administration is offered for the training of auxiliary personnel.

The program for financial and technical aid sets up standards for the granting of federal subsidies to the agencies created for the protection of mothers, children, and adolescents. It contains rules for controlling the use of federal subsidies and those obtained through the help of the federal government. The department encourages private initiative toward the solution of all problems, and even helps in the establishment, organization, and functioning of agencies set up for that purpose.

The department supports the Fernandes Figueira Institute and a Center of Orientation for Young People.

The National Department of Childhood attempts to solve the problems of children and mothers through objective and cooperative action in collaboration with similar organizations and social agencies.

The National Foundation for the Welfare of Minors, the bylaws of which were approved by the President of the Republic on July 14, 1965, is another important organization in this field. It is officially responsible for the task of furthering and developing, in the whole country, a policy for improving the welfare of minors. In order to implement this policy, it studies the problems, makes plans for solutions, takes charge of the orientation, coordination, and financial administration of the agencies which are entrusted with execution of the plans.

Among other fundamental principles adopted by the Foundation we can list:

1. Take steps to comply with the provisions of the international agreements concerning the protection of children which Brazil has signed or intends to sign

2. Grant priority to the program for relocating the minors within the communities, especially through: social work within the family; adoption in conformity with the law; placement in foster families; and the creation, throughout the country, of institutions for juveniles which will duplicate as much as possible the conditions of family living

3. Take into account, when granting aid, the idiosyncrasies and special needs of each region and encourage local initiative, both public and private; in other words, try to act as a catalyst for self-help.

Research and statistical studies followed by careful planning are the basis of all the activities of the Foundation.

The main organ of the Foundation is its National Board, composed of twenty-one members, twelve of whom represent other national agencies active in the same field, including the Brazilian

League of Assistance. The Board has defined the welfare of children as "the result of the satisfaction of their basic needs through the utilization of whatever is necessary to their subsistence, to the development of their personality and to their integration in the community."

The purpose of the Brazilian League of Assistance is the protection of mothers, children, and juveniles though protection of the family. The League's function is to plan, orientate, supervise, and implement the program which promotes its goal. Since the most acute problems concerning children are found in the lowest income brackets, the League studies national economic problems in order to be able to help bring about their solution. For the same purpose it mobilizes and coordinates all the resources of the community in order better to develop the existing programs at the national, regional, and local levels by integrating them within the activities of their area.

The League, a private, nonprofit organization, was founded on August 28, 1942, under the leadership of Mrs. Darcy Sarmanho Vargas, wife of the President of the Republic. Its offices and headquarters are in Rio de Janeiro, but its field of action is nationwide. With the support of public authorities and business leaders, Mrs. Vargas succeeded in creating an institution which counts among the most important in the world in its field.

The Federation of the Business Associations of Brazil and the National Confederation of Industry gave their support to the League. They made possible the passing of a law which forced the federal government to match with public funds the 0.5 percent paid to Social Security out of salaries. This matching 0.5 percent is given to the League for its operation and functioning. At the time of its foundation, the League concentrated on helping the families of men mobilized during the Second World War, which Brazil had entered one week before the League was founded. After the war, it specialized in the protection of mothers and children through protection of the family and the work of social agencies.

The League implements programs of family placement and help to the child within its own family, adoption or, when necessary, placement in institutions (schools, hospitals, sanatoria). The help it provides is either direct or through the action of other agencies. For direct help, it maintains maternity hospitals, shelters for mothers, child care centers, clinics, work clubs, mothers' clubs, children's hospitals, emergency centers, milk centers, and so on.

The Brazilian League of Assistance provides help for anybody who needs it but cannot receive it from the Social Security services. It thus offers hope to families where the mother is an unmarried juvenile. In addition to medical assistance, we provide drugs, milk, clothing, rent and food money, money to buy working tools. Our collaboration with other agencies takes the form of subsidies or technical help for those which function in the same field as the League and whose program fits into ours. We either provide staff or help to build, equip, organize, and improve their services.

In addition to free courses in homemaking, child care, recreation, and manual skills the League offers courses in professional skills to prepare mothers for better jobs which will give them more independence and make them able to contribute to the national wealth as well as to the enrichment of their family life.

In accordance with its bylaws, the League grants scholarships for the professional training of its personnel and that of other agencies in Brazil or abroad. At its own headquarters, it organizes seminars, classes, panel discussions, round tables, and field trips for the improvement of the staff, the modernization of its techniques, exchanges of ideas, evaluation and analysis of the problems of each region.

The League has played an important part in the organization of conventions, conferences, seminars, and field trips at home and abroad, through financial or technical participation. It plays a vital part in relief when there are natural catastrophies and disasters such as droughts, floods, fires, epidemics. It helps greatly in the northeast which is periodically stricken by severe droughts. The League provides food, powdered milk, clothing, drugs, and medical assistance and gives financial help to the local governments.

The League has 26 state and territorial offices, 672 municipal commissions, and 34 regional centers. It operates or supports child care and day care centers, medical clinics, dental care centers, and centers of social medicine, associations for the protection of mothers and children, recreation centers for children, children's hospitals, infirmaries, and homes, sanatoria, shelters for mothers, maternity hospitals, centers of family placement, social centers, community centers, social service agencies, rotating funds, milk centers, several types of schools, mothers' clubs, emergency centers, orphanages, homes for the aged, and a kindergarten.

The League is active in 1,630 welfare units scattered all over the country, and there are very few agencies which have not received help from the League at some time between 1942 and 1966. The two-year plan for 1965–67 provides for reforms and expansion of the League's activities. It is based on rational and technical planning and covers ten priority programs which are being implemented:

1. Expansion of the League's field of action
2. Creation of agencies under the exclusive authority of the League
3. Distribution of additional resources according to the needs of the state or territorial offices
3. Rehabilitation of human resources
4. Renovation of plants and equipment
5. Reorganization of the administration and work methods on a more efficient basis
6. Research, evaluation, and planning
7. Program coordination
8. Promotion of a national program
9. Redrafting of the bylaws and regulations
10. Assistance to women as human beings, through education toward careers.

This last point is given special emphasis because it provides the clients of the League with the means of becoming independent of welfare agencies. Thus the Brazilian League of Assistance promotes the harmonious adjustment of women within the frame of family life and within the economic frame of the community by giving them a professional training compatible with their aptitudes and preparing them for their double role as wives and mothers.

The League is also involved in community action. It helps to coordinate the activities of agencies devoted to the protection of mothers and children, through joint action with the public authorities, especially the National Department of Children, and the state and municipal administrations. It participates as well in the campaigns of international agencies within this field.

II. IN HONG KONG

PATRICIA NYE

EXECUTIVE DIRECTOR, INTERNATIONAL SOCIAL SERVICE
HONG KONG

SHANTYTOWNS are known in Hong Kong as "squatter areas." The official definition of a squatter is "any person who occupies any land without lawful authority or without the consent of the person entitled to the beneficial occupation of such land." I could not trace the reason behind the choice of the term "squatter," but presumably it means a person who squats on a piece of land and refuses to move on.

The problem of Hong Kong is that of population. The root of the problem goes back to the Second World War and the immediate postwar period. During the Second World War many residents left Hong Kong, so that the population by the end of the war had dropped to 600,000. The population began to build up immediately, and within one year 1,000,000 people had entered the colony. Many were prewar residents returning home; the rest were people trying to escape unsettled conditions in South China. Every postwar year brought more people into Hong Kong. Then with the change in government in China in 1949, an even greater influx began. By 1950 the population was 2,360,000; it is now close to 4,000,000. Fully 80 percent of the inhabitants dwell in only fifteen square miles of land in the twin cities of Kowloon and Victoria, although the total land area of Hong Kong is 398.25 square miles.

Existing accommodations, already overcrowded before the war years and badly depleted during the war, were completely unable to cope with the number of people involved. The result was that those who could not find conventional housing took to building shacks illegally wherever they could find space for them, at first in urban areas and then along the hillsides around those areas. In spite of the tremendous amount of home building which has taken place in recent years by both government and private enterprise, squatting continues on a large scale and is one of our major problems. A recent survey showed that almost 620,000 persons still inhabit squatter accommodations either in shacks or on roof tops and that this number grows by 30,000 each year—the result of natural increase, since new domestic squattering has practically ceased, due to tight government control.

There are three major categories of squatters: land squatters, roof-top squatters, and boat squatters.

Land squatters.—There are two types of land squatters: those, the majority, who live in illegal squatter areas; and those who live in resite areas which are controlled by the Squatter Control Unit of the Hong Kong government.

Because of the shortage and high cost of housing a good proportion of the immigrants who enter Hong Kong live for some time, often the entire time, in squatter shacks on the hillsides of Victoria and Kowloon. The early squatter "townships" were nearly all on steep hillsides because that was the only land not in use. The huts are usually made from scrap lumber, corrugated iron, and sacking. Some huts are built of bricks and cement, but these are in the minority. In general, the huts are erected haphazardly, with no pattern or any form of orderliness, and perch precariously on the hillsides. There is usually no drainage, water supply, or electricity. Sanitation is primitive or nonexistent. In most cases, the houses are packed tightly together like matchboxes, for every bit of available land is used. Some squatter districts have populations of 40,000 or more people. There are no fire lanes, and only narrow lanes or streets hacked out of the hillside separate some houses from one another.

Despite the overcrowding, some squatter areas contain packets of level or terraced land on which families can have a patch of vegetable garden and can raise pigs and chickens. Some sections even have open spaces which serve as informal playgrounds for the children.

Some squatter areas are self-contained communities with their own markets, shops, places of worship, clinics, and schools of sorts, as well as their own neighborhood associations. Most squatters own the huts in which they live, although squatter landlords are not uncommon. Hut owners do not usually pay rent for the land they occupy; for those who do not own their huts, rent is relatively lower than in the tenement districts of Hong Kong and Kowloon. Although sometimes a whole family lives in one small room, it is generally accepted that overcrowding is not as severe as in the city's old tenements.

Because it is the government's policy to discourage squatting, government-supervised clinics, schools, nurseries, and social centers, which are now commonplace in resettlement estates and tenement districts, are nonexistent in squatter areas. Although the squatter population is served by governmental and voluntary welfare agencies outside, very few agencies actually operate within the squatter areas themselves.

"Resite areas" are areas selected by the government on which squatters are permitted by law to erect their temporary structures. These sections, usually quite remote from the urban areas, are made available to people who are genuinely homeless. This category includes: (1) people moved from squatter areas because the land they occupied is required for redevelopment; (2) victims of natural disasters whose homes have been destroyed; and (3) residents of condemned tenement houses or those demolished for redevelopment.

Some basic facilities are provided in resite areas, such as concrete paths, essential sanitary services, and water supplies. The structures are of a standard size, and there is some control over the use of materials for building so as to insure a minimum risk of fires. A license fee of HK$4.00 is charged on each structure.

Although the normal services of preventive medicine, such as inoculations or vaccinations under threat of an epidemic, are available in resite areas, clinics or other medical services, education, and welfare services are not introduced by the government. However, the establishment of such facilities by voluntary agencies is permitted, provided they accept control of the size, type, and location of their buildings.

Because of their temporary nature, and because people are thrown together without much choice of where they can live, resite areas are not self-sufficient communities, and lack the feeling of neighborliness found in other squatter communities. They are dependent on markets, shops, and other facilities located quite a distance away.

Roof-top squatters.—If one were to fly over Hong Kong and Kowloon in a helicopter, one would see that most of the roof tops of the old tenements are covered with small huts and shacks. These are our roof-top squatters, of whom there are over 58,000. Like their counterparts on the hillsides, they build their huts with scrap lumber, corrugated iron, and sacking. Sometimes they are there with the permission of the landlord, and sometimes without permission. They squat on the roof tops aggressively, and it is difficult to move them away once they have established themselves. Here again there is no sanitation, running water, or electricity, although occasionally it is possible to make arrangements individually with the tenants downstairs for water and some electricity. Garbage is disposed of in the easiest way possible by throwing it into the street. Unlike the other squatters, these people on the roof tops do not form separate communities. They are part of the larger tenement community in which they live, they use all the facilities available to that area, and they belong to the same neighborhood associations.

Boat squatters.—A small but significant group of people live on boats, usually unseaworthy derelicts moored on the foreshore or in the typhoon shelters near the urban areas. This group must not be confused with the Tanka or boat people who live all their lives on the sea and who are mainly fishermen. Most boat squatters are people who have their occupation on the land but live on the small sampans or junks because of the overcrowding on land, very much as people live in houseboats along the Thames, but of course not under as favorable conditions.

Boat squatters are by far the worst off of the three groups. There is serious overcrowding, for the boats are for the most part very small. There is no running water, electricity, or any form of sanitation. All refuse is thrown overboard but is seldom washed away because the boats are usually located in shallow, static water. With the exception of a few clinics and schools operated by missionaries for the Tanka community, all facilities have to be obtained on land.

I must stress that the people who live in squatter areas are not the dregs of our society. They have not gone to live in these districts because their families have failed in life. Though poverty is quite commonplace in squatter areas, not everyone who lives there is desperately poor. Squatter communities are busy communities with many kinds of trades and industries, with various kinds of family-type factories and shops. Those who do not make their living within the squatter areas work outside as white-collar workers, teachers, skilled and semiskilled laborers, in much the same way as the rest of the community. A number of our university students live in squatter areas. From this description of squatter areas it is easy to define some of the obvious hazards to the health and welfare of the children who live there.

There are the natural hazards of typhoons and rainstorms prevalent during the summer months, when a large section of a hill can be washed away. There is the constant danger of landslides, falling boulders, and collapse of their flimsy structures under strong wind and rain. During the dry winter months, the risk of fire is ever present. Our largest squatter fire in 1953 swept away acres of homes, making 50,000 people homeless.

The lack of running water, poor sanitation, and overcrowding are obvious health hazards, particularly in the hot summer months when there is constant threat of epidemic disease. Among communicable diseases, pulmonary tuberculosis poses the greatest health problem to the young population. Because there is a lack of over-all government supervision in these areas, unregisterable clinics with unregistered doctors are not uncommon, and children are sometimes exposed to medical malpractice.

Although there are schools in these areas, they are mostly family-type schools—not registerable with the Education Department—which seldom employ trained teachers. Consequently, the education obtained in these schools is usually below the standard of that outside. As an alternative, children sometimes travel long distances to schools outside the squatter areas.

The overcrowded conditions often deprive a child of a favorable environment wherein he can do his homework. Facilities which have become common for children in resettlement estates, such as libraries, clubs, and supervised play areas, do not exist in squatter areas.

Because of the lack of supervision and the abundance of family-type factories, squatter children are sometimes hired below the legal age for employment, and work illegally long hours under unfavorable conditions. Since everyone works very hard in these communities, the children too work hard, helping with the family chores, which very often includes carrying heavy buckets of water up a steep hill from the street taps to their homes.

Again because of the lack of police patrol, drug trafficking and drug addiction are more prevalent in squatter areas. Children are sometimes used to carry narcotics. Because of constant exposure to the use of drugs, addiction seems normal, and children perhaps grow up with different moral standards than they would otherwise have.

The needs of children in squatter areas, as well as those of the adult population, are of great concern to the Hong Kong government and to voluntary agencies. As a result, we have in Hong Kong one of the world's largest resettlement programs, whereby hundreds of thousands of people have been provided with low-cost housing since 1955. By the end of 1965 the government of Hong Kong had become, through this plan, the direct landlord of about 815,000 people, or 20 percent of the population. An expanded building program aims at providing space for over 900,000 by 1970. In addition, a number of voluntary organizations have built housing for lower- and middle-income groups. The Hong Kong Housing Society has now housed 82,632 people, and other voluntary agencies have also made contributions toward housing Hong Kong's squatter population.

In the beginning, because of the urgency of the problem, resettlement estates provided only approximately 120 square feet for a family, and many hundreds of residents have to share communal washing and toilet facilities. However, improvements have been made in the design of the buildings, to provide more comfort and privacy, and the size of the accommodations has been varied.

Many of the resettlement estates are self-contained little towns with a wide range of community facilities. Ground-floor rooms are set aside for shops or restaurants to permit the settlers to continue their business in the resettled area. Provision is also made for the small factories which have operated in squatter areas. To enable those resettled from such factories to continue earning a livelihood, multistory resettlement factory blocks have been built.

Everyone in the squatter areas is registered with the government and will eventually be given a chance to resettle. It is true that some may still have to wait quite a while for this opportunity, but the ultimate aim is to provide adequate housing for everyone.

III. IN NIGERIA

G. N. AGBIM

PRINCIPAL SOCIAL WELFARE OFFICER,
MINISTRY OF LABOR AND SOCIAL WELFARE
NIGERIA

YOUNG children all the world over have special needs. These needs can only be understood in relation to the nature and structure of the family, which is the basic unit of our society and to which every child belongs. The needs can also be understood in relation to the culture of the people.

In Nigeria if a child misbehaves, we say that he has had no home training from his family. The family pattern in Nigeria is highly extended. It includes a man, his wife, their children, cousins and uncles, and those who have the same blood relationship. There are very strong family ties, and the family is therefore cohesive.

Every young child belongs to an extended family. He is economically dependent upon its members for his support and well-being. As a corollary, he is bound to abide by the rules and requirements of the family. The young child is trained to be obedient, respectful, and to carry out instructions in the home without refusal or question.

He is like an apple on the tree which ripens, falls on the soil, germinates, and grows side by side with the parent tree. He is trimmed, watered, and protected against destructive insects—undesirable adults. He is expected at growth to contribute toward the material development of the family members.

He is regarded as immature and is not qualified to enter into active social interaction with adults. He has to play with his age group and cannot argue with his parents or teachers. He is regarded as disrespectful if he joins adult conversation or talks back to people. He should prostrate to older persons or stand up for them as signs of respect in his greetings either at home or outside. He just greets people and respects them anywhere he goes.

Family rules tend to be too rigid and control tends to be too restrictive, so that young children do not enjoy the freedom of movement which town and city life attract. The child has to consult his parents on everything he wants to do. He cannot make an independent decision. This is why a young man cannot decide alone on whom to marry. The family must be consulted and their approval obtained before marriage can be consummated.

Amidst all these pressures of family control and inhibitions lie the unexpressed emotional needs of young children. Neither the school nor the home can provide avenues for the expression of these needs. Children need social activities which will be complementary to those of the school and the home. Experience has shown in Nigeria that well-organized youth clubs can go a long way toward enabling the young child to give vent to his feeling of frustration at the prohibitive controls of the family.

In Lagos, the capital city of Nigeria, there are provisions for youth clubs and centers in the urban development program.

Young people make known their need for these centers, but the difficulty is that there are no adequate funds to develop the plots of land and put up buildings.

In the new developing areas of the city are youth club houses. In these centers, children practice the art of democratic government, planning their own programs of social activities with the help of social workers. Here they organize debates, dancing, boxing, cycling, and other activities, such as writing poems and stories and holding public speaking contests. They have the liberty to organize and manage their own affairs—a situation which does not exist in the home.

Children like to dance to the tune of melodious Nigerian high life music, but the school does not provide dances as a form of relaxation and recreation. The families deplore night club dancing, and young children are not permitted to engage in it. The most frustrating aspect of this is that there are night clubs where band music is played, and adult groups go there for relaxation. By law, children are not allowed to go to such places, and in any case have no means to do so even if they were permitted. They cannot reconcile adult night club dancing with the morals to which they are exposed at home. The result is that children who are beyond parental control hang about the streets where there are night clubs in order to enjoy the music.

The Social Welfare Division in Lagos recognizes this need and the fact that social controls exercised by the families are no longer effective in stemming the natural impulse of youth to frequent undesirable places. Since the families cannot satisfy these needs, the Social Welfare Division encourages the youth to have their own groups and occasions when dances are organized with the help of group workers. This affords youth the opportunity to engage in social activities that enable them to give vent to their frustrations in a most rational way.

One of the most urgent problems of young people who drift into the cities in Nigeria is lack of employment opportunities. This is one of the serious sources of frustration which has to be reckoned with in proposals for urban development.

Young children in Nigeria need to travel to other parts of the country on educational excursions. They need to learn more about their country and to keep abreast of social and economic developments.

Many young children who have lived in central Lagos, where opportunities for creative leisure activities are not available, like to engage in camping. Equally, children in the rehousing area of Lagos welcome camping for the many opportunities it affords them for swimming at the beach.

The Social Welfare Division runs two camps in Lagos: one is at Tarkwa Bay, across the lagoon; the other, which is popularly called the boys' holiday camp, is at Kuramoh Waters. Children are taken to the camps during their holiday periods by the group workers. Camping affords young children an opportunity to be on their own, to plan their own meals, and to have a sense of independence of thought and expression, thus providing an opportunity for testing whether or not they can play the traditional roles of motherhood and fatherhood within the extended family structure.

There are children in Nigeria who need care and protection due to some form of social disorganization resulting in urbanization. A very negligible number of children are neglected. Yet there are increasing numbers of young people who without parental knowledge desire to venture into the cities. They drift into urban centers where members of their family are not residents. These children are deemed to be in need of care and protection and constitute a problem for the Social Welfare Division.

The Social Welfare Division runs six institutions in Lagos for children who are committed by the order of the juvenile court as being beyond parental control or in need of shelter, children who are found wandering, children who fall out with the law by committing offenses, and children who are exposed to moral danger.

Perhaps one of the greatest needs of the teeming population of young children in Nigeria is for adequate health and medical facilities. Infant mortality is very high.

One of the most important special needs is a good education for the young children of Nigeria to enable them to be citizens of tomorrow.

On the whole, I would say that children need special love, affection, and warmth. They need good food, shelter, clothing, and opportunities that will enable them to develop physically, mentally, socially, and spiritually. They need adequate medical care and protection against undesirable association with adults. They need their own youth clubs and should not be given too much liberty in their early growth and development.

There should be open spaces in urban areas to provide effective recreational activities designed to enable children to develop proprely.

Equally, there is need to strengthen the economy so that families can continue under the extended pattern.

Reports of
Commissions, Study Groups, and
Special Meetings

Commission I. The Impact of Urbanization

Chairman: Stelio de Alencar Roxo, *Brazil*
Vice-chairman: Genevieve W. Carter, *United States*
Rapporteur: Rev. Alister G. Dunn, *New Zealand*

Kathleen Dawe, *Australia*
Maria Helena Brotmann Loureiro, *Brazil*
Lauri Tarvainen, *Finland*
Michel Piquard, *France*
Marcelle Trillat, *France*
Martha Krause, *Germany*
Dorothea Von Caemmerer, *Germany*
Areti Mermiga, *Greece*
Louise She, *Hong Kong*
Mrs. Zarina Currimbhoy, *India*
Nina Sutaria, *India*
Hai Halevi, *Israel*
M. Cifarelli, *Italy*

Takeko Matsumoto, *Japan*
Mrs. Dieuke Heroma, *Netherlands*
Fred H. Landsman, *Netherlands*
Firoza Ahmed, *Pakistan*
Mrs. G. Pecson, *Philippines*
Filipe Mario Lopes, *Portugal*
Antonio del Olmo Parra, *Spain*
Charles Pean, *Switzerland*
Mrs. Fahrunnisa Saeden, *Turkey*
Maurice Broady, *United Kingdom*
W. George Swann, *United Kingdom*
Clifford C. Ham, *United States*
John B. Turner, *United States*

THIS commission, after a brief exploration of concepts and definitions of urbanization, decided to direct its attention to first-hand descriptions of the effects of urbanization experienced by the various countries represented. This inevitably led into inquiries about the policy and program actions now under way or under consideration by the countries involved.

Because of the excellent documents and reports already available to participants, discussion was focused more on the variations in the social dimensions of urbanization, as witnessed by the individual delegates, than on detailed accounts of demographic or geographical changes. Their vivid accounts of the human effects of urbanization opened up a panoramic view of a world-wide urbanization process. It is from these descriptive accounts concerned with some twenty-four countries that the high points of the commission's deliberations are drawn.

COMMON THEMES

The world-wide scope of the problems in the rapidly growing megalopolises of all countries, in advanced societies and developing nations alike, creates a powerful sense of the interdependency and interrelationships existing among all countries. One of the most interesting aspects, central to all countries, was the repeated theme of hope and aspiration for a better life, common to all human beings as they join the population stream toward this new life of "urbanism." One of the most positive elements in the descriptions of urbanization was this motivating force to better one's position and seek a more equitable share of the resources available within one's own country or elsewhere.

There was widespread assertion that, for good or bad, city life has a marked impact on the traditional patterns of family life. There were vivid illustrations from a number of countries of the chain of consequences set into motion when newcomers with these traditional patterns try to cope with the constraints of city living.

Perhaps the third significant observation was the common awareness of the natural processes present in the urbanization phenomenon. This was reflected in descriptions of the indigenous pathways of the population movement to and within cities. It was also introduced from another point of view—the rights of individuals and families and their freedom to move and live by choice. The controls and shaping of the urbanization process through urban development and national urbanization policies bring concomitant restraints on the range of choices for people. Generally, it was thought that sound planning could take into account the pull and force of natural, spontaneous population movement. The issue was troublesome and not easily resolved.

The various impacts, such as the balance between job opportunities and the influx of newcomers or the lack of proper housing and amenities, were important and common to most countries, and the impacts on the individual or family struck a note of general response in the commission.

In particular, the social worker is concerned with how the major national or world-wide forces of urbanization affect the social and psychological state of the individual human being. Four types of impact were cited: there is a change in patterns of family life; man must again ask who he is, for he feels a loss of self-identity when familiar supports of family and village are lost; he must adapt himself to a new kind of interdependence with community institutions and organized services; and an adjustment must be made to the anonymity of big city life. There is a breakdown in the ability of individuals in subcultural groups to see and understand the responsibility that they now share for a larger community.

There is great variation in the capacity of people to cope and adapt. Nevertheless, to many the city offers the promise of a rich and exciting life—in material advancement and in breadth or quality of living.

Among the positive aspects, one should remember the cultural horizon which is opened to all by a large city, making it possible to get free from the "social control" of the small town. It is interesting to note that in developing areas it is the psychological factor more than the economic factor that influences the move to the large cities, mainly by the young and more ambitious people. There is also the possibility of broadening their perspective; of living a more "modern" life; of getting away from the monotony, and sometimes the misery, of the countryside.

A final subject of discussion which appeared to cut across all countries was the recognition of the importance of the social worker as a member of the team of experts concerned with urbanization. Other reports have defined the respective roles of the various disciplines and professions in urban development—in analysis, planning, and implementation. There was general agreement that plans for improving the quality as well as the quantity of social workers must receive greater emphasis in all countries. In order for social workers to adapt their skills or to innovate and create appropriate programs, there must be greater understanding on the part of the social worker regarding the social-change dynamics associated with urbanization. There must be recognition of the importance of the social worker who is a specialist in social planning and social policy, as a member of a team of planners. There was concern expressed, however, that the respective disciplines and professions should maintain the integrity of their own type of contribution without too much dilution, which would create generalists of all and specialists of none.

DIFFERENCES AND VARIATIONS

Because of differences in stages of urbanization and the disparities in available resources, the emphasis on action priorities differed greatly. Urbanization heightens the differentials between the "have" and the "have-not" countries. World-wide resources must be marshaled to provide food, shelter, and health at a level that will insure human dignity for all mankind.

The problem of assimilation and integration of identifiable groups of people who are dissimilar in religion, color, social class, or culture is one of the aspects of urbanization with considerable variation among countries. In some countries there have been serious reactions of nonacceptance, threat of job competition, and even punitive responses.

Several illustrations of successful absorption of such groups were reported. Comparisons between countries were difficult, however, because each country has its own scale for measuring the intensity of the problem and the means for coping with it.

It was generally agreed that effective measures for absorption, other than in job opportunities, are not well developed and that there is an urgent need for both research and program innovations to meet the assimilation and integration problems accentuated by urbanization.

The variations in urbanization impacts between the newly developing countries and the older industrialized nations were so striking that many comparisons were meaningless. One country reported no problems: cities have developed in an orderly fashion, with no megalopolis, no housing problems, no overemployment, no burden on resources, and no problems of integrating new population groups from other countries.

War-torn countries had unique problems when new slums followed emergency housing developments after the war.

The trend toward "new towns" appeared in a number of reports. Discussion of the nature and success of these settlements brought out the need for organized preparation of newcomers. This lack of preparation for adaptation was emphasized by the commission, and there was consensus that the planned movement of a community's population should include preplanning for "new town" residents built into the urban design.

The deliberations of the commission touched on nearly every dimension of urbanization. The commission wondered if there is a possibility of limiting the size of any city, in relation to resources. The reports of participants acknowledged the serious social problems associated with urbanization around the world but were also explicit about the positive effects and the potential for desirable social changes.

We need not look forward with gloom to the future of the city. Rather, we should advance to meet the challenge of creating a life in the city which will match the hopes and aspirations of its people.

Commission II. Social Policy and Strategy for Urban Development

Chairman: Hans Reschke, *Germany*
Vice-chairman: Mrs. Maragatham Chandrasekher, *India*
Rapporteur: Mrs. Renate Langohr, *Germany*

Maria Catalina Trillo, *Argentina*
Monnoyer de Galland, *Belgium*
Newton B. Cotrim, *Brazil*
Armando Telini, *Brazil*
John Morgan, *Canada*
W. W. Struthers, *Canada*
Mme. Lefebvre, *France*
M. Trintignac, *France*
Reinhard Schnabel, *Germany*
Mrs. M. Angelopoulos, *Greece*
Alastair Todd, *Hong Kong*
M. Wertheimer, *Israel*

Totaro Okada, *Japan*
W. van der Zwaen, *Netherlands*
A. J. M. van Tienen, *Netherlands*
Begum Noon, *Pakistan*
Maria Palmira Morais Pinto Duarte, *Portugal*
Lee Beng Guan, *Singapore*
Mrs. Renu Jotidilok, *Thailand*
E. Gittus, *United Kingdom*
David R. Hunter, *United States*
Kurt Reichert, *United States*

THE GROUP agreed to base the discussion upon an outline prepared by the chairman of the commission and given to the members of the group at the first meeting. This outline, in turn, was based on an expansion of the six main headings given by the Program Committee and published in the Preliminary Program.

There was lengthy consideration as to the right, or duty, of social workers to engage in discussions and policy-making in a field wider than that normally recognized as social work; whether, in fact, social policy on a broad basis is the social worker's concern. It was finally concluded that the social worker has a very definite contribution to make to the formation of social policy. He should give his expertise to the decision-making bodies and take responsibility in policy. At the same time, other disciplines have their contributions to make, and the social worker should not have an overriding, or exclusive, responsibility. Furthermore, it was recognized that the involvement of social workers in decision-making and in planning may be different in developing countries and in developed countries. Finally, it became clear that if the social worker is to participate in policy-making on a wide basis, social work training must be so constructed as to make this practicable.

VALUE ASSUMPTIONS AND GOALS

The group was concerned with this question: What are the basic values in urban development?

It was agreed that, ideally, there should be as much freedom as possible for the individual and his family. This gave rise to two problems: the reconciliation of personal choice with the practical needs of the planner; and the means of determining the alternatives wanted by the population.

It was agreed that there should be an equilibrium between the needs of the population and the opportunities that the community can provide. Research could help to determine this, and to such research the social worker could make, if trained and encouraged to do so, an important contribution.

It was accepted as an over-all goal in urban development that social policy should make it possible for man to meet the demands of modern techniques in the best possible way so that he is able to adjust himself to conditions which prevail in urban areas—he should feel at home in his surroundings. More especially, it was recognized that:

1. Human life has an essential dignity that should be preserved.

2. Individuals, for the most part, can best realize themselves as members of groups, including those of family, employment, and community; but in planning for group interest, one must not lose sight of the inherent worth of the individual.

3. Individuals and groups have the right to make choices which should be protected by the community; but the community should also take responsibility in achieving an equilibrium between conflicting choices.

4. The objective of the community should be to foster the economic, social, and cultural development of its individual members.

5. The weight to be attached in planning to the economic, social, political, and cultural factors should be determined by the community; but consideration should be given to them all.

6. The community should be so structured and developed that

the individual may enjoy reasonable choice of shelter, employment, leisure pursuits, and so forth, as well as protection from want and fear.

The social worker has a responsibility to make values known and, if necessary, to exert political pressure toward their recognition.

THE NATURE OF THE "GOOD COMMUNITY"

The neighborhood was recognized from the physical point of view as a basic community unit. Its size can vary according to physical, social, and economic circumstances and to the situation in particular countries. But we should not foster a romantic idea of the neighborhood. In order to provide certain social services, a certain size of community unit is required, though in bigger towns it may be necessary to subdivide the town into smaller units. To know the right size of the unit, it is necessary to carry out research, and every planning body has a responsibility to carry out this research by the best possible means in order to assess the success of the plan and its impact on the population.

During the process of planning, it might become necessary to vary the method of research and even the steps of planning.

Plans for the community life should not be restricted to physical aspects; they should cover the many aspects of human relations.

Variety in the composition of the population—age groups, social groups, income groups—should be made possible, even if initially that is difficult to achieve.

Variety of educational opportunities should be provided, even if they do not seem to be successful when they are started. It was agreed as a principle that a mixture of residential and selected industrial areas is desirable, though here again people may not be willing to accept this at first. It is desirable to include light industry in order to provide employment for women and young people.

IMPLICATIONS OF CONFLICTS OF INTERESTS

The commission recognized that in every country, whatever its political system, property rights and the interest of the community in providing good housing for all its members are a continuous problem, manifested in three aspects: ownership of land; control over the use of land; and control over the price of land. Although the group recognized the political, economic, and social difficulties, it was agreed that some legal measures to control land use and acquisition should be assured.

It cannot be said whether priority should be given to the building of one-family detached houses or to blocks. Different types of housing and social amenities will be necessary to meet the different needs of the people.

POLICIES TO EXPLOIT THE POSITIVE FACTORS IN URBANIZATION

Since there is a greater variety of opportunities and facilities in urban situations, specialized services are possible, and it is necessary to coordinate these services. It seems to be more effective, for example, to provide a certain multipurpose, family casework unit rather than several services to care for the different needs of a family. But this should be combined with the work of the specialist.

In developing countries, very often the economic factor is the determining one. After the economic question has been settled, social welfare projects are planned, and if they are to be effective it is important to gain the interest and influence of policy-making bodies. Against this situation, the commission members wanted to emphasize that economic values will not be produced until we take simultaneously into consideration the relevant social needs and social implications.

In providing facilities for cultural activities, the concept of culture should not be taken too narrowly. There should be an endeavor to look for new forms of cultural activities. Some countries cited as an example the construction of multifunctional buildings to be used by all kinds of activities. For better use by the people, it seemed advisable to concentrate the specialized services of welfare centers, health centers, credit unions, legal aid, and so on, in one place.

One of the tasks was seen as encouraging and providing possibilities for celebrations and festivals for different groups in urban areas. This could be achieved by community centers, and it could help to develop a certain kind of community spirit.

These projects are encouraged when people make their own contribution and become involved, even in financial matters.

POLICIES TO MINIMIZE THE NEGATIVE EFFECTS OF URBANIZATION

In all metropolitan areas it seems difficult to coordinate social services, transportation, and educational institutions with those of surrounding rural areas. There should be certain administrative arrangements to secure their cooperation, but the self-responsibility of the community—rural as well as urban—should be kept as a principle.

The commission recognized that in a large urban area the individual may lose his sense of identity and belonging, and that the planning process must be designed to counter this tendency.

The group distinguished between two levels of planning. For many services, such as transportation and traffic control, hospitals, universities, secondary schools, and so forth, it is necessary for the sake of efficiency to plan on a large scale. Smaller units should be kept for a limited range of functions, such as family services, child care, local recreation. Which services can be provided at which level is a subject for continuous consideration. It will be different in various countries and various areas and at various times.

It was emphasized that even if some services might be provided at the local level, the financing cannot always be settled on a local basis. In developing countries where generally plans are carried out on a more central level, efforts are made to involve local people, sometimes in an advisory capacity.

Apart from the activities carried out by the state or governmental bodies, churches have a good opportunity to contribute to many aspects of community life, physically as well as spiritually. In some countries, developing as well as developed, religious institutions provide a considerable amount of social services. It was recognized that good cooperation of government bodies, churches, and private organizations is absolutely necessary to provide social services.

SOCIAL SERVICES REQUIRED IN URBAN AREAS

In addition to specialized services—health services, education, social work, housing, social security—it was stressed that there is a particular need to inform the population. Citizens' advice bureaus (information centers) are a good means for reaching people, but there should be another kind of informing which perhaps could be compared to aggressive social work; that is, information has to be communicated to the people, even if they do not come to ask questions because, in many cases, they do not even know where to go to get information.

The commission recognized a need for the development of local planning structures to facilitate the linking of physical and social planning. In such structures, a wide representation of public and private bodies should be secured.

Commission III. Patterns of Intervention— Structures and Process for Urban Development

Chairman: Mrs. Minerva G. Laudico, *Philippines*
Vice-chairman: Juan Lopez Cano, *Spain*
Rapporteur: Pierre Laplante, *Canada*

Mark Neutze, *Australia*
Frans Wastiels, *Belgium*
Clovis Garcia, *Brazil*
Ana Adelina Lina, *Brazil*
Mrs. Rachel Prochnik, *Brazil*
Antonio Paulo de Silva, *Brazil*
Alan Armstrong, *Canada*
Alice Smout, *Canada*
R. B. Splane, *Canada*
Marjatta Sarves, *Finland*
M. R. Lecourt, *France*
Marie Montagne, *France*
K. Elsholz, *Germany*
Lee Hei Man, *Hong Kong*
Armatiy Desai, *India*
Mrs. M. Clubwala Jadha, *India*

Mrs. Dina Lieberman, *Israel*
Sadatoshi Sukegawa, *Japan*
G. Rekkebo, *Korea*
Ghassan Rubeiz, *Lebanon*
N. F. A. de Graan, *Netherlands*
M. J. W. Nijkamp, *Netherlands*
Mrs. Rosa C. de Herrera, *Panama*
Mrs. Maria Raquel Riveiro, *Portugal*
Miss Lotti Brunnschweiler,
  Switzerland
S. Piamsilpa, *Thailand*
Ralph Iredale, *United Kingdom*
E. Littlejohn, *United Kingdom*
Bertram M. Beck, *United States*
Mrs. Inabel Lindsay, *United States*

THERE was a clear consensus among the members of the commission that if the cities of tomorrow are to provide a healthy environment for families, children, and the aged, our present patterns of intervention, in terms of both structures and processes for urban development, must be very much strengthened and the participation of the social disciplines and professions, as well as of the citizens concerned, must be more systematic than it is at present.

One has only to look at what is happening in the slum areas of many cities in developed countries, or in the bidonvilles or favelas of rapidly expanding urban areas in the developing countries, to realize some of the consequences of a policy of *laisser-faire* without clear concepts, or without systematic patterns of intervention, to make sure that the cities are built and equipped to meet the needs of their citizens. And here we do not mean only physical planning and material equipment; we also include a rational policy of distribution of population and of migrations to urban areas and the provision of adequate services for health and sanitation, work and recreation, education and cultural activities, income security, social counseling, and other services which should be a normal part of the social infrastructure of any city.

It is obvious that the members of this commission cannot be specific about the structures and processes required in each country to implement policies of urban development. Patterns of intervention must take into account not only the cultural values and the political context prevailing in each country, but also the specific goals to be achieved and the available resources.

In a general way, however, it is felt that urban development is such a complex and vital matter that the responsibility for planning and implementing it must rest ultimately with the central government of each country. If we want to do comprehensive planning for urban development, the central government is usually in an advantageous position to provide the financial means and to pool the best specialists required for that purpose; and thus the policy of urban development can be appropriately integrated within the over-all plan for the economic and social development of the country.

But taking the ultimate responsibility does not mean that the central government must control everything in detail. It was felt that local organizations are often in a better position to know local needs and voluntary organizations are often in a better position to do pioneering work before the government is ready to take over new responsibilities. In any case, it seems obvious that both voluntary and public agencies must work as partners. In several countries, local councils equipped with professional staff and broadly representative of various local groups help develop appropriate services and policies at the local level.

One of the crucial problems of urban development is that the goals of our policies cannot be met without a very close cooperation among various disciplines and among specialized departments. In practice, however, each profession, or agency, tends to work in isolation, with the result that planning endeavors do not take into account all the aspects of the situation. An additional problem is that the people are often bewildered by, and sometimes suspicious of, the jungle of bureaucracy. Recent trends, however, were noted with hope:

1. There is a tendency, at university level, to develop a common core of knowledge among the various professions and also an awareness of the need for a teamwork approach in the solution of complex problems.

2. New programs are being experimented with in several countries to bring as close as possible to where the people live a more integrated pattern of social services with emphasis on prevention and social enrichment.

The commission also examined the role that social welfare workers could and should play in a more systematic policy of urban development.

The social worker is often identified by other professions as being competent to deal with the social problems of individuals and families. It is sometimes felt also that he is more competent to deal with the pathological problems of the disadvantaged portion of the population and that he is of little help in guiding the planners in building new towns for the benefit of future citizens. It is, however, generally accepted that the policy of urban development must not be left in the hands of physical planners alone, or economists or engineers alone, if the city is to meet the needs of its citizens. It is believed that social welfare workers are in a strategic position to interpret the needs of the people or to help the people voice their own concerns. But, if the social worker is to play a vital role in social planning, social legislation, and public administration, he must be better trained in indirect methods of intervention.

Finally, it is obvious that especially in the less developed countries a sound policy of urban development is impossible unless there is a reservoir of qualified staff to plan and implement such a policy. It was noted with great anxiety that these countries find it difficult not only to train enough qualified workers but also to prevent the loss of personnel to more developed countries.

Since urbanization is an irreversible trend which is already affecting the way of life of millions of citizens, both in developing and developed countries, it is important to make sure that the positive values of this phenomenon are strengthened and its undesired consequences either prevented or controlled to the largest extent possible. Therefore, the commission recommends:

1. That the governments of each country take the leadership in promoting an integrated policy of urban development for its own population.

2. That effective means of communication be established at national, regional, and local levels to facilitate the teamwork required among the various disciplines and agencies for planning and implementing such policies.

3. That qualified social welfare workers be urged to share their knowledge of human needs and to help formulate the policies and implement the concerted programs of urban development with the participation of the people concerned.

It is also recommended that the members of the ICSW accept responsibility for promoting such policies through their local and national organizations; that the same recommendations be forwarded to the United Nations Bureau of Social Affairs, and that reports of action taken be heard at the next meeting of the ICSW.

Commission IV. Maximizing the Participation of Citizens in Urban Development

Chairman: C. F. McNeil, *United States*
Vice-chairman: Chang Shub Roh, *Korea*
Rapporteurs: Johanna Boer, *Netherlands*
Violet M. Sieder, *United States*

Emina Carrasco, *Argentina*
Raymonde Hontoir, *Belgium*
Elza Prado Suzuki, *Brazil*
Nylto Mobeira Velloso, *Brazil*
Annie Black, *Canada*
Audrey Burger, *Canada*
Denise Raveau, *France*
Pierre Viot, *France*
Liisa Hakola, *Finland*
Ferdinand E. Blotz, *Germany*
Arno F. Kosmale, *Germany*
Dora Papaflessa, *Greece*
Frances Chen, *Hong Kong*
Halaswamy Gupta, *India*
N. F. Kaikobad, *India*
Jona M. Rosenfeld, *Israel*
Mrs. Sybil E. Francis, *Jamaica*

Yuichi Nakamura, *Japan*
Aij Takeuchi, *Japan*
Tarek M. Shuman, *Lebanon*
Senator G. Shelley, *Malaysia*
Gemma Zaeth Guerrero Lopez,
    Mexico
Clarita Navarro de Riba, *Panama*
Mrs. Elena Perez-Ompoc, *Philippines*
Eunice de Santa Rita Vieira Ereire,
    Portugal
Suzanne Bonnard, *Switzerland*
Prakhin Xumsai, *Thailand*
Norman Longley, *United Kingdom*
John Mack, *United Kingdom*
Richard W. Boone, *United States*
Herman C. Kruse, *Uruguay*
Lila Mateo Alonso, *Venezuela*

THE COMMISSION accepted the Pre-Conference Working Party's assumption that in urban development citizens should have the opportunity to participate in planning for improvement of their physical and sociocultural environment. Citizens' participation in urban development was universally recognized as a desirable goal, based on such democratic values as social responsibility and equal opportunities, as well as a possible means to achieve social change.

The fact that physical and economic planning is usually presupposed, while social planning, until recently, tended to be neglected, led to the conclusion that on behalf of the people's welfare, social planning should be included in the process of urban development.

Attention was paid to the fact that a wide variety of forms and ways of citizens' participation exists in different countries. The nature of the participation seems to be defined by the economic, political, and cultural situation of the country concerned.

Some difficulties arose on the concept of "the sense of community," often referred to as a desirable goal. The group agreed that a "sense of community," in terms of urban development, is a complex concept which involves:

1. A common interest—the feeling of belonging which results from being part of a valued group, accounts for motivation for participation, provides for the exercise of choice and for the right to differ with those in power

2. A geographic entity which may have political boundaries, is part of a larger system, and, in turn, has subparts, including individuals, groups, and organizations.

One expresses his sense of community by taking responsibility for social action through both communities of interest and geographic communities operating at various levels and in combinations appropriate to the problem. The level and the relationships of a community determine the type of influence its citizens can exert on decisions that affect urban development.

Problems that affect citizen participation in a dynamically changing society include the following:

1. *Environmental factors*

   a) Industrialization, broadly interpreted, induces: mobility; high degree of bureaucratization; and concentration of population in urban areas.

   b) Various political systems either enhance or inhibit participation.

   c) Financial resources for social planning and citizen participation are limited.

   d) Cultural patterns are often unstable and changing.

   e) Regional or metropolitan planning networks are generally lacking.

   f) Citizens generally lack a sense of community and either are apathetic or feel powerless to deal with societal problems.

2. *Planning practices*

   a) Social planning frequently does not exist or is inadequate.

b) Social planning, physical planning, and economic planning frequently are not integrated.

c) Citizen participation is limited in numbers, in quality, in leadership, and in continuity.

d) Plans tend to be irrelevant, short-range, and opportunistic rather than long-range efforts to deal with major problems by making changes in basic social institutions.

e) Plans are not implemented because of lack of substantive knowledge, skillful practical intervention, communication, research, technical knowledge, public understanding, and citizen action and support.

f) There is a lack of appropriate channels of participation for various subgroups, such as youth, age, ethnic, racial, and the poor.

3. *Social work practice*

a) Ties to the "establishment" override concern for organizing the community to meet client needs.

b) Goals are limited when there is preoccupation with traditional professional methods to the exclusion of concern for social cause, citizen participation, and the development of leaders in all walks of life.

c) There is a lack of essential training in political process, group process, and administration.

d) The lack of status of the profession limits interaction with other professions, particularly with economic and city planners.

e) Lack of sophistication in political organization and practice can result in the political and economic exploitation of citizens' organizations which social workers have helped to create. Social workers themselves might be misused by political leaders or systems.

f) Social work agencies are not structured so as to motivate, guide, or reward community work undertaken by staff.

g) Social work has not adequately evaluated the consequences of its programs, including those which involve citizen participation.

Commission IV discussed three main issues:

1. *The citizen's role.*—Who is "the citizen"? Everyone who lives in the community concerned? Are there any restrictions as to age, sex, or membership in other subgroups, such as political, denominational, and racial groups?

Theoretically, maximizing citizens' participation would require involving as many citizens as possible. However, several countries reported that they work through councils and other social structures representing subgroups in the community. Unaffiliated people, particularly those characterized as "the poor," were thus not involved; for although these councils traditionally claim to represent everybody, they tend to represent middle- and upper-class groups. Maximizing citizen participation calls for other structures in the community, some of which are now in an experimental stage. Minority groups, particularly youth, lack opportunities for meaningful participation in urban development.

Several research approaches were mentioned as the means of investigating the citizens' needs as the basis for determining planning goals. It was recognized that often what the citizen wants is not the basic solution to his problem. Critical remarks were made about getting people to want the goals set by the experts. Social scientists and social workers should be more consciously trained, or "untrained," to undertake a special kind of research which involves close cooperation both with the people concerned and with professional experts and policy-makers.

The professional could interpret the expressed needs of the people to the experts and the planners by explaining professional insights and economic policies, as well as explaining the financial consequences to the citizens concerned. It was generally felt that maximizing citizens' participation requires information, explanation, and communication between those responsible for, and those affected by, urban planning and development. It also demands sophistication in the political process and the mobilization of countervailing power to achieve change.

The goal for social work should be to maximize citizen participation in urban development. Too often there is a premature assumption as to the limitations of such participation. The quality, degree, and form of participation are all legitimate areas for social work study and action.

This does not obviate the difficulty of finding consensus on what people need, based on the expressed needs, the professional insights, and the economic and political possibilities in a given situation. The problem still remains one of how to create a desire for improvement that will motivate citizens to act to change their social conditions.

2. *The social worker and his contribution.*—The discussion was complicated by the fact that in different countries social work education differs greatly. As a result, there are different areas of specialization, and the status of professional social workers varies. The group agreed that all professional social workers should take responsibility for community life and should help create channels through which citizens' participation can be promoted. In several countries, social workers inform the people on social affairs, but it was generally felt that information alone is not enough. By demonstrating the consequences of participation in terms of personal rewards, such as more money, less work, more leisure, apathy may be overcome. In order for the social worker to assist citizens to participate, he requires a continuing flow of information from policy-makers, planners, legislative and administrative bodies, and related interest groups. Most of the countries represented thought that social workers in general have only piecemeal information on social planning, urban development, and social affairs.

Another handicap for the social worker is the high turnover of professional personnel. Urban development is a complicated and long-term affair; in order to acquire enough insight into the social problems and to gain the citizens' confidence, the worker needs continuity of relationships. Stability and continuity of participation could also be assured by citizens' advisory groups, and the agency is a means of overcoming transitory staff service.

Although social workers were repeatedly identified with social caseworkers, the group defined the role of the social worker as one in which casework, group work, community organization, research, administration would be used as the problem demanded and agreed that the worker should be able to deal with the client systems and the social systems necessary to the support of urban development programs. It was remarked that social work students should be required to participate in social action programs as part of their training. In discussing the relationships of the social worker to other professionals engaged in urban development, it was agreed that the problem is in part that of status, which, in turn, is determined by the level of social work education. Social work training should include exposure to physical planning. Joint courses for physical planners, social scientists, and social workers have proved effective. It was noted that physical planners have equally as much to learn from social work.

The training of social workers should equip them to be critical of established ways for delivering services, to initiate new structures, to be flexible in adapting to new structures, to work with other disciplines, and to collaborate with, and work in, urban development planning bodies.

3. *The social structures.*—Structures through which citizens can participate can take many forms and should operate at all levels of society. The traditional councils need to be both broadened and augmented. A major question concerns the relationship of function and auspice. Questions were raised as to the strengths and limitations of tax-supported programs for the stimulation of citizen participation, even when this takes the form of protest movements. Professional staff is important to stimulate and guide effective participation so as to avoid the possible exploitation of inexperienced citizens and maximize the effectiveness of their efforts. When such efforts tend to threaten the establishment, support tends to be withdrawn. A basic issue is how to secure adequate financial support and freedom of action.

A common problem is the adjustment of the rural citizen who moves to an urban area. Programs to prepare him in advance and to guide his move were cited. Once he has become part of urban society, he should be involved in programs of community development.

Citizens' organizations dedicated to developing an informed

citizenry prepared to take constructive action in important social issues are necessary at every level of society. Although programs of this nature now exist in the middle class, even here the extent of popular participation is minimal, and all classes could benefit from the assistance of informed social workers.

Social workers have a special responsibility to enlighten their boards, volunteers, and committee members. In many countries there is a social distance between board and staff which limits the professional contribution to social policy or change of program. The social worker has a responsibility not only to his clients but to the agency and its relationship to the community. This calls for restructuring the agency in such a way as to make community work integral to the administrative system. It should be taken into account in staff assignments, training, evaluation, and promotion.

Should the proposal for a new consolidated international social welfare body eventuate, Commission IV recommends that citizen participation be specifically provided for in the new structure.

Along with professional social workers, economists, and other experts, representatives of consumers, volunteers, and the financial supporters of welfare service should participate in evolving and implementing international social welfare policy.

Commission V. Interrelatedness of Urban and Rural Development

Chairman: Graham M. Lomas, *United Kingdom*
Vice-chairman: Carola Ravel, *Venezuela*
Rapporteur: Ato Shimelis Adugna, *Ethiopia*

Ana Rosa Canclina, *Argentina*
Marie Teltschmer, *Australia*
Tania de Valle Antunes, *Brazil*
Darcy Mesquita da Silva, *Brazil*
Trevor Pierce, *Canada*
D. J. Rooney, *Canada*
Paulette Bernard, *France*
Hanna Behrends, *Germany*
Ursula Pietsch, *Germany*
Mrs. Skassi, *Greece*
Pushpa Gandhi, *India*
Mary Arbid, *Israel*
Rimma Del Vivo, *Italy*
Sadao Tanigawa, *Japan*
Man Choon Kang, *Korea*
Gemma Zaeth Guerrero Lopez,
    Mexico

P. Kessler, *Netherlands*
H. P. A. van Roosmalen, *Netherlands*
C. D. Saal, *Netherlands*
Aquila Kiani, *Pakistan*
Maria de Lourdes, *Portugal*
Pereira da Rocha, *Portugal*
Pilar Lago Nunez, *Spain*
Elizabeth Mueller, *Switzerland*
R. M. Clarke, *United Kingdom*
H. S. E. Snelson, *United Kingdom*
Mary E. Duren, *United States*
Harvey S. Perloff, *United States*
Marisa Izaguirre, *Venezuela*
Victor Lopez, *Venezuela*
Sheila Manzo, *Venezuela*

URBANIZATION is affecting every country in the world. The growth of cities and the spread of urban ways of life constitute an important dynamic for social change. In the developing countries, migration from the land to the cities is a dominant factor in social transformation. Yet, though urbanization is proceeding at an accelerating pace, these countries are still predominantly rural. In the highly developed countries, flight from the land has lessened; the population is still highly mobile, but migration is more between cities and within urban regions. Because of the interrelatedness of town and country, factors such as rates of economic growth, industrialization, migration, and urbanization are as significant for rural development as for urban development. It is the importance for rural areas that we wish to stress.

In planning both for the present and for the foreseeable future we must recognize that the flight from the land will continue and

that urbanization is irreversible. Indeed, in many of the developing countries, migration is speeding up. We must clearly acknowledge these facts if we are to cope with the problems raised.

Technological advances can more than make up for the manpower lost through outmigration. Nevertheless, in some developing countries too many people are chasing too few jobs. The
capacity to earn in the countryside must be increased. In these
circumstances, land reform, cooperative producing arrangements,
intensive labor methods on the farm, and other improvements in
production deserve top priority. Similarly, the crowding of people
into fast-growing cities, especially where jobs are not available in
sufficient quantity, demands special policies in rural development
as a means of countervailing the pull of cities.

BALANCED DEVELOPMENT

What the "right" balance is between urban and rural in terms
of percentage of population or resource allocation is hard, if not
impossible, to define. It would certainly vary by country and by
region, and the economic optimum may not be the social one.

This commission's stress on rural development is not to be seen
as anti-urban but is grounded in the belief that the rural dweller
in modern times is entitled—has the right—to greater parity of
services and amenities with his urban counterpart. Migration is
as often an exodus—a push—from rural conditions which offer
meager opportunities as it is a pull to an urban situation where
jobs seem more plentiful and varied, where there is a better
chance for schooling, a greater variety of social services, and—especially for the young—the promise of a more glamorous way of life.
In these days of intensified mass communications, and in a world
of highly mobile people, rural development policies should offer
equality of opportunity in housing, education, welfare, and jobs.
This will not only ameliorate conditions for those who remain in
the countryside, but might help smooth out the pace of migration
and alleviate the strain on city services.

Urban and rural changes are being simultaneously influenced
by basic forces in a nation's economy and technology. Thus, both
urban and rural problems must be dealt with in a coherent and
coordinated way.

MEASURES NEEDED IN RURAL AREAS

Land reform programs, various cooperative arrangements, and new farming techniques have an essential part to play. There is need for imaginative programs of industrial development geared to rural conditions. There is scope for opening up sparsely populated, and even some declining, agricultural regions, by constructing new communication networks. But we stress that all these policies must be applied simultaneously. To institute only one could be self-defeating. Better communications alone might speed up migration. Better education without jobs raises aspirations without hopes of fulfillment in a rural community.

Education policies for rural areas must have at least two goals. First, the countryman's training must equip him to meet day-to-day living more competently. Secondly, recognizing the pull of the cities, schooling should be basic enough to prepare man for an urban way of life. But we must stress also that if the countryman is becoming daily more urbanized, the townsman needs to be "ruralized," at least to the extent of learning to understand the legitimate aspirations of rural man and his requirements.

It may well be necessary to offer special incentives to induce social workers, teachers, doctors, and other professional groups, as well as government officials, to live and work among rural people. Some countries will feel the need to go further and will make a term of service in rural areas compulsory. Provision of services to rural communities will necessarily take different forms from those in urban areas. However, we stress that the standard must be higher than in the past.

SERVICES IN RURAL AREAS

Closer attention must be paid to the location and distribution of services in rural areas. Rationalization can take many forms, but it must always be attuned to the local situation. Planning must start with a study of the settlement patterns. There is nearly always a hierarchy from hamlets, villages, and small towns to medium-sized towns and large cities. Building upon the best practices in this regard, the network of services should be fitted to the network of settlements. It will help to locate a group of key services together at a focal point. With regard to new industries, closer attention must be paid to the existing centers which show potential for further growth. Failure in the past to recognize all these factors has led to wasted resources, conflicting policies, and often to accentuated migration. Even new city projects need to be decided with these facts in mind.

We think that the medium-sized town in a rural area has a vital part to play, not only in stimulating economic development over a wide area, but in being a focal point for services, both social and cultural. Also, such towns can be centers from which services can radiate to the surrounding countryside. Mobile services, such as traveling nurses, specially equipped vehicles for clinics, together with the usual bus transportation, can operate from these localities to the rural dweller.

PLANNING AND ADMINISTRATION

One trend is toward larger units of local administration that often require the amalgamation of small units; at the same time, there is a trend toward more decentralization from headquarters. These trends converge at the regional level. But efficiency and good administration pull one way; tradition and vested interests, the other. The neat dovetailing of boundaries is not always possible, but at least the range and interrelatedness of all the problems involved in economic, physical, and social policy-making at the regional level should be recognized.

In the modern world, planning must be flexible. We must plan with growth and change in mind. The scale of action required today necessitates greater coordination of efforts, more extensive and more centralized decision-making. We see no alternative to greater responsibility on the part of central governments in giving direction and purpose to the economic, social, and physical goals. The danger is that the administration will run the people and not the reverse. What are needed are better channels of communication between the planners and those who are planned; and genuine subregional interests should be recognized and articulated. Public initiative must not be seen as excluding private initiative, and at all levels we believe there is a special role for the private and voluntary organization to play.

We see four types of communication problem: (1) between the different tiers in the hierarchy of plan-making—central, regional, and local; (2) between the different types of planner—physical, economic, and social; (3) between the middle-class values of planners and administrators and the working-class nature of those in greatest need of help; (4) in common with all professional groups, the need for social welfare workers to communicate among *themselves* about planning.

Clearly, this involves more consultation, more interdisciplinary training, more research, more interpretation of the results of research to the public, and, above all, a willingness on the part of each planner to appreciate the approach, ideas, and terminology of the others. Without all these things, policies conflict, precious resources are wasted, goals are blurred.

The commission believes that in claiming a place in the planning teams concerned with urban and rural development the social work profession must do two things: it must clarify and articulate what it thinks its special contribution is; and it must make known its experience and knowledge gained in solving problems of human resources.

Commission VI. Social Aspects of Urban Renewal and Redevelopment

Chairman: Albert Rose, *Canada*
Vice-chairman: Giorgio Cigliana, *Italy*
Rapporteur: Olive Miles, *Australia*

Gloria Di Paola, *Argentina*
Andre Opstaele, *Belgium*
Maria Luiza Arago, *Brazil*
Douglas McConney, *Canada*
Jacqueline Ancelin, *France*
E. Chouffier, *France*
Mrs. Ingeborg Blauert, *Germany*
Mrs. Kathe Rawiel, *Germany*
C. Misrahi, *Greece*
Eiichi Isomura, *Japan*
Lester Jaffe, *Israel*
M. G. van der Flier, *Netherlands*

R. Schippers, *Netherlands*
Theodora de la Cruz, *Philippines*
Rosa Maria Ferreira Correia, *Portugal*
Thung Syn Neo, *Singapore*
Ruth Staehelain, *Switzerland*
Chek Dhanasiri, *Thailand*
D. Jones, *United Kingdom*
John Nicholson, *United Kingdom*
Margaret Berry, *United States*
Paul Ylvisaker, *United States*
Mrs. Carmen Giroux, *Catholic International Union Social Service*

THE CONCEPTS of urban renewal and redevelopment are the most sophisticated in a series of attempts to initiate and implement a revitalization of urban communities. These concepts imply the renewal, replanning, rehabilitation, indeed the reconstruction of substantial areas, whether viewed individually as a geographical entity or as a human community. In a world as varied in its development as ours, these phrases may serve well as a basis for public and voluntary action in the more developed nations, but may be of less utility and have a different meaning in the less well developed countries.

Nevertheless, the members of the commission agreed that urban renewal must be described as the totality of all coordinated public and private action that must be taken to create the conditions for sound maintenance and development of the built-up area. It is an attempt to correct some of the errors of the past, to prevent continuation of these errors, and to renew the urban core as a place where people may live, work, and play within a physical and social environment planned to meet their needs. It is clear that in North America, Western Europe, and other developed areas these definitions may be related to specific programs of legislation and community action. In many other nations, however, urban redevelopment means little more than the pressure to meet every conceivable social problem which is the consequence of rapidly developing urbanization.

PROBLEMS, PRINCIPLES, AND POLICIES

The commission examined the impact of urbanization and its implications for urban renewal and redevelopment within a framework bounded by the terms "problems, principles, and policies." The experience of a great many nations indicates that the combination of deteriorated physical environment and inadequate living conditions normally described as "slums" may well be becoming the norm in many large urban centers rather than the exception. It is true that in some of the more advanced countries blighted areas are developing more rapidly than they can be treated. The situation is much more difficult in less well developed nations where urbanization, while of shorter duration, is having a more profound impact upon the society. It is conceivable that only in the more affluent and highly developed nations can we truly speak of a broad approach to the treatment and prevention of slums and blighted areas; in the less affluent nations of the world, urban renewal may well be viewed as a dream of the distant future because the immediate problems, such as food supply, provision of water and sewer facilities, educational facilities, and public health services, are so overwhelming that the miserable structures which now serve as housing accommodations must continue in use for a long time.

This approach leads inevitably to a serious consideration of values and goals. The principles which may be applied will depend upon the values and objectives of the society as a whole, expressed through legislation and bureaucratic arrangements. The over-all community seeks the eradication of slums and the development of decent communities for those who now live in gross deprivation. These objectives may be fundamentally esthetic, economic, or social in nature, or any combination of these and related goals. At the same time, however, there is another system of goals and objectives embodied in the network of social and familial relationships retained or developed within high-density urban neighborhoods. We have come to realize that urban dwellers do not live in isolation from their neighbors but, in fact, have developed patterns of living in which mutual assistance and social relationships are easily accepted. The great challenge for programs of urban renewal throughout the world is to insure the maintenance of significant values within the patterns of living previously followed by the residents of seriously deteriorated areas, whether these be within the urban core in Western countries or on the fringes of rapidly expanding metropolitan cities elsewhere. These values must somehow be transmitted as individuals and families are uprooted, dislocated, and sometimes moved long distances from their family homes.

The members of the commission considered the perpetuation of these values within the new settings to be crucial. While every family should have a decent, safe, and sanitary dwelling, it must also have a nurturing social environment; a constellation of social and health services and opportunity to utilize these effectively; and a host of social relationships and friendships. The neighborhood and neighborliness are concepts which can be made manageable for planning purposes. They can be conceived as units within which communication can exist between people toward the organization of mutual assistance.

The participation of citizens who are affected by urban renewal is one of the most important values to be fostered and expanded. In the formulation as well as the implementation of plans and proposals there must be the maximum feasible participation of the residents. This principle implies the maximization of freedom of choice with a wide degree of tolerance in economic matters, patterns of living, and social behavior. The question is whether programs are to be imposed by the society and its institutional structure or to be implemented as a process of mutual discussion and decision. The members of the commission understand clearly that there exists wide variation in literacy, education, and understanding among the mass of urban dwellers throughout the world. Nevertheless, they believe that the majority can be helped to understand and appreciate the choices that are possible and to participate in making them. There are various levels of participation and, as well, there are different social structures through which participation will be fostered. The question for social workers is how to intervene and yet preserve the major values within the family. The experience in many countries suggests that the following proposals would be of substantial assistance in meeting the impact of urbanization as well as that of urban renewal:

1. Alternative supports must be provided for the loss of the extended rural family as migration continues from rural areas to metropolitan centers.

2. A set of required urban skills, including those of the most simple and pragmatic nature, must be taught before migrants move to the urban area.

3. Programs must be developed to prevent both physical and social contagion of newcomers within high-density slums.

4. Opportunities must be afforded for upward social and economic mobility within the expanding urban centers.

5. There must be preparation of the established urbanites (the "receivers") toward acceptance of newcomers.

The totality of urban social problems is both seriously complicated and deepened by the variety of mass movements throughout the world. In addition to the commonly understood population explosion and the mass movement to urban areas there is the further substantial movement of workers from less developed nations to highly industrialized societies that face vast shortages of labor. It is the view of the commission, however, that its proposals will serve in all these situations.

IMPLICATIONS FOR SOCIAL WELFARE

Welfare is merely a small part of the total picture within the expanding urban society, even in the most affluent societies. The central problem may be seen as that of the delivery of the social services to those individuals and families most in need. In the view of the commission, the requirements of urban renewal make it essential that the social worker be viewed as a generalist rather than a specialist. The commission recognizes that this requires a more flexible administrative structure within the social services.

The emergence of the community development worker, or change agent, makes it entirely clear that the proliferation of agencies and the dead hand of overspecialization must be overcome. Nevertheless, the leaders in social welfare are not merely required to provide services which are comprehensive and accessible; they must in many situations attempt to change the institutional structure of the society. They must confront the educational system which resists change, the power structure which monopolizes the decision-making process, and the governmental structure, because it is not merely the policy but the structure of authority which must be altered.

The major recommendation of the commission concerns the need for social welfare workers to develop the competence for, and to assert themselves more forcefully in the process of, urban decision-making. Social workers are too deferential to those they consider to be more scientifically oriented practitioners. The physical planner is not necessarily more certain of the scientific basis of his proposals, but he adopts a posture of confidence in these proposals. The planner may truly not know what he does *not* know. The social worker, on the other hand, knows what he does not know and lacks confidence in his own judgment. This has for too long inhibited the profferment and development of proposals which must be attempted if we are to learn what truly helps and what does not.

There is more than ever the need for interdisciplinary teams in the rebuilding of the cities of the world, teams in which the social worker is an equal partner. The social worker must serve as the spokesman and advocate of the future population in the area; he must verbalize the needs and aspirations of the people to be served. The practitioner of social work, or social welfare, must penetrate and participate in the power structure where social policy decisions are made. This penetration will not occur unless we are prepared to demand it.

Study Group 1. Shelter

Chairman: Mrs. Marina Cordova De Ferreira, *United Nations*
Vice-chairman: Father McLellan, *Peru*
Rapporteur: John Turner, *United States*
Resource: Hans Harm, *United States*

Maria Virginia Gomes DaSilva, *Brazil*
Michael J. Audain, *Canada*
Mrs. Moira Mosher, *Canada*
Ligorina Cordaro, *Chile*
Irma Sierralta, *Chile*
Ester De Munora, *Colombia*
Jose A. Villeyes, *El Salvador*
Paul Bernard, *France*
Fernand Bocquet, *France*
Jean Defresne, *France*
William H. C. Wan, *Hong Kong*
Onesimo Rios, *Mexico*
Bernard Korstanje, *Netherlands*
Manuela Donayte, *Peru*
Bertha Bringas De Del Favero, *Peru*

Daniel McHellan, *Peru*
Otilia Velasco, *Peru*
Malin Calissendorff, *Sweden*
Sister Louise Collins, *United Kingdom*
Marjorie Noble, *United Kingdom*
Fern M. Colborn, *United States*
Jack Fasteau, *United States*
Mrs. Olive W. Swinney, *United States*
Figueroa Cuisa, *Venezuela*
Maria Josefina Alvarey Gomez,
  Venezuela
Luisa Helena Sosa, *Venezuela*
Charles D. Spangler, *World Health
  Organization*

SHELTER and its solution must be envisaged in a global context: city-region. The region is the reason the city exists, while, at the same time, the city pours back into the region the energy which it has received from it, making a dynamic unity from the economic, sociocultural, physical, and political-administrative points of view.

The discussion was limited exclusively to the experience of the developing countries and to a search for the most effective systems and methods.

ANALYSIS

The concept of shelter is not limited to housing but includes also the social and urban services which are indispensable to the development of community life, taking into account the geographic location and social status of the family and its expectations. Looked at in this way, shelter constitutes a positive element of change and growth in a country's over-all development.

There are several reasons why a man migrates to the city: (*a*) to seek a better job; (*b*) to benefit from the social services which are lacking or limited in rural areas; (*c*) the demographic explosion and the lack of adequate planning for urban and social development within the context of the over-all development of the country.

Statistics show that the growth of the population in marginal areas is two to three times greater than that of the urban population. At the same time, the growth of these areas exceeds that of the rural areas in most Latin American countries. A similar phenomenon exists in Asia and in the Near East.

The problem of "marginality" is an important factor to take into account when we consider the socioeconomic, cultural, and political aspects of the developing countries.

RECOMMENDATIONS

1. The integration of the efforts of the people with the policies of their governments in order to solve the problem of shelter requires the establishment of a decision-making structure that will permit contact between all groups of the population and the institutional structure.

2. It is imperative to stimulate integrated and systematic action on the part of technicians, with objectives subordinated to the socioeconomic development of the region and the country.

3. It is important that the people participate in projects and systems at the local level, tending toward a functional adaptation between the methodical activities of the technician and the dynamics of the group. Within the limits of the political structure of each country, it is useful to encourage cooperation and mutual trust between the people and governmental organizations in order to facilitate joint efforts, promoting a flow of communication between the groups and the institutional structure.

4. It is necessary to search for methods and procedures which will facilitate this interrelationship.

5. With respect to shelter as an instrument of growth and change, the functions of proximity to the public services of the community or of elements of investment have to be defined in relation to the social and economic class of various groups, taking

into account their socioeconomic differences: (*a*) the function of proximity to the public services of the city which force the economically weak groups to establish themselves in the urban area; (*b*) the function of convenience and comfort of the shelter, necessary for middle-class groups because of their occupations, prestige, and development; (*c*) the function of shelter as an element of investment for the economically strong groups.

6. Recognizing the importance of finding a methodology to solve the problem of marginality in all its aspects and manifestations, the group recommends that a seminar be held to study the problem. The objectives of the seminar would be to analyze the problem, using case studies prepared by the participating countries, and to work out systems and procedures based on the realities of each country. All the Latin American countries would participate in the seminar, which would be financed by international organizations and a contribution by the host country.

Study Group 2. Employment and Unemployment

Chairman: Anna Maria Cavallone, *Italy*
Vice-chairman: Jose F. Rodrigues, *Portugal*
Rapporteur: France Helmer, *France*

Doris de Souza Amaral, *Brazil*
Mrs. Claire Arsenau, *Canada*
Real Rouleau, *Canada*
B. R. Tobar, *Ecuador*
Mrs. Suzanne Ivanovic, *France*
Andree Moinet, *France*
Chae Jang Suck, *Korea*
Aurora Arellanes, *Mexico*
Renee O. de Siller, *Mexico*
A. M. R. Alam, *Pakistan*
Laura Gonzales, *Peru*

Yolanda Gonzales, *Peru*
Otilia Valesco, *Peru*
Severlina Monte-Mayor, *Philippines*
D. M. Bentley, *United Kingdom*
Rev. Michael Forrer, *United Kingdom*
Christine Railton, *United Kingdom*
M. Cannon, *United States*
Raymond F. Clapp, *United States*
Mrs. Regina W. Saxton, *United States*
Ralph Wright, *International Labor Office*

THE GROUP discussed the effects of urbanization upon employment and unemployment and the resulting problems which affect different categories of workers, such as the unskilled, youth, women, and older workers. Also discussed were different forms of intervention on the part of society in order to offset or lessen the problems: legal action; social security programs; activities of welfare organizations; and the part played by several types of social workers, professional and volunteer.

The effects of urbanization differ greatly according to the degree of economic development of a country. All countries have called attention to the problems connected with the lack of training of many workers.

Rural migration toward cities is a universal phenomenon and brings forth problems common to all countries: the difficulty of adapting to city life aggravated by illiteracy and the difference of languages and dialects; economic difficulties caused by unemployment or insufficient wages. The serious consequences of such problems affect the life of the worker and of his family.

Next, we discussed the problems of youth: premature entrance into competition; unsuitable types of work; insufficient training; psychological results of a too quickly acquired independence.

New family problems were examined: the handling of finances; the necessity of redefining relations between members; and separation (sometimes due to the distance between home and work or to difficulty in securing lodging).

Also discussed were problems relating to women, their classification, their changing status. Last came the problems of older workers who cannot easily secure employment.

Solutions to all these problems differ according to the historical, political, and economic background of each country, Government, industry, and social organizations do their share in bringing about proper solutions.

In every country represented one has noted the help offered by governments who constantly strive to better working conditions. Everywhere there is also a growing tendency to plan economic development which will bring forth full employment. To obtain this result new jobs have to be created, better training offered, efforts to resettle people who move about within a country have to be made, and external migrations must be regulated.

More and more studies are made on the lack of qualifications of workers. They point to the necessity of early training and call attention to the need to coordinate labor and educational policies.

Social service groups whose aim is the betterment of conditions for the working class were studied, and two tendencies were noticed. In North America one finds few social services organized within industry. Problems come to the attention of well-qualified heads of personnel, experts in industrial relations, and psychologists, who refer the workers to public or private social agencies.

In Latin America and in Europe social services within private enterprises are quite well developed. Such services are in charge, first of all, of the worker's problems in relation to his work and secondarily in relation to his family. Technical consultants and liaison officers between employers and employees have as their objective the well-being of the workers.

The role played by trade unions in social affairs and in the training of the workers was also brought forth. Unions offered their members legal protection and information. There was some discussion about the clarification and definition of responsibilities concerning labor policy and the welfare of workers.

The importance of governmental action at several levels was recognized and also the importance of private social services which contribute to building a sound national labor policy. It was pointed out that coordinated international action is also a necessity.

All these efforts should result in helping each person to find his latent qualities and to develop through his work his full personality.

Study Group 3. Health

Chairman: Milton Wittman, *United States*
Vice-chairman: Harvey I. Scudder, *United States*
Program Organizer: Dorothea L. Dolan, *United States*

Valerie Douglas, *Australia*
Iran Beghin, *Belgium*
Romain Verbeke, *Belgium*
Maria Amelia Medeiros, *Brazil*
Shirley D. C. Passos, *Brazil*
C. Maria Santos, *Brazil*
Maria Helena Villar, *Brazil*
Mabel H. Crolly, *Canada*
Gladys Reid, *Canada*
Somavati Mekgana, *Ceylon*
Helen Dugripon, *France*
Jacques P. Godard, *France*
Ganga Shahani, *India*
Mohammed R. Taleghani, *Iran*
Mrs. Sumiko Kono, *Japan*
Miss Hideko Tamura, *Japan*
A. A. Sandosham, *Malaysia*
Maria Luise Flores de Vazquez, *Mexico*
Lucila Bolvarte de Rodriguez, *Peru*
Savela Hurtado Guzman, *Peru*
Rennie A. V. Lanatta Zeballos, *Peru*
Nilo Vallejo, *Peru*
Esperanza Yalan Catano, *Peru*
John Cameron, *United Kingdom*
Robert Gore, *United Kingdom*
Madeleine E. L. Malherbe, *United Kingdom*
Enid C. Warren (Session Chairman), *United Kingdom*
Janet Anderson, *United States*
Marion Andrews (*Rapporteur*), *United States*
James Brindle, *United States*

Bertram S. Brown, *United States*
Rose Brunson, *United States*
Paul Cornely, *United States*
Mildred Cunningham, *United States*
Melvin A. Glasser (Session Chairman), *United States*
Ira V. Hiscock (Session Chairman), *United States*
Ruth F. Knee, *United States*
Lucy M. Kramer, *United States*
Blanche Parcel (*Rapporteur*), *United States*
Edgar Perretz (*Rapporteur*), *United States*
Hildrus A. Poindexter, *United States*
Mazie F. Rappaport, *United States*
Russell H. Richardson, *United States*
Harriet Rinaldo (*Rapporteur*), *United States*
John Roatsch (*Rapporteur*), *United States*
Herbert Rooney (*Rapporteur*), *United States*
Sue Sadow, *United States*
Charles I. Schottland (Session Chairman), *United States*
Eugene H. Skinner, *United States*
Ruth P. Smith, *United States*
Ruth Taylor (*Rapporteur*), *United States*
Flor Alvaredo de Trujillo, *Venezuela*
Olga Betilde Ojeda, *Venezuela*
René Gonzales, *Venezuela*

SIXTY representatives of fourteen countries, in their common interest in health, achieved a high level of fruitful communication. The entire field was recognized by sampling the problems of urban man and his environment. With a different chairman, speaker, resource, and *rapporteur* for each half day, the sessions initially focused on health education, tuberculosis, family planning, nutrition, and mental health. The keynote at the final session cited as the unifying purpose of all urban health work the goal of bringing urban man to the stage of enjoying a confident, happy, and healthy old age.

The initial foci for session discussions did not remain discrete subjects but were interrelated. Health education, the subject of the first presentation, was repeatedly referred to as other topics were discussed. Rural health issues were not on the program but were raised as inseparable from urban health. The growth of cities has resulted in part from migration from rural areas; nutrition depends on food produced by a steadily shrinking rural population; health education must help rural man cope with his new environment. Indeed, health issues are public health issues: public health is concerned with people wherever they live, and the unit for consideration must be the family.

The speakers and participants referred to conditions within their knowledge in the seven continents of the world. There were important differences, but these emerged as matters of degree and not of kind or quality; similarities were more striking.

To meet and conquer or control the common public and personal health problems of infectious diseases, nutrition, family planning, and physical and mental health, all countries struggle to varying degrees with insufficient manpower, facilities, and resources and with obstacles presented by economic, social, moral, religious, and educational conditions and limitations. Everywhere, health goals are approached not only by physicians, nurses, and social workers but also by a wide variety of other professional and lay people. And everywhere great improvement is needed in communication; in organization, integration, and coordination of efforts; and in methods of reaching target groups more effectively.

Infectious diseases remain significant public menaces which are accentuated as cities become more populous. The teamwork of health educator, social worker, physician, and nurse is essential for effective prevention, case-finding, and rehabilitation.

The fantastic population growth in recent decades is not equally shared by all countries. For example, Australia actually needs more people to achieve its potential. France has a relatively stable population, but India's people are increasing beyond her capacity to maintain them. We have the technical knowledge for family planning for contraceptive measures can be nearly 100 percent effective. Health education and the teamwork of many are important to the success of family planning. Elsewhere, whether family planning is seen as a public or a personal health problem, social workers are beginning to take positive action and now face the task of learning to work cooperatively with others in this endeavor.

Nutrition problems include endemic goiter, vitamin *A* deficiency, and anemia. Problems of malnutrition include obesity and involve all age groups, especially infants, teen-agers, "machine-fed" office workers, and aged widowers. Nutritional supplements are available, but there are distribution problems and we must rely on effective health education to overcome the resistance of established food habits. Social workers have not given this subject sufficient attention; it should be stressed in professional training. There is a need for social workers to work more closely with nutritionists.

Throughout the world, mental illness remains a problem and mental health an elusive goal. Here, the teamwork required is that of professionals and laymen, business, industry, the clergy, and public and private agencies. The comprehensive mental health center concept is endeavoring to organize and integrate all relevant services so that those in need can move freely between hospital and community, using the resources of each appropriately and with continuity.

The threats to the health of urban man are many and varied; the resources to be used in time of need are increasing as we develop new knowledge and new methodology; problems of distribution, resistance, organization, and coordination will require all the skills at our command. The goals of health are not those of any one profession. Social work has an obligation to share responsibility and to seek the active collaboration of all disciplines concerned. As we succeed, we shall have contributed to the process by which many more people may enjoy not only meager survival but an old age of happiness and great good health.

Study Group 4. Income Maintenance

Chairman: Fred Steininger, *United States*
Vice-chairman: Robert Duvivier, *France*
Rapporteur: John Osborne, *Canada*

Heloisa C. deP. Oliveira, *Brazil*
J. Rodolphe Forest, *Canada*
Boyde Gill, *Canada*
Real Roleau, *Canada*
Charles de Catheu, *France*
Charles Gatinel, *France*
Rene Quillier, *France*
Anna Generalis, *Greece*
Ivor Cassam, *United Kingdom*
Eleanor Copnall, *United Kingdom*

Della Nevitt, *United Kingdom*
Florence Waldron, *United Kingdom*
Eveline Burns, *United States*
James Dumpson, *United States*
Lenore Epstein, *United States*
Rowena Friedman, *United States*
Wilbur Schmidt, *United States*
Alvin Schorr, *United States*
Stephen Simonds, *United States*

IN AN urban society, the maintenance of a regular and sufficient income is one of the most basic human needs. Income support is required by all those who have insufficient income to allow them and their families to live in health and decency, whether by reason of age, sickness, disability, undereducation, lack of skill, lack of employment, family responsibilities, or size of family.

The amount of support needed cannot be related to man's biological needs but must be determined in relation to the average level of income—what most people in that society have. Each society should try to establish standards of living below which it will not permit its residents to fall. Such standards need to be expressed in terms relative to the nation's total income. For example, a modest goal might be to insure that the lowest income group receives some minimal share of total national income. Social capital—housing, schools, hospitals—should also be considered in determining the distribution of a nation's resources. The fair distribution of income and resources among the needy—the aged, families with children, the disabled—must also be insured.

As price levels rise and productivity increases, fixed income-maintenance payments should also be automatically increased, by relating them to an index of wages or to an index of prices. Payments should be made mostly in cash to preserve a sense of dignity and self-reliance, and to allow free consumer choice. Health care and welfare services should be provided free of charge. Special subsidies may be needed for construction or rental of housing, for state-owned housing at low rents, or for rent controls, as well as for construction incentives.

THE METHOD

In modern urban communities the role of organized charity is to provide not income maintenance but emergency financial aid. Voluntary organizations can be more flexible than state agencies in helping those in need, and can focus attention and effort on specific problems as they emerge. Casework counseling, provided by voluntary as well as state agencies, is important, for social rehabilitation and public funds should be made available to support such services.

Labor unions have achieved higher wage rates and a range of fringe benefits, including programs for maintaining members' incomes during sickness and unemployment, and after retirement. They have also pressed for state-supported unemployment, health, sickness, and disability insurance, and retirement and survivors' pensions for all. In agreement with unions, some employers have introduced income-maintenance programs for their workers, supplementing state programs. However, such plans lead to higher prices, and thus to lower tax payments by the industries whose net income is thus reduced, and so the consuming, tax-paying public is forced to meet these costs for the benefit of workers who receive such preferential treatment.

Government income-maintenance programs require a combination of social insurance, universal payments, and social assistance. Social insurance, including workmen's compensation, unemployment insurance, sickness and disability insurance, and old-age and survivors' insurance, can provide stable income based on past earnings. Universal payment plans can provide flat-rate income to all aged, or all children, or all widows, regardless of past or current earnings, setting a floor on which other benefits can be built. But, since no social insurance or universal flat-rate payment program can hope to meet all needs, there will be a continuing demand for social assistance programs related to family means or needs, including special vocational training, relocation, and rehabilitation. Social assistance must recognize the necessity for a family to have adequate income for the maintenance of personal dignity and independence, and must encourage self-reliance. This may involve special training projects to improve motivation and vocational skills after lengthy unemployment. Minimum wage legislation, though a necessary protection against exploitation, is not sufficient to maintain adequate income levels. Guaranteed minimum income legislation or negative income taxes may be potentially useful, and their economic and social implications deserve further study.

THE IMPACT OF URBANIZATION

Urbanization has, on the whole, reduced the role of privately organized charity in the income-maintenance field by expanding problems beyond its scope. But urbanization has enhanced the strength of labor unions by concentrating the labor force and paying it in cash. As strong labor unions have achieved better wages and fringe benefits for their members, they have concerned themselves with social betterment, participating in community efforts to solve social and economic problems affecting families, such as housing, transportation, recreation, and urban redevelopment. Urbanization unaccompanied by industrialization leads to greater concentrations of unemployed people, weaker unions, and, therefore, to more state initiative in meeting basic income needs.

An unfamiliar urban environment means an unfamiliar distribution system, coupled with sharp selling and credit practices and special budgeting problems. The poor cannot take full advantage of mass production and retailing techniques, owing to lack of storage and refrigeration facilities and lack of access to supermarkets. Therefore, consumer education and special counseling are required on budgeting techniques and buying habits and the effective registration of complaints. Legislation is needed to prevent sharp selling practices, such as the invalidation of contracts issued by high-pressure door-to-door salesmen for forty-eight hours. Packaging and labeling techniques should be regulated to require the disclosure of contents and weights of packages. Solicitation by loan companies should be limited, and the misleading credit terms employed in installment buying should be prohibited. Urbanization costs people more to live and reduces the value of their incomes. For income-maintenance payments to be fully effective, special legislation regulating retail sales and credit is needed, and so is special social work counseling on purchasing, budgeting, and adaptation to the general problems of urban community living.

Study Group 5. The Role of the School

Chairman: M. P. Roest, *Netherlands*
Vice-chairman: Jose Pernau-Llimois, *Spain*
Rapporteur: Mrs. Nava Arach, *Israel*

Isabel Rocha Braga, *Brazil*
Maria Novais Filha, *Brazil*
Mrs. Pierre Laplante, *Canada*
Mrs. Menona Logan, *Canada*
Mary MacGregor, *Canada*
Maria Elsa Catalan, *Chile*
Mrs. M. Balme, *France*
Beatrice de Cacqueray, *France*
Manfred Moersenee, *Germany*
Ali-Asphir Sultani, *Iran*
Yushihmo Kobaski, *Japan*
Hidezo Nakazawa, *Japan*

Griselda Alvarez Ponce de Leon, *Mexico*
Mrs. Jean Dunn, *New Zealand*
Mrs. Lilian Bye, *Norway*
Hafizol Islam, *Pakistan*
Mrs. Mercedes Vilardaga, *Spain*
Mrs. J. Nurstin, *United Kingdom*
M. L. Kellmer Pringle, *United Kingdom*
Winifred Bell, *United States*
Virginia Burns, *United States*
Charles Chakerian, *United States*

IN ORDER to identify the principles of urban development in different parts of the world, and the implications of urban development in the role of the school, each member of the group gave some information about the subject. The group discovered some common elements in philosophy, programs, and practice, and agreed on the following assumptions:

1. While facing the rapid changes derived from urbanization, we cannot differentiate between social and economic developments. The planning for growth should be based on both economic and social aspects, and serious attention should be given to the problem of education in urban development.

2. Education is one of the main tools which is of vital importance to economic development. In planning for growth, serious attention should be given to the problem of education.

3. The school is of vital importance in the process of community development.

4. Teachers are social channels of influence, transferring not only scientific knowledge but also basic human attitudes and values.

5. The present situation, and the character of educational methods today, is not only the responsibility of the teachers but, in fact, reflects the policy of the government in every country.

6. In the present situation, there is an obvious connection between the social status of the parents and the achievements of their children in school.

We all feel that there is a gap between the responsibility of the school—to give equal educational opportunities to everyone in society—and its real achievements that arises from lack of tools and manpower, from its conservative value system, and from orientation toward the past rather than toward the future and the changes to come.

We all feel that schools are still in the position of waiting on the sidelines for changes to happen, and then trying to adjust to these changes, rather than taking a leading role in the process of change, especially in connection with the migration of masses from the rural areas to urban surroundings.

We feel, too, that neither the teachers nor social work education has kept pace with the development program or with anticipated needs, and there is not enough preparation for the broad tasks or for dealing with anticipated needs.

Analyzing the present distressing situation, we suggest the following:

1. There is a need to reorganize both the content and the methods of teaching and education, in order to cope with the new needs.

2. Research has an important responsibility in assessing the impact of various educational problems.

3. There is a need to emphasize preventive methods in order to avoid drop-outs, maladjustments, and so on.

4. There is a need for qualified teachers, especially for those who can teach the newcomers to urban areas and the less privileged in society—teachers with the professional experience and ability to cope with social problems and other special handicaps.

5. There is need for flexibility in methods and in the structure of education in its various types.

6. Changes in preschool education have to be followed up by changes in education in elementary and high schools.

7. Only interprofessional collaboration and teamwork can improve the functioning of the schools.

8. There is a need to emphasize both in teaching and in social work education: (*a*) the importance of broad general education and role motivation; (*b*) methods and processes of interdiscipli-

nary communication, in order to be equipped to communicate with greater confidence with specialists from other disciplines; (*c*) the importance of education toward self-management, self-responsibility, and social responsibility, and an appreciation for the service one gives rather than for his degrees, class, and so forth.

9. The school has to be an educational center dealing with the whole field of education and concerned with the problems of interrelationship between parents and children, the difficulties of adjustment of both parents and children, bringing information and consultation to the parents, creating the same educational atmosphere in the home, and informing the other institutions in society about special problems, such as housing, sanitary conditions, and so forth.

10. The school has to include in its curriculum real responsibilities and ways to bring about active participation of the pupils in decision-making.

11. Social workers have to work on the team, assuring the welfare of the pupils, the allocation of needed resources and supplementary tools for fulfillment of the role of the school and for creation of equal opportunities for the educational progress of all pupils.

12. Seeing education as a continuing process, there is need for serious planning for the continuous use of educational facilities which represent huge social and financial investments.

Further problems which warrant discussion are:

1. The need for, and the ways of, linkage between private and public enterprise and between the labor market and education

2. Ways of keeping the balance between the rights and goals of the individual, the needs of the community, and the economic needs of society

3. Ways to solve the problems of inequality of educational opportunities because of different cultural backgrounds

4. The nature and content of preventive methods to deal with the problems of school drop-outs, identification of the pupils with the school, and so on

5. Planning for institutions for vocational training

6. Ways to foster interdisciplinary collaboration between the various professions connected with schools (including identification of their roles, work with volunteers, and so on).

Study Group 6. Leisure

Chairman: K. M. Reinold, *United Kingdom*
Vice-chairman: M. Margot-Noblemaire, *France*
Rapporteur: Charles Berman, *United States*

Nazle Barzilay, *Brazil*
Rozinha Barzilay, *Brazil*
F. F. Braga, *Brazil*
F. M. H. Silva, *Brazil*
Anne Davison, *Canada*
Jeanne Michener, *Canada*
Eliana G. Gonzalez, *Chile*
Maria-Teresa Gnecco, *Colombia*
Jean Busson, *France*
Renee Garrouste, *France*
Maria-Ann Gilbert, *France*
Jean Lagarde, *France*
M. Mouillard, *France*
Rita Kandzia, *Germany*
Gerhard Mueller, *Germany*
A. Sax, *Germany*
Chi-Kin Law, *Hong Kong*

Rosa Nachargo, *Mexico*
A. de Gier, *Netherlands*
W. van Stegeren, *Netherlands*
Stella P. Kwiers, *Netherlands Antilles*
Farida Abubekar, *Philippines*
M. Calissendorff, *Sweden*
Gunvor Lundgren, *Sweden*
Marie Lewis, *United Kingdom*
Charles Morris, *United Kingdom*
Mabel Tylecote, *United Kingdom*
Thelma Mills, *United States*
Marjorie Montelius, *United States*
Joseph Prendegast, *United States*
Siglinde Ruehl, *United States*
Minnie Williams, *United States*
Millicent Yater, *United States*

THE BACKGROUND of the discussion was based upon the belief that a forty- to forty-five-hour working week is general, that settlement houses have a duty to provide for leisure, as has the state, and that a proper relationship between settlement house, state, and people is essential, although differences in educational, economic, and cultural backgrounds must be taken into consideration. It was recognized that there is a need for relaxation; it was also felt, however, that since spare time can be used both creatively and constructively, the basis of any provision might be educational in the widest sense.

The principal points in the discussion concerned: provision for family activities; the need for a place to meet; financial resources; the professional worker and his training; and provision for specific groups.

The group considered it important to provide activities for the whole family, whether the family is involved as a unit or participates in different group activities. The growth of urbanization necessitates provision for leisure-time pursuits in the countryside. Consideration must also be given to the requirements of various age and interest groups. Activities of this type afford opportunities to bring together people of unlike ethnic, economic, and cultural backgrounds.

Suitable facilities are essential. Professional workers should be recognized as having an equal responsibility with town planners, and the views of the inhabitants must be taken into account when these are set up. The premises should allow for multipurpose activities. They must be so designed as to permit use by handicapped and old people and be managed with maximum participation by the users. Urbanization necessitates bridging the gap between the residents and newcomers.

Financing should be available from the state on the basis of need for specific programs and without unreasonable conditions. It should also be forthcoming to provide maximum opportunities for training professional workers of every social discipline. To attempt to compete with commercial enterprises is thought to be unwise. With this type of help it would be possible to set up more challenging programs than now exist.

Since the basic task of a professional worker is to inform, counsel, help, and train other people, the art of negotiation in relation to people, other agencies, and public authorities should be considered an important subject in his own education. The need to stimulate individuals and groups, and the development of consequent relationships, makes it desirable for the worker to live in the neighborhood.

In planning leisure-time activities, handicapped, lonely, and old people must be borne in mind and good preparation for retirement must not be neglected. It is preferable that housing for old people should not be segregated but that it be planned as a part of the community. It was thought that more use could be made of aged people.

Recent experiences indicate that a well-planned program can have considerable value in preventing social breakdown, particularly among young people. There is also much evidence that provision of opportunities for young adults to serve the community is of growing importance.

Since the group members assumed in their discussion that education is concerned with every aspect of life, they felt that the program should result in a broad training for participation in a democratic society and for good citizenship, and be a basic factor in the development of personality and character. It should, therefore, directly reflect the needs of the people and, as far as possible, be planned and carried through by them. A direct objective of leisure-time activity should be to enable the individual to feel needed as a valuable member of society.

Study Group 7. Family Life

Chairman: Olga Sidebottom, *Argentina*
Vice-chairman and Rapporteur: Marilia Diniz Carneiro, *Brazil*

Margarita Calvento, *Argentina*
Marilia Diniz Carneiro, *Brazil*
Noemia Vieira de Moraes Lourenco, *Brazil*
Ronald Avellano, *Canada*
Edith Moore, *Canada*
Nidia A. de Barros, *Chile*
Maria Jimenez de Vega, *Chile*
Alejandrina Lopez Aguirre, *Chile*
Clara Navon Ergas, *Chile*
Rene Danes, *France*
Jacqueline Perles, *France*
Hannelore Philipps, *Germany*
Hannelore Schoberl, *Germany*
Illona Jernvall, *Finland*
Yukiko Mizushima, *Japan*
Elizabeth S. Nagata, *Japan*
Kai Ohama, *Japan*
Emma Adamo, *Mexico*
Ana Maria Lopez, *Mexico*
Carmen G. Valdez, *Mexico*

H. van den Berg, *Netherlands*
Lola E. deHundskopf, *Peru*
Martha Zevallos, *Peru*
Fe M. Daludado, *Philippines*
Hans Jensen, *Sweden*
Amicia Carroll, *United Kingdom*
Margaret Coltart, *United Kingdom*
Sister Clare Sweeney, *United Kingdom*
Clark W. Blackburn, *United States*
Mrs. Elizabeth S. Collins, *United States*
Rev. Bernard J. Coughlin, *United States*
Marie E. Kelly, *United States*
Wallace H. Kuralt, *United States*
Kathleen M. Powers, *United States*
Benjamin R. Sprafkin, *United States*
Lila de Caceres, *Venezuela*
Bolivia Ostos de Urbina, *Venezuela*
Gema Ramirez, *Venezuela*
Antoinieta Ruocco, *Venezuela*

THE FAMILY is society's recognized and approved basic and primary unit that has as its purpose the following functions: procreation; socialization; informal education; physical protection; economic and psychological well-being; and maintenance of its cultural heritage. Therefore, society has a duty to preserve the values of this primary group.

Analyzing the impact of urbanization on the family, the various countries represented saw similarities in the problems presented:

1. Urbanization intensifies the conflicts between generations: parents tend to keep the values of rural life, while the children adapt themselves more quickly to the habits, language, and resources of urban life.

2. In urban life family ties are broken and replaced by less

stable ties. The main reason for leaving rural life in developing countries is, generally, the necessity of earning a living.

3. The need to train wage earners and young people for skilled labor deserves the attention of public and voluntary agencies in urban areas.

4. Urban living and better opportunities attract the male wage earner who, as head of the family, often leaves his wife and children in an enforced separation, or abandons them altogether. Proper measures should be taken to maintain family ties.

5. Living in the city brings problems for children, who need love, proper care, security, and well-being. Most countries stressed the need for more planned preparation for family life, not only in the home, but also in courses within the educational system and under the auspices of lay and religious agencies.

6. It was felt that a unified social security system, with proper allowances for various categories—dependent and crippled children, the unemployed, the aged—should provide for adequate care for the needy. Until the social security system provides adequately, measures should be taken for proper allowances to be given through direct payment by business firms, voluntary agencies, and, of the utmost importance, through the cooperative effort of the people in programs of self-help.

7. The working mother needs the protection of additional services to safeguard herself and the life of her family. These should include the full range of maternal and child welfare, supervision and services, with homemakers, nurseries, and foster homes.

8. There should be family welfare services, youth clubs, transient homes (hostels) for working boys and girls, and other agencies, such as the Big Brothers.

9. Family planning is the responsibility of the parents, within the pattern of their religious beliefs.

It was gratifying to learn that in some countries efforts are being made to plan new cities, taking into consideration the social, educational, and economic as well as physical aspects of planning. These models should be imitated all over the world.

In the planning of cities, resources that directly affect the family should be developed. Especially important are: educational, health, recreational, and employment opportunities that are reasonably accessible to good housing; transportation that is safe as well as efficient; and open spaces.

Professional social work should stimulate in the citizenry qualities of self-help by encouraging the development of voluntary associations that contribute to the social welfare goals of the community.

Social work should more clearly define its function in relation to other disciplines and professions, working in an interdisciplinary team that also promotes an integrated family and community life.

Social workers should take a much greater part in the formulation of social policy and in social action that promotes the welfare of the community.

Study Group 8. Government Structures

Chairman: Carel Eckhart, *Netherlands*
Vice-chairman: Mrs. Maria Jacobi, *Austria*
Rapporteur: Priscilla Young, *United Kingdom*

Rudolph Oberhoffer, *Austria*
John B. Lanctot, *Canada*
Marie H. Lanctot, *Canada*
Renee Gerard, *France*
Solange Nerot, *France*
Hans Hummel, *Germany*
Guillerma Batto, *Philippines*

Maria Asuncion Martinez, *Spain*
Edith O. Mercer, *United Kingdom*
Thomas Tinto, *United Kingdom*
Ewan Clague, *United States*
Joseph Meyers, *United States*
Wayne Vasey, *United States*
Randolph E. Wise, *United States*

THE GROUP drew up the following agenda for its five meetings, based on the material presented in the chairman's discussion outline:

1. Central and local government structure and power in relation to urban development; vertical and horizontal communication and coordination; problems of centralization and decentralization

2. The role of semipublic and voluntary organizations; the involvement of citizens at the local level

3. Problems of finance, guidance, and control of local organizations in the field of urban development; the functions of social service departments in local authority administration

4. Interdisciplinary approaches to urban development; problems posed by the establishment of organizations concerned with a specific field of action

5. Methods of providing communication, consultation, and coordination at all levels; stimulation of development in rural areas to counteract the growth of existing urban areas; services to special groups in the community.

The group was conscious of the limited representation from developing countries. Although it had the benefit of the experiences of some of those countries, most of the discussion was based on North American and Western European experience.

In all the countries represented, a number of central government departments could be said to be concerned with some aspect of urban development. The extent to which there was any official coordination of their activities varied considerably. It was generally agreed that some machinery for this is essential and is probably best provided by an impartial body, not itself responsible for any particular aspect of urban development. The powers of local and regional authorities also vary in different countries, and some representatives thought that insufficient power is vested in their municipal authorities.

The group agreed that total centralization and total decentralization are both unworkable. The following elements were identified as crucial in any discussion on this topic: (*a*) quality (flexibility and attitudes) and training of executive staff; (*b*) structure of the organization and relationships within it; (*c*) degree of financial responsibility; (*d*) degree and duration of delegation of powers; (*e*) recognition of the realities of the total economic situation; and (*f*) involvement of population through formal and informal channels.

Discussion revealed that although all the members accepted the need for citizen participation in urban development, means of achieving this were very different. For example, in Austria participation would be achieved through political activity; in the Netherlands, the government deliberately encouraged the establishment of voluntary agencies as a means of involving local citizens. The importance of recognizing formal and informal leadership at the local level was emphasized.

In the United States and in the Western European countries represented, there appears to be a trend toward acceptance by the central governments of the responsibility to provide financial support for local authorities. The exception is Canada, where the trend is in the direction of increasing the responsibilities of provincial government in urban development. It seemed that some degree of support, control, and guidance by central government would be necessary in any country, in order to insure reasonable standards of housing, education, and recreation at the local level.

The group agreed that the social service department of a local authority should normally be responsible for the provision and administration of social services set up in accordance with legislation. Stress was laid on the need for a flexible approach which would take into consideration the needs of the situation and the resources available. For example, there might be situations where services could best be provided by voluntary agencies which might, where suitable, be supported by public funds.

Some members of the group reported encouraging examples of attempts to use an interdisciplinary approach to urban development, such as sociological studies undertaken in France as part of the planning for new development areas. However, with a few exceptions, as in Vienna, there was little evidence of coherent interdisciplinary planning in practice. Members of the group, recalling Hugh Wilson's plea for the cooperation of social scientists and social workers, stressed the need for an interdisciplinary approach at the planning stage. It was recognized that there are difficulties in achieving cooperative planning, particularly in so far as social work is not accorded equal status with other professions.

The group used the planning process which is likely to be gradually introduced in the Netherlands as a basis for discussion on problems of consultation and coordination at all levels and at all stages of planning and implementation in urban development:

The Planning Process

Level	Phase A: Survey	Phase B: Planning	Phase C: Implementation	Phase D: Evaluation	Phase E: Policy Adjustment
National	1 Preliminary policy	5 Final policy decisions	9 Determination of directives and means	12 Checking of aims and means	16 Policy revision
Provincial	2 Testing of objectives	6 Coordination of plans; consultations	10 Programing information guidance	13 Research and co-ordination determination	17 Adjustment of programing, etc.

	3	7	11	14	18
Regional	Assessment of needs	Deter-mination of needs	Imple-mentation	Determina-tion of short-comings	Adjust-ment of imple-mentation
Municipal	Ditto	Ditto	Ditto	Ditto	Ditto
	4	8		15	
Lowest	Self-survey	Self-planning		Supple-mentary self-survey	

Note: In theory, the process goes through stages 1–18; in practice, some stages may be omitted or combined.

In a brief discussion of measures designed to promote urban development in rural areas, examples were cited of the planning of new towns in the United Kingdom, the Netherlands, France, and Israel.

Study Group 9. Groups Needing
Special Attention: Children

Chairman: Mrs. Katherine B. Oettinger, *United States*
Vice-chairman: Dr. Hugo Solms, *Switzerland*
Rapporteur: Maria Amelia Leite, *Brazil*

Susana Blanco, *Argentina*
Norma Tomadonide Martinez,
  Argentina
Andre Opstaele, *Belgium*
Rachel M. Gomales, *Brazil*
Doris Harjes, *Brazil*
Maria Helena Baptista Silva, *Brazil*
Gabriela Gallagher, *Canada*
Eric Smit, *Canada*
Robert Wan, *Canada*
Astria Rotleigch, *Finland*
Monique Liddell, *France*
Louis Van Herck, *France*
Marianne Backer, *Germany*
Ludwig Pfau, *Germany*
Ruby Huang, *Hong Kong*
Patricia Nye, *Hong Kong*
Homai S. Dalal, *India*
R. S. Pandey, *India*
Kusum Shah, *India*
Niru Shah, *India*
John S. Kikawada, *Japan*
Margaret Hopper Taylor, *Japan*

Samira Saad, *Lebanon*
Gemma Zaeth Guemero Lopez,
  Mexico
Chandra Thapa, *Nepal*
Mary B'nan Hessen, *Netherlands*
Estelita G. de Leon, *Philippines*
Florence Montandon, *Switzerland*
Maria von Poeschl, *Turkey*
F. Alice Carter, *United Kingdom*
Dr. R. J. Donaldson, *United Kingdom*
Lesley Maddock, *United Kingdom*
Rose Alvernaz, *United States*
Doris Bender, *United States*
Fred DelliQuadri, *United States*
Harriet Haas, *United States*
Paula L. Haas, *United States*
Mrs. Rosalind W. Harris, *United
  States*
Frank Newgent, *United States*
Dorothy Self, *United States*
Dr. Alfred Yankauer, *United States*
Carmen Liuna de Verde, *Venezuela*

THE GROUP was composed of forty-five participants from twenty countries and seven specialist consultants. For the purpose of the discussion, the group accepted the following broad definition: Children are persons who, by reason of age, need some sort of protection; in other words, minors—children and youth.

Discussions focused on needs of children, how the various countries are meeting these needs, and some steps taken, or projected, toward achieving these aims:

1. The importance of the family and the need of services to strengthen and preserve family life

The representatives from all twenty countries still felt that the family is the most effective unit for child-rearing.

2. The need for governmental and other services to supplement family care and family life in the urban complex

3. The importance of planning comprehensive care for the child-health programs, including preventive, curative, and educational services, and their interrelationship

4. The cost of services and the need to establish priorities, taking into account needs, resources, cultural patterns, and the stage of development of the country

The need to emphasize human investment programs.

Such programs still compete for priorities in relation to other developmental activities.

5. New programs reported, reflecting the trend toward supportive measures for the family designed to prevent family breakdown, delinquency, and social maladjustment

6. The importance of research in all spheres of social work

7. The responsibility of helping professions in changing their own attitudes and those of the people they serve, the public, and legislative bodies in relation to such problems as family planning, adoption, illegitimacy, and the differential approach to boys and girls

8. Reaffirmation of the group's adherence to the United Nations' Declaration of the Rights of the Child

9. Efforts to consider through what means countries can develop a national social policy in relation to children.

The U.S. decennial White House Conferences on Children and Youth and other countries' approach through UNICEF or other means to assess needs was discussed, as each country evaluated the content of programs for their children.

The contributions of the group illustrated the current transition toward new legislation and its implementation, aimed at more wholesome growth of the child. The specific programs each country selected upon which to place emphasis varied with its stage of development and the cultural pattern; homemaker service, for example, which is aimed toward individual families, is not needed in countries with extended families. However, day care is emerging in many countries because of the increased number of women in the labor market and the growing recognition of the needs of the child in an urban setting. In constructing programs, the basic needs of all children for health, education, and income maintenance must be the foundation on which to build further specific programs.

Each country concentrated on reporting how the process through which achievement in the area of opinion-making, changing legislation, and appropriations (both public and voluntary) has occurred with the involvement of lay citizens, professional people, and government in promoting these movements.

The necessity for all countries to train professional personnel and supervise nonprofessional personnel and volunteers was recognized.

Throughout the meetings, the group and consultants praised the Pre-Conference report and emphasized the need for an interdisciplinary team approach to early participation in planning for both physical and social aspects of urban development.

Study Group 10. Groups Needing
Special Attention: the Aging

Chairman: Isabel de Hurtado, *France*
Vice-chairman: Dr. Robert Olin, *Sweden*
Rapporteur: Charles Schaefer, *Switzerland*

Simone de Nave, *Belgium*
Lt. Col. Ernest Fitch, *Canada*
Hope Homested, *Canada*
Mrs. Viarma Kastari, *Finland*
Mrs. Yvonne Colas Derrey, *France*
Jean Maume, *France*
Jean Timmel, *France*
Mrs. Anna Weihl, *Israel*
Nawofumi Nakajima, *Japan*
Chizuko Takase, *Japan*
Mrs. Victorina Alvarez, *Philippines*
Mrs. Brita Bergwall, *Sweden*

Beatrice Koslover, *United Kingdom*
M. H. Slater, *United Kingdom*
James Burr, *United States*
Anna Harrison, *United States*
Mrs. Ethel Mathiasen, *United States*
Helen Morton, *United States*
Marjorie Poole, *United States*
Ethel Shanas, *United States*
Clark Tibbitts, *United States*
Monique Esnard, *League of Red
Cross Societies*

SINCE the members of the group tried to keep the discussion within the limits of the general theme, they excluded consideration of such problems as the increased length of life, demographic data, and so forth. The group successively took up the following points:

URBANIZATION AND ITS EFFECTS ON THE AGING

The group stated that a serious aftereffect of urbanization is the progressive isolation of the aging. They tend to remain where they have spent at least part of their lives, while the younger people move, most often because of their work, either from rural surroundings into the cities or from the centers of the cities into new residential districts. However, in certain countries, the traditional custom of having old people live with their families markedly lessens the problems noted below.

The following principles were listed:

1. The aging should be kept, so far as possible, where they have been accustomed to live. To this end the following measures

should be adopted: medical-social assistance provided in their own homes; the physical arrangements of their apartments adapted to their needs; and increased legal protection against harmful displacement, particularly in urban renewal.

2. If it is impossible to keep elderly people in their old quarters, society has the obligation of offering various types of arrangements suited to their individual preferences, while honoring the following principles: the aging should be allowed to make their own choice of new quarters; too great a concentration of old persons in the same place should be avoided; special houskeeping arrangements should only be made progressively in relation to their decreasing capabilities in order to help them keep up healthful activities in their homes as long as possible.

The group discussed three categories of housing:

a) Individual units reserved for those in good health

These should include at least 5 percent of the total number of units in the new housing constructions

b) *Logements foyers,* groupings of individual units which benefit by certain optional community services.

Occupancy should be reserved for those who require certain material, social, or psychological help. These groups benefit from having specialized personnel attached to them. The number of *logements foyers* should not be too great, and in some countries there is now being substituted a much more elaborate home-care service for those who live in simple individual units.

c) Homes for the ages which include a full complement of services

The group could not give detailed consideration to this category.

FINANCING HOUSING FOR THE AGING

The methods of financing vary greatly from country to country. In some the state takes full charge; in others, it only supports private groups or local communities by subsidies or loans. Sometimes this is done only where the size of the problem exceeds the capabilities of private organizations. In countries where private initiative is customary, there is the problem of coordination of activities. These generally call for some form of state control, especially as regards housing for those with low incomes. This discussion on methods of finance and coordination of work led the study group to say that medical-social assistance in the home is the least costly in the instance of those in good health, or in temporary difficulties, while hospitalization is necessary and effective only for those who are seriously ill either physically or mentally.

PREVENTIVE MEASURES

The group considered preventive measures to be the best means of offsetting concentration of the aging and displacement—the evil consequences of urbanization. The measures include among others:

1. *Periodic health examinations.*—In some countries these are obligatory. If the aging are only "invited" to take advantage of such consultations, even without charge, they often fail to do so.

2. *Courses in preparation for retirement.*—Such courses have been in existence in various countries for some years; however, no precise methodology has as yet appeared.

3. *Employment.*—Here a distinction must be made. Therapeutic work has as its objective the reeducation of the aging who suffer from diminished physical and mental health. This kind of help, often provided in institutions, tends to develop also in the growing number of day centers. This evolution should be encouraged as being beneficial not only to the aging themselves but to their families, who find this treatment and supervision helpful in keeping their older parents with them.

Income-producing employment has the twofold objective of giving the old person a reason for living and of providing supplementary earnings. Often in conflict with outworn concepts of retirement, this can cause conflict with labor unions, which should be solved by rearrangements in social assistance and pensions and modifications in employment legislation.

4. *Leisure-time activities.*—It is in the community at large that there are the most problems. The general tendency is toward opening special old age clubs, but the opinions expressed by several group participants was that it is preferable for the aging to join in recreational activities open to everyone. It also seems

that the aging themselves should take responsibility for their leisure time along with volunteers and trained workers.

5. *Social services.*—The discussion showed that while many of the participants felt that casework is useful, they insisted that a knowledge of gerontology be integrated into the curriculum in schools of social work.

Existing social services should be carried on in close collaboration with the specialized agencies that serve the aging, such as home-medical care, homemakers, and so on. They should also establish close collaboration with volunteer workers, whose activities they should sustain and support.

Finally, the group expressed three wishes:

1. That social welfare for the aging be intensified in every respect

2. That social workers would be able to make their opinions count in all that concerns assistance to the aging, as much for home-care services as for the construction of housing or institutions and for social legislation

3. That the national organizations specializing in work with the aging should come together in some form of international federation.

Study Group 11.[1] Groups Needing Special Attention: the Physically Handicapped

Chairman: Eric T. Boulter, *United States*
Vice-chairman: J. A. Carmichael, *Canada*
Rapporteur: Harold G. Roberts, *United States*

Ruth Cleary, *Australia*
Noemia Neves, *Brazil*
Marie Salgado, *Brazil*
Mrs. Constance Meyers, *Canada*
Annette Grumbach, *France*
Anita Gerdes, *Germany*
Mrs. Kamala D. Kulkarni, *India*
Mrs. Raya Fine, *Israel*
Hirokuni Dazai, *Japan*
Hajime Ogawa, *Japan*
Michiko Uehara, *Japan*
Mrs. On Soon Whang, *Korea*
Mrs. Dora Martinez Palacios, *Mexico*
Mrs. Maria Spratley, *Portugal*
Phan Van Nhan, *South Vietnam*
Hazel Day, *United Kingdom*
Elizabeth Gloyne, *United Kingdom*

Doris Thornton, *United Kingdom*
Leland Ahern, *United States*
Mary Ahern, *United States*
M. Robert Barnett, *United States*
Virginia Denton, *United States*
Cecelia Dwyer, *United States*
Regina Goff, *United States*
Sally Headsten, *United States*
Paul Langon, *United States*
Dr. Douglas MacFarland, *United States*
Mrs. Ferne K. Root, *United States*
Margaret Ryan, *United States*
Mrs. Doris P. Sausser, *United States*
Mrs. Patricia Smith, *United States*
Julian G. Stone, *United States*
Mrs. Ingeborg Bessin, *Venezuela*

THE GROUP's deliberations were directed to the theme of the Conference, with special reference to the impact of urbanization upon the handicapped. It is universally true that one of the major obstacles to be overcome by handicapped persons is a deep sense of isolation and alienation from the general community. The process of urbanization intensifies this problem for all people but especially for the disabled. Our rapidly growing cities will contain ever larger numbers of disabled persons. Contributing also to the size and complexity of the problem are mounting industrial and traffic accidents, prolongation of the life span, and the salvaging of severely injured individuals through advances in medical knowl-

[1] This study group was planned by the Conference of World Organizations interested in the handicapped in cooperation with the World Council for the Welfare of the Blind, the American Foundation for Overseas Blind, and the American Foundation for the Blind.

edge. Thus, there is an urgent need for planners of urban development to recognize these factors if handicapped persons are to be helped to achieve their maximum potential for satisfying and useful lives within the complex structures of the communities of the future. It also will be necessary to conduct research and to develop new methodologies for rehabilitation of the disabled. While this will be especially difficult in developing nations, in which it is often not easy to assign a high priority to the needs of the handicapped in the light of limited resources, we believe it is important that adequate measures be taken to meet their needs.

Social workers throughout the world bear a heavy responsibility for interpreting the needs of the disabled to the planners of newly designed or redeveloped cities. Concomitantly, continuing public education programs must interpret the capabilities of the handicapped and overcome the prejudice and ignorance which lead to discrimination and segregation.

The study group considered the following basic factors: health services; provisions for handicapped children; physical planning; transportation; vocational services; and leisure—all within the philosophical framework of the desirability of integrating handicapped individuals into the main stream of urban life to the fullest extent possible.

HEALTH SERVICES

Basic to any systematic approach in dealing with disability are prevention, early detection, and treatment of the handicapped. To further the early application of health and rehabilitation services in large and complex urban areas, the study group recommends grouping such services so as to facilitate the full utilization of specialized personnel and services. Except where highly specialized arrangements and personnel are required, rehabilitation services should be provided at the neighborhood level.

HANDICAPPED CHILDREN

It is important that the earliest possible detection of disability or potential disability be assured and that adequate diagnostic services and counseling of parents be provided. We recommend the use of assessment teams composed of members of all appropriate professional disciplines so that there may be comprehensive planning to meet the medical, psychosocial, educational, and vocational needs of each individual child. Well-planned preschool programs should be followed by sound educational services which would, wherever possible, enable the child to live with his family while attending regular community schools. At the same time, special classes or schools should be available for some severely or multihandicapped children.

PHYSICAL PLANNING

Buildings should be designed so that they can be used easily and safely by the disabled, both the young and the aged. This is true equally for all types of construction, including housing, government buildings, offices and factories, schools, hospitals, churches, museums, libraries, theaters, concert halls, stadia. Public buildings would then be truly public. Although special residential arrangements will be required for some severely handicapped persons, most disabled people are able to live in ordinary residential areas if architectural barriers are removed. We welcome the prospect that in the future city planners will increasingly locate "clean" industries nearer to residential areas, since this will facilitate the employment of the disabled.

TRANSPORTATION

Since one of the most important goals in the rehabilitation of the handicapped is the ability to travel independently, and this is often costly, it is important to recognize their special transportation problems. Where there are separate vehicle and foot roads, the disabled may require special permission to drive into otherwise restricted areas. Minor modifications of buses, subways, streetcars, and automobiles will make them usable by an aging population as well as by the handicapped. Licensing authorities which legally bar deaf persons from operating automobiles should examine recent studies which indicate that they can indeed drive safely. We also support the promotion of safety measures both with respect to auto construction and to traffic regulations, and hope that authorities will increasingly provide driver education and modified vehicles to handicapped persons. Funds should be provided to meet the transportation needs of the disabled wherever necessary.

VOCATIONAL SERVICES

We are firmly convinced that disability is not a bar to successful employment if well-planned vocational rehabilitation services are available. It will be the responsibility of employers to accept competent handicapped workers. This can be achieved either through legislative requirements, voluntary efforts, or both. Vocational objectives must reflect the changing economic patterns resulting from urban developments with heightened demands for technical, professional, and service skills. Professional training programs for vocational rehabilitation personnel should be constantly reviewed to keep abreast if not ahead of the occupational opportunities of the future.

We do not view automation as a threat to the disabled, but rather as a challenging opportunity to elevate their status as workers. However, there will be a continuing need for sheltered workshops, conveniently located, for some disabled persons.

LEISURE

All people, including the handicapped, will in the future have more leisure. The most constructive use of this time by the disabled will be greatly furthered by recommendations already made with respect to the elimination of architectural barriers, the improvement of transportation facilities, and the modernization of rehabilitation programs. While special circumstances may require the organization of certain activities specifically designed for the severely disabled, we encourage the fullest participation of the handicapped in the normal family, social, recreational, and cultural pursuits of the community.

As required by the Conference theme, our recommendations reflect our concern for the problems of the handicapped in urban development. Nevertheless, we are equally aware of the needs of the disabled in rural settings and urge that wherever possible special services be provided in their own localities. This would prevent the unnecessary migration of handicapped people to urban centers and the resultant weakening of family ties.

Study Group 12. Groups Needing
Special Attention: Juvenile Delinquents

Chairman: D. V. Kulkarni, *India*
Vice-chairman and Rapporteur: Thomas Lee, *Hong Kong*

Yolanda Mirco de Mouzo, *Argentina*
Isabel Pura Torres de Villalba, *Argentina*
Ian Cox, *Australia*
Lieut. Col. Frank Moulton, *Canada*
Z. M. Staron, *Canada*
Mrs. Betty Thomas, *Canada*
Mrs. L. F. DeLathrop, *Chile*
Linos Shacallis, *Cyprus*
Suzanne Chalufour, *France*
Elizabeth Hirsch, *France*
Angelika du Mont, *Germany*
Lisel Werninger, *Germany*
Joachim Wieler, *Germany*
Dorothy Cohen, *Israel*
Winifred Hewitt, *Jamaica*
Zenichi Hiramoto, *Japan*
Olga Matamoros y Esperanza Dominquez, *Mexico*

Josefina Morales de Sotelo, *Mexico*
Cesar Avalos Arenas, *Peru*
Elena Colina Casas, *Peru*
Carmen Luz Peralto, *Peru*
Nguyen Yuan Cao, *South Vietnam*
Valere Sulle, *Switzerland*
Joan Hasler, *United Kingdom*
R. Parsons, *United Kingdom*
Mrs. E. V. Road, *United Kingdom*
Albert Hess, *United States*
S. D. Nixon, *United States*
A. G. Novick, *United States*
Howard Ohmhart, *United States*
Milton Rector, *United States*
William H. Sheridan, *United States*
Erica Sucher, *United States*
Rosario Cardenas, *Venezuela*
B. Cordero Velaquez, *Venezuela*
Hilarion Guevara Belisle, *Venezuela*

THE FACT that urbanization is associated closely with the problem of juvenile delinquency was corroborated by the participants of the group. It was further felt that juvenile delinquency needs special attention if the inevitable urban development is to be made more functional to the goal of satisfactory community living for all.

It was the consensus of opinion that the maladjustment and deviant behavior of adolescents pose a challenge to planners of urban community development, and the group strongly felt that voluntary and public agencies should work toward bringing about planned social change by paying special attention to the problem.

The phenomenal growth of urban populations throughout the world has necessitated that the field of social work should accept the responsibility of meeting many of the dysfunctional situations generated by urbanization. It was felt that the time has come when some of our traditional institutions should modify and amplify their functions so that they can meet problems like juvenile delinquency, while it may also be necessary to evolve new services to meet certain situations.

In the light of this, the group agreed that as the background of our quest for modernization, which necessarily takes into account the growth of industrialization, urbanization, and a complex competitive way of life, it is essential to examine how far our existing social apparatus with its various parts, such as the family, schools, recreational programs, the employment structure, needs to be modified or augmented. It was further felt that though there is scope for augmentation of some of these institutions, it will be necessary to build new institutional structures to face the problems of urban development. One of the important considerations, however, was that since there are appreciable variations in the development patterns among various countries, each culture may have to meet these special problems in a manner based on its social, political, and economic background, though the goal attainment may be the same.

Since available resources for dealing with such problems as juvenile delinquency are insufficient, it is imperative to develop such resources. In this context the need for research is paramount, especially in the developing countries, which offer a vast scope for research to understand the structures, functions, and processes of juvenile delinquency. It is also necessary to further professional training at the community, local, national, and international level so that maximum resources will be available to meet the problems of juvenile delinquency.

In spite of this, however, unless the grass roots are involved in organizing a change and eliminating the dysfunctional side effects of urbanization, it will be difficult to make progress in dealing with juvenile delinquency. With this end in view it was felt that avenues of community involvement should be explored. The group offered the following recommendations:

1. In addition to governmental activities, the gathering of information and the sponsoring of fundamental and applied research projects and programs of evaluation on the subject of juve-

nile delinquency, with particular emphasis on the developing countries, should be one of the main functions of the ICSW.

2. With a view to exploring additional training resources which will help to increase trained personnel, both in the voluntary and the public sector, there should be more exchanges of trainees between the developed and developing countries. The ICSW should be a clearing house for this purpose and should suggest criteria for suitable candidates and programs.

3. When planning new communities or renewing existing ones, there should be consultations between planners and social welfare agencies. It is particularly desirable that a network of youth services be designed in a creative and imaginative manner to insure the involvement and participation of youth.

4. In order to insure maximum community involvement, it is recommended that participation of local residents from all segments and the use of volunteers should be encouraged in the implementation of ongoing youth and correctional services.

5. Governments should assume responsibility for the development and implementation of adequate minimum standards for youth correctional services.

6. Steps should be taken to exchange ideas and information on a regional basis.

Study Group 13. Groups Needing
Special Attention: Newcomers to Urban Centers

Chairman: Mrs. Yedda Nellie Benzercy, *Brazil*
Vice-chairman: L. K. Northwood, *United States*
Rapporteur: Charlotte Maher, *Canada*

Maria Julieta Galzaus, *Brazil*
Bill Dales, *Canada*
Bernard R. Lournier, *Canada*
Edgurd Boutillin, *France*
Andre Guichand, *France*
Henri Petit, *France*
Francis Lerda, *Hong Kong*
Taketeshi Sasake, *Japan*

Midori Takashina, *Japan*
Gaston Martinez Matello, *Mexico*
Rose Marie R. Ocompo, *Philippines*
O. Doreen Clarke, *United Kingdom*
Joan Court, *United Kingdom*
Jacqueline Knight, *United Kingdom*
Howard Adelstein, *United States*
John F. Thomas, *United States*

VERY BROAD and complex problems need to be seen in very broad context. On the other hand, it is necessary to bring discussion down to particulars. Population movements, for instance, may be rural to urban, urban to urban, or country to country. Some reasons for movement are: automation, resulting in shifts in manpower requirements; expansion of communication and transportation; expansion of geographic horizons due to economic or educational opportunities, increased comfort and luxury, adventure and excitement, desperation, anonymity (sometimes because of illegal activities), protection, and greater freedom.

Growth of cities is a very complex phenomenon. The list of causes as identified is valid but incomplete. Motivations are often contradictory. The problems often encountered by newcomers are: lack of suitable employment; unmet physical needs (housing); difficulty in utilizing unfamiliar services and facilities due to exploitation, discrimination, anomie, loneliness, isolation, frustration, and breakdown of family because of new situations and different stresses which often result in social ills, such as juvenile delinquency, prostitution, addiction.

Possibilities for preventive action include: preparation of migrants or immigrants; preparation of receiving communities in order to prevent or control exploitation; directed movement (most countries have some control over immigration and a few control or even direct migration).

Examples from many countries showed similar kinds of problems. The differences were in intensity and in available resources. Although there are some qualitative services specifically designed for newcomers, quantitatively these are very inadequate. In many instances help stems primarily from families or friends within the slum or squatter communities.

Assistance from government seems to come after these communities have become well established and have generally taken the form of some large clearance or relocation scheme. Although private agencies or societies, in a very few instances, may initiate these schemes they are all primarily government-financed. The private sector, because of its closeness to people, has a great responsibility to influence government to give increased consideration to social and psychological needs.

Most frequently, group and individual services within this general plan are provided by private agencies. Extensive coordination between all aspects of the schemes (economic, social, physical) before, during, and after implementation is felt to be vital in every instance.

There is considerable variation in the amount of involvement of the population or the indigenous leadership in development of the plan and its implementation. This seems to relate to the degree of emergency and the long-term objectives. In some cases these primarily relieve basic physical hardship and sometimes they become more comprehensive human rehabilitative efforts. Some concern was expressed about the immediate pressures that force governments into physical urban rehabilitation or renewal schemes which are primarily related to physical structures.

There seem to be two general ways of combating or preventing urban metropolization: (1) rehabilitation or relocation within the urban area; (2) new towns, expanded towns, and urbanization in rural and/or semirural areas.

There is considerable variation in social needs due to particular social systems, such as extended families, joint families, the *compadrazgo* system. There seems to be a tendency for some of these systems to break down because of economic urban stresses.

This is often a facet of the total transition, which was seen as a vital period, a time when many personal problems develop or emerge.

The transition period has been handled in several ways, sometimes experimentally, sometimes as an emergency. One experiment has been to provide housing which offers modern urban facilities but also allows for the continuation of some rural habits, such as keeping chickens and some livestock in the courtyard. It was emphasized that while the pressure to change must not be too great, it obviously must exist. Perhaps temporary communities of homogeneous migrants or immigrants are helpful in the transition period, but these must be followed by planned integration. Personal and educational services to individuals and groups are of utmost importance both by way of preparation for, and of integration into, the new or rehabilitated community.

It should be possible to take action before emergency situations arise or intolerable conditions develop. Oddly enough, this seems to be inhibited by a lack of organization in some countries and by excessive organization and bureaucracy in others.

The group agreed to the following recommendations:

1. Social work with newcomers to the urban setting must be directed toward the social network as well as to the individual.

2. More systematic research into the effects of movement upon people is needed. The intuitive approach has validity, but it needs to be supported by systematic documentation. Evaluation of program impact has often been lacking.

3. Social development programs should provide for all newcomers irrespective of their economic circumstances. In this planning human aspirations and values must be taken into consideration.

4. Good social welfare, health, and education services for all people would prevent much of the difficulty experienced by people when they move.

5. This problem has common denominators across the world. The degree of stress, the social systems, and the resources available all vary, but we learn much from each other. We recommend that such conversation be continued or perhaps expanded.

Study Group 14. Use of Multipurpose Workers at the Local Level

Chairman: P. D. Kulkarni, *India*
Vice-chairman: Mrs. Suparb Visessurakarn, *Thailand*
Rapporteur: A. Murdock Keith, *Hong Kong*

Mary A. Davis, *Canada*
Nora Fox, *Canada*
Jane Taylor, *Canada*
Helene Gausseres, *France*
Sicard Odette, *France*
Gendreau Simone, *France*
Elizabeth Buschmann, *Germany*
Sigrid Meyer, *Germany*
Maria Chryssoverghi, *Greece*
Pei-Ngor Chen, *Hong Kong*
Trissie J. Aranha, *India*
Jerbanoo D. Irani, *India*
Junko Yamaka, *Japan*
Anna Margadant, *Netherlands*
A. M. Shafiq-Ul-Haque, *Pakistan*

Araceli Querido, *Philippines*
Pilar P. Iturbe, *Spain*
Gunnel Swedner, *Sweden*
Burapa Chanpong, *Thailand*
Modeleine Malherbe, *United Kingdom*
Norman Scotney, *United Kingdom*
Muriel Smith, *United Kingdom*
Margaret C. Browne, *United States*
James Hackshaw, *United States*
John McDowell, *United States*
Thomas D. Sherrard, *United States*
Beatrice Werble, *United States*
Mrs. Corinne H. Wolfe, *United States*
Domingo Morales, *Venezuela*

THE GROUP was composed of twenty-nine members drawn from various countries representing both the developed and the developing parts of the world.

The discussion focused on neighborhoods in urban settings. While recognizing that great differences exist, the group addressed itself to delineating the common factors. It was agreed that the basic neighborhood is one in which there is a high degree of face-to-face contacts and in which relationships can develop through propinquity. No attempt was made to define a neighborhood by the number of inhabitants because this is markedly affected by special considerations, density of population, and social conditions.

A variety of factors which operate in any community must be taken into account: housing conditions and physical environment; economic conditions; educational levels; variety of cultural backgrounds; presence of "islands" of people with similar language, cultural heritage, and economic interests; value structure and goals of the people; mobility; presence, or lack, of indigenous leaders; attitudes to others in the same urban area and particularly to the authorities; and forces which impinge on the community from outside the neighborhood.

The group used the term "multipurpose worker" to designate a person who attempts to work with the neighborhood as a whole and as an instrument of intervention, dealing with people in the totality of their needs. They envisioned two categories of multipurpose workers: a neighborhood agent who works directly with the community; and a worker who may be placed in a supervisory position to provide technical and professional services at the wider community level.

The term "specialist" referred to persons trained in a specific social work technique or in other disciplines. Indigenous volunteer leaders will also be involved in the neighborhood work. The discussion was primarily focused on the multipurpose worker in community development settings.

NEEDS TO BE MET

1. Physical needs
2. Need to relate to others, to offset isolation
3. Cultural needs
4. Need for social and physical change
5. Need to develop the leadership potential
6. Need for cohesion
7. Need to know about and understand community services, resources, and so forth

ROLES AND TASKS OF THE MULTIPURPOSE WORKER

Roles.—The multipurpose worker is regarded as an essential member of the social work personnel operating at the community level.

The neighborhood agent or worker should be drawn whenever possible from the same, or similar, background as that of the local people. He should be able to identify as closely as possible with their aims and aspirations.

The neighborhood agent should be backed up by a professionally trained multipurpose worker who will collaborate with other members of the team who have specialist training. All the personnel will be complementary to one another.

Variations in the work in the field are affected by the physical, cultural, economic, political, and philosophical context of each country or urban area. The variety of settings also depends on the organizational structure in different parts of the world.

The activities of the multipurpose worker can be: process-oriented, program- or project-oriented, or statutory based. The process orientation, while slower, may produce more lasting results, but it is advisable to promote an integrated approach combining the process, the program, and, where applicable, the statutory; only the emphasis would differ in accordance with the setting. The use of government-based multipurpose workers is affected by the relationship of the public with the government and the responsiveness of government to changing needs.

The role of the multipurpose worker is that of a catalyst in the process of bringing about citizen participation on the basis of aided self-help. In addition, wherever appropriate, the multipurpose worker may also provide community services.

Tasks.—The tasks of the multipurpose worker are many. He must first make a preliminary assessment of the needs and problems of the community and the factors operating therein. He should then identify, encourage, and train the indigenous leadership, as well as the people in general, in the skills of working with others and of planning, organizing, and administering projects. When he has helped the community to single out and articulate its needs and problems he must locate and mobilize the appropriate resources available both within and external to the neighborhood.

Another important task is to assist the process of social change and influence social policy. Furthermore, he must be available to individuals who have problems and, of course, he must provide specific services.

TRAINING OF THE MULTIPURPOSE WORKER

In the light of the tasks envisaged for the multipurpose worker, his training should be comprehensive and interdisciplinary. That of the neighborhood agent or worker should be brief and should comprise: basic principles; skills necessary for community work; and field work.

The training of the professional multipurpose worker should be on a generic base, providing the basic techniques of social work and an adequate grounding in behavioral dynamics, with some emphasis on the behavior of individuals in organizational relationships, and skill in identifying and fostering indigenous leadership. Training should result in the capacity to select an appropriate role or roles in the specific community setting in which he is employed.

The personnel policies of the agencies should provide a graduated salary scale so that workers in these categories may make careers in their positions and not be compelled to resign in search of better prospects elsewhere.

The tasks performed by the multipurpose worker and the results obtained must be evaluated periodically. While it is true that no government or organization should set up such a program without understanding that startling results may not be immediately evident and that numerical counting of successes is difficult, some bench marks must be established and instruments of judgment devised. Such evaluation would be helpful in bringing about continuous improvement in methods and programs and would also provide evidence for the justification of the expenditures incurred on neighborhood or community projects.

The result of these discussions indicates that schools of social work should seriously consider providing training for the two categories of multipurpose workers. The variation that exists in different communities and countries indicates the need for further study and thought on the concepts and roles recorded in this report.

Study Group 15. The Role of Social Work with Other Disciplines in Providing Service in Urban Areas

Chairman: John W. Frei, Canada
Vice-chairman: Hugh Sanders, United Kingdom
Rapporteur: Marie-Louise Cornaz, Switzerland

Hilda El-Jaick, Brazil
Robert Chagnon, Canada
Imelda Chenard, Canada
M. Cornwall-Jones, Canada
Cecilia Valdiri, Colombia
Eliane Brunner, France
Christiane Delalande, France
Jacqueline Perles, France
Christiane Willot, France
Hilda Raj, India
Ioshio Morii, Japan
Maria Luisa Adame, Mexico
Berta C. Hernandez, Mexico
Ahmadullah Mia, Pakistan
Ellya Carola de Ruzo, Peru

Teresita Silva, Philippines
Juana Elizondo, Spain
Ingrid Gunnas, Sweden
Derma Barin, Turkey
Sevin Guven, Turkey
X. Kowgar, Turkey
Joan Cooper, United Kingdom
Margaret Eden, United Kingdom
Hobart Burch, United States
Lyman Ford, United States
Murray Meld, United States
M. Louise Porcelli, United States
Jack Stumpf, United States
Ana Aseraje, Venezuela

THE STUDY METHOD chosen by this group was the problem approach. Low-rental housing was selected for analysis as one of the urgent urban problems that involves many social welfare disciplines. Each national delegation gave a condensed report on cooperation with other professions in the solution of this problem. Generally, cooperation between the social work profession and other disciplines ranges from full involvement even at the planning stage to complete lack of involvement.

The reasons for this divergence are manifold: the low developmental stage of the profession; lack of professional education; the resulting great differences in the quality of services rendered, leading to great differences in role and status, and in the acceptance of the profession by the community at large. With a few exceptions, it seems that even in the countries where social work has been known for a longer period of time, there is a lack of cooperation with the other professions involved in urban development.

Analysis of the national reports resulted in identification of some major factors that affect interprofessional cooperation. Each profession:

1. Has its own primary concerns, philosophies, and priorities.
2. Has a different perception of reality and causation and expresses them differently.
3. Has a different status and power base in different cultures and times.
4. Has a different technology and different processes of work.
5. Differs in the capability to measure the quality and effectiveness of its work.
6. Approaches the problem from a different platform, under different auspices, and with different sanctions.
7. Has a different function assignment and frequently an overlapping span of responsibility.
8. Differs in the degree of influence wielded over the use of available gross national income for urban development.
9. Has inadequate methods of training its novitiate for interprofessional collaboration.
10. Tends to become less flexible in acceptance and respect of other professions as it develops specialization and expertise.
11. Tends to engender pride and/or professional jealousy and can become overanxious to assert its uniqueness, which results in lack of flexibility.
12. Has its rules of confidentiality which eliminate, in many cases, the accessibility of necessary information to other professions.

The study group recommends:

1. Organization of informal courses by the professional associations of social workers for other professions involved in social welfare, and vice versa, to facilitate interprofessional understanding and communication
2. Organization of formal lectures on social work in the schools of other disciplines at the university level, and vice versa
3. Organization of informal and formal joint conferences with other professions for exploration of, and action on, mutual

problems in the delivery of social welfare services on local, national, and international levels

4. Publication of brochures demonstrating the role and function of the profession and distribution throughout the various professions of reports on interdisciplinary conferences

5. Definition and detailed interpretation by the professional associations of the roles and services the social worker can render in traditional and other settings

6. Development, by the schools of social work, of knowledge of, and skill in, working in and through task groups which involve other professions

7. Acceptance by individual workers, schools, and agencies that the best interdisciplinary coordination and understanding occur within oneself and through a better grasp and use of a knowledge of interdisciplinary resources

8. General acceptance of the value of the interdependence of specialists in the complex urban society and full commitment to this value

9. Systematic work toward the development of central principles, knowledge, and skills of the social work profession that will lead to its recognition as a professional whole which can be easily and generally identified by other disciplines and the community at large as one profession, no matter in what specialty individuals are practicing

10. Preparation of all recommendations or documents submitted to authorities by social welfare organizations in a clear language focused on the specific problem

11. Action by social workers on both the national and the local level to demonstrate to other disciplines and governmental bodies the importance of the social worker's role in urban planning

12. Organization of national professional associations in the countries where these do not exist and strengthening of present associations.

The group also suggests that social workers should enhance their status and their acceptance by other professions by demonstrating their capabilities, leading by example, being more humble and yet self-confident. All professional and interprofessional decisions in urban development must be ultimately accepted by the broader citizenry.

Finally, the study group earnestly recommends a thorough follow-up of its work to be organized in special conferences by the national and international associations. The discussions of the representatives of seventeen national delegations resulted in unanimous recognition of the extreme importance of this problem for further development of the social work profession and integration of interprofessional cooperation and for improvement of conditions of life of all people.

Special Meeting 1. Pre-Conference Seminar on Social Welfare in the United States

PLANNING COMMITTEE

Chairman: Dr. Mildred F. Woodbury
Secretary: Eleanor L. Ryder

Dr. Roland J. Artigues
Edmund N. Bacon
Stanley J. Brody
Owen R. Davison
Carl Dellmuth
Mrs. John V. Hastings III
Robert N. Hilkert
Mrs. Theodore J. Kauders
Dr. Katherine E. Lower

C. F. McNeil
William L. Rafsky
John F. Reichard
Dr. Kurt Reichert
Dr. Ruth E. Smalley
Robert E. Taber
Randolph E. Wise
Mrs. Elias Wolf
Mrs. Howard A. Wolf

DISCUSSION LEADERS

Dr. Merrill B. Conover
Manuel Kaufmann

Braulio Lopez
Mrs. Hubertine Marshall

SPEAKERS

Dr. Otto Pollak, Professor of Sociology, University of Pennsylvania: "American Social Values and Social Welfare"

William Rafsky, Executive Director, Old Philadelphia Development Corp.: "Social Welfare Problems and Urban Development"

Norman V. Lourie, Executive Secretary, Pennsylvania Department of Public Welfare; Dr. John Otto Reineman, Chairman, Philadelphia Antipoverty Action Committee; and Charles W. Bowser, Executive Director, Philadelphia Antipoverty Action Committee: "Social Welfare Service to Meet Urban Needs"

Richardson Dilworth, President, Philadelphia Board of Education: "Philadelphia's Approach to Social Welfare Problems"

Special Meeting 2. Representatives of Social Welfare Ministries Concerned with International Social Welfare

THIRTY-EIGHT representatives from fifteen social welfare or related ministries, four embassies, the United Nations, and two educational institutions took part in a special meeting held in conjunction with the XIIIth International Conference of Social Work.

Although this meeting was in a sense exploratory, the representatives quickly identified common interests and concerns. As well as reviewing a number of procedural and technical subjects— including, for example, exchange of information, training of personnel, and the role of social research—they gave particular attention to a number of broader questions, such as: the need to clarify objectives and to develop strong national programs of social welfare as a prerequisite to effective international cooperation in this field; methods of achieving inter- and intragovernmental coordination; and the role of regional organizations.

While encouraged by the increasing recognition being given to social welfare at the national level (some ninety-five countries now have ministries or departments of social welfare), the representatives noted the relative lack of visibility given to this field by intergovernmental organizations at the international level. How to achieve greater recognition and what organizational devices are necessary to do so are subjects which require the most serious attention. For this and other reasons, they attached great importance to the 1968 international conference of ministers responsible for social welfare, approved by the United Nations Economic and Social Council in August, 1966. The theme of the conference will be the role of social welfare programs in national development.

As the group had not been constituted to adopt resolutions as such, it was agreed that the chairman would advise the ICSW Permanent Committee of the significance of the 1968 international conference of ministers of social welfare. The representatives stated that they would welcome and support any initiative that the Permanent Committee might take in bringing the 1968 conference to the attention of the delegates attending the XIIIth International Conference and in including, in whatever ways might be appropriate, ICSW recognition of the strategic importance of this first international conference of social welfare ministers. The group further agreed that the ICSW be requested to forward to the United Nations the summary of its discussion in order that the subjects raised therein might be taken into account when the agenda for the conference are drawn up.

Since this first meeting of representatives of welfare ministries concerned with international social welfare has proved most useful it was agreed that the Permanent Committee be requested to organize a second meeting in connection with the XIVth International Conference, and that, as the exploratory meeting has now been held, specific agenda be developed well in advance of the next meeting.

Special Meeting 3. Municipal Social Welfare Officers

A ROUND-TABLE discussion by municipal welfare officers was held during the XIIIth International Conference of Social Work to consider the social implications of urban development for local authorities, particularly public welfare officials. The discussion was based on a series of questions prepared in advance and was directed toward the responsibility for planning and implementing programs at the various levels of government. As a frame of reference, the role of the local social welfare services was emphasized as being different in the highly developed countries from that in the predominantly agricultural countries now in rapid development.

The representative of the United Kingdom pointed out that while the responsibility for social service in his country rests primarily with local jurisdictions, the broad programs, such as employment, are the responsibility of the national government. The responsibility of the national government for the formulation of national policy was described by the representatives from India, who also stressed the importance of establishing national goals.

The United States representatives pointed out that the United States is now facing not only the problems of the large cities, but also the need to plan for the metropolitan areas, which often include many governmental jurisdictions.

It was pointed out that in Brazil there are various levels of development, and that regional planning bodies have been established with the authority vested in a board composed of officials of the jurisdictions involved. The group considered this an excellent step forward.

There was also considerable discussion regarding the way in which both elected and nominated bodies could participate in planning, with the realization that the preservation and development of human resources must be given strong emphasis.

The group concluded that a national policy is essential and, therefore, that national planning is required, but that such planning must include full participation of both elected officials and citizen groups at all levels of government. It was emphasized that the national government is responsible for implementing the national programs on the local level and for providing both technical and financial assistance. This responsibility includes assuring that the program is carried out equitably for all citizens. This was described as the function of "accountability."

The group expressed agreement on the benefit of the discussions and went on record as urging that in future programs of the ICSW there be similar sessions so that municipal social welfare officers may discuss their mutual problems.

Appendices

Countries and International Organizations Represented

Countries with ICSW National Committees

Argentina
Australia
Austria
Belgium
Bolivia
Brazil
Canada
Ceylon
Chile
Denmark
Ecuador
Ethiopia
Finland
France
Germany

Greece
Hong Kong
India
Israel
Italy
Jamaica
Japan
Korea
Lebanon
Malaysia
Mexico
Netherlands
Norway
Pakistan
Paraguay

Peru
Philippines
Portugal
Singapore
South Vietnam
Spain
Sweden
Switzerland
Thailand
United Arab Republic
United Kingdom
United States
Uruguay
Venezuela
Yugoslavia

Countries without ICSW National Committees

Algeria
Bahamas
Central African Republic
China, Republic of
Colombia
Costa Rica
Cyprus
Czechoslovakia
El Salvador
Ghana
Guatemala

Honduras
Indonesia
Iran
Iraq
Kenya
Madagascar
Monaco
Morocco
Nepal
New Zealand
Nicaragua

Nigeria
Panama
Puerto Rico
Rumania
Senegal
South Africa, Republic of
Togo
Turkey
Uganda
Upper Volta
Zambia

International Organizations

Boy Scouts World Bureau
Catholic International Union of Social Service
International Association of Schools of Social Work
International Conference of Catholic Charities (Caritas)
International Conference of Jewish Communal Service
International Council for Homehelp Services
International Council of Voluntary Agencies
International Council of Women

International Federation of Settlements and Neighborhood Centers
International Federation of Social Workers
International Labour Organisation
International League of Societies for the Mentally Handicapped
International Social Service
International Society for Community Development
League of Red Cross Societies
Organization of American States (Pan American Union)
Salvation Army International
United Nations
United Nations Children's Fund
World Association of Girl Guides and Girl Scouts
World Council of Churches
World Health Organization
World Union of Catholic Women's Organizations
World Young Women's Christian Association

Organizing Committee

Chairman: Margaret Hickey, St. Louis, Mo.

Vice-chairmen: Mrs. Richard J. Bernhard, New York, N.Y., Chairman, Development Committee; Victor Reuther, Washington, D.C.; Ruth E. Smalley, Philadelphia, Pa., representing the Council on Social Work Education; Mark Sullivan, Jr., Washington, D.C., Chairman, Washington Committee; Ellen Winston, Washington, D.C., liaison with the Federal Government

Executive Secretary: Yvonne Bourguignon, New York, N.Y.

Representatives of National Organizations

Loula Dunn, Washington, D.C., American Public Welfare Association; Sol Morton Isaac, Columbus, Ohio, National Conference on Social Welfare; C. F. McNeil, New York, N.Y., National Social Welfare Assembly; Charles I. Schottland, Waltham, Mass., U.S. Committee of ICSW; Eugene Shenefield, New York, N.Y., American Council of Voluntary Agencies for Foreign Services; Herman D. Stein, Cleveland, Ohio, National Association of Social Workers

Members

Walter Barlow, New York, N.Y.

Leona Baumgartner, M.D., New York, N.Y.

Clark W. Blackburn, New York, N.Y.

Ralph Blanchard, New York, N.Y.

Ramone Eaton, Washington, D.C.

James W. Fogarty, New York, N.Y.

Lyman S. Ford, New York, N.Y.

Sam Grais, St. Paul, Minn.

Mrs. Anna Roosevelt Halsted, Washington, D.C.

Dorothy Height, New York, N.Y.

Jane M. Hoey, New York, N.Y.

Sidney Hollander, Baltimore, Md.

Charles H. Jordan, New York, N.Y.

Gordon Manser, New York, N.Y.

Leonard Mayo, Westport, Conn.

Mrs. Eugene Meyer, Washington, D.C.

Lawrence K. Northwood, Seattle, Wash.

Joseph H. Reid, New York, N.Y.

Mrs. Alexander Ripley, Los Angeles, Calif.

Mrs. Elly Robbins, New York, N.Y.

Mrs. Laurance S. Rockefeller, New York, N.Y.

Bernard Russell, Washington, D.C.

Mabel Shannon, New York, N.Y.

George Shuster, South Bend, Ind.

Sanford Solender, New York, N.Y.

Bishop Edward Swanstrom, New York, N.Y.

Charles P. Taft, Cincinnati, Ohio

Mrs. Theodore O. Wedel, New York, N.Y.

Elizabeth Wickenden, New York, N.Y.

Mrs. Joseph Willen, New York, N.Y.

Mrs. Mildred Fairchild Woodbury, Philadelphia, Pa.

Whitney M. Young, Jr., New York, N.Y.

Program Committee

Chairman: Reuben Baetz, *Canada*

Hans Achinger, *Germany*

Rivka Aronson, *Israel*

Martha Branscombe, *United Nations*

J. F. Bulsara, *India*

Johannes Gerima, *Ethiopia*

Mrs. Ilse Jaffe de Goldschmidt, *Venezuela*

Charles E. Hendry, *International Association of Schools of Social Work*

Isabel de Hurtado, *France*

Mrs. Esperanza Balmaceda de Josefe, *Mexico*

Ken-ichi Maki, *Japan*

Florence Philpott, *International Federation of Social Workers*

Eugen Pusić, *Yugoslavia, ex officio*

Charles I. Schottland, *United States*

Lauri Tarvainen, *Finland*

Executive Committee